Pentecostal Theology

Systematic Pentecostal and Charismatic Theology

Series editors
Wolfgang Vondey
Daniela C. Augustine

Pentecostal Theology

Living the Full Gospel

Wolfgang Vondey

LONDON • NEW YORK • OXFORD • NEW DELHI • SYDNEY

T&T CLARK
Bloomsbury Publishing Plc
50 Bedford Square, London, WC1B 3DP, UK
1385 Broadway, New York, NY 10018, USA

BLOOMSBURY, T&T CLARK and the T&T Clark logo are
trademarks of Bloomsbury Publishing Plc

First published in Great Britain 2017
Paperback edition first published 2018

Copyright © Wolfgang Vondey, 2017

Wolfgang Vondey has asserted his right under the Copyright, Designs and
Patents Act, 1988, to be identified as Author of this work.

Cover image © naqiewei / GettyImages

All rights reserved. No part of this publication may be reproduced or
transmitted in any form or by any means, electronic or mechanical,
including photocopying, recording, or any information storage or
retrieval system, without prior permission in writing from the publishers.

Bloomsbury Publishing Plc does not have any control over, or responsibility for,
any third-party websites referred to or in this book. All internet addresses given
in this book were correct at the time of going to press. The author and publisher
regret any inconvenience caused if addresses have changed or sites have
ceased to exist, but can accept no responsibility for any such changes.

A catalogue record for this book is available from the British Library.

ISBN: HB: 978-0-5672-7539-4
PB: 978-0-5676-8517-9
ePDF: 978-0-5673-8773-8
ePub: 978-0-5675-1684-8

Names: Vondey, Wolfgang, author.
Title: Pentecostal theology : living the full gospel / by Wolfgang Vondey.
Description: 1 [edition]. | New York : Bloomsbury T&T Clark, 2017. | Includes
bibliographical references and index.
Identifiers: LCCN 2017018372 (print) | LCCN 2017022314 (ebook) |
ISBN 9780567387738 (ePDF) | ISBN 9780567516848 (ePUB) |
ISBN 9780567275394 (hb : alk. paper)
Subjects: LCSH: Pentecostalism. | Pentecostal churches–Doctrines.
Classification: LCC BX8762.Z5 (ebook) | LCC BX8762.Z5 V66 2017 (print) | DDC
230/.994–dc23
LC record available at https://lccn.loc.gov/2017018372

Series: T&T Clark Enquiries in Theological Ethics

Typeset by Newgen Knowledge Works Pvt Ltd., Chennai, India.
Printed and bound in Great Britain

To find out more about our authors and books visit
www.bloomsbury.com and sign up for our newsletters.

In memoriam
Heinrich Vondey (1936–2016)

Contents

Systematic Pentecostal and Charismatic Theology Series	viii
Acknowledgements	x
List of Abbreviations	xii
Introduction	1
1 Prolegomena to Pentecostal Doctrine	11
Part 1 Full Gospel Story	35
2 Saved: Meeting Jesus at the Altar	37
3 Sanctified: Participating in the Life of God	59
4 Baptized: Transformed by the Holy Spirit	83
5 Healed: Manifesting Signs and Wonders	107
6 Commissioned: Enacting the Coming Kingdom	131
Part 2 Full Gospel Theology	153
7 Creation: Spirit, Redemption, and Cosmology	155
8 Humanity: Divine Image, Human Agency, and Theological Anthropology	175
9 Society: Civilization, the Common Good, and Cultural Theory	199
10 Church: Mission, Movement, and Ecclesiology	225
11 God: Pentecost, Altar, and Doxology	255
Conclusion: Living the Full Gospel	281
Index	295

Systematic Pentecostal and Charismatic Theology Series

Wolfgang Vondey and Daniela C. Augustine, *Editors*

Wolfgang Vondey (PhD, Marquette University) is Reader in Contemporary Christianity and Pentecostal Studies at the University of Birmingham, United Kingdom, and also serves as director of the Centre for Pentecostal and Charismatic Studies. He has authored and edited a variety of publications on themes related to Pentecostalism and Pentecostal theology. He is associate editor of *PentecoStudies* and coeditor of the series *Christianity and Renewal – Interdisciplinary Studies*.

Daniela C. Augustine (DTh, University of South Africa) is Associate Professor of Theological Ethics at Lee University, Tennessee. She has published with focus on public theology, theological ethics, interdisciplinary studies in social transformation, postmodernity, and globalization, theology of economics, and the intersection of religion and culture from Pentecostal and Eastern European perspective. She currently serves as associate editor of the *Journal of Pentecostal Theology*.

Editorial Advisory Board

Kwabena Asamoah-Gyadu, Simon Chan, Pamela Holmes,
Veli-Matti Kärkkäinen, Frank Macchia, Néstor Medina,
Lisa P. Stephenson, Keith Warrington, Amos Yong

Systematic Pentecostal, and Charismatic Theology provides a platform for bringing together scholars among the Pentecostal and Charismatic movements to explore core theological themes in critical and constructive fashion. The series includes monographs that offer in-depth systematic analyses and forms of constructive theology as well as edited collections that allow scholars from a variety of theological disciplines to interact under a single theme or to present different views in order to pursue, among others, the following goals:

- to coordinate the systematic presentation (broadly construed) of Pentecostal and Charismatic theology worldwide;
- to initiate critical discussion of traditional Pentecostal doctrines by Pentecostal scholars;
- to re-examine central Pentecostal or Charismatic doctrines and practices;
- to venture into new fields of study hitherto not attempted by Pentecostal and Charismatic theologians;
- to encourage younger scholars to engage in a systematic theological endeavor from Pentecostal and Charismatic perspectives;
- to provide ecumenical and interdisciplinary conversations of systematic Pentecostal and Charismatic theologies with other theological traditions;
- to facilitate the systematic and constructive development of Pentecostal and Charismatic theology.

The books in this series address issues and concerns of Pentecostal and Charismatic studies within the academy with focus on the systematic construction, evaluation, and presentation of theology. Contributing volumes explore single or interrelated theological themes: ranging from traditional and uniquely Pentecostal doctrines to theological method, hermeneutics, spirituality, ethics, liturgy, as well as interdisciplinary engagements through the lens of Pentecostal and Charismatic theology. Hence, the series fosters broad theological conversations within and outside the Pentecostal and Charismatic movements with the purpose of offering systematic and constructive presentations for Pentecostal/Charismatic and non-Pentecostal/Charismatic audiences. At the same time, the series also contributes to the shape and development of 'systematic theology' and to the ongoing question whether and in what manner this label can be applied to Pentecostal and Charismatic scholarship. While authors are encouraged to examine the doctrines, practices, and theology of the Pentecostal and Charismatic movements, contributors are sought from a variety of scientific, disciplinary and religious traditions, countries, and contexts to reflect on the growing global and interdisciplinary study of Pentecostal theology. Authors should be aware of the conversations in the field of Pentecostal and Charismatic research and bring that work to bear methodologically, theoretically, and critically in their systematic and constructive projects.

Acknowledgements

The years working on this volume were spent in conversations and debates too numerous to recount. Many of the friends, colleagues, and students involved in the development of this book were likely not aware that their thoughts would find an entry into this text. While I have tried to reference all sources that document the contributions of others, there is always help given in ways that cannot simply be referenced. To begin with, I am indebted to D. Lyle Dabney at Marquette University for challenging me to pursue systematic theology deliberately as a Pentecostal. You insisted that Pentecostals possess their own theological narrative but had neglected to articulate it. Here is my answer to your challenge! I am thankful to Skip Jenkins for comments on the manuscript and for engaging me in honest and difficult conversations about Pentecostal theology that have challenged and taught me in many ways over the years. Our conversations are a testimony to the kind of theology I hope to inspire with this book! Particular gratitude goes to Enoch Charles for reading the entire manuscript and offering invaluable feedback, corrections, and questions on each chapter. The changes to the manuscript over the years show not only your service but your friendship as well! I am also indebted to critical comments, encouragements, and suggestions on the manuscript by Kenneth J. Archer, Nimi Wariboko, and Amos Yong. You have helped me read between the lines to create a more robust work that hopefully speaks to the diverse audiences you represent! Finally, I appreciate the support and vision of my editor at Bloomsbury, Anna Turton, for her faith in this project and for allowing the book to become the inaugural volume of the Systematic Pentecostal and Charismatic Theology series!

Several institutions have been a part of this work and left their impressions on the final product: the Pentecostal Theological Seminary, or the so-called Cleveland School, where I began my theological studies; Marquette University, my postgraduate alma mater that has shaped many Pentecostal students with its ecumenical spirit and theological rigour; Regent University, and its emphasis on what has come to be called Renewal theology, which generously sponsored a research grant during work on the manuscript; and the University of Birmingham, UK, home of the so-called Hollenweger school, where I now direct the Centre for Pentecostal and Charismatic Studies. Invaluable opportunities to present and discuss portions of this work were provided by the European Research Network on Global Pentecostalism (GloPent), the Oxford Centre for Mission Studies, the Pentecostal-Charismatic Studies Consultation at the American Academy of Religion, the Regent Center for Renewal Studies, Regents Theological College, and the Society for Pentecostal Studies. In all of these places, many individuals have challenged my preconceived notions about Pentecostal theology and allowed me to reflect on my proposal in the light of different circumstances and audiences. Your voices and dialects are a tribute to the global character of the Pentecostal community that hopefully speaks through this book.

However, when I finally began writing this book, I found myself in an unexpected and lengthy season in the wilderness. During this time, I found support, prayers, and encouragements from many, but above all in the tireless ministry of my sister in Christ, Diane J. Chandler. Your faithfulness and Christian example has left a profound imprint on my life and has hopefully shaped the spiritual character of this book! Finally, I would not have completed the manuscript without my wife, Michelle, who has accompanied my theological journey since it began. Your selfless listening to endless variations of articulating the ideas of every chapter, your questions and suggestions, but most importantly, your love and prayers encouraged me to go up the mountain again and again. Thank you for walking with me!

Abbreviations

AARAS	American Academy of Religion Academy Series
AF	*The Apostolic Faith*
AJPS	*Asian Journal for Pentecostal Studies*
ARA	*Annual Review of Anthropology*
ARSR	*Annual Review of the Sociology of Religion*
ASM	American Society of Missiology
ASR	*African Studies Review*
ATJ	*Asbury Theological Journal*
BNAPTS	*Bulletin of the North American Paul Tillich Society*
BT	*Black Theology*
CC	*The Christian Century*
CDT	*Cuadernos de teología*
CEA	*Cahiers d'Études Africaines*
CH	*Church History*
CHARIS	*Christianity and Renewal-Interdisciplinary Studies*
CJPCC	*Canadian Journal of Pentecostal-Charismatic Christianity*
CS	*Caribbean Studies*
CT	*Christianity Today*
CTM	*Concordia Theological Monthly*
CV	*Communio viatorum*
EI	*Ecclesiological Investigations*
EQ	*Evangelical Quarterly*
ERT	*Evangelical Review of Theology*
ET	*Ecumenical Trends*
FR	*Fieldwork in Religion*
GPCS	*Global Pentecostal and Charismatic Studies*
HJCTS	*Horizons: The Journal of the College Theology Society*
IBMR	*International Bulletin of Missionary Research*
IJPT	*International Journal of Public Theology*
IJSCC	*International Journal for the Study of the Christian Church*

IJST	*International Journal of Systematic Theology*
IRM	*International Review of Mission*
JEPTA	*Journal of the European Pentecostal Theological Association*
JES	*Journal of Ecumenical Studies*
JPT	*Journal of Pentecostal Theology*
JPTS	Journal of Pentecostal Theology Supplement
JRA	*Journal of Religion in Africa*
JRDH	*Journal of Religion, Disability and Health*
JRH	*Journal of Religion and Health*
JRS	*Journal of Religious Studies*
JRitS	*Journal of Ritual Studies*
JSNTS	Journal for the Study of the New Testament Supplement
JSSR	*Journal for the Scientific Study of Religion*
JTSA	*Journal of Theology for Southern Africa*
KEJT	*Kairos: Evangelical Journal of Theology*
MHRC	*Mental Health, Religion & Culture*
MIR	*Missiology: An International Review*
MPT	Münsterische Beiträge zu Theologie
MS	*Mission Studies*
MT	*Modern Theology*
NIDPCM	The New International Dictionary of Pentecostal and Charismatic Movements
NPS	*New Political Science*
OIC	*One in Christ*
PE	*Pentecostal Evangel*
PEc	*Pro Ecclesia*
PM	Pentecostal Manifestos
Pneuma	*Pneuma: The Journal of the Society for Pentecostal Studies*
PP	*Pastoral Psychology*
PSCF	*Perspectives on Science and Christian Faith*
PT	*Political Theology*
PTM	Princeton Theological Monograph Series
RAC	*Religion and American Culture*
RAE	*Review & Expositor*
RT	*Rural Theology*

SAC	*The Spirit and Church*
SAQ	*South Atlantic Quarterly*
SC	*Social Compass*
SIGC	Studien zur interkulturellen Geschichte des Christentums
SJT	*Scottish Journal of Theology*
SL	*Studia Liturgica*
SM	*Svensk missionstidskrift*
SPCI	Studies in Pentecostal and Charismatic Issues Series
SPT	Series in Pentecostal Theology
SR	*Sociology of Religion*
SRO	*Sociological Research Online*
SVTQ	*St Vladimir's Theological Quarterly*
TAS	*Theology and Science*
TS	*Theological Studies*
TSR	Texts and Studies in Religion
WF	*Western Folklore*
WTJ	*Wesleyan Theological Journal*
Zygon	*Zygon: Journal of Religion and Science*

Introduction

Pentecostal theology. The title of this book, I suspect, is likely to encounter one of several responses: curiosity by those who believe that the history of Christian thought since the twentieth century cannot be written without a discussion of the Pentecostal and Charismatic movements but wonder how to articulate such an account, apprehension by those who fear that a systematic theological account might overshadow the spiritual emphasis of the Pentecostal movement, reluctance by those who anticipate that a single account of Pentecostal theology would conceal the significant diversity of the global movement, disbelief by those who doubt that Pentecostals can contribute significantly to the theological agenda or disapproval by those who think that Pentecostalism is not a theological tradition in its own right. What these reactions share in common is their observation of the absence of a grounding theological narrative and theological symbol to identify and distinguish Pentecostal theology. The majority of recent constructive proposals of Pentecostal theology are programmatic and phenomenological; the intention is to provide principles of a theological narrative yet often without telling the Pentecostal story. As a result, a comprehensive narrative for Pentecostal theology is missing. In this book, I intend to provide this theological narrative, to demonstrate its particular Pentecostal character and to exemplify its contributions to central theological conversations. The hypothesis of this book can be summarized succinctly: Pentecost is the core theological symbol of Pentecostal theology, and its theological narrative is the full gospel.

Pentecost as theological symbol

Amidst the increasingly complex contexts and challenges of the theological task, Pentecostalism has emerged with unusual vitality as a new theological tradition. However, for many, Pentecostals remain theologically enigmatic and ambiguous, inviting countless questions. Does Pentecostal theology bear witness to the essentials of the Christian faith? What are the concerns dominating the theological agenda from a Pentecostal perspective? Do Pentecostals possess a theological method that can be developed among Pentecostals and in conversation with other Christian traditions? What is the theological language and vocabulary of global Pentecostalism? How does Pentecostal theology speak to other theological confessions? Can Pentecostal theology proceed ecumenically or does it withdraw to isolated debates occupied with internal concerns? Do Pentecostals possess a core motif for their theological reflection, and can this motif be articulated constructively and systematically? How does Pentecostalism speak to global concerns for the welfare of creation, society, and human flourishing? Can Pentecostal theology speak with authority to public, cultural, economic, and political situations?

The premise of this book is that Pentecostalism as a name for a theological tradition is unusually different from most other traditions in that the label itself is already inherently theological. To state the obvious: the name 'Pentecostal' as a label for the theology of the movement suggests a close association with the day of Pentecost. Pentecostal theology from the perspective of this self-identification is reflected in an experiential spirituality rooted in the day of Pentecost and believed by Pentecostals still to be available as a continuation or repetition or expansion (sometimes all three) of that original experience. My starting point for any response to the questions raised above is the argument that Pentecostal theology reaches deep into the day of Pentecost.

The argument that Pentecostal theology emerges from the root image of Pentecost is perhaps self-evident. However, the history of modern-day Pentecostalism only recently shows signs of Pentecostals attempting to formulate a constructive and comprehensive theology for the movement.[1]

---

[1] See the typology of Pentecostal theology in Christopher A. Stephenson, *Types of Pentecostal Theology: Method, System, Spirit* (Oxford: Oxford University Press, 2013). See also Wolfgang Vondey and Martin William Mittelstadt (eds), *The Theology of Amos Yong and the New Face*

Pentecostal theology has existed for a little more than one hundred years. It emerged with a series of spiritual revivals that marked the worldwide beginning of modern-day Pentecostalism at the turn to the twentieth century.[2] At the heart of those early revivals stood a spirituality, typically transmitted orally and ritually; Pentecostalism was marked by an ad hoc doxology rather than a systematic and dogmatic theology.[3] As a result, Pentecost has not been developed consistently as a theological symbol of the Pentecostal movement. There exists no single systematic and comprehensive account of (and for) Pentecostal theology worldwide. Convictions, beliefs, and teachings among Pentecostals are often formulated in the language and structure of other theological or cultural confessions and frequently suffer misunderstanding and misrepresentation. It is only with the global emergence of Pentecostalism, the rise of the broader Pentecostal and Charismatic movements in the mainline churches, the participation of Pentecostals in international ecumenical conversations, and the rise of Pentecostal theological scholarship, that conscious steps are taken toward formulating a comprehensive and organized Pentecostal theology. My proposal is that the way forward for constructive Pentecostal theology is marked by a way inward to and outward from the concrete beliefs and practices emerging with the day of Pentecost. In other words, Pentecost, Pentecostalism, and Pentecostal theology are intersecting realities that require definition not apart from one other but as a single (theological) concern.

Pentecost, Pentecostalism, and Pentecostal theology

Pentecostalism, of course, is a perplexing phenomenon.[4] Most definitions of Pentecostalism distinguish in some form between historical, sociological,

---

of Pentecostal Scholarship: Passion for the Spirit, Global Pentecostal and Charismatic Studies 14 (Leiden: Brill, 2013), 1–24; Wolfgang Vondey, *Pentecostalism: A Guide for the Perplexed* (London: Bloomsbury T&T Clark, 2013), 133–53.

[2] See Allan Anderson, *An Introduction to Pentecostalism: Global Charismatic Christianity* (Cambridge: Cambridge University Press, 2004), 19–38, 187–205; Vondey, *Pentecostalism*, 9–27.

[3] See Douglas Jacobsen, *Thinking in the Spirit: Theologies of the Early Pentecostal Movement* (Bloomington: Indiana University Press, 2003); Douglas Jacobsen (ed.), *A Reader in Pentecostal Theology* (Bloomington: Indiana University Press, 2006).

[4] For different approaches and literature, see Vondey, *Pentecostalism: A Guide for the Perplexed*.

geographical, and confessional variances of the movement.⁵ In this book, Pentecostalism refers in a broad sense to the complex diversity of classical Pentecostals, the charismatic movement, and Pentecostal or 'Pentecostal-like' independent churches.⁶ A prominent perspective is that of the *New International Dictionary of Pentecostal and Charismatic Movements*, which identifies as 'Pentecostal' the so-called classical Pentecostals connected with the revival at the Azusa Street Mission in Los Angeles (1906–1909); the members of the so-called charismatic movements in the established Roman Catholic, Protestant, and Orthodox churches that surfaced in North America during the 1960s; and so-called neocharismatic groups, 'a catch-all category that comprises 18,810 independent, indigenous, postdenominational denominations and groups that cannot be classified as either Pentecostal or charismatic but share a common emphasis on the Holy Spirit, spiritual gifts, Pentecostal-like experiences (not Pentecostal terminology), signs and wonders and power encounters'.⁷ Hence, it is an ambitious claim that a single theological narrative exists for these movements.

However, it is my hypothesis that the identity of the Pentecostal movement lies not primarily in its historical, denominational, geographical, or sociological features but in the theology of the movement. What emerges in this book as the theological narrative of Pentecostalism functions also as a critical lens through which one can discern the diverse adherents embraced by all-too-inclusive definitions of the Pentecostal movement. The unity and strength of Pentecostal theology lies in Pentecost as its symbol. From a theological perspective, I suggest, Pentecostalism can be identified by the day of Pentecost as the concern for an immediate encounter with God through the Spirit of Christ manifested in discernible signs and wonders as evidence of God's transforming and redeeming presence directing all of life towards the kingdom of God. The articulation of Pentecostal theology consequently goes deep into the heart of Pentecost. However, to say so is to invest in a theological

---

⁵ See Anderson, *An Introduction to Pentecostalism*, 13–14; Allan Anderson, 'Diversity in the Definition of 'Pentecostal/Charismatic' and Its Ecumenical Implications', *MS* 19, no. 2 (2002): 40–55.
⁶ Walter J. Hollenweger, *Pentecostalism: Origins and Developments Worldwide* (Peabody, MA: Hendrickson, 1997), 1; idem, *The Pentecostals: The Charismatic Movement in the Churches* (Minneapolis: Augsburg, 1972), 71–72.
⁷ Stanley M. Burgess and Eduard M. van der Maas (eds), *NIDPCM*, rev. and exp. ed. (Grand Rapids, MI: Zondervan, 2002), xx.

symbol not harvested by the traditional confessions as representative of an entire theological system. Even contemporary constructive efforts among Pentecostals have focused less on the root image of the day of Pentecost than on broader pneumatological and ecumenical metaphors.[8] The challenges of using Pentecost as a symbol for Pentecostal theology are manifold. How does the historical event function as a broad theological symbol? How does Pentecostal theology employ Pentecost without the risk of being accused of theological reductionism or historical primitivism? In other words, how do we move from Pentecost to Pentecostal and back again?

I confront these and other questions in this volume along three intersecting focal points that together construct Pentecost as a theological symbol of Pentecostal theology: First, I trace how Pentecostals find in the plot of the day of Pentecost a genuine and distinct theological tradition. An initial purpose of the book is therefore to develop and articulate the sources informing Pentecostal perspectives of the day of Pentecost and to show how these can be used consistently for theological articulation. Second, I propose a theological narrative framework from the day of Pentecost in the form of the full gospel that captures the theological convictions of the movement. The central agenda of this book is to tell the story of this full gospel and to interpret and apply it to the broad contours of Pentecostal theology. Third, I analyze how the full gospel narrative is grounded in the concrete spirituality, experiences, affections, and practices of Pentecostal worship by focusing on the tangible environment of the altar. The altar as a theological metaphor displays how the Pentecostal story is able to move from the day of Pentecost (as historical event) to Pentecost (as a theological symbol), to Pentecostalism (as a theological tradition), and back again. In other words – and this also works in both directions – Pentecostal theology is an invitation to the altar, and the altar is an invitation to the full gospel and the full gospel is an invitation to Pentecost.

These intersecting focal points are presented in two parts: the first tells the narrative of the full gospel and details the practices and rituals at the altar as foundational for Pentecostal theology; the second applies the full gospel to the broad theological concerns of creation, humanity, society, church, and God. I intend to show with this account that Pentecostal theology emerging in this

---

[8] Wolfgang Vondey, 'Pentecostalism and the Possibility of Global Theology: Implications of the Theology of Amos Yong', *Pneuma* 28, no. 2 (2006): 289–312.

fashion from the day of Pentecost is hospitable to constructive ecumenical endeavours and can contribute a comprehensive theological agenda. The two parts are preceded by an account of the prolegomena to Pentecostal theology, introductory remarks on the basic principles and premises for articulating the logic and discipline of theology from a Pentecostal perspective.

A narrative for Pentecostal theology

The chief argument of this book is that Pentecostal theology reaches deep into the heart of Pentecost. In order to substantiate this claim, part one of this volume aims at providing a theological narrative for Pentecostal theology that emerges from the experiences, beliefs, and practices of Pentecost. The most consistent theological narrative emerging from the history of Pentecostalism is the so-called full gospel. The fivefold pattern of this narrative presents an inclusive framework to explore the central venues of Pentecostal thought and praxis. This basic methodological premise originated with the Pentecostal scholarship in Cleveland, Tennessee, or the so-called Cleveland School.[9] Yet, the origins of the full gospel reach far into Pentecostal history, and the application of the full gospel motif can be traced throughout recent Pentecostal scholarship.[10] This book is therefore a discovery, synthesis, and advancement of the full gospel as a theological narrative for the global Pentecostal movement through the lens of Pentecost as its core symbol and the altar as its present realization. Each of the five chapters of part one is dedicated to one element of this full gospel: salvation, sanctification, baptism in the Spirit, divine healing, and the coming kingdom. My objective is to open up the tightness of this fivefold cord to reveal the inherent hospitality, sensibilities, experiences, and intuitions of Pentecost framed by this theological narrative. Since the full gospel functions as both theological articulation of the symbol of Pentecost and core narrative of Pentecostal theology, the first part is also a historical,

---

[9] For an exposition of the Cleveland School, see John Christopher Thomas, 'Pentecostal Theology in the Twenty-First Century', *Pneuma* 20, no. 1 (1998): 3–19. For the full gospel as a methodological premise, see Kenneth J. Archer, *The Gospel Revisited: Towards a Pentecostal Theology of Worship and Witness* (Eugene, OR: Pickwick, 2010), 1–17. For the history of the full gospel, see Donald W. Dayton, *Theological Roots of Pentecostalism* (Peabody, MA: Hendrickson, 1987).

[10] See the literature in each chapter engaging the broad scholarship on particular theological issues from the perspective of the full gospel or some of its elements.

genealogical, and theological description of the particular characteristics of Pentecostal theology inherited from the day of Pentecost. However, my goal is not to summarize any particular historical account among Pentecostals but to create an inclusive theological pattern characteristic of Pentecostal theology that can be applied to any theological topic by Pentecostals and those who wish to engage Pentecostals in dialogue. Although the story of the full gospel possesses an inherent logic that proceeds through each of the five motifs, the connections between the chapters are not just linear. The primary goal is to illustrate the methodological contributions of the full gospel, a task accomplished by constructing the primary narrative of each element from Pentecostal practices to doctrinal reflection and back again. Entrance to this narrative is possible in principle not only from the first but from any chapter of the first part.

In order to craft a theological account of Pentecostal theology along the contours of the full gospel, each chapter begins with a narrative of particular foundational ritual experiences and practices among Pentecostals. These narratives identify the spiritual underpinning and motivation for Pentecostal theology and form the basis for subsequent doctrinal reflection. This reflection, analysis and articulation of Pentecostal theology is then expanded to a conversation on foundational Christian practices as they are shaped by the particular contributions of the Pentecostal experiences and doctrines underlying them. The result is an expansion not only of the original practices among Pentecostals but of Christian doctrine as a whole. This methodology ultimately wishes to take us to an encounter with God and to the renewal of ourselves embedded in the fullness of the good news of God's renewal of the whole of creation. In this sense, the account given in the following chapters suggests that the inherent dynamic of Pentecostal theology is aimed at an ecumenical renewal of Christian theology from the perspective of the fullness of the gospel.

The spirituality, experiences, affections, and practices at the heart of Pentecostal theology given hereafter adopt the altar as the context for constructing a theological narrative. The first part is therefore also a contextual exploration of the Pentecostal metaphor of the altar. Each chapter contributes to painting in swift strokes this metaphor by examining how the full gospel emerges at the altar, how Pentecostal doctrines take account of the particular experiences and practices and how the world of the Pentecostal altar can be integrated in a broader theological conversation. The chapters continue necessarily from an initially rather broad account of the altar at Pentecost and then move to a particular discussion of contemporary appropriations of the metaphor among Pentecostals. In this way unfolds a dynamic and progressive development among the chapters which indicates that the full gospel always leads to the altar, the transformation at the altar, a release from the altar and ultimately a return to the altar. This inherent direction and continuous movement of the Pentecostal narrative form the foundation for the construction of a full gospel theology in the second part of this volume.

Systematic and constructive Pentecostal theology

The second part of this book seeks to develop from the full gospel narrative a full gospel theology and aims at illustrating the shape of systematic and constructive Pentecostal theology cast in the light of the full gospel. I propose that the full gospel narrative offers a hospitable framework for doing Pentecostal theology by providing a rich material, experiential and embodied theological agenda derived from Pentecost that is able to articulate constructively and systematically the encounter with God in the world. The contours of the five chapters in part two mirror the five elements of the full gospel narrative albeit with broader constructive theological focus. Whereas the first part provides largely a historical and genealogical narrative of Pentecostal theology, the second part aims more at providing a heuristic and hermeneutical framework for a systematic and constructive approach to Pentecostal theology cast in the image of Pentecost.

Pentecostals have been slow to articulate a systematic treatment of their theology. Although the full gospel is an open narrative, which invites other passions, practices, and beliefs, Pentecostal theology for most of the twentieth century remained confined to conversations on individual doctrines and internal matters within a sometimes rather narrowly perceived four- or fivefold gospel pattern. Pentecostals in the East and the southern hemisphere have not been able to contribute significantly their perspectives and voices to a global Pentecostal theology. However, the expansion of Pentecostalism worldwide, shifts within the internal makeup of the movement, including the advent of the charismatic renewal, participation in the ecumenical movement, the development of theological scholarship and a critical reception of Pentecostal theology by the theological academy have contributed to renewed theological consciousness among many Pentecostals. Attention has shifted among younger generations to a quest for their own contributions to theology, philosophy, and the sciences; the articulation of theological hermeneutics and methodology; the revision of traditional doctrines and theological disciplines from a Pentecostal perspective; and the questions and concerns of the global Pentecostal movement. These tasks, however speculative and systematic, remain thoroughly indebted to Pentecostal practices, rituals, and liturgies at the altar, which continues to form the seedbed for the hospitality of the full gospel.

In the first part, I suggest that the full gospel is most prepared to articulate its own convictions and to engage with other confessions when it is shaped by the spirituality, experiences, affections, practices, and doctrines emerging from the altar. The Pentecostal ritual of the altar call and response, and the ensuing practices that draw Pentecostals first to assemble and then to go beyond the altar, narrated by the full gospel, stand for a theological movement from the inside to the outside, the private to the public, the individual to the social, the church to the world, the local to the global, and the gospel to creation. Part two reverses the move, mirroring part one, and begins with a theology of creation and a view of the external world in order to move back eventually to the worship of God at the altar. Even conceptualized doctrines and philosophical considerations remain grounded in this movement of the liturgies, rituals, sacraments, and practices narrated by the full gospel. All themes of the full gospel inform other practices and attempt to integrate other doctrines into the narrative. In some sense, the second part is therefore a mirror extension of the first and its themes. In this way, the second part demonstrates the return of constructive and systematic Pentecostal theology to its root symbol of Pentecost.

At the same time, the chapters of part two are more constructive, even prescriptive, than the narrative of part one, since Pentecostal systematic and constructive theologies are still very much in development. The doctrines of creation (cosmology), humanity (anthropology), society (social and cultural anthropology), church (ecclesiology), and God (doxology) hardly exist as developed disciplines among Pentecostal groups. Nonetheless, if Pentecostal theology is oriented and structured by Pentecost as symbol narrated in the full gospel, then a development of these disciplines will be sensitive to the model described in part one and thereby be able to provide a distinctively Pentecostal colour to the conversations. I reveal these Pentecostal colours also by engaging in the second part primarily with a wide range of Pentecostal literature in order to show that we are justified in speaking of Pentecostal theology as an already existing tradition as well as to indicate how this young tradition can be shaped systematically and constructively with the help of the full gospel. The structure of part two is therefore as hospitable as the narrative of the full gospel presented in part one; it addresses concerns for the world and the environment, divine action and human agency, social justice and the common good, public and political theology, the marks of the church, and the worship of God. The result is no more than an attempt to lay out the conceptual terrain of Pentecostal theology as a model. The gaps left in this model are (not always) entirely intentional – inviting the reader to think along the lines of the full gospel, to add to the experiences and practices of a global Pentecostal narrative, and to discover even within the most speculative Pentecostal doctrines the witness to the full gospel as a call to the altar. In this fashion, the chapters always return to the central claim of this book that Pentecost is the wellspring of the Pentecostal movement and its theology.

1

Prolegomena to Pentecostal Doctrine

Prolegomena are typically not expected to offer the ingredients for the most important chapters. In the vast landscape of contemporary confessional groups and theological traditions, prolegomena are rarely developed and hardly consulted. We like to skip them in an effort to get to the point, so to speak. And the point of theology, of course, is to identify a particular system of beliefs that distinguishes one group from another. Only that, in Pentecostalism, doctrine is not the point. And to explain this peculiar character of Pentecostal theology, we need to speak to the principles that precede the content of Pentecostal doctrine. The title of this introductory chapter should therefore be read quite literally as an attempt to speak about the character of Pentecostal theology 'before' we discuss the doctrines of the movement. The first question of our prolegomena is simply: what comes *before* Pentecostal doctrine? The answer that will determine the entire enterprise is: Pentecost.

Pentecost is the core theological symbol of Pentecostal theology. Such is the argument of this book. I suspect, however, that this seemingly modest proposal is easily misunderstood as an attempt to express with the term 'Pentecost' the central doctrine of the Pentecostal movement. The danger of such an approach is that it assumes Pentecostalism fits the 'grid' or 'norm' of existing theological systems. The decision to put doctrine first means that Pentecostals are seen as dogmatically conditioned and that they can be doctrinally compared and assessed, typically, in contrast to the doctrines of other traditions. The resulting theology is often derived from saying what Pentecostal theology is not, judged against the doctrinal standards and systems of the more established traditions. 'Pentecost' as a label of doctrine is then seen as the attempt to escape the apophatic lens and to say something positive, albeit without much hope to go beyond other, already existing, doctrinal proposals. If Pentecost is doctrine alone, then it is merely a replacement for prominent ideas such as the baptism in the Holy Spirit or the speaking with tongues. Instead, the intent of these prolegomena is to overcome the rule of doctrine as the sole arbiter of determining Pentecostal theology.

The primary challenge of determining the contours and content of Pentecostal theology, I want to suggest, is its foundational indebtedness to the day of Pentecost before we can arrive at any possible articulation of Pentecostal doctrine. We might say that Pentecost *is* the very prolegomenon of Pentecostal theology, because *Pentecostalism is a form of living fundamentally concerned with the renewing work of God as it emerges from the outpouring of the Holy Spirit on the day of Pentecost*. Pentecostals are in a sense 'overaccepting' the day of Pentecost in a manner that imitates the outpouring of the Spirit. Engaging with the day of Pentecost demands a 'logic' that runs askew to the ordering of traditional doctrinal expectations, and the dominant theological systems are often ill-fit for expressing a functioning Pentecostal theology.[1] The Pentecostal theology presented here is therefore deliberately cast not, as often customary, in the language and logic of other dogmatic systems, but in a 'spirit' that takes seriously the day of Pentecost as the root symbol of Pentecostalism.

Play: The spirit of Pentecostal theology

Attempts to formulate a deliberative and systematic articulation of Pentecostal theology have increased since the early twentieth century.[2] Yet, despite various proposals outlining its content, the nature, method and development of Pentecostal theology have not been widely discussed. Pentecostal theology, because it traverses a spirituality manifested in a foundational experience of the Holy Spirit, cannot simply make 'use' of doctrine as an end of theology disassociated from the original experience. In other words, Pentecostal

---

[1] D. Lyle Dabney, 'Saul's Armor: The Problem and the Promise of Pentecostal Theology Today', *Pneuma* 23, no. 1 (2001): 115–46.
[2] See Christopher A. Stephenson, *Types of Pentecostal Theology: Method, System, Spirit* (Oxford: Oxford University Press, 2012).

theology does not seek doctrine as an end in itself but upholds the possibility of the continuing actualization of the encounter with God that makes the articulation of the experience as doctrine principally unnecessary. In the midst of the global epistemic crisis laid bare by the constructs of postmodernity, Pentecostal theology does not represent simply another epistemic construct. Rather, at the root of Pentecostalism lies the Spirit of Pentecost as the spirit of unbounded (and unexpected) freedom from such constructs. Beneath the crisis, the conflicting voices and malady of multiplicity of approaches of late modern thought, a different 'logic' holds together Pentecostal theology: the spirit of play.

The notion of play can be used as a heuristic metaphor for a way of doing theology that eludes precise rules, boundaries and systems even though it can make use of them. For my purposes of identifying Pentecostal theology, play is understood as a redemptive method of living and interpreting the logic of reality by transforming and transcending its existing structures and demands towards the realm of alternative expectations motivated by an unlimited imagination.[3] In a historical sense, play is the unexpected perpetuation of the day of Pentecost, the play of the Spirit poured out. In a theological sense, play (re)orders reality with a surplus of possibilities and an imagination oriented towards the fulfilment of God's own imagination (as revealed with the day of Pentecost).[4] In a practical sense, play is the (Pentecostal) pursuit of that divine imagination, which often runs counter to existing theological interpretations and dominant articulations of reality.[5] In a methodological sense, play is therefore a way of engaging the world not exclusively through doctrine but also materially, physically, spiritually, aesthetically, morally, and socially.[6] Theology as play has the character of spontaneity, enthusiasm, improvisation, and the free engagement of others in an unbounded movement of God's Spirit.[7] With the notion of play, I suggest that an alternative

---

[3] For the application of play to Pentecostalism, see Nimi Wariboko, *The Pentecostal Principle: Ethical Methodology in New Spirit*, PM 5 (Grand Rapids: Eerdmans, 2012), 161–95; Andre Droogers, *Play and Power in Religion: Collected Essays* (Berlin: de Gryuter, 2012); Wolfgang Vondey, *Beyond Pentecostalism: The Crisis of Global Christianity and the Renewal of the Theological Agenda*, PM 3 (Grand Rapids, MI: Eerdmans, 2010); Jean-Jacques Suurmond, *Word and Spirit at Play: Towards a Charismatic Theology* (Grand Rapids, MI: Eerdmans, 1994).
[4] Suurmond, *Word and Spirit*, 75–83.
[5] Harvey Cox, *Feast of Fools: A Theological Essay on Festivity and Fantasy* (New York: Harper and Row, 1969), 131–38.
[6] Vondey, *Beyond Pentecostalism*, 41.
[7] Wariboko, *The Pentecostal Principle*, 170.

way of doing theology identifies Pentecostal theology for the sake of renewing the world and liberating theology's own symbols and practices in redemptive engagement with God. In this sense, theology as play represents a radical theological methodology.

Pentecostals traditionally have not had a theology; they have lived it. There is no premeditated response to the day of Pentecost; one must surrender to the freedom of the Holy Spirit before being able to capture its essence in any articulate sense of theological doctrines. Therefore, it would be incorrect to argue that Pentecostals have deliberatively engaged in theology through a conceptual form of play. Rather, play is a primal way of accepting the freedom of the Spirit in an attempt not to analyze the logic of Pentecost before participating in its experience. In this way, play precedes even the primacy of Pentecostal speech, piety, and hope.[8] The spirit of play finds its shape along the contours of (1) the spirituality of the Pentecostal movement, (2) the mediation of that spirituality in the experiences of the Holy Spirit, (3) the testimony to the experiences through the Pentecostal story, (4) the living expression of that testimony through the affections, (5) the participation in theological practices, and (6) the embodiment of such practices in Pentecostal life and worship. On the following pages, I will address each element in turn, identify its particular Pentecostal character, and suggest how each element contributes to the formation of Pentecostal theology.

Spirituality: The origin of Pentecostal theology

I am arguing that Pentecostal theology reaches deep into the day of Pentecost. Yet, it is not the historical or doctrinal connections, however perceived, but the spirituality of Pentecost that marks the origin of Pentecost(al) theology. To say that Pentecostalism is a form of living is to say that the possibility for articulating a Pentecostal theology is rooted in the discernible spirituality of the Pentecostal life.[9] Pentecostal spirituality arises out of Pentecost: this kind of spirituality is not simply any form of exuberant experience or revival but the expression of a personal participation of the individual and the community

---

[8] See Harvey Cox, *Fire from Heaven: The Rise of Pentecostal Spirituality and the Reshaping of Religion in the Twenty-First Century* (Cambridge, MA: DaCapo, 1995), 81–122.
[9] Land, *Pentecostal Spirituality*, 11–19.

in the biblical story of God actualized in Jesus Christ and made possible by the Holy Spirit.[10] Chief to Pentecostal spirituality is a core belief in Jesus as the centre of the gospel filtered through a heavy emphasis on the cross and the resurrection. One might say that all Pentecostal theology flows to and from Jesus Christ. At the same time, this Christocentric spirituality clearly accentuates the work of the Holy Spirit as the most essential component of living a Christ-like life. The move to theological reflection is born from this emphasis on the Spirit of Christ, and although theological articulation can begin with doctrine (or other starting points), the development of Pentecostal doctrine always passes through a personal encounter with Christ through the Holy Spirit. In this sense, Pentecostal theology begins as a spirituality consistent with the Christian mystical tradition.[11] The theology of the Pentecostal tradition is rooted deeply in the nature of the experience of Pentecost.

The beliefs, practices, sensibilities, and values of Pentecostal spirituality are defined at the core by the experience of God.[12] The heart of this experience is narrated by the biblical scriptures with the drama of salvation history unfolding in the gospel of Jesus Christ. Yet, the focus of Pentecostal theology is not the biblical narrative itself but its accessibility, that is, restoration, renewal, and revitalization in the world for the continuation of a lived encounter with God.[13] Pentecostals seek recourse in Scripture not primarily in order to interpret Scripture but to interpret their own story in an interwoven dynamic in which the biblical revelation interprets the experience of the Spirit, and that confessional (not doctrinal) experience serves as a hermeneutical filter for the reading of Scripture.[14] The resulting practices of Pentecostal spirituality tend to lead to a rather 'thick description' that needs to stay on the ground of experience even when reaching to the height of speculative abstraction.[15]

---

[10] Ibid., 71–82.

[11] See Daniel Castelo, *Pentecostalism as a Christian Mystical Tradition* (Grand Rapids, MI: Eerdmans, 2017); Simon Chan, *Pentecostal Theology and Christian Spiritual Tradition*, JPTS 21 (Sheffield: Sheffield Academic Press, 2000). See also Roger E. Olson, 'Pietism and Pentecostalism: Spiritual Cousins or Competitors'? *Pneuma* 34, no. 3 (2012): 319–44; Kenneth J. Archer and Andrew S. Hamilton, 'Anabaptism-Pietism and Pentecostalism: Scandalous Partners in Protest', *SJT* 63, no. 2 (2010): 185–202.

[12] Daniel E. Albrecht and Evan B. Howard, 'Pentecostal Spirituality', in *The Cambridge Companion to Pentecostalism*, ed. Cecil M. Robeck Jr. and Amos Yong (New York: Cambridge University Press, 2015), 235–53.

[13] Ibid., 244–51.

[14] See Kenneth J. Archer, *A Pentecostal Hermeneutic: Spirit, Scripture and Community* (Cleveland, TN: CPT Press, 2009), 89–171.

[15] See Wolfgang Vondey (ed.), *The Holy Spirit and the Christian Life: Historical, Interdisciplinary, and Renewal Perspectives*, CHARIS 1 (New York: Palgrave, 2014), 217–25.

While speculation is not a contrast to spirituality, Pentecostal theology as a form of mystical theology demands the constant availability to be practiced, and thus makes speculative theology as a purely intellectual or theoretical endeavour impossible.

The recourse to Scripture at the heart of Pentecostal spirituality is shaped by a unique hermeneutical lens adopted throughout this volume as fundamental to the functioning of Pentecost as a theological symbol. Drawing from the speech of Peter in Acts 2, Pentecostals appeal to the biblical texts by employing a tension between what may be labelled a 'this-is-that' and 'this-is-not-that' hermeneutics.[16] In what constitutes for Pentecostals the original hermeneutics of Pentecost, the apostle explains the meaning of 'this' event in terms of the fulfilment of 'that' prophecy given in the past: 'This which you see and hear today is that which was spoken by the prophet Joel' (Acts 2:16). The distance between the present and the past is seemingly eliminated as the present reality is redefined in terms of the past: 'This *is* that'! The present participates in the biblical events by fulfilling the past, which now redefines the present. In addition, this redefinition is accompanied by a rejection of the dominant understanding of the present reality apart from the past, as Peter discards the public's explanation of the disciples' behaviour as a literal drunkenness: 'This is *not* that'! (v. 15). Instead, he substitutes for the physical intoxication a sense of spiritual overflowing that draws from the biblical reality of the past by identifying it as constituting the beginning of a new age.[17] This hermeneutic of simultaneously accepting and rejecting 'that' as the determining reality for the present 'this' underscores that Pentecostal hermeneutics is not simply guided by the return to a biblical Pentecost.[18] Pentecostals relate their experience to scripture, to stories and events in the Bible, because they interpret and authenticate their present experiences as participating in the biblical events thrust anew into the present. This way of interpretation constitutes a strategic hermeneutic in Pentecostal theology. Nonetheless, the 'that' of the biblical Pentecost cannot

---

[16] Wolfgang Vondey and Chris W. Green, 'Between This and That: Reality and Sacramentality in the Pentecostal Worldview', *JPT* 19, no. 2 (2010): 243–64.

[17] See French L. Arrington, *The Acts of the Apostles: Introduction, Translation, and Commentary* (Peabody, MA: Hendrickson, 1988), 25–32; Roger Stronstad, *The Charismatic Theology of St. Luke* (Peabody, MA: Hendrickson, 1984), 55–57; idem, 'The Influence of the Old Testament on the Charismatic Theology of St. Luke', *Pneuma* 2, no. 1 (1980): 32–50.

[18] Cf. Nimi Wariboko, *Nigerian Pentecostalism* (Rochester, NY: University of Rochester Press, 2014), 101–3.

simply be carried forward into 'this' present reality without causing significant changes. Rather, the present Pentecost reenacts the past by participating in its story and simultaneously extending and adapting it to present contexts. The appeal to the day of Pentecost is not an appeal to the return to biblical history but to participation in an enduring theological symbol.

Theological articulation among Pentecostals can be speculative and systematic albeit only if that means an integration of spirituality in terms of the cognitive, affective, and behavioural dimensions of participating in Pentecost as a perpetual system of the Christian life. This kind of mystical theology always emerges from, identifies, preserves, and returns to the foundational experience of the Holy Spirit carrying the movement.[19] In this sense, Pentecostal theology is not strictly dogmatic; it does not seek articulation of doctrine as the primary task of theology.[20] Instead, Pentecostal theology seeks a relationship between spirituality and doctrine so that living theology becomes a constant and reciprocal back-and-forth movement between beliefs, affections, and actions, on the one hand, and the articulation of doctrine, on the other.[21] Doctrinal formulations, as has been observed, are 'part of a verbalization of the implications of the more general and sometimes amorphous theological views that Pentecostals already presuppose (at times unconsciously) in their spirituality'.[22] As a result, certain doctrines rely much more on Pentecostal experience than on the power of explanation.[23] However, this imbalance should not be construed as a bias of overemphasizing spirituality or as an inability to explain themselves (although both may be present in the movement); it is rather the result of not having learned consistently how to form a reciprocal bond between theology and spirituality – a problem inherited from the modern mystical traditions and accentuated by the unexpected experience of the Holy Spirit.[24] The way forward to a genuine

---

[19] See Frank D. Macchia, 'Spirituality and Social Liberation: The Message of the Blumhardts in the Light of Württemberg Pietism, with Implications for Pentecostal Theology', in *Experiences of the Spirit: Conference on Pentecostal and Charismatic Research in Europe at Utrecht University, 1989*, ed. J. A. B. Jongeneel, SIGC 68 (Frankfurt: Peter Lang, 1989), 65–84.
[20] See Vondey, *Beyond Pentecostalism*, 98–108; idem, *Pentecostalism*, 82–84.
[21] See Stephenson, *Types of Pentecostal Theology*, 114–19.
[22] Ibid., 116.
[23] Chan, *Pentecostal Theology and the Christian Spiritual Tradition*, 10. Emphasis original.
[24] See Dale M. Coulter, 'The Spirit and the Bride Revisited: Pentecostalism, Renewal, and the Sense of History', *JPT* 21, no. 2 (2012): 298–319; Joseph Davis, 'The Movement toward Mysticism in Gustavo Gutiérrez's Thought: Is This an Open Door to Pentecostal Dialogue'? *Pneuma* 33, no. 1 (2011): 5–24.

articulation of Pentecostal theology can only lead through the formative lens of Pentecostal spirituality.

Of course, Pentecostal theology is not synonymous with spirituality. The task at hand is rather to clarify what kind of spirituality underlies the reflection and articulation of Pentecostal theology, if and how that spirituality arrives at doctrinal formulation and how spirituality continues to inform Pentecostal theology. I suggest that perceiving Pentecostal theology as an expression of mystical theology has at least four immediate consequences for employing Pentecost as theological symbol. First, the process of formulating doctrine is always submitted to the experience of the Holy Spirit, or put differently, Pentecostal theology is always experiential. Second, the formulation of doctrine depends upon the articulation of that experience, that is, Pentecostal theology always leads through narrative and testimony. Third, the relationship of Pentecostal experience and Pentecostal story is integrated by the affections, in other words, Pentecostal theology is fundamentally affective. Fourth, the affections are living expressions of Pentecostal spirituality that always lead to practices – Pentecostal theology is always practiced. The current of Pentecostal spirituality moves from experience to testimony to affections to practices and returns to experiences in an ongoing dynamic that captures what might be termed the development of doctrine.[25] Pentecostals define theology not first and foremost by its outcome as a product of the encounter with God but by its nature as the expectation of the continuing experience of God in the world. That anticipation is the root instinct of Pentecost and heartbeat of Pentecostal experiences.

Experience: The playground of Pentecostal theology

The heartbeat of Pentecostal spirituality is the experience of the Holy Spirit made possible by the event of Pentecost. On the level of experience, resonating the central emphasis spirituality places on the Spirit, Pentecostal theology is both pneumatic (as the experience resulting from the encounter with the Spirit) and pneumatological (as reflection on that experience). This mystical theology derives from the actuality (not merely the possibility) of the

---

[25] For a similar dynamic, see Land, *Pentecostal Spirituality*, 46.

experience of the Holy Spirit as an immediate revelation of God that seeks mediation in the life of the human person and the community.[26] On the level of contemplation, Pentecostal theology therefore begins with the Spirit and from there, submits to the current of spirituality and doctrine. Oral narrative and testimony, proclamation, prayer, song and dance, prophecy, and speaking in tongues are some of the native expressions of the wonder of that experience. Scripture contains these expressions (or reports them) in a normative (but second-order) fashion that allows Pentecostals to reflect on and discern their own experiences. Doctrine is in this process a third-order moment of an implicit theological method that emerges from *and* aims at the experience of worship rather than systematization, abstraction, and formalization.[27] Pentecostals certainly participate in doctrinal discussion without always possessing a confessional experience, but any teaching not subjected to the primacy of the experience of the Holy Spirit cannot be attributed to Pentecost as symbol. Put differently, Pentecostal theology can maintain any Christian doctrine without claiming that they are uniquely Pentecostal in origin or character. However, for such a teaching to be called 'Pentecostal', it must pass through the inevitable and foundational moment of experience.

What exactly Pentecostals mean by 'experience' is (often intentionally) ambiguous, at least to the outside observer.[28] The appeal to experience, Pentecostals have emphasized strongly, 'demands more than *belief* in an experience – it demands the *experience of the experience* itself'.[29] In other words, for the Pentecostal, it is a particular kind of experience – not the idea of experience as such – that forms the foundational moment for articulating a Pentecostal theology. The claim of experience as foundational for theology can be found in other traditions without those traditions claiming to be Pentecostal. Rather, it is the particular set of first-hand experiences surrounding the day of Pentecost, which concentrates on the immediate encounter with God in Christ through the Holy Spirit, that form the

[26] See Giovanni Maltese, *Geisterfahrer zwischen Transzendenz und Immanenz: Die Erfahrungsbegriffe in den pfingstlich-charismatischen Theologien von Terry L. Cross und Amos Yong im Vergleich*, Kirche – Konfession – Religion 61 (Göttingen: V&R Unipress, 2013); Peter D. Neumann, *Pentecostal Experience: An Ecumenical Encounter* (Eugene, OR: Pickwick, 2012).
[27] Even when the reading of Scripture leads to that experience, Pentecostals attribute primacy to the experience of the experience.
[28] Neumann, *Pentecostal Experience*, 100–61.
[29] Mathew S. Clark and Henry I. Lederle et al., *What Is Distinctive about Pentecostal Theology?* (Pretoria: University of South Africa, 1989), 40.

foundation for carrying out Pentecostal theology. Conversion is perhaps the entrance for most Pentecostals to the particularity of these Pentecostal experiences.[30] Yet, Pentecostals shy away from conceptualizing their experiences in fear of losing the dynamism of the actual experience and of turning the uninhibited encounter with God into a mere object of doctrinal reflection distanced from a personal and communal transformation.[31] At the same time, since theology is always already a mediated experience, the articulation of Pentecostal theology also requires an indication of the framework of mediation.[32] In this volume, I use the notion of experience, in full awareness of its ambiguity, broadly as representing an epistemological appeal to a transformative encounter with the immanence of God mediated by the Holy Spirit through the whole spectrum of created existence. One might say, for Pentecostals, the entire appeal to the experience of God is grounded in the notion of Pentecost.

Pentecost, taken as a theological symbol, suggests that the particular experiences of Pentecostals, although an interruption of the status quo, can be built into a comprehensive metaphysical framework of explanation.[33] This framework arises out of the situatedness of Pentecostal experiences in the practices of Pentecostal communities where the experiences of Pentecost find their natural continuation. In other words, the framework of Pentecostal theology is bound to the biographies and ethnographies that testify to the concrete contexts of lived experiences on the ground: theological generalizations and formulations of doctrine are shaped and reshaped by personal experiences, practices, and rituals of the church in a perpetual Pentecost.[34] These shared experiences construct the playground for Pentecostal theology by shaping a historical, theological, ecclesial, and soteriological narrative of Pentecost known as the full gospel.

---

[30] See Grace Milton, *Shalom, The Spirit and Pentecostal Conversion*, GPCS 18 (Leiden: Brill, 2015).
[31] Chan, *Pentecostal Theology*, 24.
[32] See the examples suggested in Neumann, *Pentecostal Experience*, 162–330. See also the emphasis on immediate experience in Maltese, *Geisterfahrer*, 93–106.
[33] See Yong, *The Spirit Poured Out on All Flesh*, 280–92.
[34] See Peter Marina, *Getting the Holy Ghost: Urban Ethnography in a Brooklyn Pentecostal Tongue-Speaking Church* (Lanham, MD: Lexington Books, 2013); Peter G. A. Versteeg, *The Ethnography of a Dutch Pentecostal Church: Vineyard Utrecht and the International Charismatic Movement* (New York: Edwin Mellen Press, 2011); Mark J. Cartledge, *Testimony in the Spirit: Rescripting Ordinary Pentecostal Theology* (Surrey, UK: Ashgate, 2010); Margaret M. Poloma and Ralph J. Hood, *Blood and Fire: Godly Love in a Pentecostal Emerging Church* (New York: NYU Press, 2008).

Full gospel: The narrative of Pentecostal theology

A systematic articulation of Pentecostal doctrine must take account of Pentecostals' own articulation of their theological story.[35] Narrative is widely considered the native expression of Pentecostal and charismatic spirituality.[36] The framework used most consistently for narrating the set of Pentecostal experiences emerging on the ground is the so-called full gospel, which emerged historically as a four- or fivefold pattern borrowed from the Wesleyan Holiness tradition.[37] It has endured the short history of modern-day Pentecostalism as a comprehensive blueprint for expressing Pentecostal spirituality and giving theological articulation to the movement.[38] The larger, fivefold pattern proclaims, usually in kerygmatic form, the good news that Jesus Christ brings (1) salvation, (2) sanctification, (3) baptism in the Spirit, (4) divine healing, and (5) the impending arrival of the kingdom of God.[39] I suggest that these elements identify the theme, plot, characters, and setting of a theological narrative cast in the image of the biblical story of the original Pentecost. Rather than representing elements of propositional doctrine or a system of doctrines, identifying the full gospel as a narrative for articulating meaningful experiences and spirituality suggests that these theological accents build the core motivation for Pentecostal theology but not the exclusive rules or structures for articulating Pentecostal doctrine. The full gospel gives new expression to the kind of mystical theology at the core of Pentecostal spirituality. The goal of the full gospel, in the first place, is to preserve the availability of the experiences of Pentecost, the validity of those experiences, and their perpetuation. In other words, the full gospel is not a

---

[35] The notion of the Pentecostal story was developed by Kenneth J. Archer, *The Gospel Revisited: Towards a Pentecostal Theology of Worship and Witness* (Eugene, OR: Pickwick, 2010), 18–42; idem, *A Pentecostal Hermeneutic: Spirit, Scripture and Community* (Cleveland, TN: CPT Press, 2009), 128–70; idem, 'Pentecostal Story: The Hermeneutical Filter for the Making of Meaning', *Pneuma* 26, no. 1 (2004): 36–59.

[36] See Mark J. Cartledge, *Encountering the Spirit: The Charismatic Tradition* (London: Darton, Longman & Todd, 2006), 19–32; Land, *Pentecostal Spirituality*, 63–88.

[37] See A. B. Simpson, *The Four-Fold Gospel* (repr. 1925; Harrisburg, PA: Christian Alliance Publishing Co., 1890). For the history of development see Dayton, *Theological Roots*, 15–33.

[38] See Mark J. Cartledge, 'The Early Pentecostal Theology of Confidence Magazine (1908–1926): A Version of the Five-Fold Gospel?' *JEPTA* 28, no. 2 (2008): 117–30; John Christopher Thomas, 'Pentecostal Theology in the Twenty-First Century', *Pneuma* 20, no. 1 (1998): 3–19; Land, *Pentecostal Spirituality*, 183; Donald W. Dayton, *Theological Roots of Pentecostalism* (Peabody, MA: Hendrickson, 1987), 15–23.

[39] Dayton, *Theological Roots of Pentecostalism*, 21–23.

structure for explicating Pentecostal doctrine; it is a narrative for a way of living.

The order and content of the full gospel narrative is not strictly defined; it varies historically and geographically, since the pattern is not the result of systematic theological reflection or received interpretation of Scripture but functions as a descriptive mechanism of Pentecostal spirituality shaped by a range of personal and communal experiences (that often contrast with existing theologies and interpretations in and outside of the movement).[40] Some Pentecostals adjust the historical pattern and combine or include other themes to speak of a 'fullness' of the gospel.[41] Others may not readily use the phrase 'full gospel' or its relatives to identify their theology even though the elements of the narrative are clearly seen. Pentecostal groups employ the elements of the full gospel 'in a creative and not always in a constant way'.[42] At times, the patterns emerge only individually and not as a whole. Systematic proposals can lose sight of the original narrative but tend to return to it.[43] The full gospel can therefore not be understood in a reductionist fashion as a definitive formula for the content of Pentecostal doctrine.[44] Rather, the full gospel is an expression of Pentecostal spirituality and experience because it 'is based on a passionate desire to "meet" with Jesus Christ as he is being perceived of as the Bearer of the Full Gospel'.[45] When discussed as doctrine, the elements of the full gospel are therefore never logically isolated; nor do they adhere to a strict theological sequence, since the experiences underlying the narrative have occurred in diverse fashion since the day of Pentecost.

As a narrative built on Pentecost, the full gospel emphasizes the centrality of Christ identified by several underlying experiences of the Holy Spirit that form a heuristic framework for theological articulation.[46] A systematic,

[40] See John Christopher Thomas, 'Pentecostal Theology in the Twenty-First Century', *Pneuma* 20, no. 1 (1998): 3–19.
[41] See David Yong-gi Cho, *The Five-Fold Gospel and the Three-fold Blessing* (Seoul: Logos Co., 1997).
[42] Veli-Matti Kärkkäinen, '"Encountering Christ in the Full Gospel Way": An Incarnational Pentecostal Spirituality', *JEPTA* 27, no. 1 (2007): 5–19 (15).
[43] See my critique in Wolfgang Vondey, 'Pentecostalism and the Possibility of Global Theology: Implications of the Theology of Amos Yong', *Pneuma* 28, no. 2 (2006): 289–312, but subsequently Amos Yong, *In the Days of Caesar: Pentecostalism and Political Theology* (Grand Rapids, MI: Eerdmans, 2010), 111–14.
[44] Kenneth J. Archer, 'The Fivefold Gospel and the Mission of the Church: Ecclesiastical Implications and Opportunities', in *Toward a Pentecostal Ecclesiology: The Church and the Fivefold Gospel*, ed. John Christopher Thomas (Cleveland, TN: CPT Press, 2010), 7–43.
[45] Kärkkäinen, 'Encountering Christ in the Full Gospel Way', 7.
[46] See Steven M. Studebaker, *From Pentecost to the Triune God: A Pentecostal Trinitarian Theology* (Grand Rapids, MI: Eerdmans, 2012), 19–26; Yong, *In the Days of Caesar*, 95–98.

constructive or doctrinal formulation of Pentecostal theology must aspire to hold together a similar kind of dynamic narrative of expression of the personal, communal, ecclesial, cultural, and counter-cultural experiences in the diverse contexts and history of world Pentecostalism. The primary theological challenge of this narrative is that it is not based on isolated doctrines but on interconnected foundational Pentecostal experiences. Pentecostal theology unfolds along these narratives, but it is not bound by them to a strict order, rules, and regulations.

The full gospel as a way of living is consequently shaped by a correspondence between the freedom of Pentecostal experiences and practices, on the one hand, and the demands of theological reflection and doctrinal articulation, on the other. Therein lies the greatest challenge of the realization of Pentecostal theology, which exists amidst the tension between the idealized 'pure' experiences of the gospel and their counterpart as the strict dogmatic adherence to doctrine. Embodying this tension, the claim that experience holds logical and epistemological primacy over Pentecostal theology does not apply, since experience serves an epistemological and theological practice. It is also incorrect to say that Pentecostal theology exists in praxis rather than in thought, as if experience could be emptied of any thought or to think would not account for a form of praxis. The full gospel does not merely make explicit what is implicit in Pentecostal spirituality, but the experiences of the Spirit act as a unique hermeneutic in their own right, because experience is viewed as lived affirmation of the revelation of God. Hence, the four- or fivefold narratives are principally not representations of full *doctrine* but of the full *gospel*.

Nonetheless, the experiences of the elements of the full gospel cannot simply be dissolved into other sources of theology acknowledged within the Christian tradition.[47] Experience, even when not reflective, mediates and relates the self to God and others, so that theological reflection begins with the discernment of the self in the community of those who have encountered God.[48] In this sense, as medium of the human encounter with God's Spirit, experience is normative in the Pentecostal tradition. As the object of theological reflection, experience among Pentecostals is not formally normative

---

[47] See Vondey, *Beyond Pentecostalism*, 78–108.
[48] Yong, *Spirit-Word-Community*, 188–91, 247–53.

and insufficient by itself to characterize Pentecostal theology.[49] In both cases, the experience, its articulation and interpretation as the full gospel are always mediate forms of an immediate encounter with God. The life of the full gospel unfolds only on the basis of the full gospel experiences at the root of the narrative. Pentecostals speak less about salvation, sanctification, Spirit baptism, divine healing and the kingdom of God (as the elements of the Pentecostal full gospel) than about being saved, sanctified, filled with the Spirit, healed and on their way to heaven (as moments of the root experiences of Pentecost). The path of Pentecostal theology proceeds from experience to reflection, interpretation and the articulation of doctrine through the manifestation of the underlying experiences in the affections.

Affections: The energy of Pentecostal theology

If Pentecostal theology is always experiential, how does this theology communicate that experience? Although there may be a 'pure' experience of the experience, there is no immediate rational, neutral and universal reflection on experience that does not also already depend on a particular account of the world and the particular means of communication available to the subject of that experience. The full gospel narrates the Pentecostal experiences rooted in the day of Pentecost, but these experiences are not distributed by the narrative as such. Pentecostal theology is not synonymous with narrative theology. Rather, the theological perpetuation of Pentecost, identified as the spirituality of an immediate experience of God that seeks mediation, does not and cannot proceed directly as intellectual knowledge. While the articulation of the full gospel is a consequence of the demands of a variety of such interpreted experiences, the particular proposal of the full gospel is that this narrative of the experiences of God is communicated and interpreted through the affections: love, joy, gratitude, compassion, sorrow, courage and other forms of willing, feeling and desiring that make and shape an aesthetic rather than a logic, a movement of the heart driven by experience rather than

---

[49] Dale M. Coulter, 'What Meaneth This? Pentecostals and Theological Inquiry', *JPT* 10, no. 1 (2001): 38–64.

decisions of the intellect.[50] The affections mediate God's involvement in the world through manifested expressions of the passion of God's eternal being revealed in Jesus Christ and communicated by the Holy Spirit.[51] Passion is the bridge between Pentecostal experience and doctrine, since the encounter with God occurs in the human being in a manner reflecting God's eternal being and thus characterizing the human person in its disposition towards God and others.[52] The jubilant manifestations of the affections provide the energy of Pentecostal theology.

To speak of Pentecostal theology as affective is to say that the Pentecostal living of the gospel proceeds on the premise of abiding individual and communal dispositions, not mere spontaneous emotional states, but transformative manifestations of the encounter with God. Individual affections are always embedded in communal affections and vice versa, so that the communal experience of God verifies and interprets the individual experience. In turn, the ecclesial and personal encounter with God is always embedded in the biblical story of Pentecost, which interprets and discerns the contemporary experience as a faithful manifestation of the Spirit of Christ. This discernment of the present experience and participation in the story of God proceeds by way of the affections rather than intellect, reason and knowledge. The affections bring the Pentecostal imagination to the limits of speech, concepts, theory and systematization.[53] The result is a theo-logy carried out, at least initially, in the realm of spirit (*pneuma*) rather than word (*logos*). For this reason, the experience of God among Pentecostals is always pneumatic (experience *of* the Spirit), and the affections, as manifestations of and reflections on that experience, are foundationally pneumatological (directed *by* and *towards* the Spirit).[54] In Pentecostal language, the full gospel can never be exclusively a story but must always be lived experience. Reflection on the affections proceeds by way of an imagination nurtured by the encounter with the Holy

---

[50] James K. A. Smith, *Thinking in Tongues: Pentecostal Contributions to Christian Philosophy* (Grand Rapids, MI: Eerdmans, 2010), 78–79, 80–81; Land, *Pentecostal Spirituality*, 117–80. See also Dale M. Coulter and Amos Yong (eds), *The Spirit, the Affections, and the Christian Tradition* (Notre Dame, IN: University of Notre Dame Press, 2016).
[51] Samuel Solivan, *The Spirit, Pathos and Liberation: Toward an Hispanic Pentecostal Theology*, JPTS 14 (Sheffield: Sheffield Academic Press, 1998), 59–60.
[52] Land, *Pentecostal Spirituality*, 131–64.
[53] See Smith, *Thinking in Tongues*, 123–50.
[54] Amos Yong, 'On Divine Presence and Divine Agency: Toward a Foundational Pneumatology', *AJPS* 3, no. 2 (2000): 167–88.

Spirit that seeks to interpret all reality in terms of the worldview generated by that experience.[55] Image, symbol, song, poetry, prophecy, vision, dreams and testimony are the media of the imagination carried by the affections towards theological articulation. The goal of this articulation is worship – doctrine only as doxology. Pentecostal theology is affective theology that emerges from worship and returns to worship as the energy of the full gospel.

The manifestation of the foundational experience of the encounter with the Holy Spirit should not be limited to particular affections. To do so would limit the scope of the full gospel narrative to only particular forms or patterns of experience or dissolve the experiences immediately into doctrine. Although the concern of Pentecostal spirituality is clearly for the sanctified passions, the spectrum of the affections cannot be defined by the church but depends 'on the initiating, sustaining and directing of the Sovereign Lord of the church'.[56] The range of Christian affections is objective, relational and dispositional: the source and object of the affections is God as an enduring expression of the believer's relationship with God, the church and the world, and 'disposing the person toward God and the neighbor in ways appropriate to their source and goal in God'.[57] Singular affections and dogmatic expressions of their underlying experiences have been treated as the exclusive distinctive of Pentecostal theology, among them particularly the doctrine of Spirit baptism: the theological expression that the resurrected and glorified Jesus pours out the Holy Spirit on all flesh. A broad narrative is instead necessary in order to avoid identifying Pentecostal theology solely with a singular expression of a particular doctrine. Certainly, those who deny that Spirit baptism is central to Pentecostal theology are ignorant of the history of the movement and responsible for the decline of Spirit baptism in practice; yet those who insist that Spirit baptism is the only practice genuine to Pentecostalism are responsible for its theological poverty. A Pentecostal theology constructed on the basis of that doctrine alone can proceed only if the image of Spirit baptism is significantly expanded.[58] The narrative of the full gospel instead

---

[55] Amos Yong, *The Spirit Poured Out on All Flesh: Pentecostalism and the Possibility of Global Theology* (Grand Rapids, MI: Baker Academic, 2005), 27–30; idem, *Spirit-Word-Community*, 110–217.
[56] Land, *Pentecostal Spirituality*, 135.
[57] Ibid., 134–36 (136).
[58] Significant advancements have been made by Frank Macchia, *Baptized in the Spirit: A Global Pentecostal Theology* (Grand Rapids, MI: Zondervan, 2006); Studebaker, *From Pentecost to the Triune God*, 208–68.

identifies Spirit baptism as an affective lens through which Pentecostals view and order the other elements of the full gospel, yet without isolating the experience or elevating it beyond the other constituents of the full gospel. The baptism in the Spirit is not synonymous with salvation, sanctification, divine healing, or the coming of the kingdom; it complements and orients the other accents of the gospel but does not absorb their meaning or experience. The following account of Pentecostal theology should therefore not give the impression that the central experiences among Pentecostals are limited to a select few, or Pentecostals will risk being accused of a restrictive reading of Scripture, a misunderstanding of the history of their own movement, a misappropriation of the purpose of doctrine or a neglect of the narrative form of Pentecostal theology that threatens to disconnect its doctrines from the full range of practices under the symbol of Pentecost.

The full gospel motif offers a biblically, historically, theologically, phenomenologically and pedagogically inclusive framework for the Pentecostal key experiences, which have to be elucidated in this volume. The notion of a 'full' gospel signals that Pentecostal theology is not concentrated in a single doctrine but dispersed among a variety of Christian practices along a core commitment to the transforming and renewing encounter with God in Christ through the Holy Spirit. This core commitment to the immediacy of the Holy Spirit is fundamentally soteriological. The full gospel proclaims this soteriological fullness not because of its fivefold structure, but because a *full* gospel suggests the importance of any experience of the Spirit as only one moment on the way to the 'fullness' of the redemptive and transformative work of God. Salvation is thus not one moment of the full gospel but its underlying rationale. The symbol of Pentecost as the story of the Holy Spirit in the world, the church and the human person provides an archetype for narrating Pentecostal theology that extends to the transformation and salvation of the whole of life. Soteriology is limited only by an expectation of the limits of God's redemptive activity. Just as the range of Pentecostal affections can and should not be limited, so too the range of Pentecostal theology allows for potentially unlimited affective, spiritual modes of experience and expression. Pentecostal theology is in this sense an affective embodiment of the universal promise of Pentecost that the outpouring of the Spirit transcends all theological structures, norms and prejudices.

Praxis: The materiality of Pentecostal theology

The centrality of spirituality, experience, testimony and affections characterizes Pentecostal theology inherently as praxis. To argue that Pentecostal theology reaches deep into the heart of Pentecost, therefore, is to say that the day of Pentecost functions as a theological symbol because Pentecost is itself a praxis rather than a doctrine. This designation should not be misunderstood as a rejection, ignorance, or neglect of rational, theoretical, or speculative theology. Instead, those kinds of approaches to Christian thought are themselves pursued as practices of Christian experiences and affections (even if such practices may be pre-conscious or seemingly contradictory to reason). Theology as praxis is a particular orientation towards the task of theology and as such a pattern of living theology.[59] However, Pentecostal theology as praxis is challenged by the potentially unlimited modes of expression of the experience of the Spirit made possible by an affective imagination. The chief methodological consequence of this challenge is that Pentecostal spirituality cannot proceed immediately (although eventually) in the forms and customs of traditional theology, whether conceived as doctrine, propositions, or wisdom. The affective dimension contrasts with the often performative, functionalistic, rationalistic, utilitarian and competitive character of these perspectives.[60] The practical dimension of theology, on the other hand, which expresses the experience of the Holy Spirit at the root of Pentecostal spirituality, demands the continuous association of doctrine with the original experience. The development of doctrine in Pentecostalism is affected by the insight that living their theology *cannot* proceed without being practiced but *can* proceed without being articulated as doctrine.

Although the nature of Pentecostal theology as living praxis has not yet been fully examined, it is clear that Pentecostalism and its practices do not easily fit the mould of established theological methodology. Pentecostal theology cannot be performed in prescriptive ways without dismantling the affections by threatening to objectify the experience of God underlying them and dispersing the human response to the passion of God into fragments of

---

[59] See Miroslav Volf and Dorothy C. Bass (eds), *Practicing Theology: Beliefs and Practices in Christian Life* (Grand Rapids, MI: Eerdmans, 2002).
[60] Vondey, *Beyond Pentecostalism*, 13–15.

dogmatic propositions. Put more simply, Pentecostals rely on wonder; they want to remain within the realm of experience and practices, or at least return to them. Hence, Pentecostal theology does not want to be understood, it wants to be embodied and lived (as a form of understanding, yet sometimes in pre-cognitive or irrational ways). This kind of theology struggles with doctrine defined in selective, propositional and prescriptive terms because, embedded in the experiences of the whole of life, the full gospel represents and recreates the unbounded presence of God in the world. In this sense, Pentecostal theology exists more in the realm of possibilities and wonder than in the realm of already actualized and objectified projections of reality.[61] Pentecostal theology lives expectantly in a proleptic eschatological tension between the not yet and the already.[62] Amidst this tension, theology is worship, the joy of God's grace, the exuberance of life, the freedom of creation finding itself in God. The playfulness of theology collapses when this tension is resolved prematurely, either by an overrealized confidence in doctrine or an escapist appeal to a pure experience of God.[63] Although both are possible in Pentecostal theology, neither defines the methodology of the movement. Both extremes are, so to speak, embedded and implicit in the Pentecostal way of being. However, deliberative theology is not a simple process of reflecting on multiple understandings and correcting them towards a normative pattern. Rather, Pentecostal theology does not eschew the extremes – it requires them in order to remain in the realm of possibilities. Hence, the full gospel cannot be an end in itself but must be a form of 'pure means'[64] – not in the sense of 'purposelessness' but in the sense of overaccepting at all costs the 'superfluous potential' of wonder that aims at participation in the realization of the kingdom of God.

The potential of the full gospel is rooted in the experience of the encounter with God and unfolds as participation in that experience, to which Pentecostal methodology continually seeks to return. Participation in this experience is purposeful in the sense of transforming all theology into

---

[61] See Paul Alexander, *Signs and Wonders: Why Pentecostalism Is the World's Fastest Growing Faith* (San Francisco: Jossey-Bass, 2009).
[62] On how Pentecostal theology arrived here see Peter Althouse, *Spirit of the Last Days: Pentecostal Eschatology in Conversation with Jürgen Moltmann*, JPTS 25 (London: T & T Clark, 2003), 9–106.
[63] Land, *Pentecostal Spirituality*, 15.
[64] Nimi Wariboko, *The Pentecostal Principle: Ethical Methodology in New Spirit*, PM 4 (Grand Rapids, MI: Eerdmans, 2012), 163–64.

soteriology. Pentecostal theology always seeks to be redemptive: navigating between capitulation to this world and escaping to another by bringing the two worlds into a transformative encounter with God.[65] Soteriology is therefore the pervasive direction of Pentecostal theological method unfolding in the patterns of the full gospel, manifested in the concrete experiences and practices of life and seeking redemption through participation in the life of God.[66] The full gospel as a redemptive model of theology follows a comprehensive soteriological direction that oscillates between experience and reflection, theory and praxis, affection and action – not in an endless circle but in an effort to transform all reflection into participation in the experiences of the transforming presence of God. Pentecostal theology is in this sense an attempt to embody the encounter with God as on the day of Pentecost.

Embodiment: The traditioning of Pentecostal theology

The articulation of the practices, beliefs and convictions of the full gospel allows us to build a narrative historically and theologically applicable to Pentecostals worldwide. Of course, not all (Christian) practices can be considered Pentecostal, and there exists considerable debate about which practices are normative for Pentecostals. It is also impossible to address all the nuances and diverse persuasions and emphases among Pentecostals worldwide. The theological construct in the following chapters proceeds therefore necessarily from a particular set of practices and experiences of the Pentecostal life. In order to avoid arbitrary selection (regional, cultural, ethnic, or otherwise), the most comprehensive account of Pentecostal theology emerges from practices and experiences embodying the corporate worship of Pentecostal communities. As a form of mystical theology, Pentecostalism embodies a radically doxological movement. By embodiment I refer to the materiality and physicality of practices that form and are informed by the articulation of Pentecostal doctrine.[67]

---

[65] See Vondey, *Beyond Pentecostalism*, 172–82.
[66] See Yong, *In the Days of Caesar*, 115–16.
[67] See Wolfgang Vondey, 'Embodied Gospel: The Materiality of Pentecostal Theology', in *Pentecostals and the Body*, ed. Michael Wilkinson and Peter Althouse, ARSR 7 (Leiden: Brill, 2016), 102–19.

Undoubtedly, the worship service forms the wellspring of spiritual practices among Pentecostals from which doctrinal reflection can emerge. In order to illustrate the Pentecostal way of living theology, I therefore want to bring the construction of a comprehensive narrative articulation of Pentecostal theology into dialogue with the Pentecostal practices of worship.

While this process is not unusual for articulating other approaches to Christian thought, Pentecostal theology emerges in particular contexts readily identifiable as the seedbed of Pentecostal spirituality. Rituals, rites and liturgy, once foreign terms to Pentecostal worship, have become increasingly the focus of theological attention.[68] Among these practices, the altar call and response stands out as the climax of traditional Pentecostal worship.[69] Contemporary ritual, historical and phenomenological studies of world Pentecostalism affirm certain foundational rites oriented around the altar as the consistent practices and traditions of the Pentecostal movement.[70] Although theology cannot be defined absolutely by any particular ritual, doxological practices are closest to the ground of Pentecostal origins and the way Pentecostalism continues to exist across the world. The summit and source of Pentecostal worship, rituals and practices from which Pentecostalism can be grasped constructively is undoubtedly the altar service. Other practices (and their doctrinal reflections) are readily integrated in a central practice of the altar call and response. We might say that Pentecostal theology functions on the basis of an 'altar hermeneutics'[71] ('this is that' and 'this is not that') which relates the symbolic notion of participating in Pentecost to the palpable practices and experiences at the altar. In order to avoid an abstract and speculative

---

[68] Daniel E. Albrecht, *Rites in the Spirit: A Ritual Approach to Pentecostal/Charismatic Spirituality*, JPTS 17 (Sheffield: Sheffield Academic Press, 1999).

[69] Wolfgang Vondey, 'The Theology of the Altar and Pentecostal Sacramentality', in *Scripting Pentecost: A Study of Pentecostals, Worship and Liturgy*, ed. Mark J. Cartledge and A. J. Swoboda (Aldershot, UK: Ashgate, 2016), 94–107. See also Daniel Tomberlin, *Pentecostal Sacraments: Encountering God at the Altar* (Cleveland, TN: Center for Pentecostal Leadership and Care, 2010).

[70] See Wolfgang Vondey, 'The Making of a Black Liturgy: Pentecostal Worship and Spirituality from African Slave Narratives to Urban City Scapes', *BT* 10, no. 2 (2012): 147–68; Martin Lindhardt (ed.), *Practicing the Faith: The Ritual Life of Pentecostal-Charismatic Christians* (Oxford: Berghahn, 2011); Cartledge, *Testimony in the Spirit*, 29–54; Donald E. Miller and Tetsunao Yamamori, *Global Pentecostalism: The New Face of Christian Social Engagement* (Berkeley: University of California Press, 2007), 129–59; Elisabeth Arweck and William Keenan (eds), *Materializing Religion: Expression, Performance and Ritual* (Aldershot, UK: Ashgate, 2006), 74–88, 138–60; Bobby C. Alexander, *Victor Turner Revisited: Ritual as Social Change*, AARA 74 (Atlanta, GA: Scholars, 1991).

[71] For this term see Rickie D. Moore, 'Altar Hermeneutics: Reflections on Pentecostal Biblical Interpretation', *Pneuma* 38, no. 2 (2016): 148–59.

account of the full gospel, the following chapters adopt the altar as the context for constructing a theological narrative from the ground up.

At the altar, Pentecostal theology implements the practices of the full gospel through several native, adopted and enculturated rites. This adoption of foundational rites should not be misunderstood as advocating that such practices are *the* rituals genuine to global Pentecostalism, that they are the only rites of Pentecostalism, that the descriptions given here are complete or that they attempt to give some idealized notion of a single performance of the ritual. Pentecostals resist 'ritual' as the strict ecclesiastical performance of a liturgical script within a fixed semiotic system of sacerdotal or sacramental regulations. Instead, Pentecostal rituals are often playful, improvised and unstructured.[72] My goal is simply to build a theological narrative that emerges out of a critical interpretation of these embodied practices among Pentecostals with a view to implicating their theological consequences, which in turn leads to a revision and expansion of those practices along the much broader playing field of global Pentecostalism.

Global Pentecostal theology has been slow to produce or integrate other doctrines outside of the traditional full gospel pattern. The full gospel narrative is close to Pentecostal experiences, whereas many contemporary Christian doctrines reflect conceptual propositions not immediately driven by practices and experiences of the Holy Spirit that can be readily embodied in worship. Nonetheless, the full gospel is an open narrative; it invites and requires additional practices and interpretations. Since the most widely accepted Pentecostal doctrines have emerged from the elements of the full gospel experienced in the context of the altar, Pentecostal theology is most prepared to engage other doctrines from the practices and concerns of the altar space. In turn, conceptualized doctrines and philosophical considerations have to be brought into the embodied world of the liturgies, rituals, sacraments and practices surrounding the altar. In this embodied environment of worship, the full gospel can expand into a constructive and systematic framework for the traditioning of Pentecostal Theology.

Pentecostals have struggled with the question of whether their embodied theology can (or should) be systematic.[73] Part of the difficulty is concentrated

---

[72] See Vondey, *Beyond Pentecostalism*, 109-40.
[73] See Kenneth J. Archer, 'A Pentecostal Way of Doing Theology: Method and Manner', *IJST* 9, no. 3 (2007): 301-14; Terry L. Cross, 'The Rich Feast of Theology: Can Pentecostals Bring the

in the need for an orderly, rational and coherent method that would allow for the transposition of the full gospel into formulations of doctrine without threatening the integrity of the narrative. Another concern is that systematic theology is dominated by Western ideas and constructs that are not always readily shared by the Pentecostal experiences in the East and the global South. If we identify Pentecostal theology with the embodied spirituality, experiences, affections and practices narrated by the full gospel, then a systematic account of Pentecostal theology may threaten to institutionalize, theorize, disimpassion and disembody the demand for the immediacy of the human encounter with God. A systematic Pentecostal theology must endeavour to embody Pentecostal spirituality, experiences, affections and practices which engage the world not exclusively through doctrine but also materially, physically, spiritually, aesthetically, morally and socially. Only together can we speak of Pentecostalism as a theological tradition.

To illustrate this challenge, the narrative of the full gospel in part one is cast in the language of verbs, the native language of Pentecostal worship, whereas the theological account given in part two is cast in the language of nouns, the propositional language of established theological conventions brought into dialogue with the full gospel. Inadvertently, the two parts of this book show that Pentecostal theology has both narratival and conceptual qualities. Both qualities are necessary for Pentecostal theology to proceed constructively and systematically in the diverse contexts of contemporary contextual theologies and the possibility of global theology. On the one hand, the narrative quality holds Pentecostal theology accountable to the Pentecostal story patterned after the biblical events of Pentecost. The full gospel is fundamentally a living narrative experienced among Pentecostals. On the other hand, the conceptual quality is necessary for Pentecostal theology in order not to lose itself in its own narrative. Conceptualization is a critical reflection upon one's own testimony unfolding within the larger Pentecostal story that is itself participation in the story of God. In its narrative quality, Pentecostal theology unfolds among the diverse experiences of Jesus Christ as saviour, sanctifier, Spirit baptizer, healer and coming king. Nonetheless, this theological

Main Course or Only the Relish?' *JPT* 8, no. 16 (2000): 27–47; Amos Yong, 'Whither Systematic Theology? A Systematician Chimes in on a Scandalous Conversation', *Pneuma* 20, no. 1 (1998): 85–93; David Bundy, 'The Genre of Systematic Theology in Pentecostalism', *Pneuma* 15, no. 1 (1993): 89–107.

narrative always remains tied to its origins in the day of Pentecost, which is the chief symbol of the tradition we call Pentecostal.

The continuing challenge of Pentecostal theology as a persistent tradition is a reduction of the full gospel to the propositional ideas of salvation, sanctification, Spirit baptism, divine healing and the coming kingdom, or worst, to merely one of these elements or sub-elements. What is lost in any reductionism is the dynamic of experience, reflection, practice and transformation at the core of each element and of the full gospel narrative as a whole. What is tempting is to label the Pentecostal gospel not as seeking fullness (and thus a hospitable invitation to participate) but as already complete (a fullness that requires no further transformation). At stake is the temptation to let Pentecostal theology merely perform in front of us so as to observe its various qualities as an object of scrutiny. Reduced to a bystander and observer, we may overlook that the underlying intention of Pentecostal theology is not merely to display itself as a truthful projection of the fullness of the gospel but to invite us to participate in the fullness of the redemptive life with God. The theological symbol for entering into this transformative encounter with the divine life is Pentecost. And to this core symbol of Pentecostal theology we must now turn.

Part One

Full Gospel Story

2

Saved

Meeting Jesus at the Altar

A narrative account of Pentecostal theology begins with soteriology. The full gospel lends five dominant metaphors for this narrative: salvation, sanctification, Spirit baptism, divine healing, and glorification. The articulation of these themes underscores the dominance of salvation for Pentecostal theology not merely by its primary position in the narrative but by its distribution throughout. The full gospel is soteriological from beginning to end. This first chapter consequently faces the twofold task of presenting salvation as a primary metaphor for Pentecostal thought and as a dominant theological theme throughout Pentecostal theology. Since I am suggesting that Pentecostal theology reaches deep into the heart of Pentecost, this chapter also presents much of the groundwork for subsequent chapters by beginning with the biblical and experiential perspective of Pentecost in order to allow for an articulation of the theological practices underlying Pentecostal soteriology. The first part of the chapter shows how the plot of Pentecost is appropriated by Pentecostals through the dominant practice of the altar call and response. On this basis, the second part of the chapter articulates a Pentecostal soteriology in the image of Pentecost. The final part elevates this discussion to the broader realm of Christian practices and crystallizes the Pentecostal contributions to both an understanding of and participation in the Christian notion of salvation. This discussion forms the basis for exploring the other themes of the full gospel narrative in subsequent chapters.

Experiencing salvation at Pentecost

The biblical day of Pentecost represents the foundational symbol for Pentecostal theology. As a theological symbol, Pentecost is significant for Pentecostals first and foremost because of the experiences and practices recorded in the biblical texts of Luke-Acts.[1] While we can also speak of a Johannine and Pauline Pentecost,[2] the development of Pentecost as a theological symbol of Pentecostal theology originates with the Lukan trajectory. Nonetheless, such preferences for particular biblical texts are not indicative of the broad interests of Pentecostal theology. I do not intend to provide here a biblical theology of salvation or full interpretation of biblical passages concerning the day of Pentecost. Rather, my intention is only to trace the narrative contours of Pentecost as symbol of Pentecostal soteriology and thereby to offer a symbolic plot for more detailed exegetical and theological discussion. The focus on the book of Acts I have adopted throughout the first part of this book serves not to restrict Pentecostal exegesis but rather to indicate that the day of Pentecost offers the central hermeneutical lens for Pentecostal theology, which will be expanded in the subsequent chapters and constructively utilized in the second part of this volume.

The core narrative plot of Pentecostal theology is situated within the celebration of Pentecost, a ritual event on the calendar of ancient Israel commemorating the reception of the Law (see Exod. 34:22; Deut. 16:10).[3] However, the planned celebration of this particular Pentecost meets with the fulfilment of the announcement, made by Jesus, that an unusual significance would mark the coming days following his resurrection and ascension for those tarrying in Jerusalem who are promised power from the Holy Spirit and effective witness to the gospel (Luke 24:49; Acts 1:8).[4] The disciples accordingly assemble in preparation and prayer in Jerusalem (v. 14) and meet 'all together in one place' (Acts 2:1). The events then unfolding during the day of Pentecost follow

---

[1] See Martin William Mittelstadt, *Reading Luke-Acts in the Pentecostal Tradition* (Cleveland, TN: CPT Press, 2010), 18–45.
[2] See Raniero Cantalamessa, *The Mystery of Pentecost*, trans. Glen S. Davis (Collegeville, MN: Liturgical Press, 2001).
[3] Rejecting this connection is Roger Stronstad, *The Prophethood of All Believers: A Study in Luke's Charismatic Theology* (Sheffield: Sheffield Academic Press, 1999), 54.
[4] See Robert P. Menzies, *Empowered for Witness: The Spirit in Luke-Acts* (London: Continuum, 2004), 168–201.

not the traditional expectations of the festival but are later interpreted by the apostle Peter as the unexpected fulfilment of the prophecy of the outpouring of God's Spirit on all flesh (Acts 2:16–21; see Joel 2:28–32). The unprecedented events form an archetype of practices and convictions for Pentecostal soteriology, reshaped and multiplied today by the vast diversity of global Pentecostal expressions and lived experiences on the ground. Pentecost as the beginning of Pentecostal theology is not merely a thematic locus, but it elicits an experiential identification with the biblical events of the day as well. The 'plot' of Pentecost, the internal 'logic' of the practices of the event, forms the foundation for any Pentecostal theological narrative.[5]

The narrative plot of Acts 2:1–47 gleams with incidents of 'conflict' and divine 'interruption'.[6] The expected ritual character of the day is interrupted by the outpouring of the Holy Spirit on 'all of the disciples', in a place 'where they were sitting' initiated by the sudden sound of 'a violent wind' filling 'the entire house' (v. 2) and the appearance of divided tongues 'on each of them' accompanied by the speaking in other languages 'as the Spirit gave them ability' (v. 4). A crowd gathers at the sound of the languages spoken (v. 6) and articulates the disturbance of the day with expressions of confusion and bewilderment, amazement and marvel, culminating in a series of questions concerning the identity, origins and abilities of the disciples, and thus the meaning of the entire affair (vv. 5–13).[7]

The interruption caused by the outpouring of the Spirit and its physical manifestations is accentuated by the apostle Peter who, 'standing with the eleven' (v. 14), issues an explanation and interpretation of the events (vv. 14–36) to those drawn by the unusual occurrences:[8] the day of Pentecost is a witness to the crucified Jesus Christ who has been raised from the dead and exalted to the right hand of God, who has poured out the Holy Spirit on all flesh (vv. 32–33). The work of the disciples, now fulfilling Jesus's anticipation of their witness to the gospel, proceeds in the power of the Spirit, proclaiming, exhorting, and testifying to the diverse population in attendance

---

[5] See Ju Hur, *A Dynamic Reading of the Holy Spirit in Luke-Acts* (London: Continuum, 2004), 181–278.
[6] Ibid., 183–91.
[7] See Carl Brumback, *'What Meaneth This?' A Pentecostal Answer to a Pentecostal Question* (Springfield, MO: Gospel Publishing House, 1947), 13–22.
[8] Craig S. Keener, *Acts: An Exegetical Commentary*, Volume 1, *Introduction and 1:1–2:47* (Grand Rapids: Baker, 2012), 862–85; Arrington, *Acts of the Apostles*, 26–40.

(vv. 38–40) of the 'wonderful works of God' (v. 11). The audience, devout Jews from every nation (v. 5), astonished and perplexed by their witness of the events and the redefinition of their faith in light of Peter's words, is 'cut to the heart' (v. 37) and raises the fundamental question regarding their own participation in the work of God: 'What should we do?'[9]

The apostle's answer is a call to the audience to 'repent, and be baptized' (v. 38) followed by the promise of the gift of the Holy Spirit.[10] With this action, Peter beckons 'each person' to 'turn around' and to put into practice such 'repentance' with an outward act of faith: water baptism in the name of Jesus Christ. The call is coupled with a further promise to those who respond: the outpouring of the Holy Spirit on the audience, their children, and 'all who are far away' (v. 39).[11]

The plot of the day of Pentecost ends with a collective response by the audience, several thousand who 'welcome' the call, accept the Christian teaching, and enter into fellowship with the church (vv. 41–42). The response is accompanied by continued signs and wonders (v. 43). Teaching and formation, communion, water baptism, the breaking of the bread, the sharing of possessions, and the worship of God (v. 47) are all integrated in the comprehensive conclusion of the biblical records concerning the day of Pentecost.[12]

The biblical foundations of Pentecostal soteriology are, of course, much broader than the narrative traced here.[13] The modest goal of the preceding outline was only to tell the basic plot of Pentecost taken as the core narrative of the Pentecostal tradition. This basic plot of the biblical events is embodied in various forms by contemporary Pentecostals in a foundational rite typically labelled the 'altar call'.[14] The altar is a theological metaphor; most Pentecostal churches do not have a physical altar, neither in the sacrificial sense of the biblical writings nor in the sacramental sense of the liturgical traditions.[15] Rather,

---

[9] See French L. Arrington, *The Spirit-Anointed Church: A Study of the Acts of the Apostles* (Cleveland, TN: Pathway, 2008), 65–89.
[10] See Keener, *Acts*, 862–85.
[11] Amos Yong, *The Spirit Poured Out on All Flesh: Pentecostalism and the Possibility of Global Theology* (Grand Rapids, MI: Baker Academic, 2005), 83.
[12] See Arrington, *The Spirit-Anointed Church*, 93–96.
[13] See, for example, J. Rodman Williams, *Renewal Theology: Systematic Theology from a Charismatic Perspective* (Three Volumes in One), vol. 2 (Grand Rapids: Zondervan, 1996), 13–136; Guy P. Duffield and Nathaniel M. Van Cleave, *Foundations of Pentecostal Theology* (San Dimas, CA: L.I.F.E. Bible College, 1987), 173–260; French L. Arrington, *Christian Doctrine: A Pentecostal Perspective* (Cleveland, TN: Pathway Press, 1993), 157–269.
[14] See Albrecht, *Rites in the Spirit*, 165–70.
[15] See Cyril E. Pocknee, *The Christian Altar: In History and Today* (London: A. R. Mowbray, 1963), 33–50.

imitating the events of Pentecost, the altar is a ritual metaphor for salvation experienced through the human encounter with God. Although Pentecost as theological symbol exceeds an exclusively anthropocentric idea of salvation (which is arguably dominant in the history of Pentecostalism), and the altar has often been historically and conceptually identified with a particular space and time of corporate worship, liturgy, and ritual, the Pentecostal altar is a theological metaphor of the kingdom of God, which is 'neither here nor there' (see Luke 17:21) but which comes into existence, as on the day of Pentecost, through the unexpected outpouring of the Holy Spirit and the participation of creation in response to the divine presence.

The altar as a soteriological metaphor has transitioned throughout Pentecostal history. In classical Pentecostalism, derived from the plantation prayer grounds of African slaves, the camp meetings of the rural American south, and the influence of the Church of England and early Methodism, the altar can be identified by a walking of the aisle or jumping on pews or less dramatically the simple assembly of people at the end of a church building where the Word of God is preached.[16] In charismatic churches with historical roots in the established liturgical and sacramental traditions, the architectural space of the sanctuary, including the altar and tabernacle, often delineate the spatial boundaries of the divine-human encounter.[17] In neopentecostal communities, the idea of the 'sacred space' with a central focus point ('altar') is shifting from clear architectural identifiers at the back end of a church building to the more symbolically and experientially identified centre of worship of the congregation.[18] Indeed, in the vast diversity of physical space found among Pentecostal churches worldwide, from megachurches to rooms in shopping malls, sheds on the outskirts of a village, or open-air benches, the human-divine encounter is primarily identified by the congregation's activity of worship.[19] In all its variances, the altar is inherently an ecclesial metaphor

---

[16] Vondey, *Beyond Pentecostalism*, 122–25; Ian H. Murray, *Revival and Revivalism: The Making and Marring of American Evangelicalism 1750–1858* (Banner of Truth Trust, 1994), 185–87.

[17] Jacqueline Ryle, 'Laying Our Sins and Sorrows on the Altar: Ritualizing Catholic Charismatic Reconciliation and Healing in Fiji', in *Practicing the Faith: The Ritual Life of Pentecostal-Charismatic Christians*, ed. Martin Linhardt (New York: Berghahn, 2011), 68–97.

[18] Malcolm Gold, 'From the "Upper Room" to the "Christian Centre": Changes in the Use of Sacred Space and Artefacts in a Pentecostal Assembly', in *Materializing Religion: Expression, Performance and Ritual*, ed. Elisabeth Arweck and William Keenan (Aldershot, UK: Ashgate, 2006), 74–88.

[19] See Donald E. Miller and Tetsunao Yamamori, *Global Pentecostalism: The New Face of Christian Social Engagement* (Berkeley: University of California Press, 2007), 129–59.

emphasizing salvation as a ritual of the entire community in which the individual response to God is embedded. The altar call as a collective practice acknowledges the need of a ritual space for the entire community's participation in embodying the human response to the salvation offered by God.

The altar call, reenacting the day of Pentecost, is typically an invitation issued by the pastor or evangelist to the congregation to 'bring themselves' (their lives, faith, sins, circumstances, illnesses, problems, fears, hopes, etc.) to a meeting with God.[20] The call from the platform or the front of the church may be a general invitation or follow a specific emphasis of the service; at other times, the call may not be voiced explicitly from the leaders of worship but erupt spontaneously through a tongue, prophecy, or revelation in the congregation.[21] The altar call can be made to begin a new dimension in the worship of the community (e.g. communal prayer) or to initiate the main focus of the service (e.g. a healing service) or to integrate other ritual practices (e.g. celebration of the sacraments).[22] The acceptance of the invitation is displayed in some form of audible or visible response, often accompanied by other physical and charismatic manifestations of individuals or the entire congregation. The abundant response of the worshippers includes sometimes a congregational move forward into the 'holy place', sometimes a gradual reorientation of some, at other times a jumping and running on the aisle by individuals. Responses vary from the assembly of the entire congregation at the altar to some remaining in their pews or falling on their knees in the aisle or stretching out their hands towards the perceived presence of God at the altar. The bringing of oneself to the altar may be the actual walk of a person or manifested only by a groaning in the spirit, a singing of the congregation into the perceived presence of God or the eruption of tongues and prophecies, prayers and songs, that in a manner of speaking bring the altar to the people. Pentecostals flock to the altar in expectation of a divine, often supernatural, interruption of their circumstances and in that sense of an initiation or repetition or revival of Pentecost in their own lives. The expectation of the altar involves as much the renewal of the individual as the transformation of the community.

---

[20] See R. Alan Streett, *The Effective Invitation* (Old Tappan, NJ: Fleming H. Revell, 1984), 81–107; William Oscar Thompson Jr., 'The Public Invitation as Method of Evangelism: Its Origin and Development' (PhD diss., Southwestern Baptist Theological Seminary, 1979).
[21] Albrecht, *Rites in the Spirit*, 165–66.
[22] See Tomberlin, *Pentecostal Sacraments*, 1–88; Chris E. W. Green, *Toward a Pentecostal Theology of the Lord's Supper: Foretasting the Kingdom* (Cleveland, TN: CPT Press, 2012), 74–181.

To welcome the altar call and to respond to the interruption of the Holy Spirit is to respond to the invitation of God and the proclamation of the gospel and to embark on a new life. The altar provides Pentecostal theology with a foundational ritual environment that allows us to cast Pentecostal soteriology in the image of the day of Pentecost. The pneumatological entrance to this soteriology of the altar demands further that the way of salvation is cast as wide as the way of the Spirit poured out.

Salvation in the image of Pentecost

The altar call and response as a foundational ritual of Pentecostal theology is a core expression of the path to salvation. The practice demonstrates that an encounter with God is always soteriological, always redemptive, transforming, converting, correcting, and delivering. Moreover, salvation from the perspective of the altar is always an experience that requires active participation. The experience of God's redemptive presence and activity is manifested at the altar in the call of God and its invitation to respond. The archetype of this perspective is found in the biblical narrative of Pentecost and Peter's sermon, which accentuates the church's emphasis on a theological process by which salvation is realized. This process centres on the proclamation of the gospel of Jesus Christ (Acts 2:22–36): the rationale for salvation from the perspective of Pentecost is unequivocally the life, death, and resurrection of Jesus of Nazareth. The proclamation of the cross leads to a crisis among the spectators, who identify with the process of salvation presented in the gospel but cannot bring it to a resolution in their own lives.[23] The Pentecostal reading of the biblical texts, much like the Pietistic tradition, accentuates that the initial confrontation with the narrative of salvation results in a crisis, a challenge, a struggle, and confrontation with the human self and with God.[24] The biblical narrative accentuates this crisis in the crowd's culminating question, 'what should we do'? Peter's response crafts the parameters of today's Pentecostal

---

[23] See Mark J. Cartledge, *Testimony in the Spirit: Rescripting Ordinary Pentecostal Theology* (Surrey, UK: Ashgate, 2010), 55–80; Donald E. Miller and Tetsunao Yamamori, *Global Pentecostalism: The New Face of Pentecostal Social Engagement* (Berkeley: University of California Press, 2007), 39–67.

[24] See Frank D. Macchia, *Spirituality and Social Liberation: The Message of the Blumhardts in the Light of Wuerttemberg Pietism* (Lanham, MD: Scarecrow, 1993).

soteriology: 'Repent, and be baptized every one of you in the name of Jesus Christ so that your sins may be forgiven; and you will receive the gift of the Holy Spirit. For the promise is for you, for your children, and for all who are far away, everyone whom the Lord our God calls to him' (v. 38–39). Salvation in Christ is with Pentecost thoroughly related to the outpouring of the Holy Spirit in its broadest dimensions (everyone), yet through a distinctive response (repentance) and experience (baptism) situated within the particular framework of God's initiative (the call) and act (forgiveness of sin).[25] Central to Pentecostal soteriology is the potential that the objective historical reality of Christ's death becomes an objective positional reality for the believer who can subjectively appropriate and experience Christ in the Holy Spirit.[26]

The experience and appropriation of the gospel by the believer is expressed among Pentecostals in a holistic, embodied participation of the entire person turning from sin to God. It is a coming to the altar as from 'far away', or with another Lukan narrative, the long walk of return by the prodigal child to the father (see Luke 15:11–32), a crying out to God in which we exclaim, 'Father, I have sinned against heaven and before you; I am no longer worthy to be called your child' (v. 21).[27] In the paternal and filial encounter, God responds with embrace, compassion, forgiveness, and restoration. Salvation is 'a coming to our senses' (v. 17). Leaving behind our old ways of living, the way to the altar is a return to God and the beginning of a new life. Our return 'back safe and sound' (v. 27) is celebrated by the whole household as what 'was dead ... is alive again' (v. 24) and who 'was dead ... has come to life' (v. 32). Reflecting these biblical patterns, the Pentecostal practice of altar call and response is centred on Christ and carried out in the Spirit understood as the factual experience of initiation into a newness of life, a regeneration or new birth, which marks a radical renewal, a change, transformation, and new beginning.

Equally important as the going to the altar is a person's return from the encounter with God. More exactly, it is the moment *between* the going and returning that marks a key soteriological event in Pentecostal theology, typically identified with conversion but described more broadly as the experience

---

[25] See Yong, *The Spirit Poured Out on All Flesh*, 81–82.
[26] Gordon Fee, *God's Empowering Presence: The Holy Spirit in the Letters of Paul* (Peabody, MA: Hendrickson, 1994), 854.
[27] See Amos Yong, *Who Is the Holy Spirit? A Walk with the Apostles* (Brewster, MA: Paraclete, 2011), 135, 204.

of being 'saved'. A dominant metaphor used by Pentecostals for this conversion experience is found in Jesus's conversation with Nicodemus in John 3:2-21.[28] In his exchange with the Pharisee, Jesus states, 'no one can see the kingdom of God without being born from above' or 'born anew' (v. 3). For Pentecostals, this 'new birth' represents the regeneration of the individual through the personal, conscious appropriation and response to the 'clear proclamation that, in Jesus Christ, the Son of God made man, who died and rose from the dead, salvation is offered to all humankind, as a gift of God's grace and mercy'.[29] While the notion of the new birth may have been adopted from Evangelicals, Pentecost as theological symbol defines the experience further as a decisive moment between the going to and returning from the altar, where divine invitation and human response meet in the encounter with the Spirit of Christ. Meeting Jesus at the altar marks the beginning of the soteriological direction of Pentecostal theology, a stepping forward into salvation by the Spirit as the entrance to the full gospel.[30]

When Pentecostals say that salvation marks the beginning and overall direction of theology, this should not be construed as a definitive Pentecostal *ordo salutis*. The full gospel motif as the framework for Pentecostal key experiences may give the impression that the good news of Jesus Christ as saviour, sanctifier, Spirit baptizer, divine healer, and coming king is marked by an uncompromising fivefold order. Indeed, classical Pentecostals have adopted in their history a Protestant *ordo salutis* that obscured the full gospel motif and its hospitality to many experiences as possible moments on the way to the 'fullness' of the redemptive and transformative work of God.[31] The global Pentecostal movements accentuate the single importance of conversion for Pentecostal theology, the centrality of Jesus Christ and the pneumatological orientation reflected in the full gospel. However, a much broader palette of soteriological experiences becomes visible among Pentecostals worldwide that suggests that *all* elements of the full gospel are

---

[28] R. Hollis Gause, *Living in the Spirit: The Way of Salvation* (Cleveland, TN: Pathway Press, 1980), 15-24.

[29] 'Evangelization, Proselytism, and Common Witness. Final Report of the Dialogue between the Roman Catholic Church and Some Classical Pentecostal Churches and Leaders', no. 14, in *Pentecostalism and Christian Unity: Ecumenical Documents and Critical Assessments*, ed. Wolfgang Vondey (Eugene, OR: Pickwick, 2010), 163.

[30] Veli-Matti Kärkkäinen, '"Encountering Christ in the Full Gospel Way": An Incarnational Pentecostal Spirituality', *JEPTA* 27, no. 1 (2007): 5-19.

[31] See Steven Studebaker, 'Pentecostal Soteriology and Pneumatology', *JPT* 11, no. 2 (2003): 248-70.

works of grace and thus possible entrance points to conversion and the way of salvation.[32] This soteriology by means of an expanded lens of the full gospel forms the basis for the larger theological narrative constructed in the second part of this book.

Salvation in the image of Pentecost is the conscious response to the diverse proclamations of the full gospel. The heart of this response, and thus the core of the transformative moment, is the conversion of the person encountering the presence of God.[33] For many Pentecostals, conversion consists of a hearing of the good news of Jesus Christ, a response in faith, and a definitive encounter with God, all typically subsumed in a unique personal testimony.[34] Pentecostals undoubtedly place the death and resurrection of Jesus at the heart of their soteriological witness. Classical Pentecostal pioneers widely accepted the theology that Christ's work of salvation was 'finished' on the cross.[35] Pentecostals have typically embraced 'Jesus' as the exclusive saving name of God in whom the whole content of salvation is subsumed.[36] For Oneness Pentecostals, this strong confession has led to a Christomonism widely rejected by trinitarian Pentecostals despite the recognition of different soteriologies existing globally among Pentecostal groups.[37] Faith in Jesus Christ is central to the new birth, yet the full gospel casts Jesus as saviour amidst his proclamation as sanctifier, Spirit baptizer, divine healer, and coming king. Put differently, the Pentecostal response to the gospel is motivated by

---

[32] For an example of the impact of this extension on Pentecostal doctrine see Linda Flett, *A Full-er Gospel? Pentecostal Proclamation in New Zealand 1990–2008* (Auckland, New Zealand: Archer Press, 2015).

[33] See Gwendoline Malogne-Fer, 'Genre, conversion personnelle et individualisme en pentecôtisme: les Assemblees de Dieu en Polynésie française', *SC* 60, no. 2 (2013): 189–203; Matthias Wenk, 'Conversion and Initiation: A Pentecostal View of Biblical and Patristic Perspectives', *JPT* 8, no. 17 (2000): 56–80; Nils G. Holm, 'Pentecostalism: Conversion and Charismata', *IJPR* 1, no. 3 (1991), 135–51.

[34] See, for example, Milton, *Shalom, the Spirit, and Pentecostal Conversion*, 105–7; Cartledge, *Testimony in the Spirit*, 55–80; Henri Paul Pierre Gooren', Conversion Narratives', in *Studying Global Pentecostalism: Theories and Methods*, ed. Allan Anderson et al. (Berkeley: University of California Press, 2010), 93–112; J. Kwabena Asamoah-Gyadu, 'Your Body Is a Temple: Conversion Narratives in African-led Eastern European Pentecostalism', *PP* 58, no. 1 (2009): 1–14; Elaine J. Lawless, '"The Night I Got the Holy Ghost": Holy Ghost Narratives and the Pentecostal Conversion Process', *WF* 47, no. 1 (1988): 1–19.

[35] See D. William Faupel, *The Everlasting Gospel: The Significance of Eschatology in the Development of Pentecostal Thought*, JPTS 10 (Sheffield: Sheffield Academic Press, 1996), 229–70.

[36] See David A. Reed, *'In Jesus' Name': The History and Beliefs of Oneness Pentecostals*, JPTS 31 (Blandford Forum, UK: Deo, 2008), 308–9.

[37] See 'Final Report of the Oneness-Trinitarian Pentecostal Dialogue, 2002–2007', in *Pentecostalism and Christian Unity*, vol. 2, *Continuing and Building Relationships*, ed. Wolfgang Vondey (Eugene, OR: Pickwick, 2013), 284–87.

a broad range of personal or communal contexts that aim not always immediately at conversion, but often more immediately at the restoration or resolution of spiritual, physical, social, economic, and other problems or critical needs.[38] Hence, the walk to the altar is a conversion experience when it functions as an acknowledgement of the sovereignty of God, the lordship of Jesus Christ, and the continuing power and presence of God's Spirit manifested in a response to one's needs, petitions, prayers, and offerings. These manifestations are not salvific by themselves, and a healed body or restored relationship does not constitute conversion; they point to the need for a lingering at the altar, as Pentecostals put it, an extended or repeated response to the call of God that is justified only if the human being as a whole person has come to the faith. Nonetheless, conversion as the response of faith to the encounter with God within the framework of the full gospel is perhaps best described as 'initial salvation' or an 'initial participation in salvation',[39] an 'entry level'[40] that longs for its ultimate completion. Classical Pentecostal theology, through its emergence from the nineteenth-century Holiness Movement and its revival of Wesleyan theology, speaks here of the 'first work' of grace to be followed by others.[41] The new birth emerges from a conflict of the existing life and nature of the world with the beginning of a new life, where conversion is a fundamental step towards the restoration and renewal on the way to the fullness of redemption.

The conflict apparent on the day of Pentecost is symptomatic for the need felt among Pentecostals for a radical and complete change symbolized by the new birth. This conflict is a separation from the 'old' birth, the sinfulness of human nature affecting all who are first born into this world.[42] The new birth is marked by a rupture and discontinuity with a person's past habits, practices, culture, and traditions.[43] The apostle Peter paints this conflict in

---

[38] Milton, *Shalom, the Spirit, and Pentecostal Conversion*, 185; Cartledge, *Testimony in the Spirit*, 59; Wilma Wells Davies, *The Embattled But Empowered Community: Comparing Understandings of Spiritual Power in Argentine Popular and Pentecostal Cosmologies*, GPCS 5 (Leiden: Brill, 2010), 221–28.

[39] Douglas Jacobsen, *Thinking in the Spirit: Theologies of the Early Pentecostal Movement* (Bloomington: Indiana University Press, 2003), 174–79.

[40] Cheryl J. Sanders, *Saints in Exile: The Holiness-Pentecostal Experience in African American Religion and Culture* (New York: Oxford University Press, 1996), 58.

[41] See Vinson Synan, *The Holiness-Pentecostal Movement* (Grand Rapids, MI: Eerdmans, 1971), 13–32.

[42] Gause, *Living in the Spirit*, 15–24.

[43] Joel Robbins, 'The Globalization of Pentecostal and Charismatic Christianity', ARA 33 (2004): 117–43 (127).

pneumatological and eschatological terms (see Acts 2:17–21) articulated in the full gospel motif by the portrayal of Jesus in the central roles of saviour, sanctifier, Spirit baptizer, healer, and coming king.[44] While salvation is at the core centred in Christ, for Pentecostals, it is by the Spirit that Christ accomplishes his work, and salvation is made available in the present to the human being and to creation in multiple forms.[45] Christology is interpreted pneumatologically (and vice versa): from the perspective of Pentecost, the activity of Christ and the Holy Spirit are united in God's work of redemption and its experience by the believer.

There are mutual implications of seeing the experience of salvation from a Pentecostal perspective 'in stereo'[46] as the work of both Christ and the Spirit. The language of 'conversion' tends to restrict soteriology to the realm of conscious human behaviour. In contrast, the Christological emphasis requires, on the one hand, the perpetuation of Christ's atoning work across all dimensions of life through the Holy Spirit: personal, familial, ecclesial, material, social, cosmic, and eschatological salvation.[47] The pneumatological orientation, on the other hand, requires that the redemptive act of Christ be maintained in its various present dimensions.[48] Consequently, Pentecostal expressions of salvation always manifest in some form a cosmic Spirit-Christology.[49] Responsible for this direction are the concrete experiences among Pentecostals of the saving power of God manifested without a dichotomy between Christ and the Spirit, a reading of the biblical texts, particularly Luke-Acts, that speaks of the saving work of Christ in terms of the anointing with the Spirit, and a pneumatological interpretation of salvation that understands the Holy Spirit as the gift of regeneration to the whole creation. The result of this

---

[44] See Peter Althouse, 'Pentecostal Eschatology in Context: The Eschatological Orientation of the Full Gospel', in *Perspectives in Pentecostal Eschatologies: World without End*, ed. Peter Althouse and Robbie Waddell (Eugene, OR: Pickwick, 2010), 205–31.

[45] Cf. Matthew K. Thompson, 'Eschatology as Soteriology: The Cosmic Full Gospel', in ibid., 189–204.

[46] Myk Habets, 'Spirit-Christology: Seeing in Stereo', *JPT* 11, no. 2 (2003): 199–234.

[47] See Yong, *The Spirit Poured Out on All Flesh*, 91–98.

[48] Some Pentecostals have distinguished between the work as Christ's provisional atonement and the Spirit's application; see Duffield and Van Cleave, *Foundations of Pentecostal Theology*, 179–260. In contrast, see Larry D. Hart, *Truth Aflame: Theology for the Church in Renewal*, rev. ed. (Grand Rapids, MI: Zondervan, 2005), 279–363.

[49] See Sammy Alfaro, *Divino Compañero: Toward a Hispanic Pentecostal Christology*, Princeton Theological Monograph 147 (Eugene, OR: Wipf & Stock, 2010), 52–93; Yong, *The Spirit Poured Out on All Flesh*, 83–91.

universal emphasis of joining together Christology and the pneumatology is a charismatic soteriology.[50]

A charismatic soteriology from the perspective of Pentecost interprets the new birth as participation in the promise of the universal outpouring of the Holy Spirit (Acts 2:38–39). Soteriologically, the gift is the regeneration of the human person; pneumatologically, the Spirit is both the gift and the promise of this regeneration. The charismatic dimension identifies this pneumatological perspective of salvation as a concrete experience of the human being in a personal encounter with God, who at the altar offers the gift of regeneration as the gift of the Holy Spirit. The 'moment' of conversion, often identified by Pentecostal testimonies with the exact date and time, refers to a person's reception of the divine grace – a charismatic moment that can be manifested in manifold forms along the spectrum of the full gospel. The new birth is thus not another term added to the soteriological vocabulary; it embraces the moments of redemption, atonement, reconciliation, expiation, justification and others towards the expectation of the fullness of salvation.

The cultural diversity of Pentecostalism articulates conversion in a variety of ways, often in the vernacular, sometimes through inherited Christian traditions, at other times with strong indigenous religious roots.[51] The altar calls people from all places and positions of life to a 'meeting with the Lord'.[52] From the perspective of Pentecost, this call is a broad invitation confronting all creation with the particular gift of salvation provided in the person of Jesus Christ and made present by the Holy Spirit poured out on *all* flesh. Nonetheless, the way to an encounter with God in Jesus Christ is as broad as the road to Pentecost. Two dominant metaphors for salvation in North American Pentecostalism are the participation in the divine life and the liberation from sin, both emerging with often different doctrinal emphases.[53] African American Pentecostals widely emphasize sanctification, divine healing, and personal piety as starting points for the path of salvation.[54] The

---

[50] Cf. the emphasis on pneumatological-charismatic Christocentrism in Veli-Matti Kärkkäinen, *A Constructive Christian Theology for the Pluralistic World*, vol. 1, *Christ and Reconciliation* (Grand Rapids, MI: Eerdmans, 2013), 207.
[51] See Clifton R. Clarke, *African Christology: Jesus in Post-Missionary African Christianity* (Eugene, OR: Wipf & Stock, 2011), 106–21.
[52] Kärkkäinen, 'Encountering Christ in the Full Gospel Way', 13–16.
[53] Dale Coulter, '"Delivered by the Power of God": Toward a Pentecostal Understanding of Salvation', *IJST* 10, no. 4 (2008): 447–67; Land, *Pentecostal Spirituality*, 23.
[54] See Estrelda Y. Alexander, *Black Fire: One Hundred Years of African American Pentecostalism* (Downers Grove: InterVarsity, 2011), 61–63.

black Apostolic denominations, on the other hand, uphold water baptism as a prerequisite for regeneration.[55] Salvation among Pentecostal groups in Southern Appalachia means supernatural deliverance from the powers of the devil and the world ritualizing the promises of Mark 16:18.[56] In Latin America, to be born again can also be understood in terms of spiritual and ideological, economic, and political deliverance.[57] Pentecostalism in Africa has engaged African traditional religious thought in ways that emphasize empowerment as a prerequisite for the daily struggle for salvation.[58] Pentecostalism in Asia emphasizes the need for holistic salvation amidst the concrete situations of diverse religious and secular contexts.[59] Pentecostalism in New Guinea highlights salvation as a deliverance from existing cultic and spiritual forces.[60]

Further examples could be added, yet this list remains both superficial and incomplete; it merely signals a desire among Pentecostals for a complete soteriology in terms of a materiality of salvation, which reaches the soul not only through inward repentance and spiritual conversion, as suggested by traditional Protestantism, but through a whole range of experiences marking the personal-spiritual, individual-physical, communal, socioeconomic, and ecological aspects of the full gospel.[61] The reception of salvation in the image of Pentecost is manifested both cognitively and affectively; the human being 'knows with certainty' (Acts 2:36) and is 'cut to the heart' (v. 37) by the reality of God's grace. The Holy Spirit is this divine grace manifested in liberating physical, mental, emotional, spiritual, and social passions.[62] Some Pentecostals have expressed these salvation experiences with the theological concept of the

---

[55] See James C. Richardson, *With Water and Spirit: A History of Black Apostolic Denominations in the U.S.* (Washington, DC: Spirit, 1980), 107.

[56] See Dennis Covington, *Salvation on Sand Mountain: Snake Handling and Redemption in Southern Appalachia* (Reading, MA: Addison-Wesley, 1995).

[57] See R. Andrew Chesnut, *Born Again in Brazil: The Pentecostal Boom and the Pathogens of Poverty* (New Brunswick, NJ: Rutgers University Press, 1997).

[58] David Tonghou Ngong, *The Holy Spirit and Salvation in African Christian Theology: Imagining a More Hopeful Future for Africa* (New York: Peter Lang, 2010); cf. Wariboko, *Nigerian Pentecostalism*, 30–33.

[59] See Allan Anderson and Edmond Tang (eds), *Asian and Pentecostal: The Charismatic Face of Christianity in Asia* (Oxford: Regnum Books International, 2005).

[60] Andrew Strathern, 'Fertility and Salvation: The Conflict between Spirit Cult and Christian Sext in Mount Hagen', *JRitS* 5, no. 1 (1991): 51–64.

[61] Miroslav Volf, 'Materiality of Salvation: An Investigation in the Soteriologies of Liberation and Pentecostal Theologies', *JES* 26, no. 3 (1989): 447–67.

[62] See Samuel Solivan, *The Spirit, Pathos and Liberation: Toward an Hispanic Pentecostal Theology*, JPTS 14 (Sheffield: Sheffield Academic Press, 1998), 93–118.

finite grasping the infinite (*finitum capax infiniti*).[63] The awareness of this encounter is the felt divine embrace of the human person.[64] The effects of this encounter are not only instantaneous but progressive; the altar both calls to an encounter with God and releases the human person transformed by the experience into the world. Pentecostals go to the altar with the expectation to be transformed, and they leave the altar with the expectation to return.

Salvation as praxis

The concern for redemptive practices identifies the heart of Pentecostal contributions to contemporary soteriology. All Christian theological discourse is fundamentally soteriological. However, in contrast to the dominant tendency to identify salvation with a relational disposition of the human being towards God usually directed towards one's state after death and thus primarily a positional eschatological concern,[65] soteriology in Pentecostal perspective attempts to grasp a present reality in which the future eschatological state is not only anticipated but already experienced and practiced. The experience at the altar represents the exchange of the divine invitation and the human response to the proclamation of the full gospel. As a soteriological symbol, in this exchange of invitation and response, salvation is characterized fundamentally as an experience identifiable by personal, public, and ecclesial practices. In the experience of salvation, as nowhere else, it is evident that theology and religious practices shape one another, and that such practices represent not merely the motivation or application of theological reflection. From the viewpoint of Pentecostal theology, salvation in all its dimensions, even in its cosmic scope, is in the fullest sense theological praxis.

The prevailing Christian soteriological narrative in the West typically contains a rationale for why salvation is necessary (i.e. sin and the Fall), the process by which salvation is realized (i.e. the life, death, and resurrection of Jesus

---

[63] See Terry L. Cross, 'The Divine-Human Encounter: Towards a Pentecostal Theology of Experience', *Pneuma* 31, no. 1 (2009): 3–34; Frank Macchia, 'Finitum Capax Infiniti: A Pentecostal Distinctive?' *Pneuma* 29, no. 2 (2007): 185–87.

[64] Frank Macchia, *Justified in the Spirit: Creation, Redemption, and the Triune God*, PM 2 (Grand Rapids, MI: Eerdmans, 2010), 76–80.

[65] See, for example, Clark H. Pinnock, Alister E. McGrath, Dennis L. Okholm and Timothy R. Phillips, *Four Views on Salvation in a Pluralistic World* (Grand Rapids, MI: Zondervan, 1996).

Christ), the extent of human participation (i.e. baptism, confession, faith), and the final state of salvation (i.e. resurrection, glorification, eternal life).[66] In the dominant theological story in the West, salvation, although historically accomplished by Christ, refers to a desired state in a future, post-mortem eschatology.[67] The atonement traditions are primarily 'objective' by locating the origin and effect of salvation in the activity of God, and most particularly in Christ, with little integration of the church's mission in the world and the active participation of the world and the human being.[68] The church's mission is a fulfilment of Christ's mission and thus exists as the continuation of the Incarnation as 'God's "embodied" saving activity'.[69] Although often thoroughly embedded in the language of the West, the Pentecostal approach to soteriology is more subjective, that is, salvation is based on the gospel of Christ in terms of the participation of God in creation and of humanity in the divine work of salvation. The focus of Pentecostal soteriology is not on salvation but on the saviour, not on the act itself but on the actor: Jesus, at the heart of the gospel, is the initiator and example of a soteriological praxis that involves him as a person anointed with the Spirit on the essential ground that is common to all: his own existential transformation. In turn, the narrative of Luke-Acts suggests that the church's praxis of salvation is based not solely on a view of the Incarnation and the cross but also on the outpouring of the Holy Spirit. These reflections have led Pentecostalism in often critical opposition to contemporary soteriological practices of the West.

Salvation in the East is more closely tied to the concept of deification (*theosis*) as an ongoing process of transformation into the likeness of Jesus Christ. Deification, possible because of the image of God found in humanity but deterred by the Fall, is reinstated with the Incarnation and the joining of human and divine natures in Christ.[70] The process of *theosis* is intended to 'begin here and now in the present life'[71] in a 'cooperation' between God

---

[66] See Wayne Morris, *Salvation as Praxis: A Practical Theology of Salvation for a Multi-Faith World* (London: Bloomsbury, 2014), 37–64.
[67] Ibid., 42.
[68] Veli-Matti Kärkkäinen, *Christ and Reconciliation* (Grand Rapids, MI: Eerdmans, 2013), 294–403.
[69] John Webster, *Word and Church: Essays in Christian Dogmatics* (Edinburgh: T&T Clark, 2001), 226. See also Michael S. Horton, *People and Place: A Covenant Ecclesiology* (Louisville, KY: Westminster John Knox, 2008), 166–76.
[70] Athanasius, *On the Incarnation*, 54.3.
[71] Kalistos Ware, *The Orthodox Church*, rev. ed. (New York: Penguin, 1993), 236.

and the human person so that 'our voluntary participation in God's saving action is altogether indispensable'.[72] This process is a human participation in the uncreated energies, the life, power, and glory of God.[73] Salvation is the participation in the transformation of the divine life through a perpetual process of being saved. Human participation in this process and the convergence of divine grace and human freedom are at every point the work of the Holy Spirit.[74] Although therefore entirely God's gift, salvation is a continued process of repentance exercised by the human being who is thoroughly embedded in the life of the community: going to church, receiving the sacraments, prayer, reading the Scriptures, and following the commandments are central practices of deification.[75] The Eastern view of salvation is eminently personal and practical, hesychastic and mystical on the one hand, as well as prosaic and active on the other.[76] Moreover, this personal transformation always remains embedded in the ecclesiastical, liturgical, and sacramental practices of the Orthodox Church and thus heavily depends on its sacerdotal and institutional traditions.[77] In this identification of salvation as praxis, Pentecostalism finds both its affinity to and distinction from the Orthodox tradition.

Pentecostal soteriology, although typically presented in the language of the West, is closer to the Eastern understanding of salvation as praxis.[78] The theological point of convergence is most visible in the pneumatological dimension of salvation.[79] For Pentecostals, salvation as praxis is Spirit-filled at the core because such practices depend on the outpouring of the Holy Spirit as the gift of regeneration. In other words, Pentecostals hold to a strong synergistic understanding of salvation:[80] the human being participates in the work of redemption through a joining of the Spirit of God with the human

---

[72] Kalistos Ware, *How Are We Saved? The Understanding of Salvation in the Orthodox Tradition* (Minneapolis: Light & Life, 1996), 34.
[73] Ibid., 58.
[74] Ware, *How Are We Saved*, 43.
[75] Ware, *The Orthodox Church*, 236.
[76] Ibid., 237.
[77] See Morris, *Salvation as Praxis*, 111–32.
[78] See Edmund J. Rybarczyk, *Beyond Salvation: Eastern Orthodoxy and Classical Pentecostalism on Becoming Like Christ* (Milton Keynes, UK: Paternoster, 2004); Walter J. Hollenweger, *Pentecostalism: Origins and Developments Worldwide* (Peabody, MA: Hendrickson, 1997), 253–55.
[79] Veli-Matti Kärkkäinen, *One with God: Salvation as Deification and Justification* (Collegeville, MN: Liturgical Press, 2004), 129–31.
[80] See Kenneth J. Archer and Andrew S. Hamilton, 'Anabaptist-Pietism and Pentecostalism: Scandalous Partners in Protest', *SJT* 63, no. 2 (2010): 185–202.

spirit, and such participation is affective and experiential because 'it is that very Spirit bearing witness with our spirit that we are children of God' (Rom. 8:16). Salvation is understood pneumatologically because of the Pentecostal emphasis on these experiences of salvation as experiences of the Spirit at the moment of conversion and beyond, and in a manner to which the believer's spirit can clearly testify.

At the same time, Pentecostal experiences of salvation are based on a different theological outlook at the saving work of Christ from the perspective of the Holy Spirit. The Pentecostal perspective begins with a narrative of Jesus that is thoroughly imbued with the narrative of the Spirit. The Incarnation, as the entrance point for the eternal Son of God into history, is marked by a codetermining agency of the Son and the Spirit in the economy of salvation: The Spirit creates and unites the humanity of Jesus with the Son, and the Son's action through Jesus is determinative for the Spirit.[81] This pneumatological Christology is evident in Jesus's life logically from the moment of the Incarnation. However, the ministry of salvation made possible by this union is manifested outwardly by Jesus's obedience to the leading of the Holy Spirit. Historically and practically, this public ministry begins not at Jesus's conception but at his baptism and anointing with the Holy Spirit (see Acts 10:38). The Christian practices of salvation accordingly originate with the Incarnation only insofar as the event becomes, soteriologically speaking, public property with the baptism of Jesus, so that the church and its practices are literally a continuation of the anointing of Christ.[82] Consequently, for Pentecostals, the Incarnation and Pentecost are often insufficiently linked in theological reflection.[83] Furthermore, while the history of the Holy Spirit in the earthly Jesus continues in the church, Christian soteriological practices have insufficiently accentuated the anointing with the Holy Spirit.[84] Pentecostalism, itself subject to the history of neglect,[85] has emerged as a theological critique of

---

[81] Steven M. Studebaker, *From Pentecost to the Triune God: A Pentecostal Trinitarian Theology*, PM 5 (Grand Rapids, MI: Eerdmans, 2015), 177–81.

[82] See Heribert Mühlen, *Una Mystica Persona: Die Kirche als das Mysterium der heilsgeschichtlichen Identität des Heiligen Geistes in Christus und den Christen: Eine Person in vielen Personen*, 2nd ed. (Paderborn: Schöningh, 1967), 194–96.

[83] Andrew K. Gabriel, *The Lord Is the Spirit: The Holy Spirit and the Divine Attributes* (Eugene, OR: Pickwick, 2011), 160–62.

[84] See Wolfgang Vondey, *Heribert Mühlen: His Theology and Praxis. A New Profile of the Church* (Lanham, MD: University Press of America, 2004), 196–211.

[85] Studebaker, 'Pentecostal Soteriology', 252–57.

Christendom and its neglect of the development of salvation as praxis not merely in the image of Christ but in the image of Christ anointed with the Holy Spirit. From this image of Jesus as the messiah who pours out the Holy Spirit, the reach of salvation extends beyond the human realm to the whole of creation.

The theological critique of Pentecostal soteriology is firmly embedded in an institutional critique of Christendom and its structured ritual and liturgical practices.[86] Pentecostal synergism, when understood as human participation in the saving work of Christ anointed with the Holy Spirit, demands ecclesial practices that are open to the whole range of human experiences.[87] The altar call represents this broad entrance of human participation in the divine gift of salvation in the church. The altar rite highlights the tensions between private and public conversion, sacramental and spontaneous forms of initial confession, Calvinist and Arminian distinctions of divine and human initiative, and debates about the role of catechesis and spiritual formation.[88] However, the immediate motivation of this practice is not the certainty of salvation but the initiation into participation with the full salvific work of God. The call to the altar is a call from the kingdom of God, from the throne of heaven, from Jesus Christ, through the church to the world, and in the Spirit back to Jesus Christ and to the kingdom of God. This soteriological plot involves a 'meeting with God' where 'the altar space functions symbolically as an *axis mundi*... [that] most clearly symbolizes and helps to focus the human-divine convergence'.[89] The knowledge of salvation involves a 'knowing the Lord' by the human person who engages in salvation with an epistemology that is thoroughly pneumatological because it is experiential and practical. In other words, salvation is not given and received at a distance but is always directed towards the prospect of a direct encounter with God. The praxis of salvation is itself the eradication of the distance between the human being and the saviour.

The altar call as a central theological ritual of Pentecostal soteriology reflects in the broadest sense salvation as a praxis of hospitality. The soteriological

---

[86] Vondey, *Beyond Pentecostalism*, 109–40.
[87] Yong, *The Spirit Poured Out on All Flesh*, 119.
[88] See David Bennett, *The Altar Call: Its Origins and Present Usage* (Lanham, MD: University Press of America, 2000); Dickson D. Bruce, *And They All Sang Hallelujah: Plain-Folk Camp-Meeting Religion, 1800–1845* (Knoxville: University of Tennessee Press, 1981).
[89] Albrecht, *Rites in the Spirit*, 133.

practices of the church and the human being are fundamentally a reflection of the abundant hospitality of God.[90] For Pentecostals, the paradigm of divine hospitality is Jesus Christ, whose embodied life of self-giving for the world is extended by the Holy Spirit towards the whole of creation.[91] The praxis of salvation proceeds as hospitality through the mode of exchange in 'the redemptive economy of the triune God [who] invites our participation as guests and hosts in the divine hospitality revealed in Christ by the power of the Holy Spirit'.[92] Emulating the anointing of Jesus, the human person becomes obedient to the leading of the Spirit and thus remains not merely passive-receptive but becomes participatory in the divine work of salvation. Oneness Pentecostals consequently require both water baptism and the baptism in the Holy Spirit as integral parts of conversion.[93] For most Pentecostals, participation in salvation is bound up with human, social, moral, ecclesial, sacramental, and eschatological contexts in which we find ourselves not as owners of the divine hospitality but nonetheless as participants, witnesses, and enactors in the economy of salvation.[94] The call to the altar as a call to salvation is consequently cast in the terms of hospitality as a call to the lost, the stranger, the outcast, and the other. This universal hospitality of God extended to the whole world always calls creation to the particular altar of the Lamb of God, Jesus Christ. The altar call as a call to Christ is always a call to repentance, deliverance, and spiritual transformation albeit cast beyond the narrow net of conversion and a strict order and object of salvation.[95]

Pentecostal theology spans the gap between Christ and history, and hence the way of salvation, with the Holy Spirit. While this can be said for other Christian traditions, Pentecostal soteriology operates on the explicit assumption of the Spirit's immediacy in the world that invites and enables the human being to experience a salvific encounter with God through Christ. More precisely, the experience of the hospitality of God epitomized in Jesus

---

[90] See Wolfgang Vondey, *People of Bread: Rediscovering Ecclesiology* (New York: Paulist Press, 2008).
[91] See Amos Yong, *Hospitality and the Other: Pentecost, Christian Practices, and the Neighbor* (Maryknoll, NY: Orvis, 2008), 118–28.
[92] Ibid., 127.
[93] See 'Final Report of the Oneness-Trinitarian Pentecostal Dialogue', 286.
[94] See Wolfgang Vondey, 'Pentecostal Ecclesiology and Eucharistic Hospitality: Toward a Systematic and Ecumenical Account of the Church', *Pneuma* 32, no. 1 (2010): 41–55.
[95] See Thomas E. Trask and David A. Womack, *Back to the Altar: A Call to Spiritual Awakening* (Springfield, MO: Gospel Publishing House, 1994).

Christ is always an encounter with the immediacy of the Holy Spirit. The altar as a ritual metaphor of Pentecostal soteriology represents the point of that encounter, the space and time, where the Spirit enables the human being to participate in the redemptive work of Christ. The altar is constituted by the practices of this encounter, which are as varied as the manifestations of divine hospitality: the altar is the holy and anointed habitation of God,[96] the place of Christ's sacrifice,[97] the presence of the Word of God and of the Holy Spirit,[98] instrument of evangelization and the proclamation of the gospel,[99] the anxious bench of the sinner,[100] public confession of faith,[101] invitation for baptism,[102] gift of sacramental worship,[103] the eucharistic table,[104] fellowship and revival of the faithful,[105] anointing of the church,[106] and thus home to a myriad of soteriological practices. The altar stands as the source and summit of Pentecostal theology, a metaphor of the salvific work of God into which all other theological concerns can be integrated.[107] Pentecostal theology is thus by nature hospitable to the theological constructs of other traditions, inviting and transforming them through exposure to salvation at the altar as the central locus of the Christian life.

The following chapters of part one both clarify and expand the basic soteriological reflections of this chapter along the metaphor of the altar. A complete picture of Pentecostal soteriology in the image of the full gospel can be seen only at the end of the first part. The perspective of Pentecost as the core symbol of Pentecostal theology extends the metaphor of the altar through its

---

[96] See Gerd Johannes Maurer, *'Der Altar aber ist Christus': Zur symbolischen Bedeutung des christlichen Altares in der Geschichte* (St. Augustin: Steyler, 1969).

[97] See Joseph Braun, *Der christliche Altar in seiner geschichtlichen Entwicklung*, vol. 1 (Munich: Guenther Koch, 1924), 750–55.

[98] See Samuel Fisk, *The Public Invitation: Is It Scriptural? Is It Wise? Is It Necessary?* (Brownsburg, IN: Biblical Evangelism Press, 1970).

[99] Donna Schaper, *Altar Call: Inviting Response to the Gospel* (Nashville: Abingdon, 2001).

[100] J. W. Nevin, *The Anxious Bench* (New York: Garland, 1843).

[101] See Street, *The Effective Invitation*,109–38.

[102] See Thomas H. Olbricht, 'The Invitation: A Historical Survey', *Restoration Quarterly* 5, no. 1 (1961): 6–16.

[103] See Daniel Tomberlin, *Pentecostal Sacraments: Encountering God at the Altar* (Cleveland, TN: Center for Pentecostal Leadership and Care, 2010), 73–106.

[104] See Eugene La Verdiere, *The Eucharist in the New Testament and the Early Church* (Collegeville, MN: Liturgical Press, 1996), 148–66.

[105] Bennett, *The Altar Call*, 177–90.

[106] Thomas G. Simmons, *Holy People, Holy Place: Rites for the Church's House* (Chicago, IL: Liturgy Training Publications, 1998), 49–51.

[107] See Wolfgang Vondey, 'The Theology of the Altar and Pentecostal Sacramentality', in *Scripting Pentecost: A Study of Pentecostals, Worship and Liturgy*, ed. Mark J. Cartledge and A. J. Swoboda (Aldershot, UK: Ashgate, 2016), 94–107.

Christocentric and pneumatological vision of the redemptive work of God to the whole of creation. The second part of this book brings out the cosmological, anthropological, social, ecclesiological, and theological scope of a broad Pentecostal theology. Nonetheless, the contours of this constructive journey remain anchored in the elements of the Pentecostal vision of salvation as praxis.

3

Sanctified

Participating in the Life of God

A second motif in the narrative account of Pentecost is sanctification: Jesus Christ is saviour and sanctifier. In Pentecostal articulations of the full gospel, Jesus's work of redemption is experienced at conversion, sanctification, Spirit baptism, divine healing, and the coming kingdom. Sanctification as a distinct work of grace is arguably the most contested teaching among Pentecostals; it follows salvation in the account of the fivefold gospel but is visibly absent in the fourfold pattern.[1] Although the historical discussion on sanctification is dominated by doctrinal disagreements, the different emphases on sanctification as a distinctive moment in the Pentecostal understanding of salvation are practically motivated. Within the soteriological practice of the altar call, which serves as my theological metaphor for grounding a theology around the symbol of Pentecost in the tangible practices of Pentecostal communities, sanctification identifies both the call of God and the desire of the believer to holiness (see 1 Pet. 1:15–16). In light of the promise of salvation, sanctification becomes a mandate of cleansing from sin and seeking perfection (see 2 Cor. 7:1). Hamartiology and eschatology are significant markers of the Pentecostal framework for understanding holiness, which is not a consequence but a requirement of salvation (see Heb. 12:14). Although sanctification is entirely the work of God, the Christian actively participates in the divine act in a personal and experiential manner.[2] The experience of sanctification therefore continues the Pentecostal emphasis on salvation as praxis

---

[1] Donald W. Dayton, *Theological Roots of Pentecostalism* (Peabody, MA: Hendrickson, 1987), 17–23.
[2] See R. Hollis Gause, *Living in the Spirit: The Way of Salvation* (Cleveland, TN: Pathway Press, 1980), 41.

and puts into contrast how Christian practices embrace both the believer's encounter with Christ in justification and the reception of the Holy Spirit in terms of sanctification. This chapter unfolds further the theological critique Pentecostalism brings to institutional Christendom (see Chapter 2) by arguing that sanctification has a ritual character for Pentecostals that trumps its doctrinal positioning. The ritual practices of sanctification therefore receive priority in this chapter before moving to a discussion of divergent doctrinal reflections and an integration of sanctification as a ritual in other Christian traditions. The first part continues the narrative of the altar call with focus on the central theological metaphors and Pentecostal ritual practices of sanctification emerging from the day of Pentecost. The second part unfolds the distinct and dominant teachings Pentecostals hold on sanctification. In the final part, this discussion is situated among the broader teachings and practices of sanctification in the Christian world.

Sanctification at the altar

I have argued that salvation in Pentecostal theology consists of practices of hospitality. These practices are grounded in the biblical event of Pentecost and open to manifold experiences of the redemptive work of Christ encountered in the immediacy of the Holy Spirit. The Pentecostal narrative of sanctification unambiguously focuses on sanctification as the work of Christ, the sanctifier. In the biblical narrative, however, the ritual character of sanctification at Pentecost is centred in the practice of tarrying for the presence of Jesus inextricably tied up with the coming of the Holy Spirit.[3] Before the disciples were sent out (see John 20:21), before they could follow the great commission to 'go into all the world', to 'proclaim the good news to the whole creation' (Mark 16:15), and to 'make disciples of all nations' (Matt. 28:19), they had to 'tarry' (borrowed from the King James Version) in Jerusalem (see Luke 24:49). The extended record of the tarrying of the disciples begins with the day of the ascension of Christ and the commandment of Jesus to wait in order to 'receive power when the Holy Spirit has come' (Acts 1:8). Jesus 'ordered

---

[3] See Robert W. Wall, 'Waiting on the Holy Spirit (Acts 1:4): Extending a Metaphor to Biblical Interpretation', *JPT* 22, no. 1 (2013): 37–53.

them not to leave Jerusalem, but to wait there for the promise of the Father' (Acts 1:4). The disciples followed these instructions by 'constantly devoting themselves to prayer' (v. 14) and remaining 'all together in one place' (Acts 2:1). The upper room functioned for the disciples as an altar space in which, upon tarrying, they were sanctified by the outpouring of the Holy Spirit.[4] This Christo-pneumatological synopsis of the biblical accounts from a Pentecostal perspective shapes the root practices of the Pentecostal altar call and its aim to participate in the events of the original Pentecost. The pursuit of sanctification, as part of the altar call, is fundamentally the pursuit of Pentecost, the emulation and reiteration of its larger ritual space and domain in the praxis of salvation.

The 'altar' in its various forms and understandings among Pentecostals (whether in its traditional architectural presence, its symbolic representation at the steps of the preacher's pulpit, or its manifestation in the felt presence of God among the assembly) extends through the entire narrative of sanctification.[5] The crowd on the day of Pentecost also experienced this altar from the moment they gathered to observe the disciples (see Acts 2:6). Their bewilderment, amazement, astonishment, perplexity, sneering, and mocking (vv. 5–6, 11) characterize the extension of the experience. The crowd remained in the place throughout Peter's sermon (vv. 14–36); the resulting convictions in the heart of the audience (v. 37), the testimonies and exhortations of the disciples (vv. 40), and the crowd's 'welcoming' of the message (v. 41) are all descriptions of an altar call culminating in the addition of three thousand to the church.

The biblical texts illustrate sanctification as an active pursuit by the people of God. The narrative of Pentecost embeds the individual pursuit in the communal dimensions of sanctification. Situated within the soteriological environment of the altar space, the pursuit of sanctification is a threshold-practice, a transitional rite of passage identified by an initial stage of departure of the participants from their familiar world and a concluding state of the consummation of a new state of existence, joined by an intervening phase of tarrying. The response to the altar call manifests the initial departure typically

---

[4] Laurence W. Wood, *Pentecostal Grace* (Wilmore, KY: Francis Asbury Publishing, 1980), 261.
[5] See Lee Roy Martin (ed.), *A Future for Holiness: Pentecostal Explorations* (Cleveland, TN: CPT Press, 2013), 2, 41, 48, 101, 196, 231–32.

by a physical action, a shift of position, and movement of the individual or the corporate body towards the altar.[6] The altar space is accepted as a sacred space for the tarrying, 'a temporary "container" of sorts for the sacred, for the human to engage the sacred'.[7] In its ritual sense, sanctification is an active waiting for the encounter with Christ and immersion into the sacred presence of the Holy Spirit. 'Lingering' or 'tarrying' and 'laying' or 'giving yourself' at the altar are dominant metaphors that narrate this practice of sanctification among Pentecostals.

The entire tone of Pentecostal worship has been described at times as 'one of waiting'.[8] Lingering and laying yourself at the altar are metaphors for the prolonged presence of a person before God, a personal, physical, and communal expression of Pentecostal piety and spirituality. Those who 'practice sanctification' seek to participate actively in the divine presence, even though the human 'activity' implies waiting, travailing, prostrating, and submitting oneself to the holiness of God in the expectation that God would impart this holiness through the Holy Spirit to the life of the believer.[9] Pentecostals expect that this impartation of holiness can be discerned by outward manifestations and signs of the presence of the Holy Spirit similar to the day of Pentecost. The rituals of sanctification at the altar therefore recapitulate the apostles' tarrying in the upper room, reiterating the church's waiting for the promises of God, a lingering before the Lord, a seeking of and yielding to the Holy Spirit (Acts 1:13–14). For some Pentecostals, this tarrying evident in prayer, fasting, and seeking the Lord forms consistent ascetical practices that are indispensable conditions for lifelong spiritual growth.[10] Others see these practices as contemplative modes of 'deep receptivity and a sense of openness to God' that does not permeate the entire Pentecostal worship but is dominant during the altar call and response ritual.[11] Again others view these spiritual rituals

---

[6] Daniel Albrecht, *Rites in the Spirit: A Ritual Approach to Pentecostal/Charismatic Spirituality*, JPTS 17 (Sheffield: Sheffield Academic Press, 1999), 166–69.
[7] Ibid., 133.
[8] James Menzie, 'Pentecostal Principles', *PE*, 11 October 1953, 2.
[9] See Daniel Castelo, 'Tarrying on the Lord: Affections, Virtues, and Theological Ethics in Pentecostal Perspective', *JPT* 13, no. 1 (2004): 50–56; idem, *Revisioning Pentecostal Ethics: The Epicletic Community* (Cleveland, TN: CPT Press, 2012), 35–82.
[10] See Simon Can, *Pentecostal Theology and the Christian Spiritual Tradition*, JPTS 21 (Sheffield: Sheffield Academic Press, 2000), 77.
[11] Albrecht, *Rites in the Spirit*, 183–84.

as pragmatic and dramatic expressions of 'an *active* waiting, anticipating the Spirit's intervention and activity'.[12] Tarrying and lingering along with similar expressions are metaphors for the Pentecostal vision of the moral life.[13] Nonetheless, the active and tangible dimensions of sanctification are grounded in personal and congregational rituals that can take widely different forms. The most dominant altar practices are the tarrying services among African American Pentecostals, the soaking prayer among charismatic and neo-Pentecostal congregations and the practice of foot washing among classical Pentecostal groups.

The practice of tarrying at the altar forms the core of the African American Pentecostal experience of conversion, sanctification, and Spirit baptism.[14] This practice is ritually structured and set in its own environment often outside the regular worship service:[15]

> Tarrying is a spiritual practice within African American Pentecostalism wherein a person praying at the altar repeatedly recites specific phrases. While the person prays, prayer leaders stand nearby to encourage the person in this spiritual exercise. Tarrying often follows the main evening worship service, especially on Fridays and Sundays, and can last from one to two hours. The tarrying service includes a format and content of its own, consisting of its special invocations, supplications, songs, rules and religious expectations.[16]

The tarrying ritual originated with the black Christian practice of the ringshout, an ecstatic swaying and shouting practiced among black slaves that transformed them into participants in actual biblical and historical actions.[17] The shout is a 'reaching beyond the world' to God and to freedom and 'the possibility of imminent rebirth'.[18] During the nineteenth century, these practices transitioned into tarrying with its key elements including an active

---

[12] Peter Neumann, *Pentecostal Experience: An Ecumenical Encounter* (Eugene, OR: Pickwick, 2012), 115–16.
[13] See Castelo, 'Tarrying on the Lord', 31–56.
[14] See David D. Daniels III, '"Until the Power of the Lord Comes Down": African American Pentecostal Spirituality and Tarrying', in *Contemporary Spiritualities: Social and Religious Contexts*, ed. Clive Erricker (London: Continuum, 2001), 173–91.
[15] Cheryl J. Sanders, *Saints in Exile: The Holiness-Pentecostal Experience in African American Religion and Culture* (New York: Oxford University Press, 1996), 58–59.
[16] Daniels, 'Until the Power of the Lord Comes Down', 175.
[17] Lawrence W. Levine, *Black Culture and Black Consciousness: Afro-American Folk Thought from Slavery to Freedom* (New York: Oxford University Press, 1977), 38.
[18] Ibid., 38–39.

waiting upon God, repetition of a Christian phrase or word, concentration on these words, and entering into communion with God.[19] Industrialization and urbanization have transformed these original practices into a Pentecostal liturgy that has spread far beyond African American churches.[20] Tarrying in this sense aims at sanctification by means of repetition, fervency, interiorization, diligence, letting go of oneself, and holding on to the coming of God, anticipating a breakthrough to the participation in the sanctifying presence of the Spirit of Christ.[21]

Sanctification as a tarrying practice contains the confession of sin and the surrender of one's sinful nature to God, not only as an act of the mind but, in the concrete space of the altar, as a physical and sometimes violent struggle of the flesh.[22] Believers tarry for Jesus, both in an active separation from the world, and through participation in the sanctifying presence of Christ. There is no Pentecostal tarrying without Jesus, since believers are sanctified by his blood (1 Jn 1:7; Heb. 10:10; Rev. 1:5). At the same time, the Pentecostal experience of the Lord is accompanied by the witness of the Holy Spirit in physical manifestations that can range from the inward sense of deliverance from sin to the dramatic exorcism of a demonic spirit. Christians are sanctified by the Holy Spirit (Rom. 15:16; 1 Cor. 6:11; 1 Pet. 1:2). All Pentecostal worship is a preparing for this participation in the life of God through Christ and in the Holy Spirit (see Eph. 2:18).

In more recent years, soaking prayer has emerged as a charismatic ritual among new Pentecostal groups that emulates a variety of types of prayers and charismatic activities, including waiting, resting, hearing from God, dreams and visions, singing, prophesying, or speaking in tongues. In contrast to the older practice of tarrying, the language of soaking prayer is the contemplative activity of resting, receiving, beholding, and becoming.[23] Among classical Pentecostals, similar experiences of falling to the ground during prayer are often referred to as being 'slain in the Spirit' – a description of the intense

---

[19] Daniels, 'Until the Power of the Lord Comes Down', 178.
[20] See Wolfgang Vondey, 'The Making of a Black Liturgy: Pentecostal Worship and Spirituality from African Slave Narratives to American Cityscapes', *BT* 10, no. 2 (2012): 147–68.
[21] Daniels, 'Until the Power of the Lord Comes Down', 180–84.
[22] See James S. Tinney, 'A Theoretical and Historical Comparison of Black Political and Religious Movements' (PhD dissertation, Howard University, 1978), 240–41.
[23] See Paul Yadao and Leif Hetland, *Soaking in God's Presence* (Peachtree City, GA: Global Mission Awareness, 2011), 39–54.

experience of the presence of God as if dead.[24] Unlike the explicitly verbal and petitioning tarrying service, however, soaking prayer relies on a nonverbal, meditative, and quiet posture.[25] Forms of prayer often take place within a group of individuals who 'alternate periods of song and silence'[26] and pray in their native language or quietly in tongues. As a ritual, soaking prayer is 'part of the lived experience of the sacred ... where it is claimed that time spent resting in the loving arms of the Father fills them with God's love'.[27] Among neopentecostal groups, this practice is typically directed at the impartation of the power of the Spirit, anointing, healing, sanctification, and other manifestations of the divine love and embodiment of the presence of the sacred.[28] Soaking is an extended practice of lingering at the altar, a less structured but nonetheless ritual and embodied form of seeking the encounter with God through the Holy Spirit. Verbal activities, such as singing, praying, speaking in tongues, prophecy, and other charismatic manifestations can accompany the experience.[29] Sanctification here is an umbrella term for an array of experiences associated with seeking the presence of God that range from the assurance of forgiveness to immediate deliverance, gradual purification, the sense of transformation, and the experience of renewal.

Another ritual practice of sanctification among Pentecostals is foot washing, typically celebrated in reflection of the practice recorded in John 13 and believed to be continued by the Johannine community.[30] Affirmed as a vital part of the life of the disciples and practiced not only in their companionship with Jesus but also in the upper room and beyond Pentecost, many classical Pentecostal groups regard foot washing as an ordinance and celebrate the ritual alongside water baptism and the Lord's Supper.[31] The practice of foot washing follows generally in very strict forms the biblical account, where

---

[24] See Jerry Don Venable, 'Slain in the Spirit: Another View', *Paraclete* 22, no. 3 (1988): 21–26.
[25] See Michael Wilkinson and Peter Althouse, *Catch the Fire: Soaking Prayer and Charismatic Renewal* (De Kalb: Northern Illinois University Press, 2014), 3–11.
[26] Francis MacNutt, 'The Soaking Prayer', in *Touching the Heart of God*, ed. Leonard E. LeSourd (Old Tappan, NJ: Chosen Books, 1990), 183–86 (here 184).
[27] Wilkinson and Althouse, *Catch the Fire*, 70–71.
[28] See ibid., 86–88.
[29] Ibid., 93–112.
[30] See John Christopher Thomas, *Footwashing in John 13 and the Johannine Community*, JSNTS 61 (Sheffield: JSOT Press, 1991).
[31] See Daniel Tomberlin, *Pentecostal Sacraments: Encountering God at the Altar* (Cleveland, TN: Center for Pentecostal Leadership and Care, 2010), 193–224; Daniel Tomberlin, *Encountering God at the Altar: The Sacraments in Pentecostal Worship* (Cleveland, TN: Center for Pentecostal Leadership and Care, 2006), 73–78.

we find Jesus arising during the meal, taking off his outer garments, pouring water into a basin, washing his disciples' feet and drying them with a towel (Jn 13:4–5). When Jesus met with the reluctance of Peter to have his feet washed, Jesus responded, 'Unless I wash you, you will have no inheritance with me' (v. 8). Peter's request that Jesus then should bathe him entirely is met with Jesus's explanation that 'whoever has bathed has no need except to have his feet washed' (v. 10). This reply is interpreted by Pentecostals as an initial reference to the cleansing of water baptism and the need for foot washing as a practice and sign of the continued forgiveness of post-baptismal sins.[32] Jesus then instructs his disciples to observe foot washing as an ongoing model, a command understood as a reference to sanctification by those who have been baptized.[33]

Among the distinctive practices of sanctification, foot washing is the most overtly sacramental experience among some Pentecostals.[34] Typically following the end of an evening service or celebrated as a liturgical service in its own right, the congregation meets at the altar or designated spaces with prepared bowls or tubs and towels in front of pews or chairs. The washing is typically preceded by the reading of John 13 and can be carried out in a broader sacramental framework, including the celebration of the Lord's Supper.[35] Foot washing has become an often literal practice of cleansing; the washing of sin and dirt with water is accompanied by mutual confession, forgiveness, prayer, and tears.[36] Central for the significance attributed to the washing of feet is both the cleansing effect of the washing itself on the one whose feet are washed, and the effect of the humility and cleaning act on the one who is doing the washing.[37] Sanctification is communicated in foot washing through embodiment and touch and thus requires the self-effacing embrace of what

---

[32] Thomas, *Footwashing*, 148–49.
[33] Ibid., 199–226.
[34] Tomberlin, *Pentecostal Sacraments*, 194; Tom Driver, *The Magic of Ritual* (San Francisco: Harper and Row, 1991), 208.
[35] See John Christopher Thomas, 'Footwashing within the Context of the Lord's Supper', in *The Lord's Supper: Believers Church Perspectives*, ed. Dale R. Stoffer (Scottsdale, PA: Herald Press, 1997), 169–84.
[36] Cheryl Bridges Johns, 'Transformed by Grace: The Beauty of Personal Holiness', in *Holiness Manifesto*, ed. Kevin W. Mannoia and Don Thorsen (Grand Rapids, MI: Eerdmans, 2008), 152–65 (159).
[37] Lisa P. Stephenson, 'Getting Our Feet Wet: The Politics of Footwashing', *Journal of Pentecostal Theology* 23, no. 2 (2014): 154–70; Frank D. Macchia, 'Is Footwashing the Neglected Sacrament? A Theological Response to John Christopher Thomas', *Pneuma* 19, no. 2 (1997): 239–49 (247).

is other in order to be restored.[38] The experience of foot washing is sanctifying in its participation in the humility and forgiveness of Jesus, theologically interpreting the hands of the believer as the hands of Christ, the water as the Holy Spirit, and participants serving 'as agents of cleansing and healing as well as recipients of that grace'.[39] The mutual interracial washing of feet by white and black Pentecostal denominational leaders under tears of cleansing and prayers of forgiveness, known as the so-called 'Memphis miracle' that led to the organization the Pentecostal and Charismatic Churches of North America (PCCNA), illustrates vividly the continued commitment Pentecostals have made personally and communally to an explicit practice of sanctification.[40] The continuing debate on particular practices further accentuates the importance Pentecostals attribute to sanctification as a defining element of the church and the Christian life.

While these are by no means the only ritual practices of sanctification among Pentecostals, this short overview highlights the importance of practicing a personal and experiential application of sanctification. The ritual practices accentuate an experience of sanctification that is at least logically, if not temporally, subsequent to justification.[41] However, theological interpretations of sanctification have divided Pentecostals, often despite a shared praxis, on the exact nature of sanctification, when and to what extent it is received, and when it is completed. This theological discussion has proceeded almost entirely apart from considerations of praxis and documents the indebtedness of Pentecostal theology to modern Evangelical concerns of doctrine.

Sanctification as a concern of doctrine

For Pentecostals, holiness is the heart of the doctrine of salvation.[42] However, as the preceding account of various rituals of sanctification suggests, Pentecostals hold different views on the place and effect of sanctification in the order of salvation. Most visibly, Pentecostals are divided over the exact

---

[38] Stephenson, 'Getting Our Feet Wet', 166–68.
[39] Johns, 'Transformed by Grace', 159.
[40] See Vinson Synan, 'Memphis 1994: Miracle and Mandate', available at http://www.pccna.org/about_history.htm, accessed 1 August 2016.
[41] See Gause, *Living in the Spirit*, 40.
[42] See Dale M. Coulter, *Holiness: The Beauty of Perfection* (Cleveland, TN: Pathway, 2004), 65–92.

reception of sanctification as a work of grace; those following the Wesleyan Holiness tradition speak of sanctification as the experience of a 'second blessing' (subsequent to regeneration) while others follow the Reformed view of progressive sanctification throughout the believer's life.[43] Each alternative originates from experience and traditioned practices, whether in approval of the idea or in rejection of the conviction held by the other group. The more immediate doctrinal articulations of sanctification among classical Pentecostals have emerged from the nineteenth-century Holiness Movement, although the roots of the Pentecostal teaching reach back to Lutheran Pietism in late sixteenth- and early seventeenth-centuries.[44] The theological controversy of the movement is most evident in the debates surrounding John Wesley's teaching that 'entire sanctification' or 'complete perfection' is attainable in the present life.[45] Some classical Pentecostals have embraced the notion that entire sanctification can be received as a second work of grace or a second blessing following conversion. For others, this experience has become synonymous with justification, on the one hand, or Spirit baptism, on the other. As a motif of the full gospel, sanctification remains a theologically distinct moment on the way of salvation.

The Pentecostal holiness view on entire sanctification holds that God removes the sinful nature, which originated with the fall of Adam, in a second work of grace distinct from conversion. Amidst a range of biblical interpretations, most advocates of this position would emphasize immediately that the disciples, who already possessed faith in Jesus, were all entirely sanctified on the day of Pentecost. The subsequent outpouring of the Spirit on the disciples represents a prototype for this Pentecostal view of sanctification, which is frequently supported by giving multiple exegetical accounts. Central to the interpretation of these accounts is the equation of sanctification with the reception of the Holy Spirit. Among the most popular passages is Acts 8:1–25, which records that the Samarian Christians had already found faith

---

[43] William W. Menzies, 'Non-Wesleyan Pentecostalism: A Tradition', *AJPS* 14, no. 2 (2011): 187–98.
[44] See Melvin Dieter (ed.), *The 19th-Century Holiness Movement*, vol. 4 of *Great Holiness Classics* (Kansas City, MO: Beacon Hill, 1998). Cf. Roger E. Olson, 'Pietism and Pentecostalism: Spiritual Cousins or Competitors?' *Pneuma* 34, no. 3 (2012): 319–44.
[45] See Robert Webster, 'The Holy Spirit and the Miraculous: John Wesley's Egalitarian View of the Supernatural and Its Problems', in *The Holy Spirit and the Christian Life: Historical, Interdisciplinary, and Renewal Perspectives*, ed. Wolfgang Vondey, CHARIS 1 (New York: Palgrave Macmillan, 2014), 143–59.

in Christ and had been baptized with water but subsequently received the Holy Spirit; Acts 19:1-7 speaks of believers in Ephesus who had been baptized in water but had not yet received the Holy Spirit; the story of the apostle Paul in Acts 9:1-22 is interpreted in two stages with Saul's conversion on the road to Damascus and his subsequent sanctification at the hands of Ananias; and the reading of Acts 10:24-48 interprets the household of Cornelius as already believers when the Holy Spirit was poured out on the Gentiles.[46] The Pentecostal holiness reading of Scripture thus emphasizes the need for sanctification following conversion and identifies this second work of grace with the outpouring of the Holy Spirit. The title 'Pentecostal' is here theologically synonymous with sanctification before it is associated with other outward manifestations of the movement!

The rituals among Pentecostal holiness groups emphasize both the need for sanctification subsequent to conversion and the possibility of entire sanctification of the believer in this life. Both convictions grew out of the experience that conversion often does not mark an eradication of the life of sin (in contrast to expectations), but that such a life is indeed possible if the believer embraces a crisis with a search for entire sanctification.[47] The language of a second crisis (following the first crisis of conversion) has contributed to the practices of the altar call and response, typically identifying the altar experience with the opportunity for conversion and subsequent sanctification. Where the language of sanctification has remained in the Wesleyan-Holiness tradition, some churches allow for the interpretation of 'subsequent' as logical rather than temporal, thus shortening the distance between conversion and sanctification in practice while retaining their theological distinction.[48] Nevertheless, entire sanctification refers to a life of piety and holiness in the expectation to be fully cleansed from the imperfections of sin. This view rejects the idea of gradual purification in favour of instantaneous sanctification, similar to regeneration, by which holiness is implanted in the believer to empower a life in the grace of sanctification free from the power of original sin. While the sanctified believer does not enter into a state of sinless perfection without temptation, the

---

[46] See J. Kenneth Grider, *Entire Sanctification: The Distinctive Doctrine of Wesleyanism* (Kansas City, MO: Beacon Hill, 1980), 44-57.
[47] See Melvin E. Dieter, 'The Wesleyan Perspective', in *Five Views on Sanctification*, ed. Stanley Gundry (Grand Rapids, MI: Zondervan, 1987), 11-46.
[48] See David G. Roebuck, 'Sanctification and the Church of God', part 2, *Reflections ... upon Church of God Heritage* 2, no. 2 (1992): 1-3.

cleansing from the power of original sin enables a person to live victoriously in the fullness of the grace already received. Holiness thus precedes power, sanctification becomes the presupposition for Spirit baptism.[49] Perfection is the substance of the sanctified life, not its distant goal.

The most devastating critique to this view from among Pentecostals came from the so-called 'finished work' theology developed by William H. Durham (1873–1912), which was adopted quickly, particularly among independent churches and Oneness Pentecostal groups. As the title suggests, Durham's theology ascribed to the full efficacy of Christ's death and thus the completion of our forgiveness, justification, *and* sanctification with Christ's work at Calvary. He rejected the idea of sanctification as a second crisis and concentrated the *ordo salutis* essentially in a single conversion experience.[50] Whereas the Pentecostal holiness tradition acknowledges a distinct work to address the complete eradication of the sinful nature (even if this can logically coincide with conversion), the new teaching views the second crisis as a 'fictitious experience'[51] and rejects the idea that God does not accomplish sanctification at the moment of justification. The finished work theology shifted the concerns of sanctification from its practice to doctrinal concerns.[52]

The doctrinal battle between a 'finished work' and 'second work' of sanctification has had significant ecclesiastical and liturgical impact on Pentecostals. Those advocating a second crisis provide continuing opportunities for encountering such crisis moments at the altar, while those advocating a finished work must provide opportunities for receiving the completed work at the single moment of conversion. The liturgical practices of Oneness Pentecostals, in following Acts 2:38, have identified that moment with Christian initiation and include opportunities in the conversion experience for repentance, sanctification, and the baptism in the Spirit.[53] Holiness is

---

[49] See Henry H. Knight III, *Anticipating Heaven Below: Optimism of Grace from Wesley to the Pentecostals* (Eugene, OR: Cascade, 2014), 55–117; William W. Menzies, *Anointed to Serve: The Story of the Assemblies of God* (Springfield, MO: Gospel Publishing House, 1984), 74.

[50] See Thomas George Farkas, 'William H. Durham and the Sanctification Controversy in Early American Pentecostalism, 1906-1916' (PhD diss., Southern Baptist Theological Seminary, 1993), 109–86.

[51] Vinson Synan, *The Holiness-Pentecostal Movement in the United States* (Grand Rapids, MI: Eerdmans, 1971), 149.

[52] See Wolfgang Vondey, *Beyond Pentecostalism: The Crisis of Global Christianity and the Renewal of the Theological Agenda*, PM 3 (Grand Rapids, MI: Eerdmans, 2010), 88–98.

[53] See Thomas A. Fudge, *Christianity without the Cross: A History of Salvation in Oneness Pentecostalism* (Parkland, FL: Universal Publishers, 2003), 150–64.

therefore both the immediate result and expected life-long manifestation of the regenerating and sanctifying work of the Holy Spirit. Salvation and sanctification coincide at a single altar experience. At the same time, while the altar experience is then typically identified more strongly with conversion (and Spirit baptism), the praxis of sanctification shifts to the Christian life as a whole and to personal conduct beyond the original conversion experience.[54] Although all Pentecostal groups include in some form in their theology a teaching on proper conduct, refraining from amusement and entertainment, emphasis on hair and dress code, stewardship of the body, marriage, sexuality, and other elements of the moral life, the finished work position was eventually interpreted as a progressive form of sanctification, while the holiness trajectory expects such conduct to result from a completed second experience of sanctification.

The transformation of the finished work theology to a progressive theology of sanctification resulted from an adaptation of Durham's teaching by the British Keswick movement, which entered Pentecostalism as a 'higher life' interpretation of sanctification along Anglican and Reformed evangelical trajectories of salvation.[55] On the one hand, Keswick groups reject the holiness teaching of a second work of grace and the tendency to equate sanctification with Spirit baptism; on the other hand, Keswick doctrine does not equate sanctification completely with conversion. Instead, they identify sanctification as a life-long process of progressive growth in grace that begins at conversion but is never fully completed.[56] While Durham saw the root of sanctification in the completed work of Christ, Keswick teaching understands Christ as the foundation and the Holy Spirit as the agent of sanctification.[57] The Spirit suppresses the power of the sinful nature, which nonetheless continues to exert its influence on the Christian life.[58] The root of original sin is thus never completely eradicated and entire sanctification is reserved for our glorification. Holiness is no less important for this

---

[54] See David K. Bernard, *Practical Holiness: A Second Look*, SPT 4 (Hazelwood, MO: Word Aflame Press, 1985), 135–327.
[55] See William W. Menzies, 'The Reformed Roots of Pentecostalism', *AJPS* 9, no. 2 (2006): 260–82.
[56] Robert Mapes Anderson, *Vision of the Disinherited: The Making of American Pentecostalism* (New York: Oxford University Press, 1979), 39–41.
[57] See Farkas, 'William H. Durham', 254.
[58] David D. Bundy, *Keswick: A Bibliographic Introduction to the Higher Life Movements* (Wilmore, KY: Asbury Theological Seminary, 1975), 153.

trajectory of Pentecostal theology, yet sanctification is understood less in terms of the cleansing and purification from sin than the empowerment for mission and evangelism. Hence, there is no separate crisis experience for sanctification sought at the altar, and this detachment of sanctification from a distinct moment in the *ordo salutis* led to its theological equation with conversion or Spirit baptism and eventually its visible absence from the fourfold gospel motif.[59]

Despite the negative effects of this division, the controversy has significantly expanded the views on sanctification in Pentecostal theology. Key elements of Pentecostal teaching include Christology, with its emphasis on the work of Christ as the ground of sanctification; pneumatology, with its emphasis on the Holy Spirit as the agent who applies the work of Christ to the person; anthropology, with its emphasis on the weakness and ability of the human being; ecclesiology, with its emphasis on the church as the community of saints; and eschatology, with its outlook to glorification as the final sanctification of all creation. While one trajectory views holiness in terms of sanctification as an inward cleansing and a form of personal and ecclesial piety, the other sees it more in terms of 'consecration for the purpose of empowerment for evangelization to the ends of the earth'.[60]

All Pentecostal groups locate initial sanctification at conversion and distinguish then between entire sanctification (instantaneously at a second crisis) or progressive sanctification (ongoing and culminating in glorification).[61] The Reformed evangelical trajectory, however, interprets the instantaneous moment of sanctification at conversion as positional sanctification through which the believer is enabled to begin a sanctified life, whereas the Pentecostal holiness trajectory views sanctification as instantaneous in terms of immediate, actual and complete sanctification. Both trajectories understand sanctification as a work of the Holy Spirit that transforms the human being in the holiness of God, but the Reformed evangelical position views this transformation in largely juridical terms, while the Pentecostal holiness view focuses

---

[59] See Donald W. Dayton, *Theological Roots of Pentecostalism* (Peabody, MA: Hendrickson, 1987), 19–23.
[60] Amos Yong, *In the Days of Caesar: Pentecostalism and Political Theology*, The Cadbury Lectures 2009 (Grand Rapids, MI: Eerdmans, 2010), 170.
[61] See Stanley M. Horton, 'The Pentecostal Perspective', in Gundry, *Five Views on Sanctification*, 105–35; Harold D. Hunter, *Spirit-Baptism: A Pentecostal Alternative* (Lanham, MD: University Press of America, 1983), 253–81.

more on ontological transformation.⁶² The need for an ongoing actualization of the sanctified life is recognized by both trajectories, yet the Reformed groups interpret progressive sanctification as a gradual increase of holiness, while the holiness groups can speak of progression only in terms of a continuing actualization of the full sanctification already obtained. Both groups can speak of entire sanctification, yet the former interprets this in eschatological terms (the believer seeking maturity) and the latter in historical terms (the believer living out the mature life). Both trajectories identify sanctification as the work of Christ and the Spirit, but the Reformed view tends to see sanctification as a work accomplished by the encounter with Christ, while the holiness perspective identifies sanctification more closely as a distinct work experienced in the Holy Spirit. That is, both emphasize the need for the application and actualization of sanctification in the human life, yet the Reformed perspective is more overtly Christological (in accomplishment and expectation of sanctification), while the holiness perspective is more pneumatological (in pursuit and application of sanctification). The evangelicalization of Pentecostalism since the second half of the twentieth century has contributed to the sharpening of theological debates over doctrinal differences at the cost of neglecting the practical impact of the different positions. These doctrinal differences tend to overshadow attempts at reconciliation and the integration of Pentecostal rituals of sanctification in the broader Christian landscape.

Sanctification as ritual

Situated among the Christian traditions, the Pentecostal rituals of sanctification are distinctive, if not unique, in practice and theological perspective. The dominant narrative in the West, in Roman Catholic, Protestant, and Evangelical traditions identifies sanctification typically with justification and hence more with the giving than the reception of the divine activity and grace in distinct ritual practices of the church.⁶³ The Catechism of the Catholic Church emphasizes that 'justification is not only the remission of

---

⁶² See Edmund J. Rybarczyk, *Beyond Salvation: Eastern Orthodoxy and Classical Pentecostalism on Becoming Like Christ* (Milton Keynes, UK: Paternoster, 2004), 213–39.
⁶³ See the overview in Amos Yong, *Renewing Christian Theology: Systematics for a Global Christianity* (Waco, TX: Baylor University Press, 2014), 103–30.

sins, but also the sanctification and renewal of the interior man'.[64] Through justification, we are 'detached' from sin and enabled to 'cooperate' with God's grace.[65] The Holy Spirit gives birth to our new nature and thus imparts actual sanctification at the moment we are justified.[66] As an act of divine grace, justification is effected at conversion, and the Christian cooperates with the sanctifying grace through participation in water baptism.[67] The Catholic narrative here distinguishes between the habitual grace, given at baptism to provide the permanent disposition to live a sanctified life, and actual graces, which signify God's interventions in the course of sanctification, as well as sacramental graces and special graces or charisms, which 'are oriented toward sanctifying grace'.[68] Nonetheless, a particular ritual of sanctification apart from the sacraments is not included in regular Catholic praxis; rather, all sacramental practices of the church serve the sanctification of the body of Christ. Foot washing is practiced as a ritual only on Holy Thursday, and the participation of a lay person or entire congregations is highly debated.[69] For Pentecostals, the accepted Catholic sacraments, which do not include foot washing, are too unspecific to aid the Christian in the conscious pursuit of a sanctified life. While in principle amicable to a sacramental worldview, Pentecostal theology would require a reordering of sacramental practices to fit the Pentecostal *ordo salutis*.[70]

In comparison, the Protestant view of the relationship between justification and sanctification is perhaps best described as imputed righteousness.[71] Martin Luther's image of the Christian as simultaneously just and a sinner captures the essence of sanctification as entirely the work of God imputed to the human being through justification by faith.[72] Put differently, the Lutheran emphasis on justification by faith alone is reiterated in a

---

[64] *Catechism of the Catholic Church* (Washington, DC: United States Catholic Conference, 1994), no. 1989.
[65] Ibid., nos. 1990 and 1993.
[66] Ibid., no. 1995.
[67] Ibid., nos. 1989 and 1999.
[68] Ibid., no. 2003. See also ibid., no. 2000.
[69] See Peter Jeffrey, *A New Commandment: Toward a Renewed Rite for the Washing of Feet* (Collegeville, MN: Liturgical Press, 1992).
[70] See Wolfgang Vondey, 'Christian Amnesia: Who in the World Are Pentecostals?' *AJPS* 4, no. 1 (2001): 21–39.
[71] Frank D. Macchia, *Justified in the Spirit: Creation, Redemption, and the Triune God* (Pentecostal Manifestos 2; Grand Rapids: Eerdmans, 2010), 38.
[72] See Martin Luther, *Lectures on Romans*, vol. 25, *Luther's Works*, ed. Helmut T. Lehman (St. Louis, MO: Concordia, 1972), 322–23.

teaching of sanctification by grace alone. Sanctification is not an additional process added to justification but rather 'the art of getting used to justification'.[73] Sanctification therefore cannot be worked out by the human being, since that would ignore the central importance of faith and become a form of legalism or a theology of works. Instead, sanctification is passive and alien to the human person who can grow in grace only by letting go of one's own attempt at achieving holiness.[74] The means of sanctification are the preaching of the Word, baptism, the Lord's Supper, the keys, ministry, public worship, and the cross.[75] Foot washing is celebrated on Holy Thursday or in the context of ordination by Lutherans and various other Protestant groups, yet the practice is typically symbolic and offers little ritual structure for the purpose of sanctification. The Lutheran practices are strictly speaking acts of the Holy Spirit and not distinctive rituals of sanctification acted out by the church. No ritual of the church or the individual can produce or add to the imputed righteousness of Christ. While Pentecostals would agree here with Lutherans, the acknowledgement that we do not sanctify ourselves does not preclude for Pentecostals the responsibility to participate in the divine holiness through particular practices of sanctification. Justification indicates a positional change to which the believer does not 'get used' without acting out the justified position throughout a sanctified life.

In a slightly different way, John Calvin emphasized the righteousness of the Christian by imputation.[76] Sanctification is learning to live out the implications of the fullness of God's grace given to us at conversion in a journey of continual growth.[77] Central to the Calvinist view is the conviction that human righteousness is located only in Jesus Christ, and that our sanctification is accomplished through union with Christ.[78] In contrast to Luther, justification is not found in a legal declaration of God but located in the actual life, death, and resurrection of Christ.[79] The Christian is thus reconciled (i.e.

---

[73] Gerhard O. Forde, 'The Lutheran View', in *Christian Spirituality: Five Views on Sanctification*, ed. Donald Alexander (Downers Grove: InterVarsity, 1988), 13–32 (27).
[74] Philip S. Watson, 'Luther and Sanctification', *CTM* 30, no. 4 (1959): 243–59.
[75] Ibid., 250.
[76] John Calvin, *Institutes of the Christian Religion*, ed. John T. McNeill (Philadelphia: Westminster, 1960), 3.11.11.
[77] Cf. Miyon Chung, 'Conversion and Sanctification', in *The Cambridge Companion to Evangelical Theology*, ed. Timothy Larsen and Daniel J. Treier (Cambridge: Cambridge University Press, 2007), 109–24.
[78] Sinclair B. Ferguson, 'The Reformed View', in Alexander, *Christian Spirituality*, 47–76 (48).
[79] Calvin, *Institutes*, 2.16.19.

justified) with God by the righteousness of Christ and at the same time made righteous (i.e. sanctified) by his Spirit.[80] Despite this integration of justification and sanctification, Pentecostals would argue that it is not explicit what exactly connects the imputation of Christ's righteousness with the Christian's participation through union with Christ by faith.[81] No particular practices are associated with that union and thus invite to a participation in the divine life of holiness.

In contrast, Pentecostal theology can distinguish between Christ's work of justification and the Spirit's application of that work through sanctification, which opens the doors for the notion of sanctification as a second blessing subsequent to conversion, even though this practice subordinates pneumatology to Christology and denies the Spirit a constitutive function in justification.[82] The Reformed perspective is attractive to Pentecostals because it speaks of human involvement in the process of sanctification in particular by means of the Word, the providences of God, the fellowship of the church, and the sacraments, which can be appropriated as rituals of sanctification.[83] The pressures of finding a 'second' blessing can thus be dispersed into a lifelong process that finds its final goal only in our glorification.[84] This dispersion, however, can eliminate the need for distinctive ritual practices of sanctification subsequent to justification and divert attention from an empowering and sanctifying experience of the Holy Spirit. While sanctification is not strictly identical with justification in the Reformed view, it is difficult to distinguish sanctification from other everyday practices of the Christian life. Without a ritual identity of sanctification in the order of salvation, however, Pentecostal soteriology would remain in principle a Christological affirmation and afford the pneumatological dynamic characteristic for Pentecostal theology little role in carrying the Christian life further towards glorification. The adoption of the Reformed perspective by some Pentecostals has consequently led to a weakening of the ritual practices of sanctification.

---

[80] Ibid., 1.3.11.
[81] Macchia, *Justified by the Spirit*, 62.
[82] Studebaker, 'Pentecostal Soteriology and Pneumatology', 260–65.
[83] See Ferguson, 'The Reformed View', 67–74.
[84] See Anthony A. Hoekema, 'The Reformed Perspective', in Gundry, *Five Views on Sanctification*, 59–90.

Perhaps closer to Pentecostal theology, the Eastern Orthodox view does not strictly distinguish between justification and sanctification as different dynamics of the *ordo salutis* but focuses on the connecting practices of the spiritual life. In contrast to Protestant views, the whole of salvation is an 'ongoing process that leads from initial salvation, through sanctification, and on to a "deification by grace" of the human person'.[85] Sanctification is an ontological participation in the divine life that does not follow justification, but both are integrated in the deifying transformation of the Christian.[86] The means of sanctification interpreted as deification are thoroughly embedded in participation in the life of the church through the liturgy, the sacraments, and diverse ascetic practices.[87] Foot washing as a ritual practice is generally reserved for the ordained priest or bishop.[88] Pentecostal theology, particularly the Wesleyan-Holiness tradition, stands in a certain continuity with the Orthodox view.[89] Ritual practices, revivals, personal piety, and ascetic discipline, although often with stronger emphasis on the individual, are the tributaries to sanctification from a Pentecostal viewpoint.[90] However, sanctification is interwoven in the rituals of the Orthodox Christian life as the process whereby one is deified and not as the goal of any ritual practice itself. In other words, Orthodox theology is by nature concerned with sanctification, yet the Orthodox Christian does not typically seek to be sanctified, in the pragmatic sense of Pentecostals, by any one particular experience. The pragmatic Pentecostal approach to sanctification may be the result of the young movement's inherent struggle to be at home in so many cultural and ecclesial traditions while emerging historically (at least in the West) in an environment heavily influenced by a modernist rational and pragmatist mindset. The heartbeat of this mentality is the conviction that sanctification is an existential reality that can be grasped fully only by concrete,

---

[85] John Breck, 'Divine Initiative: Salvation in Orthodox Theology', *Salvation in Christ: A Lutheran-Orthodox Dialogue*, ed. John Meyendorff and Robert Tobias (Minneapolis, MN: Augsburg, 1992), 116.
[86] See Ross Aden, 'Justification and Sanctification: A Conversation between Lutheranism and Orthodoxy', *SVTQ* 38, no. 1 (1994): 87–109.
[87] See Rybarczyk, *Beyond Salvation*, 127–71.
[88] Except in the Coptic Orthodox Church.
[89] See David Bundy, 'Visions of Sanctification: Themes of Orthodoxy in the Methodist, Holiness, and Pentecostal Traditions', *WTJ* 39, no. 1 (2004): 104–36.
[90] See Rybarczyk, *Beyond Salvation*, 271–323.

deliberate, and repeated practices, which focus on the sanctification of the individual in a manner that such ritual practices spill over into the whole of the Christian life.

Although these characterizations of sanctification in the Christian traditions are highly simplified, the Pentecostal tradition speaks to the traditions primarily from the perspective that salvation is praxis, and hence sanctification, as an instrument of salvation, must also be practiced. The communal practices of sanctification form the ritual bedrock among Pentecostals for pursuing and living a sanctified life. The ritual practices of the congregations reinforce the conviction that sanctification (whether personal or communal) always involves consistent embodied actions of the believer. Sanctification is understood as purification and cleansing from sin, involving an intellectual, moral and physical washing as well as a consecration, often in terms of distancing oneself from the world and its pollutants. Tarrying services, soaking prayer, and foot washing achieve little without personal discipline, including abstaining from sin and establishing a disciplined life within moral boundaries that limit a person's exposure to temptation (e.g. abstaining from drugs, sexual misconduct, etc.). In turn, personal discipline is reinforced by communal prayer, revival meetings, fasting practices, and ritual celebrations of the congregations.[91] Practicing sanctification takes the person, while remaining in the world, into a different reality from the world, a sanctified world with its own prohibitions, loyalties, and commitments that aim at personal transformation as well as communal and social change.[92] Ritual should therefore not be understood here as the structured performance of a regulated practice produced by the church's liturgy.[93] Rather, ritual is the response to the grace of God throughout the life of the believer manifested in persistent dispositions and practices. Worship functions as an expression and extension of the ritual life with its charismatic manifestations often believed not only to express but to validate the sanctity of the believer. At the same time, if the Catholic perspective argues for the importance of sacraments for justification, and the

---

[91] See Anthea D. Butler, 'Observing the Lives of the Saints: Sanctification as Practice in the Church of God in Christ', in *Practicing Protestants: Histories of Christian Life in America, 1630–1965*, ed. Laurie F. Maffly-Kipp, Leigh E. Schmidt and Mark Valeri (Baltimore, MD: Johns Hopkins University Press, 2006), 159–76.

[92] See Anthea D. Butler, *Women in the Church of God in Christ: Making a Sanctified World* (Chapel Hill: University of North Carolina Press, 2007).

[93] See Vondey, *Beyond Pentecostalism*, 129–40.

Protestant views emphasize the importance of the Word of God, then the Pentecostal perspective is closer to the Orthodox view of transformational practices that bridge the Word and the sacraments.[94] Pentecostal theology advises the Christian world to heed the importance of sanctification in piety, doctrine, and practice. The emphasis of doing theology by means of transformational rituals is therefore placed not only on the nature of sanctification as an overarching term for the Christian life as a whole but on particular ecclesial and individual practices of the Christian life that initiate and sustain such transformation.[95] Sanctification is not contained in the Christian life in general or subsumed under other ecclesial practices but pursued as a goal in its own right.

To speak of sanctification as ritual can be understood as the performance of a sequence of practices determined by cultural, ecclesial, and doctrinal processes.[96] In this sense, sanctification reveals the dependence of Pentecostal theology on performance-oriented mechanisms. Nonetheless, this does not mean that Pentecostals embrace a works-righteousness theology.[97] Rather, the performance of sanctification is a rite of passage in the *ordo salutis* and as such marks both an entrance point on the way to salvation and a bridge to glorification. Put differently, sanctification as ritual carries ontological rather than doctrinal or functional status.[98] In this sense, sanctification is both positional and instantaneous, as well as practical and progressive.[99] The ritual move forward to the altar and thus to the presence of God is a shift of position that symbolizes the believer's participation in the divine life; it anticipates and practices separation from sin and unto God as an act of Christ-like obedience through the Holy Spirit as it is needed in everyday Christian living.[100] As a ritual, the reception of sanctification must be instantaneous for the practice to be considered efficacious, since the fullness (not a portion)

---

[94] Frank D. Macchia, 'Justification and the Spirit: A Pentecostal Reflection on the Doctrine by Which the Church Stands or Falls', *Pneuma* 22, no. 1 (2000): 3–21 (19).

[95] See Chris E. W. Green, '"Not I, but Christ": Holiness, Conscience, & the (Im)possibility of Community', in *A Future for Holiness: Pentecostal Explorations*, ed. Lee Roy Martin (Cleveland, TN: CPT Press, 2013), 127–44.

[96] Victor Turner, *The Anthropology of Performance* (New York: PAJ Publications, 1987), 75.

[97] Studebaker, 'Pentecostal Soteriology and Pneumatology', 267.

[98] See Bobby C. Alexander, 'Pentecostal Ritual Reconsidered: Anti-Structural Dimensions of Possession', *JRS* 3, no. 1 (1989): 109–28 (especially 113–16).

[99] See William W. Menzies and Stanley M. Horton, *Bible Doctrines: A Pentecostal Perspective* (Springfield, MO: Gospel Publishing House, 1993), 147.

[100] See French L. Arrington, *Christian Doctrine: A Pentecostal Perspective*, vol. 2 (Cleveland, TN: Pathway Press, 1993), 233.

of sanctifying grace is poured out by the Holy Spirit. Pentecostals speak of this aspect of sanctification as 'deliverance' and being 'set free', code words that can indicate the experience of justification, typically at a person's conversion, or the affirmation of justification in a subsequent experience, and that refer to a concrete and repeated sense of liberation from sin, addiction, sickness, and even demon-possession.[101] Sanctification is practical in the sense that it is practiced by the believer, or more precisely, the believer practices participation in the sanctifying grace given by Christ. In that sense, sanctification is practical because it is personal (practiced by the believer), pragmatic (practiced for the purpose of being sanctified), ecclesial (practiced by the congregation and in a particular space and time), and missional (empowering the believer to be a witness to the kingdom of God).[102] Sanctification is progressive in the sense that rituals are repeated practices that maintain and reaffirm the efficacy of the ritual in the life of the individual and the community. While some Pentecostals understand the progressive character as practicing growth in increasing holiness, others have cautioned that 'without a coherent theology, beliefs like ... progressive sanctification become isolated from the main body of the Pentecostal belief system'.[103] The ritualization of sanctification integrates these practices, despite different interpretations, in the Pentecostal worldview.

The emphasis on sanctification as a ritual practice is first and foremost an emphasis on the need to practice holiness. The aversion Pentecostals typically show to historically established rituals of the church is overcome by an interpretation of the ritual that points beyond itself into daily life, where Pentecostals practice sanctification 'accompanied by their altered understanding of reality and with the experience of the ritual, in order to interact better and affect their world'.[104] The rite, in this sense, serves the learning of sanctification for the whole of the moral life. Sanctification is play rather than performance, creative and imaginative rather than constraining and

---

[101] See Gwendolyn Heaner, '"Fieldworking" Deliverance Rituals in a Liberian Pentecostal Ministry', *FR* 5, no. 2 (2010): 193–206.

[102] See Albrecht, *Rites in the Spirit*, 124–35; Monte Lee Rice, 'The Pentecostal Triple Way: An Ecumenical Model of the Pentecostal *Via Salutis* and Soteriological Experience', in Martin, *A Future for Holiness*, 145–70.

[103] Chan, *Pentecostal Theology*, 77.

[104] Albrecht, *Rites in the Spirit*, 135.

demanding, relational and participatory rather than solitary.[105] Pentecostal theology advises other traditions to develop and maintain particular rituals of the sanctified life. This emphasis on the doing of theology accentuates the ritual character of the Christian life and the nature of the fullness of the gospel. Only within this practical and pragmatic framework can we explain what is arguably the central ritual of the full gospel among Pentecostals: the baptism in the Holy Spirit.

---

[105] See Stephen Parker, 'Holiness as Play: A Developmental Perspective on Christian Formation', in Martin, *A Future for Holiness*, 312–32.

4

Baptized

Transformed by the Holy Spirit

A third, and typically central, motif of the full gospel, the narrative account of Pentecostal theology, is the baptism in the Holy Spirit. Called by various names – including baptism with the Holy Spirit, baptism with (or in) the Holy Ghost, Spirit baptism, baptism with fire, the Pentecostal baptism, and a variety of other biblical terms – the personal, institutional, denominational, and ecumenical accounts of the phenomenon are numerous and varied. I have maintained that Pentecostal theology is embedded deeply in the day of Pentecost, which as a theological symbol accentuates the practical and pragmatic character of the Christian life and requires a ritual framework for its explanation. Following this premise, this chapter argues that Spirit baptism emerging from Pentecost is first and foremost an experience characterized by distinctive practices. However, echoing the full gospel motif of sanctification, the conversation on Spirit baptism has been overshadowed by doctrinal debates, which often function primarily as an apologetic but rarely as an explanation of or invitation to Pentecostal theology. In light of the multifarious experiences of Spirit baptism existing, not only among Pentecostals, the altar offers a concrete heuristic and hermeneutical context through which we can portray a theological understanding of these Pentecostal practices. On the tangible grounds of the altar, Spirit baptism can be identified as a lens through which Pentecostals view and order the other elements of the full gospel. In the narrative of the full gospel, this means, the baptism in the Spirit is a transformative experience most intimately tied to the altar as a metaphor for the encounter with God to which the other elements point and in which they receive their meaning. Yet, this important position does not elevate Spirit baptism above the other elements. Rather, this transformative experience marks a turning point in the narrative of the altar: with the baptism in the Spirit, those who have come to the altar are transformed to leave the altar. Part one of this chapter therefore begins with a presentation of diverse altar practices of the baptism in the Spirit. The second part examines the theological debates surrounding Spirit baptism, and the final part offers an ecumenical portrayal of Spirit baptism that redirects the doctrinal debates to the practices at the altar and thereby further extends the Pentecostal notions of salvation as praxis and sanctification as ritual in the direction of a sacramental encounter with God.

Spirit baptism at the altar

The baptism in the Spirit is a deep, personal experience in which the regenerated and sanctified believer receives in an unprecedented encounter with the Holy Spirit empowerment for the Christian life. Pentecostals have looked consistently to the day of Pentecost as the root symbol for understanding Spirit Baptism. The biblical narratives of Luke-Acts serve as primary sources to identify the experience, and most Pentecostals consult the Pauline corpus, Johannine texts, and historical literature only secondarily for an explanation and defence of maintaining the contested practice.[1] While Luke-Acts offers numerous places for doctrinal debate, a few select narratives typically function as the framework for the ritual practices surrounding Spirit baptism. These practices further illustrate the significance of the altar call and response that forms the overarching metaphor for Pentecostal practices identified by the full gospel: beginning with the move to the altar (conversion), continuing with the tarrying at the altar (sanctification), and culminating with a transformation at the altar (Spirit baptism). Each narrative identifies at least one central practice of Spirit baptism manifested in this unfolding of the gospel at the altar.

The Pentecostal experience of Spirit baptism is first and foremost an encounter with Jesus Christ. In the full gospel, Christ is always the acting

---

[1] See William P. Atkinson, *Baptism in the Spirit: Luke-Acts and the Dunn Debate* (Cambridge: Lutterworth Press, 2011), 92–122; Martin William Mittelstadt, *Reading Luke-Acts in the Pentecostal Tradition* (Cleveland, TN: CPT Press, 2010), 68–76; Harold D. Hunter, *Spirit-Baptism: A Pentecostal Alternative* (Lanham, MD: University Press of America, 1983), 22–116.

subject and the one who saves, sanctifies, and baptizes with the Holy Spirit. At the same time, in the unfolding narrative of the full gospel, the motif of Spirit baptism is also the most obviously pneumatological.[2] This dual emphasis is important at this point, as Spirit baptism marks a shift in ritual dynamic, a culmination of the encounter with Christ in which the person who has come to the altar and tarried at the altar is transformed by the Holy Spirit to leave the altar. The work of Christ and the Holy Spirit are united in this transformation, as much as they are in the work of salvation and sanctification. Pentecostal theology at the crossroads of Spirit baptism emphasizes the essence of salvation as both the redemptive work of Christ and the gift of the Holy Spirit. The altar is therefore a place of refuge to the lordship of Jesus, who baptizes with the Spirit, and to the Holy Spirit, who transforms the believer after the manner of Christ. While the Christian is thus in a passive-receptive sense 'being baptized' in the Spirit at the hands of Jesus, the believer seeks to be baptized in an active-contributing sense emerging from the practices of sanctification exemplified in the command of Jesus to wait for the Spirit. This expectation of participatory transformation forms an interpretive horizon for the Pentecostal reading of the biblical texts (see Chapter 1).

The most immediate biblical report of a baptism in the Spirit is the outpouring of the Holy Spirit on the day of Pentecost recorded in Acts 2. Shaped by the motif of sanctification that forms a foundation for the reception of the Spirit, the Pentecostal reading of this passage accentuates the waiting and tarrying of the disciples. However, the disciples reshape Jesus's command to wait into an altar practice of joining together constantly in prayer (v. 14) in the upper room. In the subsequent development, the brief statement that 'all of them were filled with the Holy Spirit' (Acts 2:4) identifies most closely the experience of the baptism in the Spirit. The origin of this baptism is attributed to Christ and the Holy Spirit, while the disciples themselves participate in this divine activity seemingly only by being filled. Nonetheless, Pentecostals read this passive-receptive participation in light of the disciples' preceding action of prayer carried out in the upper room. More than inactive waiting, the disciples actively pursued the promise of the Spirit through prayer. To use

---

[2] Amos Yong, *In the Days of Caesar: Pentecostalism and Political Theology* (Grand Rapids, MI: Eerdmans, 2010), 95–98.

Pentecostal lingo, the disciples had 'prayed through' to the baptism in the Holy Spirit.

The practice of praying through is essentially an emphasis on sustained prayer until the results of that prayer are manifest. Prayer meetings, tarrying services, prayer revivals, prayer camps, outdoor and indoor prayers, corporate and individual forms of praying are typical events among all Pentecostals.³ Yet, while prayer is of course a central practice throughout the Christian life, praying *through* requires a focused attention and dedication to a particular request or desire.⁴ For Pentecostals, praying through emerges from a tarrying heart in the 'upper room'; the prayer is carried out by a soul yearning for fulfilment until the prayer is answered. Although praying through frequently emerges from an attitude of lament, the perceived absence of God, and emptiness of the human life, it eventually moves from anguish to praise.⁵ It is a raw form of prayer, firm and straight to God.⁶ Praying through (for whatever desired result) is always a praying for the manifestation of the Holy Spirit (who alone can bring about the desired result). Persistent prayer for the gift and the gifts of the Spirit is the heartbeat of the Pentecostal movement.⁷ The pursuit of prayer is modelled on the biblical image of a hospitable God who as a generous Father is eager to give the gift of the Spirit to those who diligently and persistently seek him (see Mt. 7:11; Lk. 11:13).⁸ Praying through, in this sense, is not so much a conscious ritual than an embodied affection that is carried out as much in a mode of celebration as in contemplation, penitence, ceremony, ecstasy, pragmatism, or spontaneous improvisation.⁹ The practice focuses the attention on God, decreases preoccupation with the self, intensifies sensitivity for others, lowers defensiveness and restraint, increases

---

³ See Keith Warrington, *Pentecostal Theology: A Theology of Encounter* (London: T& T Clark, 2008), 214–19.
⁴ See E. J. Dabney, *What It Means to Pray Through* (Memphis, TN: COGIC Publishing Board, 1987).
⁵ See Narelle Jane Melton, 'Lessons of Lament: Reflections on the Correspondence between the Lament Psalms and Early Australian Pentecostal Prayer', *JPT* 20, no. 1 (2011): 68–80; Larry McQueen, *Joel and the Spirit: The Cry of a Prophetic Hermeneutic*, JPTS 8 (Sheffield: Sheffield Academic Press, 1995): 76–82.
⁶ Rickie D. Moore, 'Raw Prayer and Refined Theology: "You Have Not Spoken Straight to Me, as My Servant Job Has"', in *The Spirit and the Mind: Essays in Informed Pentecostalism* (Lanham, MD: University Press of America, 2000), 35–48.
⁷ C. P. Wagner, 'Americas Pentecostals: See How They Grow', *Christianity Today* 31 (October 16, 1987): 28–29.
⁸ Kim Dongsoo, 'Lukan Pentecostal Theology of Prayer: Is Persistent Prayer not Biblical?' *AJPS* 7, no. 2 (2004): 205–17.
⁹ See Daniel E. Albrecht, *Rites in the Spirit: A Ritual Approach to Pentecostal/Charismatic Spirituality*, JPTS 17 (Sheffield: Sheffield Academic Press, 1999), 179–89.

openness and spontaneity, and births a longing and expectation for the kingdom of God.[10] Praying through embodies the baptism in the Spirit when it becomes a transformative ritual identified by a transformation of the practice itself as the praying *for* the Spirit becomes a praying *in* the Spirit (see Rom. 8:16, 26).

The transformation from praying for the Spirit to praying in and with the Spirit manifests the baptism for Pentecostals most clearly in the disciples' speaking with other tongues (see Acts 2:4). Such tongues are a manifestation that the prayer for the Spirit has been answered by the giving of the Spirit. A twofold emphasis has persisted among Pentecostals by interpreting this manifestation of Spirit baptism: either in the terms of sanctification or of charismatic empowerment.[11] Undoubtedly, the practice of praying through ushers out of a sanctified life into a charismatic life, yet the distinction between the two should not narrowly construct sanctification only as an inward cleansing and the baptism in the Spirit as an outward empowerment.[12] As an altar experience narrating the full gospel, praying through is both a sanctifying tarrying for and an empowering demonstration of the encounter with the Holy Spirit.

A second practice of Spirit baptism is the proclamation of the gospel in preaching. While typically a focal point of the Pentecostal service as a whole (especially since the influence of modern-day Evangelicalism), the pastoral message plays a particular role in conferring the baptism in the Spirit.[13] The biblical background for this connection is drawn from the conversion of the Gentiles recorded in Acts 10 and Peter's account of the event in the following chapter. Summoned to Cornelius's household by the Holy Spirit, the apostle proclaims the gospel of 'how God anointed Jesus of Nazareth with the Holy Spirit and with power' (Acts 10:38), that Jesus was crucified and raised from the dead and that faith in Christ leads to forgiveness of sins (vv. 39–43). The records then state that 'while Peter was still speaking, the Holy Spirit fell upon

---

[10] Thomas I. Devol, 'Ecstatic Pentecostal Prayer and Meditation', *JRH* 13, no. 4 (1974): 285–88.
[11] See Frank D. Macchia, 'The Kingdom and the Power: Spirit Baptism in Pentecostal and Ecumenical Perspective', in *The Work of the Spirit: Pneumatology and Pentecostalism*, ed. Michael Welker (Grand Rapids, MI: Eerdmans, 2006), 109–25.
[12] Ibid., 122; Hollis Gause, *Living in the Spirit: The Way of Salvation* (Cleveland, TN: Pathway, 1980), 49–57, 79–94.
[13] See Timothy Yeung, 'The Characteristics of William Seymour's Sermons: A Reflection on Pentecostal Ethos', *AJPS* 14, no. 1 (2011): 57–73; Donald R. Wheelock, 'Spirit Baptism in American Pentecostal Thought' (PhD diss., Emory University, 1983), 182–83.

all who heard the word' (v. 44) and the disciples acknowledged the event as a Pentecost-like outpouring of the Holy Spirit 'for they heard them speaking in tongues and extolling God' (v. 46). In his account of the event to the council of Jerusalem, Peter reemphasizes that it was the Spirit who directed him to the Gentiles (Acts 11:12) and that *when* he 'began to speak the Holy Spirit fell upon them just as it had upon us at the beginning' (v. 15). In one of the central passages for Pentecostals, Peter here describes the event explicitly as a 'baptism' in the Holy Spirit (v. 16).

Testimony, prophecy, and prayer are the most basic forms among Pentecostals that function as a personal witness to the work of God and thus to the gospel. Preaching is understood as an oral embodiment of the gospel that involves a narrative of speaking, hearing and then, again, speaking and hearing.[14] In worship, the immediate goal of this witness is an appeal to the affections (rather than the intellect), a directing of the audience's desire to the gift of God's Spirit.[15] Preaching as an appeal to the affections is a transformational practice in which the initial proclamation of the outpouring of the Spirit (by the preacher) and the hearing of the message (by the audience) shifts in the actual baptism to a speaking by the audience (which has received the Spirit) and the hearing of that speaking (in tongues and exaltation) by the preacher. Preaching is thus seen as a charismatic ritual evidenced in the transformation of the practice itself, involving the joining of Word and Spirit beginning with the proclamation of the gospel through the anointing of the preacher, directed to a re-experiencing of the biblical event, shifting to the anointing of the audience, the outpouring of the Spirit, and the response of the recipients.[16] Preaching as transformational practice is an affirmation of the biblical promises (by speaker and hearer), prophetic pronouncement (on behalf of God) of the extension of the promise to the contemporary audience, and invitation to experience these promises (as

---

[14] See Jerry Camery-Hogatt, 'The Word of God from Living Voices: Orality and Literacy in the Pentecostal Tradition', *Pneuma* 27, no. 2 (2005): 225–55.

[15] See Lee Roy Martin (ed.), *Toward a Pentecostal Theology of Preaching* (Cleveland, TN: CPT Press, 2015); Ray H. Hughes, *Pentecostal Preaching* (Cleveland, TN: Pathway Press, 2004); Guy P. Duffield, Jr., *Pentecostal Preaching* (New York: Vantage Press, 1957).

[16] See Albrecht, *Rites in the Spirit*, 162–64; Ian Stackhouse, 'Charismatic Utterance: Preaching as Prophecy', in *The Future of Preaching*, ed. Geoffrey Stevenson (London: SCM Press, 2010), 42–46; Vincent Leoh, 'A Pentecostal Preacher as an Empowered Witness', *Asian Journal of Pentecostal Studies* 9, no. 1 (2006): 35–58; Joseph Byrd, 'Paul Ricoeur's Hermeneutical Theory and Pentecostal Proclamation', *Pneuma* 15, no. 2 (1993): 203–14; H. W. Steinberg, 'Anointed Preaching', *Paraclete* 24 (1990): 6–9.

given by the Spirit).¹⁷ The baptism in the Holy Spirit as the expected experience resulting from the act of proclamation is a distinctive characteristic of Pentecostal preaching.

A third vital altar practice for the baptism in the Spirit is often derived from two biblical narratives: Peter and John's visit to Samaria (Acts 8:14–17) and Paul's encounter with disciples at Ephesus (Acts 19).¹⁸ In both events, the reception of the Holy Spirit is attributed to the laying on of hands. Peter and John were sent to Samaria upon reports of conversions in the region and there discover that the believers already had been baptized in water but 'the Spirit had not come on any of them' (v. 16) – an obvious reference back to the day of Pentecost. In response, the apostles 'prayed for them that they might receive the Holy Spirit' (v. 15) and *when* they 'laid their hands on them, [. . .] they received the Holy Spirit' (v. 17). Similarly, Paul, learning that some disciples were unaware that there was a Holy Spirit (often seen by Pentecostals as symptomatic of believers), baptizes the disciples in water (Acts 19:1–5), and *when* 'Paul had laid his hands on them, the Holy Spirit came upon them, and they spoke in tongues and prophesied' (v. 6). Again, there exists an explicit causal correspondence between the practices of the disciples and the reception of the Spirit: the baptism in the Spirit is seen as an immediate result of the laying on of hands.¹⁹ Among the different altar practices, the laying on of hands, a longstanding Christian altar ritual, demands the most physical contact among believers.

The biblical records identifying the laying on of hands as a ritual practice reveal no formal liturgical pattern other than the imposition of hands.²⁰ At the same time, this imposition is exceptionally concrete in its material, physical, physiological, spiritual, and relational dimensions. The ritual is further embedded in other practices, including prayer or proclamation, and it represents for many Pentecostals the most expressive and efficacious rite to confer the baptism in the Holy Spirit.²¹ Echoing the events of Pentecost, the laying on of hands by the believer represents the unrepeatable outpouring of

---

[17] See Ray J. Hughes, *Pentecostal Preaching*, rev. ed. (Cleveland, TN: Pathway Press, 2004).
[18] See Hunter, *Spirit-Baptism*, 79–89.
[19] John Fleter Tipei, 'The Function of Laying on of Hands in the New Testament', *JEPTA* 20 (2000): 93–115.
[20] Rudolph D. González, 'Laying-on of Hands in Luke and Acts: Theology, Ritual, and Interpretation' (PhD diss., Baylor University, 1999), 161–71.
[21] See William K. Kay, *Pentecostals in Britain* (Carlisle: Paternoster, 2001), 101.

the Holy Spirit on all flesh at the hands of Jesus.[22] In the ritual, the hand of the believer is the hand of Christ, who baptizes with the Spirit, and the touch of the hand is the Holy Spirit – evoking a strong appeal to the affections of the persons participating in the ritual. The baptism in the Spirit itself is the affective moment concentrated in the giving and receiving of the Spirit at the laying on of hands.

The laying on of hands can be performed by all believers, whether congregations, collective groups, or individuals, with no requirement other than that the person performing the ritual has already been baptized with the Spirit. In turn, the believer on whom hands are laid is expected to receive the Holy Spirit. Prayer, prophecy, speaking in tongues, and the use of anointing oil often accompany the ritual.[23] Although concentrated in the use of hands, the practice is a thoroughly charismatic rite in action and demonstration including characteristic Pentecostal behaviours such as shouting, jumping, dancing, swaying, bowing, praising, and falling in the Spirit.[24] The baptism in the Spirit is signalled for Pentecostals by the speaking in tongues and manifestations of other spiritual gifts (see Acts 19:6). As with the other altar rites, the laying on of hands is transformative in the transformation of the rite itself, as the laying on of hands becomes a transferring of, and endowment with, the Holy Spirit.

Praying through, preaching, and the laying on of hands are transformative practices that involve the Holy Spirit in the act of giving, transferring, receiving, and manifesting of the experience. Other biblical narratives exist, of course, to substantiate and further illuminate these altar practices or to add other practices. These practices are concentrated in an almost climactic move from praying to proclamation to the laying on of hands, from passive-receptive to active participation; the baptism in the Spirit marks a point of reversal at which the believer who has come and tarried at the altar is transformed by a participation in the spiritual presence of God. As a baptismal practice, this participation in the divine life is a transformative experience in which the passive-receptive believer becomes an active agent of the Spirit: the one who has come to the altar is now equipped to leave the altar.

---

[22] González, 'Laying-on of Hands in Luke and Acts', 164.
[23] See Walter J. Hollenweger, *The Pentecostals: The Charismatic Movement in the Churches* (Minneapolis, MN: Augsburg, 1972), 330–41.
[24] See Albrecht, *Rites in the Spirit*, 171–76.

Spirit baptism as doctrine

The intensity of ritual practices surrounding the baptism in the Spirit is further extended and accentuated by the doctrinal history of the Pentecostal movement. Among the doctrines identifying the Pentecostal theological tradition, the baptism in the Spirit has been described as the 'crown jewel' of Pentecostal theological distinctives.[25] The articulation of a theology of Spirit baptism helped constitute the Pentecostal community as a doctrinal community, directed the experience towards a shared form, encapsulated Pentecostal identity and worldview, and provided global explanatory strength for the worldwide movement.[26] However, if it is necessary to speak of Spirit baptism primarily in terms of experience, then a conversation exclusively in terms of doctrine is both problematic and limiting.[27] Such doctrinal debate should be integrated and evaluated within the contexts of global Pentecostal practices, which show a wide range of interpretations.[28]

The doctrinal discussion of the baptism in the Spirit has been dominated by three debates: (1) the distinction between sanctification and charismatic empowerment, (2) the notion of subsequence, and (3) the argument of initial evidence. The conversations on these issues have shifted the focus at times exclusively to an apologetic for Pentecostalism, often solely on the basis of biblical interpretations, and contributed to a weakened emphasis on Spirit baptism as a ritual experience.[29] Nonetheless, the doctrinal debates are at the core concerned with the vitality of the experience, that is, with the viability of Pentecostal practices and their possible integration into the structures of established Christian traditions.[30]

The theological and historical roots of much of classical Pentecostalism in the Puritan, Pietist, and Holiness traditions have contributed to the

---

[25] Macchia, *Baptized in the Spirit*, 20, 26.
[26] See Shane Clifton, 'The Spirit and Doctrinal Development: A Functional Analysis of the Traditional Pentecostal Doctrine of the Baptism in the Holy Spirit', *Pneuma* 29, no. 1 (2007): 5–23, esp. 14–15.
[27] Walter J. Hollenweger, 'From Azusa Street to the Toronto Phenomenon', in *Pentecostal Movements as an Ecumenical Challenge*, ed. Jürgen Moltmann and Karl-Josef Kuschel (Concilium 3; London: SCM Press, 1996), 7.
[28] See Amos Yong, *Renewing Christian Theology: Systematics for a Global Christianity* (Waco, TX: Baylor University Press, 2014), 81–102.
[29] Macchia, *Baptized in the Spirit*, 26–28.
[30] See Henry I. Lederle, *Treasures Old and New: Interpretations of 'Spirit-Baptism' in the Charismatic Renewal Movement* (Peabody, MA: Hendrickson, 1988), 144–212.

nomenclature of a 'baptism in the Holy Spirit'. Especially the Wesleyan, early Methodist and nineteenth-century Holiness Movement affirmed with the phrase an experience of permanent sanctification following conversion identified by biblical records of the events following the day of Pentecost.[31] Pentecostals adopted the ethos of viewing the Christian life as several distinct crisis moments in which Spirit baptism is considered a (second or third) 'blessing' to be received subsequent to conversion.[32] The biblical and theological grounds for advocating different stages of the Christian life categorize sanctification in this sense as a baptism of holiness associated with the Holy Spirit given to those who already received a baptism of regeneration at the hands of Jesus.[33] In the distinction of the Pentecostal movement from its theological predecessors, the dispensational character of this perspective became further enforced when the immediate association of the experience with the day of Pentecost directed Pentecostals beyond singular concerns about sanctification and towards the biblical rhetoric of power and charismatic endowment. In response, the baptism in the Spirit became identified with charismatic empowerment under which sanctification was now typically assumed but deemed insufficient by itself for Christian ministry and the mission of the church.[34] Pentecostals outside the Wesleyan Holiness tradition and the growth of a diverse Pentecostal movement worldwide ultimately contributed to a hardening of the separation of Spirit baptism from conversion while blurring its distinction to sanctification. Among some Pentecostal groups today, sanctification is removed from the full gospel as a distinct motif and subsumed in a fourfold scheme under the baptism in the Spirit.

The shift to the notion of charismatic endowment identifies the primary purpose of Spirit baptism with the reception of power evident in particular in the manifestation of spiritual gifts. As a consequence, the experience has been identified at times exclusively in terms of prophetic and missiological implications and with no soteriological significance.[35] However, the emphasis

---

[31] See Henry H. Knight III, *Anticipating Heaven Below: Optimism of Grace from Wesley to the Pentecostals* (Eugene, OR: Cascade, 2014), 81–96; Donald W. Dayton, *Theological Roots of Pentecostalism* (Peabody, MA: Hendrickson, 1987), 63–84.

[32] See Gause, *Living in the Spirit*, 59–72.

[33] See Steven M. Studebaker, 'Pentecostal Soteriology and Pneumatology', JPT 11, no. 2 (2003): 248–70.

[34] See Allan Anderson, *Spreading Fires: The Missionary Nature of Early Pentecostalism* (London: SCM Press, 2007), 17–31.

[35] See Robert P. Menzies, *Empowered for Witness: The Spirit in Luke-Acts*, JPTS 6 (Sheffield: Sheffield Academic Press, 1994).

on empowerment should not be misunderstood as standing in juxtaposition to sanctification or as outside the metaphor of Christian salvation. Spirit baptism perceived in terms of power includes victory over sin, charismatic life, and witness to the gospel. In Pentecostal terms, Spirit baptism is both an overpowering and empowering experience of the Holy Spirit who breaks through personal, affective, sociocultural, political, and religious dimensions of the Christian life.[36] The debate about the nature and placement of Spirit baptism emphasizes the Pentecostal concern for the process of the human awareness of God's saving grace along different moments of transformative experiences.[37] Conversion, sanctification, and charismatic empowerment can all function as metaphors for the baptism in the Spirit when viewed together and not in isolated theological categories which demand no genuine experiences.

Nonetheless, Pentecostal theology has not always emphasized the integrative nature of the fivefold gospel motifs. The distinction of sanctification and Spirit baptism from conversion, in particular, remains an isolated concern in ecumenical conversations.[38] Furthermore, the shift from interpreting the baptism in the Spirit in terms of sanctification to the idea of charismatic empowerment has led historically to a second doctrinal emphasis on the 'subsequence' of Spirit baptism. This teaching argues within a strict order of salvation for the independent temporal experience of Spirit baptism *following* conversion and distinct from its purposes.[39] Pentecostal theology, on the one hand, should not be construed as suggesting a distinctive *ordo salutis* accentuating a single Pentecostal element, but rather all motifs of the full gospel are possible entrance points to the way of salvation. On the other hand, the interpretation of biblical events in light of their own experiences raises for most Pentecostals the question of a normative logical, if not chronological, subsequence of the baptism in the Spirit to conversion

---

[36] See Wolfgang Vondey, *Pentecostalism: A Guide for the Perplexed* (London and New York: Bloomsbury, 2013), 39–47.

[37] Amos Yong, *The Spirit Poured Out on All Flesh: Pentecostalism and the Possibility of Global Theology* (Grand Rapids, MI: Baker Academic, 2005), 105.

[38] See Wolfgang Vondey, *Pentecostalism and Christian Unity*, vol. 1, *Ecumenical Documents and Critical Assessments* (Eugene, OR: Pickwick, 2010).

[39] See Atkinson, *Baptism in the Spirit*; Howard M. Ervin, *Conversion-Initiation and the Baptism in the Holy Spirit: An Engaging Critique of James D. G. Dunn's Baptism in the Holy Spirit* (Peabody, MA: Hendrickson, 1984); James D. G. Dunn, *Baptism in the Holy Spirit: A Re-examination of the New Testament Teaching on the Gift of the Spirit in Relation to Pentecostalism Today* (Philadelphia, PA: Westminster, 1970).

and regeneration.⁴⁰ Theologically, while the merging of Spirit baptism with sanctification is a less contested (though significant) issue, the identification of Spirit baptism as a distinct motif of the full gospel cannot be maintained if the experience is merged with regeneration.⁴¹ Therefore, Pentecostals argue for the separability and subsequence of the baptism in the Spirit from the baptism in water.⁴²

In general, Pentecostals contend that the baptism in the Spirit is a distinct experience from conversion: while all who are saved receive the Holy Spirit, celebrated by the baptism in water, a further baptism in the Spirit is available for the full unfolding of the Christian life and the mission of the church.⁴³ Even when it is granted that Spirit baptism and regeneration can occur simultaneously, Pentecostals retain a logical distinction of progression of both experiences. The insistence on subsequence serves to identify charismatic empowerment as a unique experiential dimension of the Christian life, emphasizing the significance of conversion and sanctification, yet contending for the importance of seeking continued spiritual progression throughout the Christian life.⁴⁴ The experience of the baptism in the Spirit thus shows a different manner of reception of the Spirit and different soteriological purpose than regeneration and sanctification.⁴⁵ This theological distinction highlights an initial experience of receiving the Holy Spirit for regeneration, an ongoing experience of being filled with the Spirit for sanctification and a distinctive experience of the baptism with the Holy Spirit for empowerment. While Pentecostal theology at times sharply distinguishes between these aspects, they remain deeply interconnected moments on the way to salvation.

Finally, the debates on subsequence and charismatic endowment are reinforced and sharpened by yet another, most visible, discussion on the experiential evidence of the baptism in the Holy Spirit. Classical Pentecostal theology, in particular, insists that the baptism in the Spirit is manifested by speaking

---

40 See Bradley Truman Noel, 'Gordon Fee and the Challenge to Pentecostal Hermeneutics: Thirty Years Later', *Pneuma* 26, no. 1 (2004): 60–80.
41 Warrington, *Pentecostal Theology*, 102.
42 See Gordon D. Fee, 'Baptism in the Holy Spirit: The Issue of Separability and Subsequence', *Pneuma* 7, no. 2 (1985): 87–99.
43 Warrington, *Pentecostal Theology*, 99–106.
44 Ibid., 105; Lederle, *Treasures Old and New*, 227–40.
45 David Petts, 'The Baptism in the Holy Spirit: The Theological Distinctive', in *Pentecostal Perspectives*, ed. Keith Warrington (Carlisle: Paternoster, 1998), 98–119; Gause, *Living in the Spirit*, 110–23.

with other tongues as the initial (physical) evidence shown in the biblical records and confirmed by contemporary experience.[46] Speaking with tongues emphasizes the observable and intensely personal nature of the baptism in the Spirit, the primacy of the affections over doctrine and the importance of the charismatic dimension for Pentecostal theology.[47] Pentecostals identify the speaking with tongues in terms of two forms of supernatural speech: the speaking in an existing human language not previously learned by the speaker but understood by the audience and the speaking in an unknown heavenly tongue that requires interpretation to be understood.[48] In theory, the former is seen as instrument for the mission of the church, while the latter is typically understood as an expression of personal piety.[49] Pentecostals see in both forms of speech a physical manifestation confirming the baptism in the Spirit and expressing its purposes, even if speaking with tongues today is widely considered no longer the only evidence of Spirit baptism.[50] Echoing the events of Pentecost, speaking with tongues is seen in diverse ways as pointing to the restoration of a biblical and apostolic life, a call to personal holiness and sanctification, the empowerment of the church, the proclamation of the gospel to the world, endowment for worship and the prophetic confrontation of social, religious, political, economic, or cultural injustices for the purpose of liberation, transformation, and renewal.[51] While speaking with tongues has always functioned to justify the biblical precedence of the baptism in the Holy Spirit and to ascertain the reception of the baptism in the life of the believer, the importance of its function as an *initial* evidence is to emphasize a necessary openness to other charismatic manifestations in the life of the believer following Spirit baptism. Tongues are not the culmination of a Pentecostal experience but a manifestation of divine sovereignty and human

---

[46] See Aaron T. Friesen, *Norming the Abnormal: The Development and Function of the Doctrine of Initial Evidence in Classical Pentecostalism* (Eugene, OR: Pickwick, 2013); Gary B. McGee (ed.), *Initial Evidence: Historical and Biblical Perspectives on the Pentecostal Doctrine of Spirit Baptism* (Peabody, MA: Hendrickson, 1991).

[47] Stanley Horton, 'Spirit Baptism: A Pentecostal Perspective', in *Perspectives on Spirit Baptism*, ed. Chad Owen Brand (Nashville: Broadman & Holman, 2004), 48.

[48] See Wolfgang Vondey, 'Glossolalia', in *Global Dictionary of Theology*, ed. William A. Dyrness and Veli-Matti Kärkkäinen (Downers Grove, IL: IVP Academic, 2008), 343–45.

[49] See Randall Holm, Matthew Wolf and James K. A. Smith, 'New Frontiers in Tongues Research: A Symposium', *JPT* 20, no. 1 (2011): 122–54; Anderson, *Spreading Fires*, 40–50, 57–65.

[50] See Cecil M. Robeck Jr., 'An Emerging Magisterium? The Case of the Assemblies of God', *Pneuma* 25, no. 2 (2003): 164–215.

[51] See Friesen, *Norming the Abnormal*, 154–93.

responsibility calling for a further unfolding of a fuller personal and spiritual life of the Christian and the community.

The global diversification and ecumenical exposure of Pentecostalism, coupled with concerns for the institutionalization and routinization of charismatic experiences, has led to reinterpretations of the notion of initial evidence in terms of a sacramental understanding of speaking with tongues. Rejecting the mechanisms of ecclesiastical initiation, manipulation, and formalization through which tongues become a condition for rather than manifestation of Spirit baptism, the interpretation of speaking in tongues as a sacramental sign offers theological grounds to view Spirit baptism less in evidential or causal categories than in existential and dialogical terms.[52] While sacramentality may be viewed by Pentecostals as supporting formal liturgical traditions, the sacramental character of speaking in tongues is here used in a broadly analogical sense as audible 'signs' of the Spirit and the grace of God.[53] Pentecostal theology thus can regard speaking in tongues as a sacramental act 'that signifies, while participating in it, the empowerment of the Spirit in the Christian life'.[54] As sacramental, speaking in tongues is a uniquely spontaneous and even critical sign protesting a stagnant liturgical life among the existing Christian traditions.[55] Tongue speech is evidential manifestation of God's presence through the freedom of the Spirit revealed in a manner that is both divine speech and a language of faith.[56]

Sacramental theology among Pentecostals has remained underdeveloped. As physical manifestation and sign, speaking with tongues cannot be considered a sacrament in itself but should be viewed rather as the visible and

---

[52] See Neil Ferguson, 'Separating Speaking in Tongues from Glossolalia Using a Sacramental View', *Colloquium* 43, no. 1 (2011): 39–58; Simon Chan, *Pentecostal Theology and the Christian Spiritual Tradition*, JPTS 21 (Sheffield: Sheffield Academic Press, 2000), 77–82; Frank D. Macchia, 'The Question of Tongues as Initial Evidence: A Review of Initial Evidence, Edited by Gary B. McGee', *JPT* 2 (1993): 117–27; William Samarin, *Tongues of Men and Angels: The Religious Language of Pentecostalism* (New York: Macmillan, 1972), 232–33; Simon Tugwell, 'The Speech-Giving Spirit: A Dialogue with Tongues', in *New Heaven, New Earth? An Encounter with Pentecostalism*, ed. Simon Tugwell et al. (Springfield, IL: Temple-gate, 1976), 150–64.

[53] See Frank D. Macchia, 'Tongues as a Sign: Towards a Sacramental Understanding of Pentecostal Experience', *Pneuma* 15, no. 1 (1993): 61–76.

[54] Ibid., 69. See also Kilian McDonnell, 'The Function of Tongues in Pentecostalism', in *Roman Catholic-Pentecostal Dialogue (1977–1982): A Study in Developing Ecumenism*, ed. Jerry L. Sandidge, vol. 2 (Frankfurt: Peter Lang, 1987), 20–56.

[55] Frank D. Macchia, 'Discerning the Truth of Tongues Speech: A Response to Amos Yong', *JPT* 12 (1998): 67–71.

[56] Frank D. Macchia, 'Groans Too Deep for Words: Towards a Theology of Tongues as Initial Evidence', *AJPS* 1, no. 2 (1998): 149–73.

audible element of the sacramental practice, which is the baptism in the Holy Spirit. Interpreted in isolation from larger spiritual realities and other theological symbols, however, seeking charismatic empowerment, pursuing an experience of the Spirit subsequent to conversion and speaking in tongues, at times, have become ritual practices in their own right. This development has stifled theological articulation of Spirit baptism in terms of actual Pentecostal practices in favour of creating a quasi-ritual reality that can substitute for the original experience. The debates on subsequence, charismatic endowment and initial evidence may identify the boundaries of the baptism in the Spirit, but they do not characterize the transforming nature of the practices of praying through, preaching and the laying on of hands. The doctrinal discussion on Spirit baptism is in the process of returning to these original practices and their reinterpretation and integration in the Christian spiritual traditions. In this (re)turn to experience, the notion of sacramentality holds primacy of place in the theological conversation.

Spirit baptism as sacrament

Although the doctrine of the baptism in the Spirit is rarely a focal point of theological discussion outside the Pentecostal movement, a sacramental interpretation of Spirit baptism has received the strongest ecumenical support. The notion of sacramentality as such is more akin to neo-Pentecostal and charismatic theologies among groups that have not severed their bond to established traditions and mainline denominations, although the global and local diversification of Pentecostalism makes any strict theological distinctions along denominational affiliation highly problematic. Especially the integration of the charismatic renewal in the Roman Catholic Church has supported the development of a sacramental theology of Spirit baptism.[57] The theological interpretation of the baptism in the Spirit in terms of the sacrament of confirmation, or the renewal of confirmation, has significantly assisted this endeavour.[58] The Malines Documents, in particular, speak of

---

[57] See Lederle, *Treasures Old and New*, 104–43.
[58] See Wolfgang Vondey, 'New Evangelization and Liturgical Praxis in the Roman Catholic Church', *SL* 36, no. 2 (2006): 231–52; idem, *Heribert Mühlen: His Theology and Praxis. A New Profile of the Church* (Lanham, MD: University Press of America, 2004), 161–262.

Spirit baptism as a conscious experience of the power of the Holy Spirit given at water baptism.[59] According to this view, the baptism in the Spirit can be integrated in the sacramental framework of Catholic liturgy if the particular experience is interpreted, not as an independent sacramental grace, but as a further realization, awareness, deepening, or fulfilling of the gift of the Spirit received at water baptism and confirmation.[60] Prominent Catholic interpretation therefore stresses that there are, in principle, no two baptisms, but that the baptism in the Holy Spirit is a renewal of the already given but latent power of the Holy Spirit from the inside rather than an independent outpouring of the Spirit from the outside.[61] In contrast to Pentecostal theology, Spirit baptism cannot be severed from Christian initiation but is an anointing received at the moment of water baptism.[62] Properly speaking, the baptism in the Spirit is not a sacrament but a sacramental act of worship, which can lead to water baptism, or for those already baptized, to a confirmation and sanctification of the Christian life.[63] As a sacramental act integrated in the fullness of the Christian life, Spirit baptism is therefore not seen as an isolated moment in the order of salvation but as identifying, in tandem with other sacramental moments, a lifelong process of conversion.[64] The charismatic movements among Lutheran, Reformed, and in other Protestant traditions, as well as Eastern Orthodox interpretations, have supported (although not significantly added to) this sacramental understanding of Spirit baptism.[65] Typically, it is the experience of the baptism that is identified in sacramental terms rather than the notion of sacramentality that is reinterpreted in light of the Pentecostal experience.

An exception and fruitful theological reinterpretation of the sacramental view can be found in the work of Catholic theologian Heribert Mühlen, who identifies the baptism of Jesus as a prototype for the baptism in the Spirit.[66]

---

[59] See 'Malines Document I', in *Presence, Power, Praise: Documents on the Charismatic Renewal*, vol. 1, *Continental, National, and Regional Documents*, ed. Kilian McDonnell (Collegeville, MN: Liturgical Press, 1980), 13–70.
[60] Ibid., 39–40.
[61] See Léon Joseph Cardinal Suenens, *A New Pentecost?* trans. Francis Martin (London: Darton, Longman and Todd, 1975), 80–81.
[62] See Kilian McDonnell and George T. Montague, *Christian Initiation and Baptism in the Holy Spirit: Evidence from the First Eight Centuries* (Collegeville, MN: Liturgical Press, 1991), 316–42.
[63] See Donald L. Gelpi, *Pentecostalism: A Theological Viewpoint* (New York: Paulist, 1971), 173–86.
[64] Donald L. Gelpi, *Charism and Sacrament: A Theology of Christian Conversion* (New York: Paulist, 1976), 150–51.
[65] See Lederle, *Treasures Old and New*, 124–38.
[66] Vondey, *Heribert Mühlen*, 196–211; Lederle, *Treasures Old and New*, 180–85.

The importance of his proposal for Pentecostal theology lies in his reformulation of the sacramental and liturgical framework, that is, the integration of Spirit baptism in a revised praxis of the church. Mühlen views Pentecost as the historical continuation of Jesus's experience of the Spirit, a corporeal, objective inner occurrence in the life of Jesus, who hears the voice of the Father and sees the Spirit descend on him (see Mt. 3:16-17; Lk. 3:21-22).[67] Jesus's baptism in the Spirit is the beginning of a personal, public, social, and communal ministry in words and signs (Acts 10:38) that also marks the origin of the church.[68] The one who baptizes with the Spirit is himself baptized in the Spirit and releases at Pentecost the Spirit into the history of the church. Jesus himself illustrates with his baptism the proper human response to God's offer of the new covenant, which is continued in the church's celebration of the sacraments. Sacramentality is the human embrace of God's covenant on the inside manifested in outward observable signs that witness to the gospel. Mühlen therefore speaks of a *'sacramental baptism of the Spirit...* since sacraments are God's *offers* effective in us only to the extent we accept that offer'.[69] The baptism in the Spirit calls for the conscious and deliberate acceptance and renewal of water baptism or confirmation in the course of a person's life. Jesus's example shows that this public acceptance is marked by a 'breakthrough' to charismatic-prophetic activity so that 'we are plunged into the divine *power for testimony,* for self-renunciation and self-surrender to others'.[70] Mühlen describes the renewal of the Spirit as a 'charismatic sacrament' in which the *'charismatic graces are sacramentally offered'*.[71] The charismatic gifts of the Spirit are not mere external signs of an internal experience but corporeal expressions of God's love and ecclesial expressions of grace through the Spirit.[72] The baptism in the Spirit is consequently as much a personal experience as it is an ecclesial event in which the individual and the

---

[67] See Heribert Mühlen, *Una Mystica Persona: Die Kirche als das Mysterium der Identität des heiligen Geistes in Christus und den Christen,* 2nd ed. (Paderborn: Schöningh, 1967), 216-86.
[68] Heribert Mühlen, *A Charismatic Theology: Initiation in the Spirit,* trans. Edward Quinn and Thomas Linton (New York: Paulist, 1978), 113-23.
[69] Ibid., 93-94. See Heribert Mühlen, *Einübung in die christliche Grunderfahrung: Lehre und Zuspruch* (Mainz: Grünewald, 1976), 92-105.
[70] Ibid., 95. Emphasis original.
[71] Ibid., 132. Emphasis original.
[72] See Heribert Mühlen, *Die Erneuerung des christlichen Glaubens: Charisma-Geist-Befreiung* (Munich: Don Bosco, 1974), 173-80; idem., *Entsakralisierung: Ein epochales Schlagwort in seiner Bedeutung für die Zukunft der christlichen Kirchen* (Paderborn: Schöningh, 1971), 140-76.

churches are renewed from within to become open to all gifts of the Spirit.[73] In this baptism, God awakens the charismatic gifts in the churches, which can now proclaim in sociocritical forms the gospel to the world.[74] For this to occur, the churches must reinforce concrete opportunities to accept the fullness of God's covenant in a liturgical framework that can renew taken-for-granted sacramental structures by allowing for a free personal, corporeal, and deliberate assent to God's grace in an inner baptism resulting from the work of the Holy Spirit.[75]

The attempt to capture the soteriological dimension of Spirit baptism by developing its charismatic, ecclesial, and critical dimensions speaks to current Pentecostal reformulations of the doctrine.[76] Still, Pentecostal theology resists the tendency evident in Catholic proposals to shift away from baptismal language or to identify the baptism in the Spirit with the baptism in water.[77] For some Pentecostals, Mühlen's identification of Jesus as the prototype of those baptized in the Spirit may also separate the identity of our experience from Jesus as the one who baptizes with the Spirit – and thus from Pentecost. Yet, the historical distance to Jesus's own baptism is overcome precisely with the day of Pentecost when the one who was baptized in the Spirit now becomes the one who baptizes with the Spirit. Only through Pentecost can the church maintain an incarnational theology of Christ as God-with-us to continue beyond the ascension.[78] Yet, the significance of Pentecost does not derive from imitation of Jesus. The reverse is true; the baptism in the Spirit takes its meaning from the unexpected and unimaginable gift of the Spirit by the ascended Christ. In this sense, Christ is present sacramentally in the mystery (*sacramentum*) of the outpouring of the Holy Spirit. To interpret

---

[73] See Heribert Mühlen, *Neu mit Gott: Grundkurs christlichen Lebens*, 4th ed. (Freiburg: Herder, 2000), 179–205; idem., *Grundentscheidung: Weg aus der Krise I* (Mainz: Grünewald, 1983), 108–34.

[74] See Heribert Mühlen (ed.), *Geistesgaben heute* (Mainz: Grünewald, 1982), 33–49, 160–74.

[75] See Heribert Mühlen, *Kirche wächst von innen: Weg zu einer glaubensgeschichtlich neuen Gestalt der Kirche* (Paderborn: Bonifatius, 1995).

[76] See Macchia, *Baptized in the Spirit*, 211–22, 241–56; Clifton, 'The Spirit and Doctrinal Development', 15–20; Chan, *Pentecostalism and the Christian Spiritual Tradition*, 41; Yong, *The Spirit Poured Out on All Flesh*, 103–9.

[77] See Macchia, *Baptized in the Spirit*, 72–75; Mark Lee, 'An Evangelical Dialogue on Luke, Salvation, and Spirit Baptism', *Pneuma* 26, no. 1 (2004): 81–98.

[78] See Odette Mainville, *The Spirit in Luke-Acts* (Woodstock, GA: The Foundation for Pentecostal Scholarship, 2016), 150–64, 205–7. The full realization of the eucharistic presence of Christ must also lead through Pentecost. See Wolfgang Vondey, *People of Bread: Rediscovering Ecclesiology* (New York: Paulist Press, 2008), 173–94.

this continuity of the messianic presence in sacramental terms is not foreign to Pentecostalism but meets with efforts among Pentecostals to expand the notion of sacramentality and sacramental practices in their own churches.[79] However, Pentecostal theology might speak of Spirit baptism less as a sacramental *act* than a sacramental *encounter* with the person of the Holy Spirit who reveals Jesus as one who baptizes with the Spirit.[80] As encounter with the mystery of the continuing presence of Christ, the baptism in the Spirit cannot be absorbed by the cultic repetitions of the church but escapes human ability to capture and reproduce its effects. Pentecostal sacramentality is an effort to preserve the mystery, not to ritualize and domesticate the divine gift.

Among these efforts, the speaking with tongues can be seen to manifest Pentecost as a radically new event that does not simply imitate the baptism of Jesus. Sacramentality can serve as a theological expression for the Pentecostal altar hermeneutics, which tends to oscillate between identifying the reality of the human encounter with the Spirit in terms of a tension between 'this-is-that' and 'this-is-not-that' (see Chapter 1). The baptism in the Spirit, understood as a sacramental encounter, functions as a mechanism for describing 'this' reality of the human life in terms of a radical openness to participation in 'that' reality of God without confounding or separating the two.[81] As a sacramental encounter, 'this' baptism in the Spirit among Pentecostals today is a palpable experience of the baptism of Jesus, who baptizes with the Spirit by giving his Spirit in a manner analogous to 'that' outpouring on the day of Pentecost. Speaking with tongues signifies this unexpected encounter and gift, and, for Pentecostals, is sacramental in this analogical sense, not as a mere sign pointing to another reality but as a participatory and experienced reality presented in the unmediated process of signification.[82] However, while the baptism in the Spirit is already participation in the life of Christ by the Spirit,

---

[79] See Chris E. W. Green, *Toward a Pentecostal Theology of the Lord's Supper: Foretasting the Kingdom* (Cleveland, TN: CPT Press, 2012); Veli-Matti Kärkkäinen, 'The Pentecostal View', in *The Lord's Supper: Five Views*, ed. Gordon T. Smith (Downers Grove: IVP, 2008), 117–35; Wesley Scott Biddy, 'Re-envisioning the Pentecostal Understanding of the Eucharist: An Ecumenical Proposal', *Pneuma* 28, no. 2 (2006): 228–51; Daniel Tomberlin, *Encountering God at the Altar: The Sacraments in Pentecostal Worship* (Cleveland, TN: Center for Pentecostal Leadership and Care, 2006).

[80] See Krzysztof Gasecki, *Das Profil des Geistes in den Sakramenten: Pneumatologische Grundlagen der Sakramentenlehre*, MPT 66 (Münster: Aschendorff, 2009), 280–365.

[81] See James K. A. Smith, *Thinking in Tongues: Pentecostal Contributions to Christian Philosophy*, PM 1 (Grand Rapids, MI: Eerdmans, 2010), 33–39.

[82] Macchia, 'Tongues as a Sign', 62–63.

'this' experience is not yet 'that' experience of the fullness of the redeemed life. Tongues are a broken symbol, transformative but apophatic reference to the divine presence, provisional but not absolute.[83] As such, speaking with tongues is complete as sign but incomplete as evidence of the sacramental encounter with the Holy Spirit.

The identification of tongues as sign rather than evidence of Spirit baptism does not distract from the importance of the experience among Pentecostals. However, this reinterpretation of the function of speaking in tongues allows the practice to be identified as the sign of the sacramental encounter rather than as the sacrament itself. The sign's value is established by the Pentecostal practices of the individual amidst the community of believers.[84] Hence, the sacramental encounter of Spirit baptism is inseparable from the Pentecostal practices, such as praying through, the proclamation of the Word and the laying on of hands. These practices manifest the corporeality of the baptism in the Spirit; they are personal and ecclesial expressions of the radical openness to the gospel of Jesus Christ. At the same time, while inseparable from the sacramental encounter, they are not identical with that encounter nor with its charismatic manifestations. Mühlen's proposal is significant here as it affords Pentecostals to speak of Spirit baptism not only as sacramental sign but as charismatic sacrament. While Pentecostals have admitted that the frequent criticism of evidential language limited to the speaking in tongues is justified, the displacement of such charismatic language and of the importance of tongues is inadmissible for Pentecostal theology. It is precisely the charismatic dimension of Spirit baptism that allows Pentecostals to speak of the experience as a sacrament.

Pentecostal theology speaks to the Christian sacramental traditions through its struggle to reconcile sanctification with charismatic empowerment. The inseparability of Spirit baptism as a theological motif from corporeal practices at the altar emphasizes the importance placed on the operation of the Holy Spirit in all practices and rituals of the church. At the same time, the baptism in the Spirit represents not simply one practice among others. As

---

[83] See Amos Yong, '"Tongues of Fire" in the Pentecostal Imagination: The Truth of Glossolalia in Light of R C Neville's Thy of Religious Symbolism', *JPT* 12 (1998): 39–65. Yong's notion borrows from Robert Cummings Neville, *The Truth of Broken Symbols* (Albany: State University of New York Press, 1996), an adaptation of Tillich's notion of 'broken myths'.

[84] Wolfgang Vondey, 'The Symbolic Turn: A Symbolic Conception of the Liturgy of Pentecostalism', *WTJ* 36, no. 2 (2001): 223–47.

a sacrament it becomes a transformative ritual that transitions the individual and the church from sanctification to charismatic ministry; at the altar, the distinction between sanctification and charisma ceases at the moment of the encounter with God. The one who is baptized in the Spirit receives by participating in the act the sacredness of God's actions.[85] For Pentecostals, therefore, sanctification is not an end in itself but always a gateway to the full hospitality of God (see Chapter 3). With the metaphor of the altar, Pentecostals can speak of a movement from altar to altar towards the holy of holies.[86] At the baptism in the Spirit, the holiness of God fills and overflows the receptive capacity of the believer and the community: the praying for the Spirit becomes a praying in the Spirit, the hearing of the gospel becomes a proclamation of the gospel, the laying on of hands becomes an endowment with the Holy Spirit. Such transformations are a consequence of the empowerment with the Spirit.[87] The sanctifying baptism is a charismatic baptism – the bursting forth of the gifts of the Spirit in proclamation, praise, and worship. These manifestations harken back to the baptism of repentance and conversion while also pointing forward to a person's full transformation in the kingdom of God.

The baptism in the Spirit transforms the identity of sacramental practices and makes charismatic manifestations indispensable. Pentecostals can agree with Mühlen's concept of Spirit baptism as an inner acceptance and breakthrough. However, for Pentecostals, Spirit baptism occurs on the inside by means of the affections, that is, abiding dispositions resulting from the encounter with the Holy Spirit and directing a person more fully towards God and neighbour.[88] As affective, the baptism in the Spirit ignites a passion directed beyond one's self to the church and to the world that seeks to overcome the isolation of a personal covenant relationship for the sake of God's promise of the redemption of all creation.[89] The charismatic dimension,

---

[85] See Adam Ayers, 'Can the Behavior of Tongues Utterance Still Function as Ecclesial Boundary? The Significance of Art and Sacrament', *Pneuma* 20, no. 2 (2000): 271–301.

[86] Frank Macchia, *Justified in the Spirit: Creation, Redemption, and the Triune God* (Grand Rapids, MI: Eerdmans, 2010), 83, citing unknown author, 'Salvation according to the True Tabernacle', *AF* 1, no. 10 (1907): 3.

[87] Albrecht, *Rites in the Spirit*, 215.

[88] Steven J. Land, *Pentecostal Spirituality: A Passion for the Kingdom*, JPTS 1 (Sheffield: Sheffield Academic Press, 1993), 136.

[89] See Kimberly Ervin Alexander, James P. Bowers and Mark J. Cartledge, 'Spirit Baptism, Socialization and Godly Love in the Church of God' (Cleveland, TN), *PentecoStudies* 11, no. 1 (2012): 27–47; Samuel Solivan, *The Spirit, Pathos and Liberation: Toward an Hispanic Pentecostal Theology*, JPTS 14 (Sheffield: Sheffield Academic Press, 1998), 93–118.

therefore, is not only a corporeal and ecclesial expression of grace but a universal and eschatological manifestation of the kingdom of God in the world.[90] Pentecostal theology highlights that through the experience of charismatic power, the transformation inherent in the sacramental encounter extends beyond the participant to the whole community and to the world (see Chapter 10). Through the baptism in the Spirit, 'the church is allowed to participate in, and bear witness to, the final sanctification of creation'.[91] Speaking with tongues is an expression of this witness within a broader network of broken symbols that call for interpretation of meaning and truth.[92] Pentecostals warn against identifying the baptism in the Spirit too narrowly with tongues alone.[93] Conversely, the emphasis on speaking with tongues as initial evidence retains the important link between the charismatic and eschatological identity of the Christian life. Spirit baptism functions as a sociocritical act in the world and a counter-critical ritual in the church because its manifestation in tongues, prophecy and other gifts of the Spirit signals the coming of God's kingdom ('this is that') while groaning in solidarity with the suffering creation ('this is not that') for the fullness of redemption.[94]

The charismatic dimension shifts Pentecostal sacramentality from an existential distinction between what is and what is not to an eschatological distinction between what is *already* and what is *not yet* participation in the kingdom of God. On the one hand, the baptism in the Spirit is a foretaste of that coming kingdom already breaking into this present world. On the other hand, the sacramental encounter with God, in all its power to make present the divine, also manifests a distance between the church and Christ overcome only in the final consummation of the kingdom. Speaking in tongues, as any other charismatic expression, is a heralding of God's kingdom and foretaste of the fullness of salvation.[95] Spirit baptism is ultimately an expression of the radical freedom of the Spirit, a counter-sacrament that resists containment in strict rituals and seeks the transformation of all soteriological practices

---

[90] Solivan, *Spirit, Pathos, and Liberation*, 112–18; Macchia, *Baptized in the Spirit*, 85–88.
[91] Macchia, *Baptized in the Spirit*, 86.
[92] See Yong, 'Tongues of Fire', 39–65.
[93] Juan Sepulveda, 'Born Again: Baptism and the Spirit, a Pentecostal Perspective', in *The Pentecostal Movements as an Ecumenical Challenge*, ed. Jürgen Moltmann and Karl-Josef Kuschel (Maryknoll, NY: Orbis, 1996), 104–9.
[94] See Macchia, 'Groans Too Deep for Words', 10–11.
[95] Gause, *Living in the Spirit*, 95–104.

in light of the coming of Christ. That the Spirit on the day of Pentecost is poured out on all flesh (Acts 2:17) challenges the church to engage with this gift all of creation.[96] With the baptism in the Spirit, the church has arrived at a threshold of its own identity: from the reception to the giving of the Spirit, from the community of saints to the community of witnesses and from the altar to the world.

---

[96] See Veli-Matti Kärkkäinen (ed.), *The Spirit in the World: Emerging Pentecostal Theologies in Global Contexts* (Grand Rapids, MI: Eerdmans, 2009); Amos Yong (ed.), *The Spirit Renews the Face of the Earth: Pentecostal Forays in Science and Theology of Creation* (Eugene, OR: Pickwick, 2009).

5

Healed

Manifesting Signs and Wonders

The central argument of this book is that Pentecostal theology reaches deep into the heart of Pentecost and that this event finds its native expression in the theological narrative of the full gospel and its application at the altar. When Pentecostals express the full gospel in testimonial phrases indicating that they are 'saved, sanctified and filled with the Holy Spirit', 'healed and delivered', or 'on their way to heaven', they express the experiences of their arrival, tarrying and transformation at the altar. Cast in the image of Pentecost, the release from the altar initiated by the baptism in the Spirit now opens the way to the fourth motif of the full gospel: divine healing. For many (if not most) Pentecostals, the experience or witnessing of divine healing distinguishes Pentecostals from other Christians.[1] On the other hand, while it is this belief and practice that has often been a cause for division, divine healing may be what most connects Pentecostals with historic Christianity.[2] Moreover, the celebration of healing miracles across diverse cultural contexts connects most deeply with indigenous peoples, offering continuity with traditional healing practices, and thereby allows Pentecostalism to function as a kind of mirror of the globalization of Christianity.[3]

This chapter traces the theological contours of divine healing through the metaphor of the altar, used throughout this book as a way to identify the practices emerging from Pentecost as theological symbol. The preceding chapters

---

[1] See Pew Forum on Religion and Public Life (ed.), 'Spirit and Power: A 10-Country Survey of Pentecostals', accessed 1 January 2016 at http://www.pewforum.org/2006/10/05/spirit-and-power/.
[2] See Kimberly Ervin Alexander, *Pentecostal Healing: Models in Theology and Practice*, JPTS 2 (Sheffield: Deo, 2006).
[3] See Candy Gunther Brown (ed.), *Global Pentecostal and Charismatic Healing* (Oxford: Oxford University Press, 2011), 4–6; Amanda Porterfield, *Healing in the History of Christianity*

have outlined the journey to the altar and its transformational experiences as a framework for Pentecostal soteriology. The day of Pentecost suggests that the believer, who comes to the altar for conversion and tarries at the altar for sanctification, is transformed through the baptism in the Spirit to leave the altar. Divine healing represents this leaving of the altar and going into the world; it is an outward oriented soteriological praxis that is tied as much to ecclesial rituals at the altar as to improvised practices among the sick and the dying in the world. In this sense, divine healing also provides significant expansion to the day of Pentecost as a root symbol for Pentecostal theology. The chapter begins by identifying approaches to divine healing in the wake of Pentecost from the perspective of specific ecclesial and sociocultural practices among Pentecostals. The second part traces the doctrine of divine healing in its central components and nuances among various Pentecostal groups. I conclude with an ecumenical proposal of divine healing built on the expanded image of Pentecost as expression of the signs and wonders of redemption.

Divine healing at the altar

When we speak of divine healing, two different dynamics represent themselves: practices by the sick to seek healing from God and practices by those who minister to the sick. Divine healing is evident both by coming to the altar and by taking the altar to the sick and the dying. At the altar, both dynamics overlap in prayer for one another's needs, various types of healing rites, deliverance, exorcism, and other restorative ministries.[4] As with the preceding elements of the full gospel, the biblical texts of Luke-Acts form a particular (though not the only) backdrop for shaping Pentecostal healing practices.[5] Suffering, sickness, and persecution are seen as consistent biblical themes

---

(Oxford: Oxford University Press, 2005), 159–85; Morton T. Kelsey, *Healing and Christianity: In Ancient Thought and Modern Times* (New York: Harper & Row, 1973), 354.

[4] See Daniel E. Albrecht, *Rites in the Spirit: A Ritual Approach to Pentecostal/Charismatic Spirituality*, JPTS 17 (Sheffield: Sheffield Academic Press, 1999), 256; James Peacock, 'Symbolic and Psychological Anthropology: The Case of Pentecostal Faith Healing', *Ethos* 12, no. 1 (1984): 37–53; William M. Clements, 'Ritual Expectation in Pentecostal Healing Experience', *WF* 40, no. (1981): 139–48.

[5] Martin William Mittelstadt, *Reading Luke-Acts in the Pentecostal Tradition* (Cleveland, TN: CPT Press, 2010), 98–103.

that evolve around concerns for the redeeming presence of God.[6] At the same time, differences in race, gender, culture, and religious formation exert a much broader dynamic on Pentecostal healing practices.[7] The contours of these practices remain thoroughly connected to the altar while diversifying rapidly through three intersecting dynamics: those saved, sanctified, and baptized in the Spirit come to the altar for divine healing, those who experience healing at the altar take the altar into the world, and those in the world who receive healing come to the altar for salvation. On the one hand, healing is seen as an extension of the biblical narratives of salvation, sanctification, and Spirit baptism, while, on the other hand, healing practices translate this narrative into the present with often unprecedented interpretation and new forms of application. If the outpouring of the Spirit identifies the origin of the church, healing is a metaphor for its purpose and function.

A motif of primary importance for Pentecostal practices of healing is the vocalization of faith. Among the central healing narratives of Acts, the healing of the crippled beggar reported immediately following the day of Pentecost sets the initial pattern for Pentecostal practices (see Acts 3:1–4:22).[8] The story shows Peter as taking the crippled man by the hand and raising him up with the authoritative command: 'In the name of Jesus Christ of Nazareth, stand up and walk' (Acts 3:6). Immediately strengthened, the man leaps up and walks. Peter explains to the astonished crowd that 'by faith in his name, this man ... his name has made strong, and the faith that comes through it has given him perfect health' (3:16). Arrested and taken before the Sanhedrin, Peter repeats that 'it was in the name of Jesus Christ ... in his name this man stands before you healed' (4:10). Subsequent reports of Peter's healing ministry continue to emphasize the importance to believe that 'Jesus Christ heals' (9:34) and connect the act of faith typically with an exhortation, such as 'get

---

[6] See Martin William Mittelstadt, *The Spirit and Suffering in Luke-Acts: Implications for a Pentecostal Pneumatology*, JPTS 26 (London: T & T Clark International, 2004); John Christopher Thomas, *The Devil, Disease and Deliverance: Origins of Illness in New Testament Thought*, JPTS 13 (Sheffield: Sheffield Academic Press, 1998), 310–19.

[7] See Brown, *Global Pentecostal and Charismatic Healing*; Donald E. Miller and Tetsunao Yamamori, *Global Pentecostalism: The New Face of Christian Social Engagement* (Berkeley: University of California Press, 2007), 149–54; Gaston Espinosa, '"God Made a Miracle in My Life": Latino Pentecostal Healing in the Borderlands', in *Religion and Healing in America*, ed. Linda L. Barnes and Susan S. Sered (Oxford: Oxford University Press, 2005), 123–38.

[8] Thomas, *Devil, Disease and Deliverance*, 30–31.

up' or 'rise up' (v. 40). Pentecostal practices identify the authoritative command frequently as the verbal expression of faith.

Pentecostal healing practices are in the first place practices of faith, evident not only in the expectation that healing results from the act of faith, but that such acts require the active participation of the believer in the pursuit of divine healing. The verbalization of faith is the most immediate ritual expression of this participation, at the most basic level understood as a vocalization of prayer.[9] Regular prayer for those sick, suffering or dying is a standard practice among Pentecostals. Practices of praying for the sick range from short commands, simple prayers of faith, speaking in tongues, testimonies and intercession, to prolonged tarrying, fasting prayer, and praying through at the altar until healing is manifested.[10] The invocation of healing 'in the name of Jesus' is a common affective exclamation across the movement.[11] It indicates belief in the abiding presence of Jesus and the continuing and consistent availability of his healing power.[12] The verbalization of this belief is not necessarily seen as producing immediate results. Instead, a longer process can involve the verbalization of faith in repeated testimonies and prayers.[13] The testimonies of healing (including its delayed process) therefore become healing practices in their own right. Divine healing is a response to faith vocalized in prayer, testimony, and other articulations of faith in the midst of opposing circumstances.

While most of these practices at the altar follow the patterns identified in the biblical scriptures, the move from the altar of the church to the sick and dying in the world has significantly expanded ecclesial practices and wedded them to particular historical, geographical, and sociocultural phenomena. For many of those standing at both sides of the altar (giving and receiving healing), these practices require a re-learning of the gestures of

[9] See Margaret M. Poloma, 'Pentecostal Prayer within the Assemblies of God: An Empirical Study', *Pneuma* 31, no. 1 (2009): 47–65.
[10] See Joseph W. Williams, *Spirit Cure: A History of Pentecostal Healing* (Oxford: Oxford University Press, 2013), 98–121; James Robinson, *Divine Healing: The Holiness-Pentecostal Transition Years, 1890–1906* (Eugene, OR: Pickwick, 2013), 183–208; Alexander, *Pentecostal Healing*, 64–194; James Randi, *The Faith Healers* (Buffalo, NY: Prometheus, 1987), 31–45; Francis MacNutt, *The Power to Heal* (Notre Dame, IN: Ave Maria Press, 1977), 47–79.
[11] Keith Warrington, 'The Path to Wholeness: Beliefs and Practices Relating to Healing in Pentecostalism', *Evangel* 21, no. 2 (2003): 45–49.
[12] See Keith Warrington, 'Acts and the Healing Narratives: Why?' *JPT* 14, no. 2 (2006): 189–217.
[13] Eva Jansen and Claudia Lang, 'Transforming the Self and Healing the Body through the Use of Testimonies in a Divine Retreat Center, Kerala', *JRH* 51, no. 2 (2012): 542–51.

faith.¹⁴ The widespread use of television and other media has shaped new, more institutionalized practices, particularly in affluent Western nations, while rural and developing countries have seen unprecedented mass-healing practices.¹⁵ Vocalized healing prayers are sometimes produced by the 'healer' following a strict format and pattern that can be reproduced through various media.¹⁶ Some Pentecostals take the vocalization of faith to heart and 'yell' or shout – in a radical form of public expression – in order to reach from the realm of the word to the realm of the Spirit.¹⁷ Historical models show that the diverse vocalizing practices can be seen through varying lenses as confrontational (to challenge evil and sickness), intercessory (to intervene on behalf of the sick), incubational (to initiate and aid a healing process over time), revelational (to speak beyond the sickness), and soteriological (to make healing a normative Christian practice).¹⁸ Equally important to the exclamation of healing on behalf of the sick is also the vocal participation by those who are suffering. Here, the word of faith is sometimes seen as a 'positive confession' despite one's physical circumstances.¹⁹ Practices can include a groaning in the spirit, prayerful agreement with the healer, shouts of praise, or a 'claiming' of healing by the sick – often despite the lack of physical evidence.

The biblical account of the conversion and healing of Saul in Acts 9 offers another dominant pattern for healing practices while also providing a connection to Pentecost in its close relation to Spirit baptism. After Saul had become blind at his encounter with the risen Jesus on the road to Damascus, he learned in a vision that he would regain his sight when a disciple of Christ, Ananias, would 'lay his hands on him' (Acts 9:12). Ananias indeed enters the

---

¹⁴ Georges Combet and Laureat Fabre, 'The Pentecostal Movement and the Gift of Healing', in *Experience of the Spirit*, ed. Peter Huizing and William Bassett (New York: Seabury, 1976), 106–10.
¹⁵ See Williams, *Spirit Cure*, 122–56; Gunther Brown, *Global Pentecostal and Charismatic Healing*, 29–126; Paul Gale Chappell, 'The Divine Healing Movement in America' (PhD diss., Drew University, 1983), 283–357.
¹⁶ Jansen and Lang, 'Transforming the Self', 547–50.
¹⁷ See Edmond Tang, '"Yellers" and Healers – Pentecostalism and the Study of Grassroots Pentecostalism in China', in *Asian and Pentecostal*, ed. Allan Anderson and Edmond Tang (Oxford: Regnum, 2005), 379–94.
¹⁸ See Ronald A. N. Kydd, *Healing through the Centuries: Models for Understanding* (Peabody: Hendrickson, 1998). The reliquarial model he also depicts is not characteristic of Pentecostals.
¹⁹ See Neil Hudson, 'Early British Pentecostals and Their Relationship to Health, Healing and Medicine', *AJPS* 6, no. 2 (2003): 283–301; Allan Anderson, 'Pentecostal Approaches to Faith and Healing', *IRM* 91, no. 363 (2002): 523–34.

house and lays hands on Saul, exclaiming that he had been sent by Jesus so that Saul may be healed and filled with the Spirit (v. 17). The text reports that Saul immediately regained his sight and was baptized (v. 18). The practice of healing through the use of hands is later seen at Paul's own ministry at Troas. After a long preaching in an upstairs room, a young man named Eutychus fell asleep and fell down from a third story window to his death (Acts 20:7-9). Paul, however, runs down to revive the young man, 'throws himself upon him' (v. 10) and in a dramatic extension of the impositions of hands, embracing him, the apostle brings the boy back to life.

These narratives identify the laying on of hands for Pentecostals first and foremost as a ritual for the baptism in the Spirit (see Chapter 4). Nevertheless, the significance attached to this ritual as a means of both sanctification and empowerment have led Pentecostals to extend its realm of influence, supported by a reading of other biblical texts. Mark 16:18, in particular, is widely understood as a mandate of those baptized in the Spirit that 'they will lay their hands on the sick, and they will recover'. The typical place for conducting this practice is at the altar or in the home of the sick, identified in James 5 as places where the elders of the church come together to pray (v. 14) and where believers pray for one another (v. 16).[20] While the imposition of hands does not differ in practice, whether intended for the baptism in the Spirit or for healing, the experience of healing, both in its giving and receiving, is directly identified with the transfer of divine power through the imposition of hands. The book of James connects this emphasis unmistakably with the 'prayer of faith' (Jas 5:15), which penetrates the entire healing ritual. At the same time, the touch is in itself anticipated as the 'remedy' where the Spirit of God engages the body of believers (individually and corporately) in the redemption and cleansing from sin and disease.[21]

In response to this reading, Pentecostals have established 'healing altars' and 'healing homes', often to replace or to supplement hospitals, and at revivals can be found 'healing rooms' dedicated to prayer and other ministries for

---

[20] Alexander, *Pentecostal Healing*, 82-84, 93.
[21] See Kimberly Ervin Alexander, '"How Wide Thy Healing Streams Are Spread": Constructing a Wesleyan Pentecostal Model for Healing for the Twenty-First Century', *ATJ* 59, no. 1/2 (2004): 63-76; Jonathan R. Baer, 'Redeemed Bodies: The Functions of Divine Healing in Incipient Pentecostalism', *CH* 70, no. 4 (2001): 735-71.

the sick.[22] Taking up the biblical mandate and carrying the healing power from the altar of the church to the homes of the sick and into the streets has caused an unprecedented expansion and transformation of altar rituals into public practices. In the diverse contexts of global Pentecostalism, the imposition of hands ranges from quick touches to long embraces to repeated and prolonged treatments, carried out by individuals to large groups, from healing evangelists and pastors to elders and entire congregations.[23] The physical touch to heal the sick is paradigmatic for the experience of the power of God. The touch is a physical extension and intensification of the prayer of faith; its importance is equaled only by an intensification of the human touch through the anointing with oil.

The centrality of Jas 5:14–16 has also directed Pentecostals to the use of anointing with oil. In response to James's rhetorical question, if any in the church are suffering and sick, the apostle instructs the congregation in the practice of an altar ritual constructed by the assembly of the elders, the prayer of faith, and the anointing 'with oil in the name of the Lord' (v. 14). Understood as a divine anointing or ointment with the Spirit, some Pentecostals substitute the use of oil for the use of medicine.[24] Typically applied not only on the skin, frequently on the forehead or hands and feet, but also directly on the place of pain and illness, and often supplemented by fragrance added to the oil, the anointing is a multisensory experience. The oil is applied gently with one or more fingers, never forceful or wasteful, as an expression of God's love and healing presence as well as of the Christian love for others.[25] The application of oil is seen as a gentle but penetrating exhibition of power and demonstration of the Spirit's anointing available to all Christians.[26]

---

[22] See Margaret M. Poloma, 'Old Wine, New Wineskins: The Rise of Healing Rooms in Revival Pentecostalism', *Pneuma* 28, no. 1 (2006): 59–71; Hardesty, *Faith Cure*, 56–71.

[23] See Pavel Hejzlar, *Two Paradigms for Divine Healing: Fred F. Bosworth, Kenneth E. Hagin, Agnes Sanford, and Francis MacNutt in Dialogue*, Global Pentecostal and Charismatic Studies 4 (Leiden: Brill, 2010), 41–72; Mark J. Cartledge, *Testimony on the Spirit: Rescripting Ordinary Pentecostal Theology* (Surrey, UK: Ashgate, 2010), 105–29; Matthew Marostica, 'Learning from the Master: Carlos Annacondia and the Standardization of Pentecostal Practices in and beyond Argentina', in Gunther Brown, *Global Pentecostal and Charismatic Healing*, 207–27; Michael Bergunder, 'Miracle Healing and Exorcism in South Indian Pentecostalism', ibid., 287–306.

[24] See Candy Gunther Brown, *Testing Prayer: Science and Healing* (Cambridge, MA: Harvard University Press, 2012), 71–74, 99–102; Warrington, 'The Path to Wholeness', 46–48; Synan, 'A Healer in the House', 197–98.

[25] See Mark J. Cartledge, 'Pentecostal Healing as an Expression of Godly Love: An Empirical Study', *MHRC* 16, no. 5 (2013): 501–22.

[26] Walter J. Hollenweger, *The Pentecostals: The Charismatic Movement in the Churches* (Minneapolis: Augsburg, 1972), 353–62.

Despite their physical intensity, Pentecostal healing practices do not exist as independent rituals. It is more accurate to speak of the prayer of faith, the laying on of hands and the anointing with oil as dimensions of a single ritual among Pentecostals. The interdependent nature of these practices, the belief that divine healing is available to all Christians, and the 'ordinary' nature of speaking, touching, and anointing have led to wide variations. Pentecostal healing practices echo the dynamics of the New Testament accounts of healing, including instances of carrying the sick into the path of the disciples, seeking healing in the shadow of the apostles and finding cure in a handkerchief or apron (see Acts 5:12–16; 14:8–18; 19:11–20). The diverse practices reflect a discernible sacramental character, embedded in the sacramentality of the baptism in the Spirit in the healing context of the altar.[27] However, while often practiced in literal interpretation of biblical healing narratives, Pentecostals have put few restrictions on practicing the healing power of Christ through the Spirit. Healing practices in the global movement can expand beyond the sacramental environment of the church and readily connect with indigenous religious identities and practices to form enculturated rituals departing from strict biblical or apostolic patterns.[28] Commercially available anointing oils have obtained an almost institutionalized character.[29] Handkerchiefs and cloths anointed with oil are sent to the sick as an extension of the healing ministry in the church.[30] Even devotional newspapers and magazines are laid on the sick and have been attributed to divine healing.[31] In many places, the materiality of healing includes not just bodily recuperation but remedies for unemployment, family disputes, racism, marital discord,

---

[27] See Kimberly E. Alexander, 'The Pentecostal Church: A Sacramental Healing Community', *ET* 41, no. 8 (2012): 1–3, 14.

[28] See Mark S. Clatterbuck, 'Healing Hills and Sacred Songs: Crow Pentecostalism, Anti-traditionalism, and Native Religious Identity', *Spiritus* 12, no. 2 (2012): 248–77; Kim Dongsoo, 'The Healing of Han in Korean Pentecostalism', *JPT* 15 (1999): 123–39; G. C. Oosthuizen et al. (eds), *Afro-Christian Religion and Healing in Southern Africa*, African Studies 8 (Lewiston, NY: The Edwin Mellen Press, 1989).

[29] J. Kwabena Asamoah-Gyadu, '"Unction to Function": Reinventing the Oil of Influence in African Pentecostalism', *JPT* 13, no. 2 (2005): 231–56.

[30] See John Christopher Thomas, 'Toward a Pentecostal Theology of Anointed Cloths', in *Toward a Pentecostal Theology of Worship*, ed. Lee Roy Martin (Cleveland, TN: CPT Press, 2016), 89–112; Katharine L. Wiegele, *Investing in Miracles: El Shaddai and the Transformation of Popular Catholicism in the Philippines* (Honolulu: University of Hawaii Press, 2005), 80–104, 142–69.

[31] See R. Marie Griffith, 'Female Suffering and Religious Devotion in American Pentecostalism', in *Women and Twentieth Century Protestantism*, ed. Margaret Lamberts Bendroth and Virginia Lieson Brereton (Urbana: University of Illinois Press, 2002), 184–208.

and other problems.³² Healing is sought as much for the human body as for the nation and the environment.³³ The path of healing from the altar to the people reflects the Pentecostal desire to revive the biblical understanding of healing as wholeness.³⁴ In the practices of divine healing, Pentecostal theology encounters not only its most intimate but also its most concrete manifestation as a global movement.

The doctrine of divine healing

The practices of divine healing, illustrated above with substantial variations and expansions, are indicative of the significant doctrinal debates that accompanied the rise of a global Pentecostal awakening. The doctrinal discussion confirms the perception that the varied soteriological practices among Pentecostals take them not only to the altar but beyond. The departure from the ecclesiastical haven of the altar has demanded a necessary realism of Pentecostal doctrine in order to situate divine healing in the unabated contexts of sin, sickness, suffering, and death – persistent opposition to divine healing that penetrates its doctrinal history. The fact that some are not healed has persuaded Pentecostals frequently to adjust their teachings in order to maintain the core belief in divine healing amidst the often devastating effects of wars, natural disasters, national epidemics, and personal tragedies.³⁵ This existential tension between expectation and experience colours the doctrine of divine healing from its Christological foundation to its pneumatological, ecclesiological, soteriological, and eschatological conclusions.

As with all motifs of the full gospel, Pentecostal theology affirms the divine initiative in all aspects of salvation. Healing and wholeness are the universal

---

[32] Harvey Cox, 'Healers and Ecologists: Pentecostalism in Africa', *The Christian Century* (9 November 1994), 1042–46.

[33] See Jill M. Wightman, 'Healing the Nation: Pentecostal Identity and Social Change in Bolivia', in *Conversion of a Continent: Contemporary Religious Change in Latin America*, ed. Timothy J. Steigenga and Edward L. Cleary (New Brunswick, NJ: Rutgers University Press, 2007), 239–55; Marthinus L. Daneel, *African Earthkeepers: Wholistic Interfaith Mission* (Maryknoll, NY: Orbis, 2001), 145–59.

[34] See Margaret M. Poloma and Lynette F. Hoelter, 'The "Toronto Blessing": A Holistic Model of Healing', *JSSR* 37 (1998): 257–72.

[35] See James Robinson, *Divine Healing: The Years of Expansion, 1906–1930. Theological Variation in the Transatlantic World* (Eugene, OR: Pickwick, 2014), 5–29, 39–68, 161–208; Donald Gee, *Trophimus I Left Sick: Our Problems with Divine Healing* (London: Elim, 1952).

will of God for all creation, even if not always experienced.[36] This existential divide between God's perfect will and the contrasting experience of continued sickness and suffering in the world is the result of the Fall. Consequently, sickness can be attributed to God, as a means of instruction, punishment, spreading the gospel, sanctification, salvation, and sign of the coming kingdom of God, or to the devil and demonic activity as an act of torment and oppression, as well as to individual circumstances and relational causes.[37] Sickness and disease are a result of the fallen human condition, which characterizes the state of creation until the fullness of redemption is achieved with the final realization of the kingdom of God. Divine healing signifies the contrast between God's will and the human condition; it is a remedy required for all of creation.

God's remedy for sickness and suffering is the atonement.[38] As a motif of the full gospel, healing is a possibility dependent on the grace of God made evident in the work of Christ.[39] The salvation of the soul and the redemption of the physical body are tied together in the death of Christ, who took upon himself human sin, sickness, and death.[40] God's will and initiative is evident in the life of Jesus who provides not only the paradigm for healing in his own ministry but whose death and resurrection also form the 'guarantee' of the continued promise of divine healing for the world.[41] Christ bridges the existential tension between God and creation in the struggle that leads to his own death and the victory over death in his resurrection. Pentecostals see themselves as participating in this twofold struggle. Still wrapped up in mortality, healing is a foretaste of the resurrection.[42]

The doctrine that divine healing is provided in the atonement is not a monolithic and naïve affirmation that faith in Jesus heals all who are sick. The teaching relies on the biblical affirmation that all who came to Jesus were healed (see Mt. 8:16; Lk. 6:19) and that the power of divine healing continued in the ministry of the church (Acts 5:16). Nonetheless, Pentecostals have

---

[36] Warrington, 'The Path to Wholeness', 45–46.
[37] Thomas, *Devil, Disease and Deliverance*, 292–93; Alexander, *Pentecostal Healing*, 75–76, 88–93.
[38] See Duffield and Van Cleave, *Foundations of Pentecostal Theology*, 388–92.
[39] Alexander, *Pentecostal Healing*, 76–78.
[40] Baer, 'Redeemed Bodies', 735–71.
[41] See Keith Warrington, 'The Role of Jesus as Presented in the Healing Praxis and Teaching of British Pentecostalism: A Re-Examination', *Pneuma* 25, no. 1 (2005): 66–92.
[42] Alexander, 'How Wide Thy Healing Streams', 66.

come to realize that Jesus's healings are not paradigmatic realizations but more anticipations of a new world order not yet fully realized.[43] God's sovereign will offers the hope and potential for the healing of all creation. The realization that some are not healed is evidence of the continued existential tension that remains in the world until the final reconciliation. Divine healing is available because of the death and resurrection of Jesus, and the atonement offers both a spiritual and physical transformation into the image of Christ, even though a life void of sickness and death may not yet be experienced in this world.[44] However, the weight of this necessary realism falls not on the continuing reality of sickness and disease but on the potential realization of healing and wholeness. Divine healing, although an eschatological promise, is embraced with unbridled optimism as a sign that the realization of that promise has already become a reality.

The focus on the atonement is both Christological and pneumatological. The experience of divine healing is ultimately rooted in the atonement, albeit indirectly as a consequence of Christ's death and resurrection.[45] The actualization of healing derived from Christ's atoning work is typically attributed to the present work of the Holy Spirit, frequently manifested in experiences of healing at the time of the baptism in the Spirit or to a more expansive work of sanctification.[46] In other words, while (and because) Christ is the anointed divine healer, Pentecostal healing is always an experience of the Spirit.[47]

The physical experience of healing is a tangible encounter, impartation, and anointing with the Holy Spirit, often manifested as a palpable force, an electrifying experience of the healing power of Christ.[48] The work of the Spirit manifests more tangibly the existential tension exposed by the confrontation of sickness and healing. The Spirit works most directly through weakness and suffering, at times, as a helping, comforting, interceding, and empowering

---

[43] See Keith Warrington, *Jesus the Healer: Paradigm or Phenomenon* (Carlisle: Paternoster, 2000), 1–29, 141–63.

[44] Robert P. Menzies, 'Healing in the Atonement', in *'Spirit and Power': Foundations of Pentecostal Experience*, ed. William W. Menzies and Robert P. Menzies (Grand Rapids, MI: Zondervan, 2000), 160–68.

[45] See David Petts, 'Healing and the Atonement' (PhD diss., University of Nottingham, 1993).

[46] Alexander, *Pentecostal Healing*, 78–79.

[47] See Margaret M. Poloma, 'Divine Healing, Religious Revivals, and Contemporary Pentecostalism: A North American Perspective', in *The Spirit in the World: Emerging Pentecostal Theologies in Global Contexts*, ed. Veli-Matti Kärkkäinen (Grand Rapids, MI: Eerdmans, 2009), 21–39.

[48] Williams, *Spirit Cure*, 48–54.

healer, at other times, to inspire and liberate amidst suffering and death.[49] Divine healing does not juxtapose a theology of the cross with a theology of glory, even though a Pentecostal theology based on both perspectives tends to interpret the former in light of the latter.[50] Healing as the Spirit's work expands beyond the physical into the spiritual world and vice versa – ranging from the conviction that sickness may be caused by personal neglect to the dramatic enactment of spirituality and healing rituals.

The pneumatological focus of divine healing in Pentecostal theology radiates a confrontational attitude that colours the existential tension in images reclaiming ancient spiritual values and biblical traditions of sickness and healing in terms of spiritual warfare. The Holy Spirit brings about God's purposes by engaging the believer's life in a holistic and relational fashion that focuses on physical illness only as a manifestation of larger spiritual concerns.[51] Divine healing is a confrontation with spiritual powers, whether perceived as a struggle with oneself, oppressive social and political structures, or demonic influence. The Holy Spirit is the power of God against these 'principalities and powers' (Eph. 6:12) which can be overcome because of the atoning work of Christ. Healing is therefore redemption experienced as deliverance, liberation, and exorcism taking place in a spiritual realm but manifested tangibly in the physical world.

Situated in the realm of spiritual warfare, divine healing occupies a central position in the Pentecostal worldview and functions as a universal metaphor for the concrete realization of redemption.[52] While this soteriological imagination may be applied to all motifs of the full gospel, the unique character of healing as a tangible experience of the divine power suggests for Pentecostals that salvation includes the physical world. This 'materiality' of salvation is an essential component of Pentecostal soteriology, which distinguishes it radically from classical Protestantism.[53] For Pentecostals, 'divine healing is divine

---

[49] See Keith Warrington, *Healing and Suffering: Biblical and Pastoral Reflections* (Milton Keynes, UK: Paternoster, 2005), 180–97; Mittelstadt, *The Spirit and Suffering in Luke-Acts*, 130–38.

[50] See Thomas Smail, 'The Cross and the Spirit: Toward a Theology of Renewal', in *The Love of Power and the Power of Love: A Careful Assessment of the Problems Within the Charismatic and Word-Of-Faith Movements*, ed. Thomas Smail, Andrew Walker, Nigel Wright (London: SPCK, 1993), 13–36.

[51] See Daiel Chiquete, 'Healing, Salvation and Mission: The Ministry of Healing in Latin American Pentecostalism', *IRM* 93, no. 370/371 (2004): 474–85.

[52] See Guy P. Duffield and Nathaniel M. Van Cleave, *Foundations of Pentecostal Theology* (Los Angeles: L.I.F.E. Bible College, 1983), 363–415.

[53] Miroslav Volf, 'Materiality of Salvation: An Investigation in the Soteriologies of Liberation and Pentecostal Theologies', *JES* 26, no. 3 (1989): 447–67.

life in the physical body'.[54] Salvation is the physical experience, at least in part, of Christ living in the mortal body of the believer (see Gal. 2:20) so that despite human mortality, the life of Jesus is already manifested in the body (2 Cor. 4:10–11).[55] Rather than interpreting these and other biblical texts (see also Isa. 53:5; 1 Cor. 6:19; 2 Cor. 6:15; Eph. 3:19, 5:30) in an exclusively spiritual sense, Pentecostal soteriology insists that the materiality of salvation is an eschatological reality already realized in the present life. As an eschatological realization, however, divine healing manifests the volatile nature of the present world, in which the kingdom of God is not yet fully realized. The realization of healing and salvation stands at war with the sinfulness, violence, corruption, and mortality of a fallen creation. The redemption of the world is not a sudden and abrupt event in a distant future, but the atonement has made possible that believers already 'are made partakers of the bodily nature of the kingdom of God'.[56] Salvation as praxis is not exclusively concerned with the healing of the soul but with the whole person, not only with the individual but with the healing of relationships, not with humankind alone but with the whole of creation. Divine healing is the realization of the divine life in the unity of material, physical, historical, sociopolitical, economic, cultural, and spiritual dimensions of the present world.

As a spiritual and material experience, divine healing is entrenched in personal, communal, and theological relationships. The goal of all healing is personal, spiritual, integrative, and holistic transformation that includes and transcends physical cure.[57] Hence, many Pentecostals resist purely biomedical approaches to health or reject medical science entirely.[58] As a divine cure, healing is experienced and expected first and foremost within the community of faith.[59] The rituals of divine healing show faith as an instrument of human

---

[54] Duffield and Van Cleave, *Foundations of Pentecostal Theology*, 403.
[55] Ibid., 404; Stanley M. Horton, *What the Bible Says about the Holy Spirit*, rev. ed. (Springfield, MO: Gospel Publishing House, 2005), 188–90.
[56] Earl P. Paulk Jr., *Your Pentecostal Neighbor* (Cleveland, TN: Pathway Press, 1958), 110.
[57] See Amos Yong, *Renewing Christian Theology: Systematics for a Global Christianity* (Waco, TX: Baylor University Press, 2014), 193–222.
[58] See Hudson, 'Early British Pentecostals', 294–97; R. Andrew Chesnut, 'Exorcising the Demons of Deprivation: Divine Healing and Conversion in Brazilian Pentecostalism', in Gunther Brown, *Global Pentecostal and Charismatic Healing*, 169–85; Catherine Bowler, 'Blessed Bodies: Healing within the African American Faith Movement', ibid., 81–105.
[59] See Nancy A. Hardesty, *Faith Cure: Divine Healing in the Holiness and Pentecostal Movements* (Peabody, MA: Hendrickson, 2003); Kimberly E. Alexander, 'The Pentecostal Healing Community', in *Toward a Pentecostal Ecclesiology: The Church and the Fivefold Gospel*, ed. John Christopher Thomas (Cleveland, TN: CPT Press, 2010): 183–206.

participation in the divine initiative. However, Pentecostals are divided over the theological significance of faith to obtain healing. While the so-called 'word of faith' movement within Pentecostalism interprets the 'principle of faith' in terms of the ability to claim one's own healing through 'positive confession', and thus blames the absence of healing on the absence or weakness of one's faith, other Pentecostals interpret faith as a gift of divine power to become channels of healing for others, making healing less dependent on one's own faith than on the promises of Scripture. Again, others emphasize the sovereign will of God and interpret faith as an essential trust in God, who desires healing for all in a universal sense even though healing may not always be realized in a particular situation.[60] Further integrative approaches understand faith as a virtue available to the Christian community, rather than a special gift to the individual, and thus requiring an environment of love in which healing may take place.[61] Similar interpretations emphasize the sacramental nature of healing, which occurs in the community of worship where faith in God's healing power is present.[62] Again, others see no strict relationship of cause and effect between faith and healing.[63] Rather, faith in healing is the same as faith that leads to salvation.[64] The divisions over the role of faith are primarily a result of overtly individualistic or anthropocentric interpretations of divine healing that neglect the role of relationships with God and others in the community of faith.

Pentecostal practices of divine healing both require the community and establish the community. They are forms of socialization at and beyond the altar and establish and integrate the individual in a network of relations with the church, society, and God.[65] These communal structures are transformative of the self and the community, empowering those who are suffering, establishing the oppressed as recipients and leaders of divine healing, and often causing a ripple effect of the experience and practices of healing beyond the original community.[66] In turn, divine healing as a communal praxis

---

[60] Cf. Henry H. Knight III, 'God's Faithfulness and God's Freedom: A Comparison of Contemporary Theologies of Healing', *JPT* 2 (1993): 65–89.
[61] Ibid., 78–82.
[62] Ibid., 82–83.
[63] See Ken Blue, *Authority to Heal* (Downers Grove, IL: Intervarsity, 1987), 78.
[64] David Yonggi Cho, *How Can I Be Healed?* (Seoul: Logos International, 1999), 71–74.
[65] See Cartledge, 'Pentecostal Healing', 506–7.
[66] Gunther Brown, 'Pentecostal Power', 40–52; Alexander, *Pentecostal Healing*, 240–41; Jansen and Lang, 'Transforming the Self', 544–50.

establishes the church also as a sociopolitical, economic, and environmental healer and liberator.[67] As a form of spiritual warfare, divine healing engages the spiritual communities of principalities and powers, devils and demons, as well as the divine community of God. Even if the full spectrum is not always realized among all Pentecostals, divine healing is empowerment for service and mission of the church in the world.[68] In this sense, divine healing forms a bridge across the existential tension towards the full realization of salvation.

The doctrine of divine healing critically questions any kind of anthropocentric and individualistic soteriology, healing focused on humanity alone, and irresponsible eschatology that ignores the redemption promised to the whole world.[69] From the outpouring of the Spirit at Pentecost emerges salvation as the possibility of divine healing for all of creation.[70] Responsible for the integrative and universal theology of divine healing among Pentecostals is its *Christological* grounding in the atonement, which brings redemption to all, its *pneumatological* orientation, which finds the Spirit as God's universal power of healing and salvation in the world, its *fideistic* centre, which allows for human participation in the divine healing, its *ecclesiological* framework, which identifies healing as the church's mission, and its *missiological* application, which seeks the entire creation as the harvest of God's salvation.[71] In the universal Pentecostal vision of realized redemption, Christ is the author and origin of salvation, healing, and restoration. The Holy Spirit is the shaper and sustainer of all habitable space, vivifying and transforming creation and its creatures in the image of Christ.[72] The church is the Spirit-filled worker of healing among the sick and dying creatures and structures of the world.[73] The Christian is a recipient and empowered catalyst of divine healing on behalf of the relationality and reciprocity of creation.[74] And creation is the realization

---

[67] Daneel, *African Earthkeepers*, 147–53.
[68] Alexander, *Pentecostal Healing*, 50–53.
[69] A. J. Swoboda, *Tongues and Trees: Toward a Pentecostal Ecological Theology*, JPTS 41 (Blandford Forum, UK: Deo, 2014), 27.
[70] See Howard A. Snyder and Joel Scandrett, *Salvation Means Creation Healed: The Ecology of Sin and Grace. Overcoming the Divorce between Earth and Heaven* (Eugene, OR: Wipf and Stock, 2011), 167–227.
[71] See John Wimber, *Power Healing* (London: Hodder & Stoughton, 1986), 292–93.
[72] Daneels, *African Earthkeepers*, 231–47; Clark H. Pinnock, *Flame of Love: A Theology of the Holy Spirit* (Downers Grove, IL: Intervarsity, 1996), 76–77.
[73] See Norberto Saracco, 'The Holy Spirit and the Church's Mission of Healing', *IRM* 93, no. 370/371 (2004): 412–13.
[74] See Joshua D. Reichard, 'Relational Empowerment: A Process-Relational Theology of the Spirit-filled Life', *Pneuma* 36, no. 2 (2014): 226–45.

of the purpose of divine healing as the manifestation of the gospel in signs and wonders.

Divine healing as signs and wonders of redemption

Pentecostal theology marks a rediscovery of signs and wonders in the late modern world.[75] While healing practices and rituals have endured throughout Christian history, it is only in modern-day Pentecostal theology that divine healing occupies a central soteriological, cosmological, and ecclesiological position. The Pentecostal doctrine of divine healing comes at the end of an era that began with the Protestant Reformers' condemnation of the cult of saints and their healing powers, the accompanying reformation of the sacerdotal system and its devaluation of the priestly role in healing rituals, continued with the politicization of healing and its prioritization of social and economic welfare throughout the modern era, the missionary rejection of native spiritual practices, and the emergence of new but isolated indigenous healing practices, and found its climax with the rise to dominance of the medical sciences, the flowering of scepticism, and the struggle between rationalism and supernaturalism.[76] At the end of this development, three dominant metaphysical claims can be said to shape the existing theological positions with regard to divine healing: supernaturalism, naturalism, and cessationism.

Unexplainable events of unexpected healing occupy by far the largest territory in documenting the miraculous throughout Christian history.[77] Divine healing, that is, any healing attributed to the direct action and intervention of God, traditionally occupies space in Christian teachings primarily in association with miracles. From this position, divine healing, unlike medical healing, is seen as 'a special or immediate act of God' often in contradistinction to 'God's continuous work of creating and sustaining the world'.[78] The unusual,

---

[75] Walter J. Hollenweger, *Pentecostalism: Origins and Developments Worldwide* (Peabody, MA: Hendrickson, 1997), 228–45.
[76] Cf. Colin Brown, 'Issues in the History of the Debates on Miracles', in *The Cambridge Companion to Miracles*, ed. Graham H. Twelftree (Cambridge: Cambridge University Press, 2011), 273–90; Porterfield, *Healing in the History of Christianity*, 93–158; Kelsey, *Healing and Christianity*, 200–42.
[77] See Jacalyn Duffin, *Medical Miracles: Doctors, Saints, and Healing in the Modern World* (Oxford: Oxford University Press, 2009), 71–111.
[78] Mark Corner, *Signs of God: Miracles and Their Interpretation* (Aldershot, UK: Ashgate, 2005), 15.

unexpected, yet observable and awe-inspiring, event of miraculous healing is typically seen as an exception and benevolent disruption of the laws of nature.[79] As miracle, to use Augustine's classic definition, the divine initiative constitutes 'whatever appears that is difficult or unusual above the hope and power of them who wonder'.[80] While Augustine suggests that miracles occur within the potentialities of creation and serve primarily the heuristic purpose to reawaken the wonder at the divine providence, he laments the fact that the rare and unusual typically identify the miraculous as something exceptional and supernatural.[81] This contrast reached its paradigmatic form with the argument of Thomas Aquinas, who defined miracles as events that surpass the power of nature and find in God their primary cause for the reason and the manner in which the miraculous occurs.[82] As a supernatural event, divine healing is a temporary manifestation of the true order of nature and of the divine as its transcendent cause and invisible sustenance. The presupposition for this position is not only a strict distinction between the natural world and the divine or supernatural but their existential division, which is bridged only in the exceptional event of the miracle. Miracles are entirely objects of faith.[83]

The difficulty to sustain the classic definition of miracles and its underlying metaphysical distinction between the natural and the supernatural became apparent only in the aftermath of the Enlightenment with its elevation of reason, rejection of the supernatural and the rise of critical methods. David Hume's critique of historical miracles exemplifies the rejection of supernaturalism and the rising dominance of evidential empiricism.[84] Within the emerging scientific worldview, theologians such as Friedrich Schleiermacher rejected the sharp distinction of the natural and supernatural as a basis for the definition of the miraculous and defined instead 'every finite thing' as 'a sign of the infinite' so that 'miracle is simply the religious name for event'.[85]

---

[79] David Basinger, 'What Is a Miracle?' in Twelftree, *The Cambrige Companion to Miracles*, 19–35.
[80] Augustine, *The Usefulness of Believing*, 34.
[81] Cf. Chris Gousmett, 'Creation Order and Miracle According to Augustine', *Evangelical Quarterly* 60 (July 1988): 217–40.
[82] Thomas Aquinas, *Summa Theologiae*, I, 105, 7; idem, *Against Faustus*, 26.3. Cf. Ralph Del Colle, 'Miracles in Christianity', in Twelftree, *The Cambridge Companion to Miracles*, 235–53.
[83] Cf. François Pouliot, *La doctrine du miracle chez Thomas d'Aquin: Deus in omnibus intime operator* (Paris: J. Vrin, 2005).
[84] David Hume, 'Of Miracles', Section X. *Enquiries Concerning Human Understanding and Concerning the Principles of Morals*, ed. L. A. Selby-Bigge and P. H. Nidditch, 3rd rev. ed. (Oxford: Oxford University Press, 1975).
[85] Friedrich Schleiermacher, *On Religion: Speeches to Its Cultural Despisers*, trans. John Oman(New York: Harper and Row, 1958), 88.

Rejecting transcendent and supernatural phenomena, naturalism identifies divine healing not in contrast to but in conjunction with the laws of nature.[86] The naturalist definition restored the discrepancy between the notion of miracle as extraordinary divine activity and the often neglected divine sustaining of creation attributed to each day that allowed for divine agency amidst a scientific account of nature.[87] However, with Schleiermacher's dominant account at the entrance to theological appropriations of the Newtonian worldview, the miraculous as event now became located in the subjectivity of religious feeling.[88] Along the naturalist line of thought, divine healing is miraculous in the shift of attitude and condition of the observer towards any event, so that any event can be considered miraculous. In the theological position of naturalism, nature does not point beyond itself to the supernatural, at best, because no such transcendent reality is necessary to explain an event, and at worst, because no such reality is believed to exist. The subjectivity of religious feeling tries to rescue the existential division between natural and supernatural from collapsing either into a deism that denies the divine involvement in the natural world or into a pantheism that knows no such distinction in the first place.

The mounting tension between modernist tendencies and religious enthusiasts eventually brought forth a third position, which accepts the authenticity of biblical miracles while rejecting their continuing possibility. Cessationism retains the distinction between the natural and supernatural, albeit confined to the biblical and apostolic world. Benjamin Warfield's important twentieth-century polemic against postbiblical miracles defined the miraculous as 'specifically an effect in the external world, produced by the immediate efficiency of God'.[89] Warfield thus returned to the idea of miracles as external, supernatural events caused by direct divine agency, albeit at the cost of denying that such events continue to exist beyond the realm of the New Testament.[90] Divine

---

[86] Stewart Goetz and Charles Taliaferro, *Naturalism* (Grand Rapids, MI: Eerdmans, 2008), 7–8.
[87] See Wolfgang Vondey, 'Spirit and Nature: Pentecostal Pneumatology in Dialogue with Tillich's Pneumatological Ontology', in *Paul Tillich and Pentecostal Theology: Spiritual Presence and Spiritual Power*, ed. Nimi Wariboko and Amos Yong (Bloomington: Indiana University Press, 2015), 30–44.
[88] Richards, 'The Nature of Miracle', 260–321.
[89] Benjamin B. Warfield, 'The Question of Miracle', in *Selected Shorter Writings of Benjamin B. Warfield*, vol. 2, ed. John E. Meeter (Phillipsburg: Presbyterian and Reformed, 1973), 167–204 (170).
[90] See Jon Ruthven, *On the Cessation of the Charismata: The Protestant Polemic on Postbiblical Miracles*, JPTS 3 (Sheffield: Sheffield Academic Press, 1993), 41–111.

healing as miracle holds an exclusively evidentialist purpose realized in their sole function to accredit revelation recorded in Scripture and thus confined to the biblical times. Warfield rejected divine healing on the grounds that no evidence exists for the immediate, transcendent, and complete efficacy of postapostolic miraculous charismata.[91] The moderate cessationist allows in principle for divine healing by adopting the classical supernatural worldview yet truncates that view by disallowing for the continued operation of such divine activity today.[92] The strong cessationist rejects with the possibility of miracles also the possibility of all charismatic activity in the history of the church.[93]

Pentecostal theology of divine healing contrasts with these admittedly superficial projections of dominant metaphysical claims. First, Pentecostal theology cannot be cessationist since a Pentecostal hermeneutic depends on the continuing, extending, or repeating possibility of Pentecost throughout the history of the church. More than a historical event, Pentecost is the metaphysical claim for a pneumatological soteriology in which conversion, sanctification, Spirit baptism, divine healing, and glorification become metaphors for the work of the Holy Spirit in Christian salvation.[94] Pneumatology leads Pentecostal theology beyond the dualism of natural and supernatural, biblical and historical, church and creation by way of the charismatic manifestations of the Holy Spirit. Cessationism not only devalues the gifts of the Spirit but demythologizes the existence of the spiritual world and the power of the demonic, sin, and sickness.[95] In contrast, divine healing emphasizes the reality of spiritual warfare, collapsed by cessationism, in which the physical and spiritual ruin of the world since the Fall and under the dominion of the demonic is displaced by the kingdom of God.[96] The Pentecostal insistence on divine healing is therefore eschatological in nature since the full redemption of creation has not yet been realized. The denial of spiritual warfare allows only for a static supernaturalism or for a naturalism disconnecting the divine

---

[91] Benjamin B. Warfield, *Counterfeit Miracles* (New York: Charles Scribners' Sons, 1918), 185–88.
[92] See Richard B. Gaffin, 'A Cessationist View', in *Are Miraculous Gifts for Today: Four Views* (Grand Rapids, MI: Zondervan, 1996), 25–64.
[93] See John F. McArthur, *Strange Fire: The Danger of Offending the Holy Spirit with Counterfeit Worship* (Nashville, TN: Thomas Nelson, 2013), 155–78.
[94] Yong, *The Spirit Poured Out on All Flesh*, 91–109.
[95] Ruthven, *On the Cessation of the Charismata*, 88.
[96] Ibid., 80, 116.

from the reality of evil and sickness and thus from the existential struggle of creation.

Second, a Pentecostal theology of divine healing cannot embrace naturalism, since the dominant altar hermeneutic of Pentecostal thought always requires an interpretation of creation in terms of its dependence on the divine. Divine healing is seen as participation of this world of sickness and death in that world of wholeness and life. The eschatological nature of divine healing exhibits an existential tension in Pentecostal metaphysics between a 'this-is-that' and a 'this-is-not-that' hermeneutic (see Chapter 1). The former realizes that this present creation is always also participation in the divine reality, while the latter demands that there cannot yet exist a complete identity. Sickness and death are signs of a world not yet redeemed (this-is-not-that), while healing is a sign of the redemption already manifested in the physical realm (this-is-that). In the sacramental reality established by the outpouring of the Holy Spirit, and realized in the Pentecostal experience of Spirit baptism, divine healing occupies a participatory character in both worlds, nature and the divine. Naturalism collapses the distance between both worlds.[97] Pentecostals, however, reject a metaphysical naturalism because it does not allow for the meeting of the human and the divine, restricting all events to the physical universe; and they reject a methodological naturalism as long as it operates on the assumption that even if the supernatural exists, it cannot be manifested in the natural world.[98] Instead, within the pneumatological soteriology of Pentecostalism, divine healing is natural only insofar as nature is imbued with the Spirit of God. This means that an affirmation of divine healing as a natural event not only cannot exclude the Holy Spirit, but that such affirmation depends on the interpretation of the event via 'both the dynamic presence of the Spirit in creation and a nondualistic emphasis on bodily healing'.[99] Divine healing is possible because nature is inhabited by the Spirit, and the Pentecostal practices of faith, anointing and laying on of hands are therefore efficacious as actions of the Spirit of God.

---

[97] See Paul Tillich, *Systematic Theology*, vol. 2, *Existence and the Christ* (Chicago: University of Chicago Press, 1957), 7.

[98] See James K. A. Smith, 'Is There Room for Surprise in the Natural World? Naturalism, the Supernatural, and Pentecostal Spirituality', in *Science and the Spirit: A Pentecostal Engagement with the Sciences* (Bloomington: Indiana University Press, 2010), 34–49.

[99] James K. A. Smith, *Thinking in Tongues: Pentecostal Contributions to Christian Philosophy*, PM 1 (Grand Rapids: Eerdmans, 2010), 104.

Third, Pentecostal theology does not support a strict supernatural worldview, although a miraculous supernaturalism is often expressed in popular Pentecostal language.[100] Pentecostals reject a strict supernaturalism from above that casts a model of creation and the divine as two parallel worlds, restricting God's creative activity to the beginning of the created order and identifying God's continuing activity as anomalous, miraculous events.[101] Nature is here portrayed as causally open to the supernatural activity of God even though we lack any predictive analogical conception of such sporadic interaction.[102] The value of divine healing from such a perspective, however, is purely evidential and excludes the expectation in advance of the probability that God will intervene with certainty.[103] In contrast, Pentecostals understand divine healing as a material dimension of salvation manifesting participation in the redeemed life (see Chapter 2). Pentecostal theology exhibits more of a supernaturalism from below, embedded in the materiality of salvation, which demands that all participation in the divine life is a form of sanctification (see Chapter 3) manifested in actual practices of transformation. Within the sacramental reality created by the outpouring of the Holy Spirit at Pentecost and expressed in the doctrine of Spirit baptism (see Chapter 4), divine healing is an eschatological manifestation of the real struggle for the union of God and creation. Healing is not an anomalous event breaking the causal chain of the laws of nature but a consistent sign and wonder manifesting the struggle for the end of the artificial division of the supernatural and the natural in the realization of the union of God and creation.

Signs and wonders are meaningful charismatic experiences of the Spirit of God at work in the world that bear witness to the messy and risky reality of redemption. A Pentecostal metaphysic depends on the pneumatological claim that the Spirit bridges the immanent physical and fallen world and the redemptive reality of the transcendent divine in the experience of suffering. This pneumatology is eminently charismatic, that is, pragmatic and material,

---

[100] Smith, *Thinking in Tongues*, 97–98.
[101] Tillich, *Systematic Theology*, vol. 3, 6. See Louis Hoffman and Katherine McGuire, 'Are Miracles Essential or Peripheral to Faith Traditions?' in *Miracles: God, Science, and Psychology in the Paranormal*, vol. 1, *Religious and Spiritual Events*, ed. J. Harold Ellens (Westport, CT: Praeger, 2008), 221–40.
[102] See Corner, *The Philosophy of Miracles*, 40–78.
[103] Cf. R. Douglas Geivett, 'The Evidential Value of Miracles', in *In Defense of Miracles: A Comprehensive Case for God's Action in History*, ed. R. Douglas Geivett and Gary B. Habermas (Downers Grove, IL: Intervarsity, 1997), 178–95.

so that 'the Spirit is at work not only in the fantastic and miraculous but also in the mundane and regular'.[104] Divine healing as a charismatic manifestation of the Spirit represents the possible union of nature and spirit.[105] Healing and other charismatic experiences reject the artificial separation of the natural and the spiritual as fundamentally opposite principles of reality.[106] The realism of Pentecostal doctrine remains hesitant to collapse the supernatural entirely into nature. The partial realization of the charismatic life, including the possible absence of divine healing, shows that the union of nature and spirit as such remains in eschatological tension.

The connotation of divine healing as 'sign' underscores the difficulty of the material realization of salvation amidst the inability of finite creation to create the presence of the infinite; it signifies, in traditional terms, the dependence of nature on grace. The practices of divine healing confront the ambiguities of life from within the union of nature and spirit by bringing to light the reality of spiritual warfare manifesting the charismatic dimension of the struggle for healing, deliverance, and wholeness.[107] The confrontation of the charismatic and the demonic constitutes a central feature of Pentecostal worldview and cosmology.[108] This confrontation represents the most concrete manifestation of the uneasy union of nature and spirit and its struggle towards identification with the divine. Here, the union is most intimate and volatile. Without the realization of spiritual warfare, the Christian gospel is romanticized, at best, and incomplete, at worst.

Divine healing as an element of the full gospel is a sign of struggle; its slogan is 'all things are possible' amidst the persistent reality of sickness, disability, despair, and death.[109] Pentecostals can acknowledge the 'dark side' of a healing theology that continues to operate on the distinction of the miraculous and the supernatural.[110] In its place, healing – realized or not – is a testimony to the

---

[104] Smith, 'Is There Room for Surprise', 44.
[105] Vondey, 'Spirit and Nature', 39–41.
[106] See Walter J. Hollenweger, '*Creator Spiritus*: The Challenge of Pentecostal Experience to Pentecostal Theology', *Theology* 81, no. 1 (1978): 32–40.
[107] Wolfgang Vondey, *Pentecostalism: A Guide for the Perplexed* (London: Bloomsbury, 2013), 29–47.
[108] See Opoku Onyinah, *Spiritual Warfare: A Centre for Pentecostal Theology Short Introduction* (Cleveland, TN: CPT Press, 2012).
[109] See Jörg Stolz, '"All Things Are Possible": Towards a Sociological Explanation of Pentecostal Miracles and Healings', *SR* 72, no. 4 (2011): 456–82.
[110] Shane Clifton, 'The Dark Side of Prayer for Healing: Toward a Theology of Well-Being', *Pneuma* 36, no. 2 (2014): 204–25.

permanence of suffering as an expression of the spiritual war waging between sickness and health, sin and salvation, good and evil, Satan and God.[111] Yet, this emphasis should not lead to a conflation of sin and disease or disability or to the idea of virtuous suffering.[112] By spiritualizing disease and disability, the physical reality and persistence of suffering is disconnected from Christian soteriology, which forms the framework for understanding the reality of such suffering. Natural, irreversible, and collective causes of suffering may lie beyond the social, political, or economic power of individuals and their faith.[113] Such a theology legitimizes an ideology of healing that is blind to the oppressive and marginalized experiences of those not healed.[114] A Pentecostal theology of divine healing is therefore also concerned with human suffering outside the experience of spiritual warfare in order to integrate all such experiences in the redemptive community of faith. Divine healing then embraces not only the possibility of the transformation of the sick into the healed but also the transformation of the entire community of redemption, which includes those with continuing sicknesses and unaltered disabilities.[115] Divine healing is not an exceptional performance of God wrought to the world and the individual from the outside – the miracle is the consistent healing of the world from the inside. The signs and wonders of divine healing are the transformations of the sick, the suffering, and the dying into the community of the redeemed.

Divine healing alerts Pentecostal theology to the existential challenges of living out the charismatic reality of the sacramental life that was introduced with the baptism in the Spirit. If signs and wonders accompany the rediscovery of primal piety and spirituality in Pentecostalism, recalling the foundations of human religiosity and forming a kind of universal grammar and syntax,[116] then such universal grammar develops only in the church as a communion of the shared struggle for redemption.[117] Healing is as much

---

[111] See Steven M. Fettke and Michael L. Dusing, 'A Practical Pentecostal Theodicy? A Proposal', *Pneuma* 38, no. 2 (2016): 160–79.

[112] Nancy L. Eiesland, *The Disabled God: Toward a Liberation Theology of Disability* (Nashville, TN: Abingdon, 1994), 70–75.

[113] See Arlene Sanchez Walsh, 'Santidad, Salvación, Sanidad, Liberación: The Word of Faith Movement among Twenty-First-Century Latina/o Pentecostals', in Gunther Brown, *Global Pentecostal and Charismatic Healing*, 151–68.

[114] Cf. Amos Yong, 'Many Tongues, Many Senses: Pentecost, the Body Politic, and the Redemption of Dis/Ability', *Pneuma* 31, no. 2 (2009): 167–88.

[115] Ibid., 177.

[116] Cox, *Fire from Heaven*, 82, 99–110.

[117] Eiesland, *The Disabled God*, 108–11.

based in the atonement as it is in search of atonement.[118] The realization of divine healing reminds us that the sacramentality of the spiritual life cannot be realized as an abstract worldview but only through participation of the community in the physicality of brokenness.[119] With divine healing, the church faces its innermost identity as the body of Christ connecting salvation to both body and soul, nature and spirit, individual and community, creation and the kingdom of God.

---

[118] See Randall Holm, 'Healing in Search of Atonement', *JPT* 23 (2014): 50–67.
[119] Ibid., 111–18; Alexander, 'The Pentecostal Healing Community', 197–202.

6

Commissioned

Enacting the Coming Kingdom

Pentecostal theology has been presented thus far as giving expression to Pentecost as theological symbol pursued through the lens of the full gospel and its identification of Jesus Christ as saviour, sanctifier, Spirit baptizer, and healer. This chapter complements those themes with the eschatological emphasis the full gospel places on Jesus as the soon-coming King. The proverbial Pentecostal testimony to being saved, sanctified, filled with the Holy Spirit, healed, and delivered typically ends with an exclamation of being part of the church and on the way to heaven.[1] However, despite its placement in the full gospel, such eschatological sentiment does not mark the completion or 'end' of Pentecostal theology. The expectation of being 'on the way', cast in the shadow of the imminent return of Christ, expresses for Pentecostals not merely a sojourning of Christians towards glory but a commissioning of the church into the world. Rather, the image of Pentecost suggests that the 'way to glory' is marked by the continuing experiences of salvation, sanctification, Spirit baptism, and divine healing. Eschatology functions as an integrating theme that returns Pentecostal theology to its central concerns, albeit transformed by an apocalyptic urgency. The apocalyptic expectation of the inbreaking of the kingdom of God already manifested in the outpouring of the Holy Spirit stands as an icon of Pentecostal theology that permeates the reading and practices of the other gospel motifs. The events of Pentecost represent the eschatological

---

[1] Steven J. Land, *Pentecostal Spirituality: A Passion for the Kingdom*, JPTS 1 (Sheffield: Sheffield Academic Press, 1993), 80–81.

centrepiece for the proclamation of the full gospel to the gathering of all creation in the kingdom of God.

Pentecostal theology finds in an overabundant apocalyptic imagination its most playful vitality. Eschatology reshapes Pentecostal theology in its orientation from and return to practices that characterize the Pentecostal gospel narrative and its doctrinal articulation. The metaphor of the altar, used throughout the previous chapters to demonstrate the dynamic of experience-reflection-practice-transformation characteristic of Pentecostal theology, finds in the eschatological motif its recurring energy. To illustrate this theme, the first part of this chapter identifies particular eschatological practices among Pentecostals and demonstrates that eschatology does not originate from a purely doctrinal mindset but from pragmatic concerns for church and mission. The second part offers an analysis of dominant doctrinal conversations among Pentecostals on eschatology and identifies the changes and challenges of apocalyptic eschatology in the history of Pentecostal theology. In the final part, the discussion turns to an ecumenical conversation on eschatological practices and the role of an apocalyptic vision for Pentecostal theology today.

Eschatology at the altar

It may be expected that eschatology is a doctrinal and propositional mindset farthest removed from the practices at the altar. In the scheme of the full gospel, laid out in previous chapters, the altar represents a metaphor for the Pentecostal way of salvation, narrating the response to a call from God (conversion), a tarrying in the presence of God (sanctification), leading to an encounter with God (Spirit baptism), and a transformation to leave the altar (healing). Eschatology in this theme may appear as the far distant goal of the altar call and response towards which all Pentecostal practices aim. However, such a scenario would be a misinterpretation of the full-gospel motif as if it represented a fixed order of elements that always resolve in an end-time scenario. Moreover, such a misinterpretation neglects the importance of practices for all Pentecostal theology by relegating eschatology to a mere belief system or a particularly hermeneutic of history. While there is an intentionality in the narrative of the full gospel of Christ from saviour to coming king, the playfulness of Pentecostal theology finds in its eschatological focus a constant way of return to the elements of the full gospel without losing itself in the idea of having comprehended or resolved the fate of the world through articulating a 'final' doctrinal proposition. An apocalyptic emphasis on the imminent return of Christ always projects Pentecostal theology back onto itself in critical reflection: eschatology not only draws Pentecostals from the altar to the ends of the earth but urges them to return to the altar for the signs and wonders of salvation, sanctification, Spirit baptism, and divine healing. Pentecostal eschatology culminates in an apocalyptic mandate to go and seek the lost, to proclaim the kingdom of God, and to bring the world to the altar.

The biblical narrative of the day of Pentecost forms the image par excellence for Pentecostal eschatology. Early classical Pentecostalism understood itself as an eschatological movement, and through the lens of the outpouring of the Holy Spirit (see Acts 2:1–22) used a variety of eschatological models to identify itself, such as the 'apostolic faith', the 'everlasting gospel', and 'the latter rain'.[2] The latter rain teaching, in particular, functions as a theological interpretation of biblical imagery (rather than purely hermeneutical assessments of history). This imagery correlates the narrative of Pentecost not only with the prophecy of Joel that 'in the last days' God would pour out the Holy Spirit on all flesh (Joel 2:28; Acts 2:16–18) but also with the experiences of modern-day Pentecostals. Whereas the apostle Peter explicitly identified the day of Pentecost as the fulfilment of Joel's prophecy, Pentecostals also see in the day of Pentecost a future promise that God 'will pour out' the Spirit 'on all flesh' (Acts 2:17). With the idea of two raining seasons in Palestine, the former and the latter rain, Pentecostals are able to identify the day of Pentecost as the former rain and the contemporary Pentecostal movement as the latter rain recipient of the biblical promises: Pentecostalism is the eschatological fulfilment of the outpouring of the Holy Spirit on all flesh.[3] The latter rain teaching culminates in the idea of a revival, return to, or final completion of the day of Pentecost in the present

---

[2] D. William Faupel, 'The Function of "Models" in the Interpretation of Pentecostal Thought', *Pneuma* 2, no. 1 (1980): 51–71.
[3] See David Wesley Myland, *The Latter Rain Covenant and Pentecostal Power* (Chicago: The Evangel Publishing House, 1910); Charles F. Parham, 'The Latter Rain: The Story of the Origin of the Original Apostolic or Pentecostal Movements', *AF* 2, no. 7 (1926): 5–6.

age of the church, manifested by the Pentecostal movement. Foundational for this eschatological correlation is the identification of experiences and practices introduced to the apostolic church with the day of Pentecost and revived in modern-day Pentecostalism.

Pentecostals find their primary eschatological practices within the biblical narratives surrounding the day of Pentecost and its impact on the apostolic community. It is the belief that these practices form the latter rain completion of Pentecost that 'gives coherence to the Pentecostal testimony, practice and affections'.[4] The opening of the book of Acts weaves together the continuing concern of the disciples for the coming of God's kingdom, which dominated Jesus's teaching in Luke's Gospel, and Jesus's announcement of the gift of the Holy Spirit (Acts 1:6–8).[5] Jesus weds the eschatological concerns for the kingdom and the Spirit by explaining the religious and sociopolitical implications of the coming kingdom through the announcement that the disciples would receive power through the Holy Spirit and become 'witnesses in Jerusalem, in all Judea and Samaria and to the ends of the earth' (1:8). These instructions hearken back to the commissioning of the disciples in the Gospel to proclaim 'repentance and forgiveness of sins ... to all nations' and to be 'witnesses of these things' after the disciples would receive the Holy Spirit and be 'clothed with power from on high' (Lk. 4:44–49). From this context emerges a fundamentally praxis-oriented eschatology based on a pneumatological framework for Pentecostal ecclesiology and mission in the Spirit.

The pneumatological lens of reading the eschatological narratives of Luke-Acts through the work of God's Spirit forms the foundation for Pentecostal eschatology and missiology, two interwoven aspects of Pentecostal theology that should not be separated.[6] The primary metaphor for this eschato-missiological focus is the notion of power, personified

---

[4] Land, *Pentecostal Spirituality*, 54.
[5] Blaine Charette, 'Restoring the Kingdom to Israel: Kingdom and Spirit in Luke's Thought', in *Perspectives in Pentecostal Eschatologies: World without End*, ed. Peter Althouse and Robby Waddell (Cambridge, UK: James Clark and Co., 2010), 49–60.
[6] See Julie Ma, 'Eschatology and Mission: Living in the "Last Days" Today', *Transformation* 26, no. 3 (2009): 186–98; Byron Klaus, 'The Holy Spirit and Mission in Eschatological Perspective: A Pentecostal Viewpoint', *Pneuma* 27, no. 2 (2005): 322–42; Dale M. Coulter, 'Pentecostal Visions of the End: Eschatology, Ecclesiology and the Fascination with the Left Behind Series', *JPT* 14, no. 1 (2005): 81–98; Veli-Matti Kärkkäinen, 'Mission, Spirit and Eschatology: An Outline of a Pentecostal-Charismatic Theology of Mission', *MS* 16, no. 1 (1999): 73–94; Andrew M. Lord, 'Mission Eschatology: A Framework for Mission in the Spirit', *JPT* 11 (1997): 111–23.

in the Holy Spirit and manifested in the charismatic gifts given to the church at Pentecost. The eschatological practices among Pentecostals are seen as the result of both the community-forming power of the Spirit and the empowerment for witness.[7] The full gospel narrates this metaphor of power in terms of the different experiences of salvation, sanctification, Spirit baptism, and divine healing. At the risk of oversimplification, the practices of the full gospel inform and are informed by a reading of the Great Commission in the biblical texts through an ecclesio-missiological hermeneutic of empowerment.[8]

Through the lens of the Great Commission, Mk 16:14-18 urges Pentecostals to "go into all the world and proclaim the good news to the whole creation" and points to practices of water baptism, exorcism, speaking in tongues, and divine healing (including, for some Pentecostals, the reference to picking up snakes without harm).[9] The commission in Mt. 28:16-20 identifies the command to go into the world through the primary actions of baptism and teaching, followed by the promise of Jesus's continuous presence.[10] In Jn 20:19-23, the disciples are sent into the world after receiving the Holy Spirit with the authority to forgive sins and to withhold forgiveness.[11] Pentecostals therefore understand the reception of the Holy Spirit as a foundational eschatological experience: salvation, sanctification, Spirit baptism, healing, and transformation by the Spirit are the presuppositions for the creation of the church and its empowerment for mission. The narrative of the day of Pentecost illustrates the eschatological consequences of experiencing the outpouring of the Spirit through a mix of ecclesiological and missiological practices: proclamation of the gospel, speaking in

---

[7] See Matthias Wenk, *Community-Forming Power: The Socio-Ethical Role of the Spirit in Luke-Acts*, JPTS 19 (Sheffield: Sheffield Academic Press, 2000); Max Turner, *Power from on High: The Spirit in Israel's Restoration and Witness in Luke-Acts*, JPTS 9 (Sheffield: Sheffield Academic Press, 1996); Robert P. Menzies, *Empowerment for Witness: The Spirit in Luke-Acts*, JPTS 6 (Sheffield: Sheffield Academic Press, 1994).

[8] See Ulrich Luz, 'Empowerment and Commission in the New Testament', *JEPTA* 26, no. 1 (2006): 49–62; Gordon D. Fee, 'The Kingdom of God and the Church's Global Mission', in *Called and Empowered: Global Mission in Pentecostal Perspective*, ed. Murray W. Dempster et al. (Peabody, MA: Hendrickson, 1991), 7–21.

[9] See Ralph W. Hood Jr. and W. Paul Williamson, *Them That Believe: The Power and Meaning of the Christian Serpent-Handling Tradition* (Berkeley: University of California Press, 2008), 1–12.

[10] See Craig S. Keener, 'Matthew's Missiology: Making Disciples of the Nations (Matthew 28:19–20)', *AJPS* 12, no. 1 (2009): 3–20.

[11] Craig S. Keener, 'Sent Like Jesus: Johannine Missiology (John 20:21–22)', *AJPS* 12, no. 1 (2009): 21–45.

tongues, water baptism, teaching and fellowship, breaking of bread, prayer, sharing and distribution of possessions, wonders and signs, and the praise of God (see Acts 2:41–47). The eschatological promises of God are fulfilled in a mission-initiated church on the day of Pentecost that anticipates the growth of the church to the ends of the earth (v.47).

This broad characterization of Pentecostal reading of the biblical texts suggests that eschatological practices are in principle any practices acted out by the church for its mission to transform the world. These practices are also always experiences at the altar, although few of them happen at a physical altar in an ecclesiastical environment. Moreover, the outpouring of the Holy Spirit grasps Pentecostals with an apocalyptic vision of the presence, power, and person of Christ that demands 'taking the altar' to the ends of the earth (in the spatial and temporal sense). It is this apocalyptic urgency that transforms ecclesial practices into eschatological ones. Pentecostals see themselves as agents of witness and worship in 'a missionary fellowship where testimonies [are] given constantly in order to develop in the hearers the virtues, expectancy, attitudes, and experiences of those testifying'.[12] The practices of this eschatological fellowship are organized along any of the central experiences of the full gospel at the altar, albeit now realized as an aspect of the imminent fullness of the kingdom of God.

In the ecclesio-missiological framework of Pentecostals, to experience *salvation* eschatologically among Pentecostals means 'an entry into the training program of a missionary fellowship'[13] where one's life is reordered and redirected by the Spirit in radical discontinuity from and as a testimony to the world. The eschatological experience of *sanctification* means a radical break and transformation of the person from a life of the flesh to a life in the Spirit as a testimony to a Christ-like standard of living.[14] The eschatological experience of the *baptism in the Spirit* means a radical equipping of the Christian as witness to the lost and spiritual battle with the enemies of God as a testimony to empowered and anointed service.[15] The eschatological experience of *divine healing* means a radical experience of encounter with the coming

[12] Land, *Pentecostal Spirituality*, 80.
[13] Ibid., 82.
[14] Ibid., 88–90.
[15] Ibid., 91–93.

Christ already manifested in the physical life of believers as a testimony to the presence of the kingdom.

These and other experiences of the full gospel, demonstrating an expectation of imminent fulfilment of the kingdom of God, reshape the practices of the church into eschatological actions that serve as signs, confirmations, and celebrations of the power and legitimacy of those experiences. Many of these practices appear in other Christian traditions, since they are in principle ecclesio-missiological actions, but the difference among Pentecostals is their 'eschatological intensification'[16] manifested in the apocalyptic urgency, anticipation, and manifestations of the outpouring of the Spirit. The gifts of the Spirit radically distinguish Pentecostal eschatology from other traditions, above all the dramatic oral gifts of speaking with tongues, prophecy, words of knowledge and wisdom, teaching, exhortation, and interpretation of tongues.[17] The global South emphasizes further the role of exorcism, deliverance ministries, and other power encounters involving spiritual warfare – warfare prayer, warfare tongues, and intercession, all done with a sense of apocalyptic urgency.[18] These eschatological gifts and activities identify the most significant eschato-missiological experiences of the apostolic church revived in the Pentecostal movement.

Eschatological practices have experienced a shift during the twentieth century with regard to the interpretation, application, and intensity of spiritual gifts and their situatedness in an apocalyptic frame of reference. Early Pentecostals interpreted the revival of charismatic gifts as missiological tools of an apocalyptic movement, confirmed by worldwide testimonies of the ability to speak in an unlearned foreign language (*xenolalia*). Convinced of the power of 'missionary tongues' and the ability to speak the languages of the nations, Pentecostals quickly set off on foreign missions to bring the gospel to the lost before the imminent return of Christ in judgement.[19] What

---

[16] Ibid., 94.
[17] Robert P. Menzies, 'The Role of Glossolalia in Luke-Acts', *AJPS* 15, no. 1 (2012): 47–72. Cf. Scott Ellington, '"Can I Get a Witness": The Myth of Pentecostal Orality and the Process of Traditioning in the Psalms', *JPT* 20, no. 1 (2011): 54–67.
[18] See Opoku Onyinah, *Pentecostal Exorcism: Witchcraft and Demonology in Ghana*, JPTS 34 (Blandford Forum, UK: Deo, 2011); Candy Gunther Brown (ed.), *Global Pentecostal and Charismatic Healing* (Oxford: Oxford University Press, 2011).
[19] See Gary B. McGee, *Miracles, Missions, and American Pentecostalism*, American Society of Missiology 45 (Maryknoll, NY: Orbis, 2010), 61–76; Allan Anderson, *Spreading Fire: The Missionary Nature of Early Pentecostalism* (Maryknoll, NY: Orbis, 2007), 40–45, 57–64.

Pentecostals had learned at the altars of the church was carried under the influence of an apocalyptic vision into the world in order to bring the nations before the altar of God. With the changes of apocalyptic urgency during the twentieth century, particularly in the West and challenged by the global South, Pentecostal eschato-missiological practices have shifted from evangelization to social action.[20] While for some Pentecostal groups, the apocalyptic urgency of a world facing judgement remains the motivation for eschatological practices, the general focus of Pentecostal eschatology has moved to the space *between* missiological and ecclesiological concerns, that is, to the space between the world and the altar: emergency services (response to floods and earthquakes), medical assistance (including medical response to disasters, preventive care, drug rehabilitation programmes, psychological services, and establishing health and dental clinics), mercy ministries (such as homeless shelters, food banks, clothing services, and services to the elderly), educational programmes (especially day care and schools), counselling services (assisting cases of addiction, pregnancy, divorce, depression, or prison ministries), economic development (including job training, housing development, youth programmes, urban development programmes, housing programmes, and microenterprise loans), policy change (with focus on monitoring elections, opposing corruption, or advocating a living wage), and services in the arts (with training in music, drama, and dance) form the new face of eschatological social commitment.[21] Eschatological practices have become redefined in terms of political activism, racial reconciliation, concerns for pacifism, economic justice, and ecological liberation.[22] The changes in eschatological practices among Pentecostals reflect the dramatic transitions in Pentecostal doctrine.

---

[20] See Byron Klaus, 'Growing Edges Have Shifted: Pentecostal Mission in the 21st Century', JEPTA 30, no. 2 (2010): 65–81; Dhan Prakash, 'Toward a Theology of Social Concern: A Pentecostal Perspective', *AJPS* 13, no. 1 (2010): 65–97.

[21] See Donald E. Miller and Tetsunao Yamamori, *Global Pentecostalism: The New Face of Christian Social Engagement* (Berkeley: University of California Press, 2007), 41–43; Wolfgang Vondey, *Pentecostalism: A Guide for the Perplexed* (London: Bloomington, 2013), 90–97.

[22] Kärkkäinen, 'Mission, Spirit and Eschatology', 82–83; Calvin L. Smith, 'Revolutionaries and Revivalists: Pentecostal Eschatology, Politics and the Nicaraguan Revolution', *Pneuma* 30, no. 1 (2008): 55–82; Peter Althouse, *Spirit of the Last Days: Pentecostal Eschatology in Conversation with Jürgen Moltmann*, JPTS 25 (London: T&T Clark International, 2003), 179–92.

Eschatology and Pentecostal doctrine

The doctrinal articulation of Pentecostal eschatology emerged primarily in the context of adopting or modifying the convictions of classical dispensationalism.[23] Although the nucleus of Pentecostal eschatology developed alongside the flourishing of dispensationalist doctrine, much of the history of articulating Pentecostal eschatology shows the influence of hermeneutical presuppositions provided by dispensationalism.[24] Three particular trajectories exist with regard to Pentecostal dispensational teachings, each identified by its position concerning an imminent futurist or apocalyptic eschatology, the millennial reign of Christ, and the identification of the church in reference to the nation state of Israel.[25]

The first trajectory essentially adopts classical dispensationalism without modification: Scripture is interpreted literally through a typology of history which follows a sequence of events typically divided into a sevenfold pattern of distinct epochs of salvation history.[26] Pentecostals in this trajectory locate themselves just before the arrival of the final dispensation of Christ's eternal reign following (1) the dispensation of innocence beginning with the creation and ending with the Fall, (2) the dispensation of conscience ending with the Flood, (3) the dispensation of human government ending with Babel, (4) the dispensation of promise ending with the captivity of Israel, (5) the dispensation of the Law ending with the death of Christ, and (6) the current dispensation of grace that will end with the tribulation and usher in the return of Christ.[27] This grounding of an eschatological interpretation of history in successive stages of epochal transitions has offered Pentecostals a biblical hermeneutical framework for the doctrinal articulation of the latter-rain motif.[28] Classical dispensational eschatology is strictly speaking a philosophy of history and a hermeneutical system, which helps Pentecostals to identify themselves as an

---

[23] See Larry R. McQueen, *Toward a Pentecostal Eschatology: Discerning the Way Forward*, JPTS 39 (Blandford Forum, UK: Deo, 2012), 5–59.
[24] Donald Dayton, *Theological Roots of Pentecostalism* (Peabody, MA: Hendrickson, 1997), 33.
[25] See Glenn Balfour, 'Pentecostal Eschatology Revisited', *JEPTA* 31, no. 2 (2011): 127–40.
[26] McQueen, *Toward a Pentecostal Eschatology*, 57–58; Althouse, *The Spirit in the Last Days*, 23–24; Faupel, *Everlasting Gospel*, 44–186.
[27] See George M. Marsden, *Fundamentalism and American Culture*, 2nd ed. (Oxford: Oxford University Press, 2006), 65–66.
[28] See Dale M. Coulter, 'The Spirit and the Bride Revisited: Pentecostalism, Renewal, and the Sense of History', *JPT* 21 (2012): 298–319.

apocalyptic product heralding the last revival before the return of Christ.[29] This influence on Pentecostal theology is largely responsible for the lack of focus on developing a long-term ecclesiological model of Pentecostalism and an accompanying sustained social ethic beyond the notion of a temporary apocalyptic movement of the last days. Classical dispensational eschatology allows Pentecostals to situate their experiences theologically in the context of premillennial expectations, which identify Pentecostalism as an apocalyptic revival movement rather than a restoration of the church.[30]

A second progressive trajectory follows a less controlling script of biblical dispensations and seeks to identify more genuine Pentecostal elements.[31] In contrast to a purely literal interpretation of Scripture, other methods offer a less immediate apocalyptic reading of dispensational history and place more value on developing a Pentecostal ecclesiology. Progressive dispensational eschatology is strictly speaking the wedding of premillennialism with a charismatic ecclesiology, which helps Pentecostals to interpret their apocalyptic beliefs through the encounter with the Spirit. The strict sevenfold pattern is substituted with a threefold pattern of overlapping dispensations corresponding to the history of Israel, the work of Jesus Christ, and the present age of the Holy Spirit.[32] The ages are held together by a progressive revelation that identifies each dispensation as 'already' revealing a kingdom 'not yet' fully realized. These ages correspond to an eschatological trinitarian process enveloping the work of creation by the Father, redemption by the Son and sustaining by the Holy Spirit so that 'salvation history is a progression from the Father through the Son in the Spirit, then in the Spirit through the Son to the Father'.[33] Progressive dispensational eschatology allows Pentecostals to escape the strict pattern of fundamentalist dispensationalism and what is essentially a cessationist ecclesiology in which the church is merely parenthetical; progressive dispensational Pentecostals, on the other hand, understand eschatology less through an interpretation of Scripture than through the

---

[29] Matthew K. Thompson, *Kingdom Come: Revisioning Pentecostal Eschatology*, JPTS 37 (Blandford Forum, UK: Deo, 2010), 49–58.
[30] See Gerald T. Sheppard, 'Pentecostalism and the Hermeneutics of Dispensationalism: The Anatomy of an Uneasy Relationship', *Pneuma* 6, no. 1 (1984): 5–34.
[31] McQueen, *Toward a Pentecostal Eschatology*, 58.
[32] Land, *Pentecostal Spirituality*, 69–71.
[33] Steven J. Land, 'The Triune Center: Wesleyans and Pentecostals Together in Mission', *Wesleyan Theological Journal* 34, no. 1 (1999): 83–100 (at 91).

experiences connected with the outpouring of the Holy Spirit.[34] The church is understood not in contrast to Israel but as the fulfilment of Old Testament prophecy.[35] And although a modified dispensationalism identifies the church as apostate since the fall of Constantine[36] – a tendency which continues to subordinate ecclesiology under eschatology – a more distinctive emphasis on the origin of the church in the outpouring of the Spirit at Pentecost reshapes the identity of Pentecostalism as an apocalyptic movement by identifying the movement as the restoration of the church in the last days.

A third trajectory shows little or no influence of classical dispensationalism on Pentecostal eschatology.[37] Instead, Pentecostal concerns here dominate over dispensational hermeneutics, eschatological vision is grounded in Pentecostal soteriology, and eschatological doctrine seeks to be a deliberate revision or abandonment of classical dispensationalism.[38] In this trajectory, the eschatological future is seen in terms of the transformation, not the destruction of the present world.[39] Sociopolitical concerns for the kingdom of God take precedence over ideological concerns for the nation of Israel; premillennialism is no longer an immediate apocalyptic hermeneutical position; and the reign of Christ, rather than postponed to the second coming, is seen as already present even though not yet completed.[40] Ecclesiology and social ethics gain priority over eschatological doctrine. The result is a transformation of Pentecostal eschatology accompanied by a reinterpretation of apocalyptic urgency. Although still in its infancy, this trajectory has allowed Pentecostals to develop the ethical implications, ecumenical opportunities, and elements of cosmic transformation in their eschatology.[41]

---

[34] Shepperd, 'Pentecostals and the Hermeneutics of Dispensationalism', 22–26.
[35] McQueen, *Toward a Pentecostal Eschatology*, 58.
[36] Coulter, 'Pentecostal Visions of the End', 85–88.
[37] McQueen, *Toward a Pentecostal Eschatology*, 58.
[38] See Althouse, *Spirit of the Last Days*, 61–107; May Ling Tan-Chow, *Pentecostal Theology for the Twenty-First Century: Engaging with Multi-Faith Singapore* (Burlington, VT: Ashgate, 2007); Thompson, *Kingdom Come*, 59–160.
[39] Simon Chan, *Spiritual Theology: A Systematic Study of the Christian Life* (Downers Grove, IL: InterVarsity, 1998), 186.
[40] See Nigel Scotland, 'From the "Not Yet" to the "Now and the Not Yet": Charismatic Kingdom Theology 1960–2010', *JPT* 20 (2011): 272–90; Wonsuk Ma, 'Pentecostal Eschatology: What Happened When the Wave Hit the West End of the Ocean', *AJPS* 12, no. 1 (2009): 95–112; Murray W. Dempster, 'Christian Social Concern in Pentecostal Perspective: Reformulating Pentecostal Eschatology', *JPT* 2 (1993): 53–66.
[41] See Irvin G. Ghetty, 'Pentecostals and Socio-political Engagement: An Overview from Azusa Street to the New Kairos Movement', *JTSA* 143 (July 2012): 23–47; Harold D. Hunter, 'Some Ethical Implications of Pentecostal Eschatology', *JEPTA* 22 (2002): 45–55.

The adaptations and modifications of classical dispensationalism in Pentecostal theology reveal an eschatology heavily dependent on a particular apocalyptic hermeneutic of Pentecostal experiences. The primary importance of a dispensational hermeneutic lies in the apocalyptic urgency with which it provided Pentecostal sensitivities.[42] However, despite the dominance of dispensational thought, it would be a mistake to portray Pentecostal eschatology exclusively in terms of fundamentalist or broadly existing evangelical themes, including the second coming of Christ, millennialism, the restoration of Israel, heaven and hell, and the kingdom of God. The varying interpretations of Pentecostal experiences show that Pentecostal eschatology emphasizes not only the apocalyptic position but more importantly the *function* of the movement as instrumental for the coming of the kingdom: the return of the Lord awaits the proclamation of the full gospel in signs and wonders to the ends of the earth.[43] The theological core of this ecclesio-missiological eschatology is a premillennial pneumatological restorationism.

Premillennialism is a dominant theme in Pentecostal eschatology because its focus on a radical and definite historical turning point, marked by the return of Christ, allows Pentecostals to identify their movement as existing 'just before' the final consummation of the kingdom of God. Theologically, the idea of the future millennial reign itself has occupied little significance in Pentecostal eschatology in contrast to the importance placed on the present age, which links the prospect of the eschatological reign with a strong apocalyptic expectancy. In principle, premillennial expectations have shown to support positions ranging from pessimistic apocalyptic scenarios to a robust optimism and a transformative social ethic.[44] In either of these interpretations, premillennialism expresses the central importance of discontinuity in Pentecostal eschatological discourse by reminding Pentecostals that the kingdom of God is realized only through a decisive inbreaking of God as

---

[42] See James J. Glass, 'Eschatology: A Clear and Present Danger – A Sure and Certain Hope', in *Pentecostal Perspectives*, ed. Keith Warrington (Carlisle, UK: Paternoster, 1998), 120–46.

[43] Grant Wacker, *Heaven Below: Early Pentecostals and American Culture* (Cambridge, MA: Harvard University Press, 2003), 253.

[44] See Frederick L. Ware, 'On the Compatibility/Incompatibility of Pentecostal Premillennialism with Black Liberation Theology', in *Afro-Pentecostalism: Black Pentecostal and Charismatic Christianity in History and Culture*, ed. Amos Yong and Estrelda Y. Alexander (New York: New York University Press, 2011), 191–206; Tobias Brandner, 'Premillennial and Countercultural Faith and Its Production and Reception in the Chinese Context', *AJPS* 14, no. 1 (2011): 3–26.

patterned by the day of Pentecost. Thus conversion, sanctification, Spirit baptism, divine healing, and other signs and wonders are not gradual transitions of this world into the kingdom but unexpected encounters with God heralding the complete salvation of creation.[45]

Pentecostal interpretations of these unexpected encounters with God, patterned after the eschatological image of Pentecost, are thoroughly pneumatological. The latter-rain motif, which identifies the day of Pentecost as the beginning and the Pentecostal movement of the twentieth century as the close of the current age, centres on the eschatological activity of the Holy Spirit. Situated between a kingdom to come and a world destined to pass away (see Rev. 21:4), Pentecostal eschatology understands the present age as the inbreaking of the Spirit in the last days. The outpouring of the Spirit serves as a central motif for understanding both the continuous presence of God in creation and the discontinuity with the coming kingdom.[46] Interpreted largely in ecclesio-missiological terms, the church stands at the centre of the activity of the Spirit. The dramatic experiences of conversion, sanctification, the baptism in the Spirit, the speaking with tongues and the gifts of the Spirit, divine healing, deliverance, exorcism, and other manifestations of signs and wonders are signals of 'a large-scale restoration of apostolic faith and power'.[47] At the heart of this restorationism stands an apocalyptic sense of both continuity and discontinuity between the apostolic community and the historical church, Pentecostalism and the institutional church and between Pentecostalism and the kingdom of God. Early Pentecostal theology emphasized this apocalyptic sense primarily by identifying the end of the current age in the same terms as it had begun: with an outpouring of the Holy Spirit and charismatic manifestations leading to an unprecedented evangelization of the world.[48] The endorsement of fundamentalist dispensationalism and the delay of the imminent return of Christ

---

[45] McQueen, *Toward a Pentecostal Eschatology*, 216–20; Peter Althouse, 'Pentecostal Eschatology in Context: The Eschatological Orientation of the Full Gospel', in Althouse and Robby Waddell, *Perspectives in Pentecostal Eschatologies*, 205–31; Shane Clifton, 'Preaching the "Full Gospel" in the Context of Global Environmental Crises', in *The Spirit Renews the Face of the Earth: Pentecostal Forays in Science and Theology of Creation*, ed. Amos Yong (Eugene, OR: Pickwick, 2009), 117–34.

[46] See Peter Althouse, 'Implications of the Kenosis of the Spirit for a Creational Eschatology: A Pentecostal Engagement with Jürgen Moltmann', in Yong, *The Spirit Renews the Face of the Earth*, 155–72.

[47] Land, *Pentecostal Spirituality*, 61.

[48] See Thompson, *Kingdom Come*, 9–58; Althouse, *Spirit of the Last Days*, 9–60.

led Pentecostal theology during the middle of the twentieth century to an apocalyptic expectation of the world's ultimate destruction and withdrawal from transformative missiological practices.[49] Contemporary Pentecostals are recovering the prophetic, socio-critical, and transformative dimensions of the early movement and emphasize a more socially and ethically responsible eschatology.[50] While a single dominant narrative of Pentecostal eschatology is difficult to formulate, all attempts remain grounded in an eschatological tension existing between Pentecostalism, the present world, the church, and the kingdom of God. This tension is bridged by the outpouring of the Holy Spirit who combines eschatology, pneumatology, and missiology into a single passion.[51]

For Pentecostals, the present age represents in principle a restoration of Pentecost by the Spirit who is the promise of God's kingdom and the gift of the coming age already present.[52] From the perspective of Pentecost, the mission of the Spirit is committed to the mission of Jesus by taking the church into the world; from the perspective of the 'end' (*eschaton*), Pentecostalism is in this sense a restoration of the mission of the Spirit in the life of the church and every believer 'to be a Christ-like witness in the power and demonstration of the Holy Spirit with an eschatological sense of urgency and passion'.[53] This pneumatological definition of restorationism embraces both the classical Pentecostal emphasis on the recovery of apostolic faith, praxis and power, and global Pentecostal interpretations of restoration in terms of pragmatic social engagement and transformation. The difference between the classical and global positions lies primarily in their advocacy of an apocalyptic urgency, which is central to Pentecostal theology but interpreted differently with regard to its ecclesiological implications and practical consequences. In the broad sense of identifying Pentecostal theology as a form of premillennial pneumatological restorationism, eschatology among Pentecostals can be described succinctly as an apocalyptic mandate of participating in the realization of the kingdom of God through the charismatic ministry of the Spirit

---

[49] See Althouse, *Spirit of the Last Days*, 36–44; Peter E. Prosser, *Dispensational Eschatology and Its Influence on American and British Religious Movements*, TSR 82 (Queenstown, ON: Edwin Mellen, 1999), 253–87; Sheppard, 'Pentecostalism and the Hermeneutics of Dispensationalism', 5–34.
[50] See Althouse, *Spirit of the Last Days*, 61–107.
[51] Land, *Pentecostal Spirituality*, 66.
[52] Thompson, *Kingdom Come*, 128–43.
[53] Land, *Pentecostal Spirituality*, 97.

unfolding in the practices of the church.⁵⁴ The expectation of the return of Christ and the inbreaking of the kingdom direct Pentecostal theology back to the practices of the full gospel, which now has become an eschatological gospel: salvation, sanctification, Spirit baptism, and divine healing lead towards and emerge from an apocalyptic vision of the kingdom of God.

Eschatology as apocalyptic mission

Apocalyptic eschatology is not a central element permeating the doctrines and practices of most Christian traditions. Despite a resurgence of Christian eschatological themes during the twentieth century, especially in popular perception, the official discussion is generally placed at the end of doctrinal systems and rarely shows significant influence on the preceding theological constructs. A strong apocalyptic emphasis of eschatology is typically ascribed most prominently to fundamentalist fringe movements in Christian history.⁵⁵ In the mainstream Christian traditions, eschatology is primarily a conceptual system for the articulation of doctrines pertaining to the future and articulated as a delineation of a sequence of events or an application of the biblical message of the kingdom of God to the present notion of the church.⁵⁶ A brief overview helps to accentuate the particular contributions of the apocalyptic vision in Pentecostal eschatology.

Roman Catholic teaching has revived its eschatological focus during the twentieth century, albeit without developing a concurrent systematic presentation of the doctrine.⁵⁷ Generally, eschatology is embedded in particular teachings on grace, original sin, and Jesus Christ.⁵⁸ More specifically, eschatology is the movement of history towards reconciliation with God manifested

---

⁵⁴ See Matthew K. Thompson, 'Eschatology as Soteriology: The Cosmic Full Gospel', Althouse and Waddell, *Perspectives in Pentecostal Eschatologies*, 189–204; Frank D. Macchia, 'Pentecostal and Charismatic Theology', in *The Oxford Handbook of Eschatology*, ed. Jerry L. Walls (Oxford: Oxford University Press, 2008), 280–94; Land, *Pentecostal Spirituality*, 95–98.

⁵⁵ See Stephen J. Stein, 'Apocalypticism Outside the Mainstream in the United States', in *Encyclopedia of Apocalypticism*, vol. 3 (New York: Continuum, 1998), 108–39; Paul Boyer, 'The Growth of Fundamentalist Apocalyptic in the United States', ibid., 140–78.

⁵⁶ See Stanley J. Grenz, 'Eschatological Theology: Contours of a Postmodern Theology of Hope', *RE* 97, no. 3 (2000): 339–54.

⁵⁷ See Peter C. Phan, 'Roman Catholic Teaching', in *The Oxford Handbook of Eschatology*, ed. Jerry L. Walls (Oxford: Oxford University Press, 2008), 215–32.

⁵⁸ See Richard P. McBrien, *Catholicism*, vol. 2 (Minneapolis: Winston Press, 1980), 1132–35.

by various stages: death, particular judgement, heaven, final purification, hell, last judgement, new heaven, and new earth.[59] Vatican II situates eschatology in ecclesiology centred along a 'pilgrim church' committed to human flourishing and transformation in history.[60] Catholic theologians have invested in the further development of eschatology.[61] We might say that eschatology is a 'constant' in Catholic theology with which theological and missionary practices are confronted.[62] However, the significance of apocalyptic urgency in Catholic eschatology remains undetermined.[63] A strong apocalypticism is limited to a minority and generally interpreted symbolically.[64] Practices are eschatological because they are ecclesiological with their summit in the celebration of the Eucharist yet without an apocalyptic emphasis on evangelization and mission.[65]

Similarly, in the Eastern Orthodox tradition, eschatology finds little doctrinal articulation in its own right but instead is dispersed predominantly among ecclesiological convictions and the liturgical life of the church. Contemporary Orthodox eschatology has shifted from a traditional emphasis on worship, prayer, and action grounded in the origins of the church to a focus on the church in the process of becoming that is grounded in the eschaton.[66] The central eschatological image is the kingdom of God, which is presented as 'heaven on earth' through the church's liturgy, sacraments, and hierarchy.[67] As an eschatological community, the church holds a missionary imperative to proclaim and communicate the eschaton as the being and fullness of the church.[68] However, the eschatological community does not

---

[59] *Catechism of the Catholic Church*, nos. 1020–65.
[60] See *Lumen Gentium*, no. 48–51; *Gaudium et Spes*, no. 38–39.
[61] Phan, 'Roman Catholic Teaching', 220–28; McBrien, *Catholicism*, 1120–25.
[62] See Stephen Bevans and Roger Schroeder, *Constants in Context: A Theology of Mission for Today*, ASM 30 (Maryknoll, NY: Orbis, 2004), 348–95.
[63] See Phan, 'Roman Catholic Teaching', 228–29.
[64] See Benjamin Peters, 'Apocalyptic Sectarianism: The Theology at Work in Critiques of Catholic Radicals', *HJCTS* 39, no. 2 (2012): 208–29; Amy Luebbers, 'The Remnant Faithful: A Case Study of Contemporary Apocalyptic Catholicism', *SR* 62, no. 2 (2001): 221–41.
[65] See Gerwin van Leeuwen, 'The Sacramentality of the Church: Its Eschatological Identity', in *The Church in India in Search of a New Identity*, ed. Kurien Kunnumpuram, Errol D'Lima, Jacob Parappally (Bangalore: NBCLC, 1997), 330–51.
[66] See Pantelis Kalaitzidis, 'New Trends in Greek Orthodox Theology: Challenges in the Movement towards a Genuine Renewal and Christian Unity', *SJT* 67, no. 2 (2014): 127–64.
[67] Timothy (Kallistos) Ware, 'The Earthly Heaven', in *Eastern Orthodox Theology: A Contemporary Reader*, ed. Daniel B. Clendenin (Grand Rapids, MI: Baker Academic, 2003), 11–20.
[68] See Alexander Schmemann, 'The Missionary Imperative in the Orthodox Tradition', in Clendenin, *Eastern Orthodox Theology*, 199–200.

transform society into the church or the world into the kingdom.[69] Rather, the kingdom is realized only within ecclesiastical structures rooted in the Eucharist through which the church participates in the kingdom of God.[70] The church thus stands in contrast to the world, and the Eucharist both establishes that contrast by forming an image of the kingdom and transfigures the world by realizing the kingdom of God in the present.[71] Practices are eschatological because the mission of the church is realized through the concurrent participation in the worship, witness, service, and fellowship of the community yet without an apocalyptic emphasis on evangelization or sociopolitical engagement and transformation.[72]

Eschatology has long occupied a central position in Protestant theologies, and an apocalyptic scenario was part and parcel of both the early and the radical Reformers.[73] However, modern Protestant theology, particularly its evangelical representation, shifted its eschatological doctrines overwhelmingly to a futurist interpretation of history and the biblicist hermeneutic of classical dispensationalism.[74] Contemporary Protestant eschatology has critically engaged these tendencies and reinterpreted the 'end' through a more realist accent on the present and transformational emphasis on Christian hope.[75] Similar to contemporary Catholicism, eschatology marks the Christian community as the pilgrim people of God, yet, the eschatological task of the church is found not in sacramental rituals but in a transforming mission to disclose Jesus Christ as the future of the world.[76] In contrast to the Eastern Orthodox tradition, the eschaton is more properly seen as the goal than the being of the church. The relationship of reality and history, future and present, actuality

---

[69] Ibid., 195–201.
[70] See Andrew Louth, 'Eastern Orthodox Eschatology', in Walls, *The Oxford Handbook of Eschatology*, 233–47.
[71] See John Zizioulas, *The Eucharistic Communion and the World*, ed. Luke Ben Tallon (London: T&T Clark, 2011), 39–82.
[72] See Anne-Christine Lindvall, 'Response to the New WCC Documents from an Orthodox Perspective', *SM* 101, nos. 3–4 (2013): 311–15.
[73] See Marius Timmann Mjaaland, 'Apocalypse and the Spirit of Revolution: The Political Legacy of the Early Reformation', *PT* 14, no. 2 (2013): 155–73; Walter Klaassen, *Living at the End of the Ages: Apocalyptic Expectation in the Radical Reformation* (Lanham, MD: University Press of America, 1992).
[74] See James H. Moorhead, 'Apocalypticism in Mainstream Protestantism, 1800 to the Present', in *Encyclopedia of Apocalypticism*, vol. 3 (New York: Continuum, 1998), 72–107.
[75] See Gerhard Sauter, 'Protestant Theology', in Walls, *The Oxford Handbook of Eschatology*, 248–62; Grenz, 'Eschatological Theology', 339–54.
[76] See Jürgen Moltmann, *Theology of Hope: On the Ground and the Implication of a Christian Eschatology*, trans. Margaret Kohl (Minneapolis: Fortress, 1993), 304–38.

and hope tends to inspire a cosmic ontology in which the church constructs a world based on the Word of God.[77] Eschatological mission is characterized by 'the weekday obedience and the worldly callings of Christians in their social roles'.[78] Yet, the image of the kingdom of God has motivated both transhistorical withdrawal and historical realism.[79] The idea of the kingdom as an ethical reality stands in place of an urgent apocalyptic vision.[80] Ecclesiology in the image of the eschaton remains more anticipatory mission and evangelization than participatory fullness of salvation in the image of Pentecost.[81] Practices are eschatological because the mission of the church is the proclamation of the gospel as an 'interim'[82] community existing 'between the times'[83] yet without an apocalyptic participation in the fullness of gifts of the kingdom of God.

In light of these brief (and overdrawn) characterizations, Pentecostal theology alerts Christianity to the ongoing significance of eschatology for ecclesiology and mission and the importance of cultivating eschatological practices in light of an apocalyptic vision. Although eschatology finds expression among Pentecostals in doctrinal articulation, theology is most thoroughly Pentecostal when eschatology is practiced as an apocalyptic mandate for the mission of the church carried out in the life, power, witness, gifts, and fellowship of the Spirit. The history of Pentecostal doctrine shows that the eschatological interpretation of mission can include both the ideas of urgent evangelization and long-term social transformation as long as these practices emerge from and lead towards an apocalyptic vision of the coming kingdom. Pentecostal theology underscores the importance of maintaining an apocalyptic expectancy amidst questions of apocalyptic sustainability that have forced Pentecostals to re-envision the church's mission beyond a dispensational sense of last-days' worldwide evangelization.[84] At the same time, the pragmatic nature of Pentecostal apocalypticism struggles with the notion that

---

[77] Grenz, 'Eschatological Theology', 347-51.
[78] Ibid., 304-5.
[79] See Christofer Frey, 'Eschatology and Ethics: Their Relation in Recent Continental Protestantism', in *Eschatology in the Bible and in Jewish and Christian Tradition*, ed. Henning Graf Reventlow (Sheffield: Sheffield Academic Press, 1997), 62-74.
[80] Morehead, 'Apocalypticism', 89.
[81] See Harry R. Boer, *Pentecost and Mission* (Grand Rapids, MI: Eerdmans, 1961).
[82] See David J. Bosch, *Transforming Mission: Paradigm Shifts in Theology of Mission* (Maryknoll, NY: Orbis, 1991), 165-70.
[83] R. Pierce Beaver, *The Missionary between the Times* (New York: Doubleday, 1968), 159-82.
[84] See Robby Waddell, 'Apocalyptic Sustainability: The Future of Pentecostal Ecology', in Althouse and Waddell, *Perspectives in Pentecostal Eschatologies*, 95-110.

Christ could return 'at any moment', which is eschatological only if the urgent sense of apocalyptic expectancy is indeed sustained through meaningful practices at every moment. The delay of the parousia has attuned Pentecostal theology to the importance of continually rediscovering eschatology as a motivation for mission coupled with a corresponding reinterpretation of the role of the church in light of sustaining apocalyptic expectations.[85] Learning the virtue of apocalyptic patience, Pentecostal eschatology has begun to embrace a larger theological understanding of mission in the economy of salvation.[86] Nevertheless, while the nature of Pentecostal apocalypticism has changed, the continued centrality of an apocalyptic vision is a key to understanding and interpreting Pentecostal theology.

In principle, all elements of the full gospel are apocalyptic visions of the church's mission thrust into a world confronted with the inbreaking of the Spirit in the last days.[87] In its doctrinal articulations, Pentecostal apocalypticism includes the emphasis on a cosmic spiritual battle between good and evil, an intensification of the powers of evil and a final victory and judgement of God.[88] Outside the dominance of dispensational hermeneutic, the Pentecostal apocalyptic vision can be more exactly defined as an affective transformation conforming the church and the individual to the pathos of God instilled by the outpouring of the Holy Spirit through experiences of the charismatic gifts creating and shaping eschatological practices.[89] These practices are eschatological because they are reconstructions of time and space by the Holy Spirit in the image of the eschaton.[90] They are apocalyptic because they are motivated and sustained by a passion for the world confronted with and ultimately consumed by the kingdom of God (see Rev. 11:15). Salvation, sanctification, Spirit baptism, and divine healing represent pneumatological actions of the church through which God enables the participation of the

---

[85] Keith Warrington, *Pentecostal Theology: A Theology of Encounter* (London: Bloomsbury, 2008), 258–59.
[86] See Daniel Castelo, 'Patience as a Theological Virtue: A Challenge to Pentecostal Eschatology', in Althouse and Waddell, *Perspectives in Pentecostal Eschatologies*, 232–46.
[87] See McQueen, *Toward a Pentecostal Eschatology*, 216–57.
[88] Amos Yong, *In the Days of Caesar: Pentecostalism and Political Theology* (Grand Rapids, MI: Eerdmans, 2010), 327–28.
[89] See Land, *Pentecostal Spirituality*, 58–121; idem, 'Response to Professor Harvey Cox', *JPT* 5 (1994): 13–16.
[90] See Wolfgang Vondey, 'The Holy Spirit and the Physical Universe: The Impact of Scientific Paradigm Shifts on Contemporary Pneumatology', *TS* 70, no. 1 (2009): 3–36; idem, 'The Holy Spirit and Time in Contemporary Catholic and Protestant Theology', *SJT* 58, no. 4 (2005): 393–409.

world in God's kingdom.⁹¹ This apocalyptic vision sustains a Pentecostal theology of the church that consists in its broadest sense in a commitment to the entire mission of the full gospel.

The apocalyptic element in Pentecostal theology stands in contrast to any purely conceptual eschatology.⁹² While all Christian theology is eschatological, few traditions embrace an apocalyptic interpretation of liturgy, rituals, and ecclesiastical practices in and outside of the church. The importance of Pentecostal theology lies in its insistence on apocalyptic fervour not merely as the end but as the motivation for the Christian life and the mission of the church. The lessons learned from Pentecostal history show that apocalypticism uninformed by the gospel leads to other-worldly passivism; the gospel, when not informed by an apocalyptic vision, leads to this-worldly activism focused only on the present redemption of the human condition.⁹³ The Pentecostal apocalytpic commitment, freed from the futurist assurances of classical dispensationalism, embraces a pneumatological apocalypticism that takes seriously the mission of the church in the world in light of the outpouring of the Spirit.⁹⁴ The apocalyptic element, not eschatology as such, insists on the endowment with the Spirit in the present as the indispensable motivation and empowerment for mission. The charismatic manifestations of the church are constant reminders of the eschaton. In other words, the church is commissioned by Christ and endowed with the Spirit because of the coming kingdom.⁹⁵ In the church as a charismatic missionary fellowship, the Spirit and the eschaton converge in the experiences and encounter with the transcendent (see Chapter 10). Transformative mission, political theology, social ethics, creation care, and other Pentecostal practices without an eschato-missiological centre motivated and sustained by a pneumatological apocalypticism undermine central Pentecostal commitments to the full gospel.

---

⁹¹ Amos Yong, *Hospitality and the Other: Pentecost, Christian Practices, and the Neighbor* (Maryknoll, NY: Orbis, 2008), 59–64; Thompson, *Kingdom Come*, 121–23.

⁹² See Huibert Zegwaart, 'Apocalyptic Eschatology and Pentecostalism: The Relevance of John's Millennium for Today', *Pneuma* 10, no. 1 (1988): 3–25.

⁹³ Macchia, 'Pentecostal and Charismatic Theology', 287.

⁹⁴ See Yong, *In the Days of Caesar*, 327–32.

⁹⁵ See Jeffrey S. Lamp, 'New Heavens and New Earth: Early Pentecostal Soteriology as a Foundation for Creation Care in the Present', *Pneuma* 36, no. 1 (2014): 64–80; Clifton, 'Preaching the Full Gospel', 129–34; Murray Dempster, 'A Theology of the Kingdom – a Pentecostal Contribution', in *Mission as Transformation: A Theology of the Whole Gospel*, ed. Vinay Samuel and Chris Sugden (Oxford: Regnum, 1999), 45–75; Brussels Consultation of the Division of Foreign Missions of the Assemblies of God, 'Brussels Statement on Evangelization and Social Concern', *Transformation* 16, no. 2 (1999): 41–43.

Apocalyptic eschatology, cast in the image of Pentecost, consists of the charismatic confrontation of the church with the world marked by the signs and wonders of the full gospel. Pentecostal theology is in this sense a recovery of the Christian apocalyptic vision of Luke-Acts in the charismatic, socio-critical, and evangelistic practices of the church around the altar.[96] This apocalyptic sense of mission is defined not exclusively by a sense of urgency but more fully by the dramatic experiences and expectations of the full realization of the outpouring of the Spirit: signs and wonders, gifts and manifestations of salvation, sanctification, Spirit baptism, and divine healing. Pentecostal apocalypticism is therefore always a call to mission, while it also realizes that change cannot be fabricated by the church but depends on the renewing work of the Spirit. The proclamation of the full gospel, when defined eschatologically, invites the full range of Pentecostal practices, since the apocalyptic vision points not exclusively to the end but also back again to the outpouring of the Holy Spirit. Eschatology therefore does not resolve the full gospel but completes it by pointing to the kingdom of God as a perpetual Pentecost.

---

[96] See Yong, *In the Days of Caesar*, 330; Althouse, *Spirit of the Last Days*, 61–107.

Part Two

Full Gospel Theology

7

Creation

Spirit, Redemption, and Cosmology

Pentecostal theology, as the title of this book suggests, can be characterized as a form of living the fullness of the gospel. The first part of this book has provided the theological narrative of the Pentecostal full gospel placed under the symbol of Pentecost and emerging from practices at the altar. The preceding five chapters have outlined this narrative along the themes of salvation, sanctification, Spirit baptism, divine healing, and the coming kingdom. Rooted in the wide-ranging soteriology of the full gospel, the second part of this book now envisions a larger theological narrative by means of expanding the lens of the full gospel to the dominant theological conversations on creation, humanity, society, church, and God. The following chapters move from the large to the small, the cosmos to the church, before returning eventually to a theological vision at the altar at which the full gospel originates. The altar thus remains the angle point for Pentecostal hermeneutics and entrance to the full gospel by charting new territory and offering direction in matters which have not yet been widely engaged by Pentecostals. The goal of the following chapters is to illustrate how Pentecostals have consistently (though sometimes inadvertently) followed the path of their theological narrative. My chief intention is to show that the full gospel can function both descriptively and constructively for developing a systematic Pentecostal theology.

Although Pentecostals have a strong and coherent cosmology underlying their articulation of the full gospel, a doctrine of creation is absent from many systematic attempts at presenting a constructive Pentecostal theology.[1]

---

[1] See Keith Warrington, *Pentecostal Theology: A Theology of Encounter* (London: T & T Clark, 2008); William W. Menzies, *Bible Doctrines: A Pentecostal Perspective* (Springfield, MO: Logion, 1993); Guy P. Duffield and Nathaniel M. Van Cleave, *Foundations of Pentecostal Theology* (San Dimas, CA: L.I.F.E. Bible College, 1983).

Traditionally, Pentecostals are not disinterested in the doctrine of creation, but cosmology is largely subsumed under the primary theological headings of salvation, sanctification, Spirit baptism, divine healing, and the coming kingdom, which tend to put the human being at the heart of doctrinal conversations. The Pentecostal concern for experience and praxis also delayed contributions to a theology of creation, which is widely considered to be of primarily conceptual interest. A biblicist hermeneutic and strong apocalyptic urgency among classical Pentecostals accentuated the anthropocentric lens through a consistent emphasis on mission and evangelization rather than ecology and creation. Constructive proposals of a doctrine of creation surfaced only during the second half of the twentieth century with the global expansion of Pentecostalism and the challenges posed by various indigenous cosmologies absorbed in diverse Pentecostal contexts. The rise of theological scholarship among Pentecostals eventually initiated engagement with the natural sciences and critical assessments of evolution, divine action, natural laws, and creation care.[2]

A pneumatological lens forms the most consistent theological foundation for a Pentecostal theology of creation. However, while a pneumatological imagination forms the backdrop for any theological pursuit born from the cradle of Pentecost, it would be misleading to equate a Pentecostal theology of creation simply with a pneumatological cosmology. The first part of this volume has argued that the particular Pentecostal character of pneumatology can be identified by the elements of the full gospel. This chapter applies the fivefold pattern articulated in part one to the constructive concerns of a theology of creation. Given the centrality of the altar for Pentecostal practices, I argue that creation can be seen as the economy of salvation, as it were, the cosmic altar of redemption, sanctification, empowerment, transformation and eschatological mission. Pentecostal experiences of the Holy Spirit provide experiential, physical, social, historical, and eschatological frames of reference for rethinking fundamental notions of God's activity in the world. The full gospel not only directs Pentecostals to the Holy Spirit, it also challenges them to move this pneumatological orientation in the spirit of Pentecost to the ends of the world.

---

[2] See the literature in Wolfgang Vondey, *Pentecostalism: A Guide for the Perplexed* (London: Bloomsbury, 2013), 133–53.

Creation as the economy of salvation

The affirmation of the full gospel that 'Jesus is saviour' forms the basis for constructing a Pentecostal narrative of the doctrine of creation. If we are correct in identifying the Pentecostal character of salvation as participating in divine hospitality (see Chapter 2), then Pentecostal theology may suggest that this Christological affirmation must ultimately find broad cosmic application. The initial ground for a hospitable soteriology is the affirmation that creation does not exist apart from but solely for the purposes of salvation. The doctrine of creation is subsumed under soteriology in Pentecostal theology as an indication that the meaning of being created is found not in the product or act of creation itself but in its redemption. From a soteriological perspective, the notion of 'creation' is inexplicably defined by the expectation of a 'new creation' brought about by the work of God.[3] In other words, creation and redemption, although temporally distinguished, are logically the same act so that all of creation reveals God's eternal saving purpose and the purposes of salvation are found throughout all creation. Since the narrative of the full gospel is Christologically articulated (*Jesus* is Saviour), the primary soteriological question is how the salvation of Christ extends to all of creation. The pneumatological orientation of Pentecostal theology, cast in the image of Pentecost, directs the answer immediately to the realm of God as spirit.

Pentecostals emphasize the significant role of the divine spirit in the creation narratives of Genesis. Read through a pneumatological lens, the biblical account of divine creativity is framed by the assertion at the beginning of the creation narrative that the spirit of God (*ruach Elohim*) 'swept over the face of the waters' (Gen. 1:2) and the added emphasis that God breathed into the human being 'the breath of life' (Gen. 2:7).[4] The presence of the spirit of God is the principal expression of God's life-giving activity at the creation of the world and is further accentuated by the assertion that the continued

---

[3] See Larry D. Hart, *Truth Aflame: Theology for the Church in Renewal*, rev. ed. (Grand Rapids, MI: Zondervan, 2005), 152–54; Timothy Munyon, 'The Creation of the Universe and Humankind', in *Systematic Theology*, ed. Stanley M. Horton, rev. ed. (Springfield, MO: Logion, 1994), 220–22.
[4] Amos Yong, '*Ruach*, the Primordial Chaos, and the Breath of Life: Emergence Theory and the Creation Narratives in Pneumatological Perspective', in *The Work of the Spirit: Pneumatology and Pentecostalism*, ed. Michael Welker (Grand Rapids, MI: Eerdmans, 2006), 183–204.

sustaining of life also demands the continuing divine presence.⁵ The core belief that God is the source and sustainer of the universe (see Ps. 33:6), and that the act of divine creation as well as its provision and sustaining are continued spiritual activities (see Job 27:3; 33:4; 34:14–15), functions as a basis for both Pentecostal cosmogony and cosmology. The theological significance of this pneumatological lens lies in identifying not only the origin of life but its continuing existence with the experiential possibility to encounter God as spirit (see Pss. 51:10–12; 104:29–30).

The pneumatological account of creation does not imply an exclusively theistic focus. Especially in African and Latin American Pentecostalism, a pneumatological discourse penetrates the entire cosmological narrative.⁶ The universe is 'spirit-filled' with a range of spiritual beings and powers that may be conceptualized into four broad spheres: (1) the divine, (2) the human, (3) the natural world, and (4) the realm of evil.⁷ The origins of this typology can be traced to the experiences among Pentecostals of diverse spirits in the universe and the interaction of human beings with different powers in the spiritual dimension of the universe. In other words, the unique contributions of Pentecostal theology are not primarily its understanding of the origins and development of the universe but the relational qualities between the various spiritual realms.⁸ In turn, salvation in a spirit-filled world must therefore be oriented towards the diverse notion(s) of spirit.

The idea of creation as a spirit-filled cosmos evokes a pneumatological imagination that considers the economy of salvation (and thus soteriology)

---

5   Scott A. Ellington, 'The Face of God as His Creating Spirit: The Interplay of Yahweh's *Panim* and *Ruach* in Psalm 104:29–30', in *The Spirit Renews the Face of the Earth: Pentecostal Forays in Science and Theology of Creation*, ed. Amos Yong (Eugene, OR: Pickwick, 2009), 3–16.

6   See Wilma Wells Davies, *The Embattled But Empowered Community: Comparing Understandings of Spiritual Power in Argentine Popular and Pentecostal Cosmologies*, Global Pentecostal and Charismatic Studies 5 (Leiden: Brill, 2010), 107–67; J. Kwabena Asamoah-Gyadu, 'God's Laws of Productivity: Creation in African Pentecostal Hermeneutics', in Yong, *The Spirit Renews*, 175–90; Emmanuel Kingsley Larbi, 'The Nature of Continuity and Discontinuity of Ghanaian Pentecostal Concept of Salvation in African Cosmology', *AJPS* 5, no. 1 (2002): 87–106.

7   Amos Yong, *The Spirit of Creation: Modern Science and Divine Action in the Pentecostal-Charismatic Imagination*, PM 4 (Grand Rapids, MI: Eerdmans, 2011), 175–84; Carolyn Denise Baker, 'Created Spirit Beings', in Horton, *Systematic Theology*, 179–94; Frank D. Macchia, 'Repudiating the Enemy: Satan and Demons', ibid., 194–213; Derek B. Mutungu, 'A Response to M. L. Daneel', in *All Together in One Place: Theological Papers from the Brighton Conference on World Evangelization*, ed. Harold D. Hunter and Peter D. Hocken (Sheffield: Sheffield Academic Press, 1993), 127–31.

8   See Scott A. Ellington, '"A Relational Theology That Isn't Relational Enough": A Response to *God and World in the Old Testament*', *JPT* 19 (2010): 190–97.

as concerned with the Spirit of God amidst and in relation to other spirits, spiritual powers, and principalities.[9] Soteriology accordingly involves a relational cosmology of intersubjectivity between otherwise disconnected entities, groups, or persons.[10] This spirit-oriented cosmology (and soteriology) emerges from an experiential metaphysics, which relies on subjective encounter and intersubjective engagement with the world rather than an objective, symbolic ontology.[11] In contrast to the traditional cosmological argument, which postulates God as the first cause of creation and places God as absolutely transcendent above the created order, Pentecostal theology insists on the operation of God as spirit (and as the Spirit) within creation and within the causal relationships of the cosmos (see Chapter 11). This pneumatological metaphysics rejects a strict distinction between the eternal being of God and the economy of salvation, particularly in Oneness Pentecostal teaching, in favour of a kenotic presence of the divine.[12] From a trinitarian Pentecostal perspective, the triune life of God is not transcendent, closed or self-contained but dynamic and open to creation: the Father, in an ecstatic movement, literally, standing outside of himself, interacts through the Spirit by manifesting God's identity as the Word in the world; in turn, Christ becomes 'paraclete' through the Spirit, while the Holy Spirit also becomes 'paraclete' through Christ, both engaging and liberating each other and the world for participation in God.[13] Creation is the economy of salvation because it is the arena of Incarnation and Pentecost. The Holy Spirit is active already in the conception and mission of the Son, and the Father pours out the Holy Spirit through the Son on all flesh and to the ends of the earth (see Acts 2:17–21). Christology and pneumatology are joint aspects of the redemptive activity of the Father in the economy of salvation.[14] Jesus is saviour precisely because he

---

[9] Cf. Veli-Matti Kärkkäinen, 'Spirit(s) in Contemporary Christian Theology: An Interim Report of the Unbinding of Pneumatology', in *Interdisciplinary and Religio-Cultural Discourses on a Spirit-Filled World: Loosing the Spirits*, ed. Veli-Matti Kärkkäinen et al. (New York: Palgrave, 2013), 29–40.

[10] Yong, *The Spirit of Creation*, 181.

[11] See Amos Yong, *The Spirit Poured Out on All Flesh: Pentecostalism and the Possibility of Global Theology* (Grand Rapids, MI: Baker Academic, 2005), 289–92.

[12] Wolfgang Vondey, *Beyond Pentecostalism: The Crisis of Global Christianity and the Renewal of the Theological Agenda*, PM 3 (Grand Rapids, MI: Eerdmans, 2010), 98–108.

[13] Frank D. Macchia, *Baptized in the Spirit: A Global Pentecostal Theology* (Grand Rapids, MI: Zondervan, 2006), 117–20; Jean-Jacques Suurmond, *Word and Spirit at Play: Towards a Charismatic Theology* (Grand Rapids, MI: Eerdmans, 1994), 180–84.

[14] Yong, *The Spirit Poured Out*, 226, 233–34.

is the incarnate Son of God who is baptized with the Spirit (Lk. 4:18–19; Acts 10:38) and who baptizes with the Holy Spirit (Lk. 3:16; Acts 1:5).[15] Pentecostal theology therefore understands creation primarily as God's activity 'for us' by giving witness to the story of God who in Christ and the Spirit is 'among us', 'with us', 'in us', and 'through us', and thereby invites all of creation to participate in the divine life.

Creation as the materialization of sanctification

Salvation as a spiritual reality does not simply disperse from God in Christ throughout creation in a universal manner. Although Pentecostals consider the world sacred because it originates from God, the existential reality of a spirit-filled universe confronts the appropriation of the work of redemption with the relational intersubjectivity of the diverse spiritual realities in terms of divine, human, natural, and evil spirits. Temptation, sin, the devil, and the demonic represent the obstacles to the realization of universal salvation. From a pneumatological perspective, the Spirit of God brings order to the chaotic waters at the creation of the world (see Gen. 1:2), yet that order is dramatically challenged by the wickedness and corruption of creation as a result of the Fall (Gen 6:3).[16] While Scripture distinguishes strictly between good and evil, God and Satan, angels and demons, divine powers and fallen principalities and powers, the manifold spiritual beings and powers interact with the physical, chemical, and biological properties of the cosmos.[17] In response, Pentecostals emphasize the importance of the spiritual reality of Christ's salvation from the cosmic powers of darkness (see Col. 1:13; Gal. 1:4; Phil. 3:21; Eph. 1:22; Heb. 2:8–9). Christology is interpreted pneumatologically (see Chapter 2). The reality of salvation wrought by the Spirit must therefore include material deliverance, healing, liberation, and sanctification from other spiritual beings and powers.[18] Since Pentecostal cosmology

---

[15] See Amos Yong, *Spirit-Word-Community: Theological Hermeneutics in Trinitarian Perspective* (Eugene, OR: Wipf and Stock, 2002), 28–34.

[16] Robin Routledge, '"My Spirit" in Genesis 6.1–4', *JPT* 20 (2011): 232–51. Not all Pentecostal scholars endorse the idea of an angelic fall.

[17] See David Bradnick, 'Spirits and the Stars: A Spirit-Filled Cosmology', in Kärkkäinen et al., *Interdisciplinary and Religio-Cultural Discourses*, 213–26.

[18] Martinus L. Daneel, 'African Independent Church Pneumatology and the Salvation of All Creation', in Hunter and Hocken, *All Together in One Place*, 96–126.

emerges from experiences of diverse and opposing spirits, and sanctification carries primarily ontological status in Pentecostal theology (see Chapter 3), a theological challenge from the perspective of the full gospel is the question of how creation can be understood as sanctified by the Spirit of God.

To speak of the sanctification of creation is to attribute to holiness not only an anthropological but cosmological and metaphysical quality. The pneumatological perspective of Pentecostalism allows creation to be perceived as a unity created and sustained by the Holy Spirit and intended for the participation of the whole cosmos in the glory and holiness of God.[19] The experiential focus of this 'material' pneumatology suggests that the contours of the sanctification of creation are drawn by a tangible encounter with the Holy Spirit (in contrast to the encounter with other spirits), the experience of the presence of the divine throughout the cosmos, the expectation that the encounter with the Spirit of God transforms the human being and the world, and the realization of thus standing in relation to the divine and the created order.[20] Human beings participate in God's sanctifying work not merely as human (anthropocentrically) but synergistically as spiritual, physical, social, and cultural embodied creatures who exist in interdependence with the materiality of creation. The artificial modern differentiation between spirit and body, animate and inanimate, natural and human, mind and matter, natural and supernatural, and similar dichotomies can therefore largely be abandoned by Pentecostals.[21]

A cosmology cast in the image of Pentecost suggests that 'spirit' is not only a literal substance but an animating teleological principle for understanding the sanctifying (and unifying) interconnectedness and purpose of matter, structure, and systems of life's history.[22] The sanctifying impact of the outpouring of the Holy Spirit transcends the Christian and the church and extends to all of life and creation. In this sense, the biblical day of Pentecost

---

[19] Wesley Granberg-Michaelson, 'Redeeming the Earth: A Theology for This World', *The Covenant Quarterly* 42, no. 2 (1984): 17–29; idem, 'Earthkeeping: A Theology for Global Sanctification', *Sojourners* 11 (1982): 21–24.

[20] Néstor Medina, 'Jürgen Moltmann and Pentecostalism(s): Toward a Cultural Theology of the Spirit', in *Love and Freedom*, ed. Abrahim Khan (Toronto: Toronto School of Theology, 2008), 101–13.

[21] See Yong, *The Spirit of Creation*, 196–207.

[22] Jeffrey Schloss, 'Hovering over Waters: Spirit and the Ordering of Creation', in *The Spirit in Creation and New Creation: Science and Theology in Western and Orthodox Realms*, ed. Michael Welker (Grand Rapids, MI: Eerdmans, 2012), 26–49.

anticipates the cosmic filling of the whole universe with the divine Spirit.[23] In turn, just as the presence of the Spirit in the individual and the church has a sanctifying effect, so the goal of pouring out the Spirit on all flesh is the entire sanctification of all creation.[24] The order of sanctification in creation proceeds from the Spirit of Christ through the church to the individual into the world. Put differently, sanctification proceeds only by way of the Holy Spirit, and the way of sanctification is fully made available in the church, which therefore participates in the sanctification of all creation. Hence, the sanctification of creation is cosmological not simply because it is pneumatological; the world is not sanctified with the day of Pentecost. Rather, a pneumatological account of creation in the image of Pentecost calls for an eschatological integration and the cumulative responsibility of humankind to enable the sanctification of creation by mediating the unrestricted presence of the Spirit in the world.[25]

When sanctification is seen as the eschatological struggle amidst continuity and discontinuity for the reconciliation of creation with one another and with God, the goal of the outpouring of the Holy Spirit can be identified as the transformation of the entire creation into a sanctified community.[26] Holiness in the image of Pentecost therefore possesses pneumatological, cosmological, anthropological, ecological, and ecclesiological dimensions: it is pneumatological because holiness is the primary attribute of the mediation of the Spirit of God;[27] it is cosmological because the whole of creation is the sacred space and intended goal of the outpouring of the Holy Spirit;[28] it is anthropological because of the human vocation to serve and care for creation;[29] it is ecological because the whole of the created order alongside human beings is a doxological and eschatological dwelling

---

[23] Macchia, *Baptized in the Spirit*, 102–4.
[24] Ibid., 204; Matthew K. Thompson, *Kingdom Come: Revisioning Pentecostal Eschatology*, JPTS 37 (Blandford Forum, UK: Deo, 2010), 137–40.
[25] See Miroslav Volf, 'The Final Reconciliation: Reflections on a Social Dimension of the Eschatological Transition', *MT* 16, no. 1 (2000): 91–113.
[26] See Matthias Wenk, *Community-Forming Power: The Socio-ethical Role of the Spirit in Luke-Acts*, JPTS 19 (Sheffield: Sheffield Academic Press, 2000), 259–308.
[27] Jason E. Vickers, 'Holiness and Mediation: Pneumatology in Pietist Perspective', *IJST* 16, no. 2 (2014): 192–206; Lyle Story, 'Pauline Thoughts on the Holy Spirit and Sanctification: Provision, Process, and Consummation', *JPT* 18, no. 1 (2009): 67–94.
[28] Macchia, *Baptized in the Spirit*, 204; Yong, *The Spirit Poured Out*, 292–302; David S. Norris, 'Creation Revealed: An Early Pentecostal Hermeneutic', in Yong, *The Spirit Renews*, 74–92.
[29] Amos Yong, 'Sanctification, Science and the Spirit: Salvaging Holiness in the Late Modern World', *WTJ* 47, no. 2 (2012): 36–52.

place for God;[30] and it is ecclesiological because the church as the body of Christ embodies the sanctifying work of the Spirit by providing sanctified practices that allow the world to participate in God's holiness.[31] Through these dimensions of a Pentecostal cosmology of sanctification, the pneumatological orientation forms the theological motif for understanding how the sanctifying activity of God can transcend the private and public, ecclesial and social, anthropological, and ecological boundaries of creation.[32] The goal of this sanctification is a cosmos filled with the Holy Spirit or, to use Pentecostal language, creation baptized in the Spirit.

Creation baptized in the Spirit

For Pentecostals, sanctification is not an end in itself but always a gateway to realizing the full promises of God. In the narrative framework of the full gospel, I have identified the baptism in the Spirit as a lens through which Pentecostals view and order the other elements of the narrative (see Chapter 4). The often central place given to the baptism in the Spirit weds the concerns of sanctification with a focus on charismatic empowerment. Within the broad cosmology attempted in this chapter, the motif of the outpouring of the Spirit orients the full gospel towards a 'cosmic Pentecost'[33] where Spirit baptism identifies the power to accomplish the transformation of the whole of creation towards its goal in Jesus Christ. The chief challenge to this perspective is the question how we can speak of a charismatic empowerment of the whole of creation. The emphasis on a pneumatological theology of creation, forged within the Christological headship of the full gospel, suggests that God creates, redeems and consummates the entire cosmos through Word and Spirit.[34]

---

[30] See Jeffrey S. Lamp, 'Jesus as Sanctifier: Creation Care and the Fivefold Gospel', in *Blood Cries Out: Pentecostals, Ecology, and the Groans of Creation*, ed. A. J. Swoboda (Eugene, OR: Pickwick, 2014), 152–68.

[31] See Torbjörn Aronson, 'Spirit and Church in the Ecclesiology of Lewi Pethrus', *PentecoStudies* 11, no. 2 (2012): 192–211; Matthias Wenk, 'The Church as Sanctified Community', in *Toward a Pentecostal Ecclesiology: The Church and the Fivefold Gospel*, ed. John Christopher Thomas (Cleveland, TN: CPT Press, 2010), 105–35.

[32] See Amos Yong, 'What Spirit(s), Which Public(s)? The Pneumatologies of Global Pentecostal-Charismatic Christianity', *IJPT* 7, no. 3 (2013): 241–59.

[33] Thompson, *Kingdom Come*, 135–37.

[34] See Amos Yong, '*Creatio Spiritus* and the Spirit of Christ: Toward a Trinitarian Theology of Creation', in *Spirit of God: Christian Renewal in the Community of Faith*, ed. Jeffrey W. Barbeau and Beth Felker Jones (Downers Grove, IL: InterVarsity, 2015), 168–82.

As a sacramental encounter, Spirit baptism functions within this trinitarian theology of creation as an embodied act fully integrated in the transformation of the world and manifesting with the charismatic dimension the universal and eschatological arrival of the kingdom of God. Such a structurally integrative perspective demands that the outpouring of the Spirit affects the relationship of nature and spirit in principle, even if such transformation is not manifested immediately across the taxonomy of the created order.

The outpouring of the Spirit on the day of Pentecost is said to be 'on all flesh' (Acts 2:17) with ramifications for the 'heavens above' and the 'earth below' (v. 19) and culminating in the judgement of the entire cosmos on the day of the Lord (v. 20). The biblical metaphor of a 'baptism' in the Spirit here identifies an intensity of the Spirit that surpasses individuals, believers, communities, churches and humanity to penetrate the whole of creation.[35] This infusion with the Spirit is different from the indwelling of the Spirit for the creation and sustaining of life; it is, as Pentecostals say, a subsequent filling or release of power.[36] The outpouring of the Spirit at creation makes possible the ontological participation of all creation 'in the divine through the animating power of the Spirit', while the outpouring of the Spirit at Pentecost marks 'a soteriological participation in the Spirit ... [that] is an intensification of just that ontological participation'.[37] Put differently, with Pentecost the presence of the Spirit intensifies throughout creation so that the Spirit, who is omnipresent with creation, now also becomes more fully active in all created beings.[38] The baptism in the Spirit thus stands for the increase of the mutual participation of creation in the Spirit and of the Spirit in creation for the purposes of cosmic redemption (see Chapter 11).

The interpretation of the sacramentality of Spirit baptism in terms of both sanctification and charismatic empowerment is significant here. Spirit baptism as a sacramental encounter and mutual interpenetration of nature and spirit allows Pentecostal cosmology to speak of the redemption of the

---

[35] Andrew K. Gabriel, 'The Intensity of the Spirit in a Spirit-filled World: Spirit Baptism, Subsequence, and the Spirit of Creation', *Pneuma* 34, no. 3 (2012): 365–82.

[36] John R. Levison, *Filled with the Spirit* (Grand Rapids, MI: Eerdmans, 2009), 12–33; Macchia, *Baptized in the Spirit*, 77.

[37] James K. A. Smith, 'The Spirit, Religions, and the World as Sacrament: A Response to Amos Yong's Pneumatological Assist', *JPT* 15, no. 2 (2007): 251–61 (at 254–55).

[38] Andrew K. Gabriel, *The Lord Is the Spirit: The Holy Spirit and the Divine Attributes* (Eugene, OR: Pickwick, 2011), 173–78.

cosmos by highlighting the continuity and discontinuity, the determinate and ambiguous nature of participating in the divine life.[39] The outpouring of the Spirit at Pentecost marks the defining moment of a new ontological reality that invites a union of nature and spirit brought about by the Spirit of God through the charismatic dimension. This union is 'simply a more obvious sign of the interpenetration of the divine and the orders of creation'[40] yet without collapsing them into a single reality. The descending order implied by the image of the 'outpouring' of the Holy Spirit on all flesh is complemented by an ascending pneumatology which acknowledges that the reception and exercise of spiritual power transforms and elevates creation bearing the Spirit.[41] This charismatic theology of creation abandons the artificial distinction between natural and supernatural (see Chapter 5) and can resist the discontinuity and hierarchy often placed between common and special grace.[42] Creation and redemption are a single activity of the Spirit.

The Pentecostal insistence that the baptism in the Spirit is of cosmic proportions emphasizes the importance of Pentecost for the redemption of creation. The creative movement of the Spirit precedes the empowerment of creation at Pentecost and its transition 'into a pneumatological horizon of redemption'.[43] Charismatic empowerment is a necessary degree in God's activity of redemption, most clearly manifested in the Incarnation of Christ and made available to all creation through the outpouring of the Spirit. Nevertheless, while all of creation can be said to participate in the presence of the Spirit, not all elements of the cosmos participate in the divine presence with the same intensity.[44] On the one hand, Pentecostal theology insists on the radically disorienting nature of the Fall, the continuing impact of evil and the struggle of creation against sin and the demonic as the antithesis to the divine Spirit. The confrontation of the charismatic and the demonic

---

[39] See Wolfgang Vondey and Chris W. Green, 'Between This and That: Reality and Sacramentality in the Pentecostal Worldview', *JPT* 19, no. 2 (2010): 243–64.
[40] Yong, *The Spirit Poured Out*, 295.
[41] Wolfgang Vondey, 'Spirit and Nature: Pentecostal Pneumatology in Dialogue with Tillich's Pneumatological Ontology', in *Paul Tillich and Pentecostal Theology: Spiritual Presence and Spiritual Power*, ed. Nimi Wariboko and Amos Yong (Bloomington: Indiana University Press, 2016), 30–44.
[42] See Steven M. Studebaker, 'The Spirit in Creation: A Unified Theology of Grace and Creation Care', *Zygon* 43, no. 4 (2008): 943–60.
[43] Ibid., 92.
[44] Smith, 'The Spirit, Religions, and the World as Sacrament', 256; Gabriel, 'The Intensity of the Spirit', 378.

realms constitutes a central feature of Pentecostal pneumatological ontology.[45] This confrontation represents the most concrete manifestation of the uneasy union of nature and spirit and its struggle towards participation in the divine. On the other hand, the charismatic manifestations are typically observed with a strong focus on the empowerment of the human being and with particular focus on the church and the Christian.[46] From a charismatic viewpoint, the directionality of the Spirit's empowerment in creation points from the Christian to the church to humanity to nature and is confronted on all levels by opposing spirits and the powers of evil. The Holy Spirit is no less present anywhere in the world, yet the difference of intensity of the Spirit suggests that the charismatic empowerment can be more fully manifested in the sanctified and Spirit-baptized person as part of the church's participation in God's purposes of salvation. While the redemption achieved by Christ is pneumatologically mediated, the Spirit works concurrently with human and divine agency to produce the desired results in the created order.[47] The metaphor of a cosmic Spirit baptism affirms this divine-human cooperation with emphasis on human agency enabled by the reception of spiritual power, which releases the charismatic gifts, signs, and wonders of the Spirit.[48]

The significance of identifying Spirit baptism as sacramental encounter lies in a charismatic extension of the metaphor from primarily anthropocentric ('only human beings are baptized in the Spirit') and ecclesiocentric definitions ('only Christians are baptized in the Spirit') to the cosmological ramifications of redemption ('all creation participates in Spirit baptism to some degree'). Pentecostal theology of creation affirms the integrative significance of human agency enabled by the power of the Spirit on behalf of the transformation of the world.[49] The baptism in the Spirit, as a human event, ignites in the person a passion directed beyond one's self to the world that seeks participation in the realization of God's promises of redemption to all of creation. As a charismatic event, the baptism in the Spirit confronts the

---

[45] Vondey, *Pentecostalism*, 29–47.
[46] See Keith Warrington, *Pentecostal Theology: A Theology of Encounter* (London: T&T Clark, 2008), 106–19; Duffield and Van Cleave, *Foundations of Pentecostal Theology*, 326–57.
[47] Mark J. Cartledge, *The Mediation of the Spirit: Interventions in Practical Theology*, Pentecostal Manifestos 7 (Grand Rapids, MI: Eerdmans, 2015), 71–75.
[48] See Joshua D. Reichard, 'Toward a Pentecostal Theology of *Concursus*', *JPT* 22 (2013): 95–114.
[49] See A. J. Swoboda, 'Eco-Glossolalia: Emerging Twenty-First Century Pentecostal and Charismatic Ecotheology', *RT* 9, no. 2 (2011): 101–16.

ambiguities of life from within the unity of nature and spirit driving the person and community towards the transcendent.[50] As an ecclesial event, Spirit baptism speaks to the cooperation of the church with the missional life of the triune God.[51] In these interconnected ways, creation is baptized in the Spirit with signs and wonders prophetically and critically announcing the coming of God's kingdom while groaning in solidarity with creation awaiting the fullness of redemption.

Divine healing and the fullness of redemption

The notion of creation baptized in the Spirit demands a cosmological reinvention of Christian practices.[52] The sacramentality of Spirit baptism, on the one hand, functions as a foretaste of the power of the kingdom already present in this world, while, on the other, it manifests the distance still existing between the present world and the new creation. In the Pentecostal worldview, Christ is healer, and the Spirit is the medicine which brings about God's purposes by engaging in a confrontation with spiritual powers manifested tangibly in the physical world (see Chapter 5). The practices of divine healing confront the existential tensions of creation by bringing to light the reality of spiritual warfare manifesting the struggle for the healing, deliverance, and wholeness of the cosmos. The chief theological question confronting this worldview is how Christian practices can be said to apply to the natural world beyond an anthropocentric theology of divine healing. Classical Pentecostalism has been hesitant to engage issues of creation, nature and ecology, particularly because of its urgent apocalypticism, which envisioned the imminent destruction of the present world.[53] However, while the early eschatological response was largely procrastinating in nature ('creation will be transformed in the end'), the global sensitivities of contemporary Pentecostal theology have redirected its attention more immediately to the active transformation of creation in the

---

[50] Wolfgang Vondey, 'Spirit and Nature as Ultimate Concern: Tillich's "Radical" Ontology in Conversation with Contemporary Pentecostalism', *BNAPTS* 39, no. 1 (2013): 30–35.

[51] See Peter Althouse, 'Towards a Pentecostal Ecclesiology: Participation in the Missional Life of the Triune God', *JPT* 18 (2009): 230–45.

[52] A. J. Swoboda, *Tongues and Trees: Toward a Pentecostal Ecological Theology*, JPTS 40 (Blandford Forum, UK: Deo, 2013), 203.

[53] Peter Althouse, 'Pentecostal Eco-Transformation: Possibilities for a Pentecostal Ecotheology in Light of Moltmann's Green Theology', in Swoboda, *Blood Cries Out*, 116–32.

present. The Pentecostal emphasis on charismatic empowerment and the mission of the church are casting the struggle for divine healing in the image of social justice, creation care, and environmental stewardship.

With the extension of Pentecostalism to worldwide proportions, Pentecostal concerns for global themes, social, and environmental issues expanded as well.[54] These concerns are widely situated within a theology of spiritual warfare that takes seriously the spiritual dimensions of created existence and the resulting interdependent (and confrontational) relationships.[55] Spiritual warfare is territorial conflict often understood in its most common form to entail demonic spirits that inhabit people (ancestral spirits, occult spirits and demons attached to vices).[56] However, human spirit-possession in the Pentecostal worldview is simply a more obvious form of territorial warfare throughout the created world. At a global level, the devil's realm of influence is seen in the biblical title 'ruler of this world' (Jn 12:31; 14:30) and of the demonic powers as 'the rulers of the darkness of this world' (Eph. 6:12). A Pentecostal theology of creation can distinguish between a vast array of territorial spirits over regions, nations, cities, people groups, tribes, neighbourhoods, and social networks.[57] Other levels may include institutional spirits (e.g. government, schools, churches), instrumental spirits assigned to buildings, tools, instruments, rituals and practices, functional spirits promoting particular actions (e.g. murder, adultery, abortion) and, finally, ancestral and ground-level spirits over families and individuals.[58]

While global Pentecostal views on the spiritual world are contextual and complex, this attention to the spiritual realm is complemented by an equally important doctrine of angels with very clear distinctions drawn

---

[54] See Michael Wilkinson, 'Globalization and the Environment as Social Problem: Assessing a Pentecostal Response', in *A Liberating Spirit: Pentecostals and Social Action in North America*, ed. Michael Wilkinson and Steven M. Studebaker (Eugene, OR: Pickwick, 2010), 213–30.

[55] Allan Anderson, 'Deliverance and Exorcism in Majority World Pentecostalism', in *Exorcism and Deliverance: Multi-Disciplinary Studies*, ed. William K. Kay and Robin Parry, Studies in Pentecostal and Charismatic Issues (Milton Keynes, UK: Paternoster, 2011), 101–19.

[56] Opoku Onyinah, *Spiritual Warfare: A Centre for Pentecostal Theology Short Introduction* (Cleveland, TN: CPT Press, 2012), 10–14. See Charles H. Kraft, *Defeating the Dark Angels* (Kent: Sovereign World, 1993).

[57] C. Peter Wagner (ed.), *Territorial Spirits: Practical Strategies for How to Crush the Enemy through Spiritual Warfare* (Shippensburg, PA: Destiny, 2012); idem, *Engaging the Enemy: How to Fight and Defeat Territorial Spirits* (Ventura: Regal, 1993).

[58] See Gregory Boyd, 'The Ground-Level Deliverance Model', in *Understanding Spiritual Warfare: Four Views*, ed. James K. Beilby and Paul Rhodes Eddy (Grand Rapids, MI: Baker, 2012), 129–72.

between demonic and angelic spirits.[59] Spiritual warfare is based on a pneumatological cosmology concerning the nature and action of powers that create and animate the universe. A certain otherworldliness, overemphasis on the demonic and pessimistic eschatological outlook has led Pentecostals in the past to neglect environmental issues.[60] For the more progressive Pentecostals, this spiritual worldview identifies the critical relationality of human, divine, and evil orders as interwoven dimensions of all creaturely existence and point to the distinctive contributions of humankind to the conservation and transformation of the ecological system.[61] The experiences and practices of spiritual warfare conceive the theological emphasis of the full gospel on salvation, sanctification and Spirit baptism in terms of the human instrumentality on behalf of the world. The soteriological orientation of Pentecostal theology leads ultimately to a praxis-centred theology of creation integrated in the anthropology and missiological concerns of global Pentecostalism.[62]

Pentecostals can speak of human instrumentality for the healing of the cosmos because the Spirit's work of redemption encompasses the origin, care and transformation of creation in which human life is embedded. The work of the Spirit in human lives corresponds to the work of the Spirit in the world, not in an abstract correlation but in a complex interrelationship with the world in which there is no such thing as 'pure' nature.[63] Instead, human destiny is tied up both with the suffering of creation, as a consequence of human sin, and with the renewal of creation as a dimension of Christian formation, sanctification and salvation. Put differently, the care for creation requires not only a universal but also an ecclesiological and personal ecological commitment.[64]

---

[59] See William K. Kay, 'Pentecostals and Angels', in *Angels and Demons: Perspectives and Practices from Diverse Religious Traditions*, ed. Peter G. Riddell and Beverly Smith Riddell (Nottingham: Apollos, 2007), 63–83; William Atkinson, 'Angels and the Spirit in Luke-Acts', *JEPTA* 26, no. 1 (2006): 76–90.

[60] See Augustus Dermawan, 'The Spirit in Creation and Environmental Stewardship: A Preliminary Pentecostal Response toward Ecological Theology', *AJPS* 6, no. 2 (2003): 199–217.

[61] See Veli-Matti Kärkkäinen, 'The Greening of the Spirit: Towards a Pneumatological Theology of the Flourishing of Nature', in Swoboda, *Blood Cries Out*, 83–97.

[62] See. A. J. Swoboda, 'Looking the Wrong Way: Salvation and the Spirit in Pentecostal Eco-Theology', in Wilkinson and Studebaker, *A Liberating Spirit*, 231–47.

[63] Studebaker, 'The Spirit in Creation', 953–54.

[64] Jean Jacques Suurmond, 'Christ King: A Charismatic Appeal for an Ecological Lifestyle', *Pneuma* 10 (1988): 26–35.

Two main trajectories guide this missiological perspective within the larger matrix of a pneumatological cosmology: a theology of social justice and the emergence of a distinctive Pentecostal ecotheology.[65] Both are relatively new commitments for Pentecostals. At first glance, a Pentecostal approach to social justice engages cosmological and ecological issues only indirectly.[66] However, a closer look suggests that both concerns are held together by a pneumatology surrounding the notions of salvation, sanctification and empowerment to a cosmic theology of the healing power of the Spirit.[67] Because of the Spirit, God experiences the pain of creation and extends the work of Christ to heal the sickness of the entire cosmos.[68] In this soteriological extension, divine healing is inherently physical, social and ecological because it emerges from the Spirit of creation. The connection is established through the kenotic relationality of the Spirit, who is poured out on all flesh both 'to be a community of the Spirit *in* the world and a community of the Spirit *for* the world'.[69] This ecological sensitivity is typically stronger among Pentecostals in the global South faced with poverty, overpopulation, drought, deforestation, natural disasters and other ecological problems.[70] In this relational cosmology, human beings are created as agents for the healing and peace of creation.[71] From a Pentecostal perspective, such agency is carried out by the church as the charismatic community through which the Spirit of creation can heal the world.[72] The charismatic gifts include not only the groaning in the Spirit in solidarity with creation but a counter-cultural activity on behalf of the cosmos, nature, the environment, and the creatures embedded within, a prophetic confrontation with the powers of exploitation and oppression,

---

[65] Swoboda, *Tongues and Trees*, 69–101; idem, 'Eco-Glossolalia', 103–11.
[66] See Wolfgang Vondey, 'The Impact of Culture and Social Justice on Christian Formation in Pentecostalism', *JPT* 24, no. 2 (2015): 201–16.
[67] Swoboda, *Tongues and Trees*, 101–4.
[68] See Matthew Tallman, 'Pentecostal Ecology: A Theological Paradigm for Pentecostal Environmentalism', in Yong, *The Spirit Renews*, 135–54; Marthinus Daneel, 'Earthkeeping Churches at the African Grassroots', in *Christianity and Ecology: Seeking the Well-being of Earth and Healing*, ed. Dieter T. Hessel and Rosemary Radford Ruether (Cambridge, MA: Harvard University Press, 2000), 533–48.
[69] Eldin Villafañe, *The Liberating Spirit: Toward an Hispanic American Pentecostal Social Ethic* (Grand Rapids, MI: Eerdmans, 1993), 196.
[70] See David Roebuck, 'Pentecostalism at the End of the Twentieth Century: From Poverty, Promise and Passion to Prosperity, Power and Place', in *Religion in the Contemporary South: Changes, Continuities, and Contexts*, ed. Corrie Norman (Knoxville: University of Tennessee Press, 2005), 53–73.
[71] R. Jerome Boone, 'Created for Shalom: Human Agency and Responsibility in the World', in Yong, *The Spirit Renews*, 17–29.
[72] Swoboda, *Tongues and Trees*, 204–16.

exorcism of spiritual forces, anointing and healing of sickness in all its forms throughout the natural world, liberation from social, political, economic, and institutional injustice and the restoration of relationships among all of God's creatures into the eternal fellowship of the Spirit.

With a raised consciousness for human responsibility, Pentecostals have begun to articulate a distinctive Pentecostal ecology based on the healing aspects of an ecotheology that is consistent with the full gospel.[73] More precisely, the Pentecostal mandate for the fullness of the gospel demands the inclusion of concerns for the ecological and eschatological well-being of creation.[74] From a pneumatological perspective, there is no closed independent ecological system: a cosmology that is pneumatologically oriented – and therefore embraces the deeply relational and interdependent as well as ambiguous and confrontational aspects of creation – crosses the borders between the local and the global, the natural and the human, the spiritual and the physical, the present and the coming world for the renewal of the entire cosmos.

Creation and the renewal of the cosmos

Cosmology and eschatology are mutually conditioning elements in Pentecostal theology, which features a strong apocalyptic vision (see Chapter 6). The narrative of Pentecostal pneumatological cosmology is very much grounded in cosmogony rather than eschatology. Nonetheless, the question of the end of creation has had decisive influence on the more recent missional theology of relational responsibility: In a world destined to pass away with a cataclysmic apocalyptic scenario and expectations of an otherworldly heavenly kingdom, few Pentecostals felt compelled to become advocates for creation care during the early twentieth century; however, with the delay of the parousia, a reinterpretation of apocalyptic urgency and a more realized than dispensational eschatology locating the kingdom of God on earth, contemporary eschatology has become a prime motivation for advocating ecological concerns for the healing and transformation of

---

[73] See Harold Hunter, 'Pentecostal Healing for God's Sick Creation?' *SC* 2, no. 2 (2000): 145–67.
[74] Shane Clifton, 'Preaching the "Full Gospel" in the Context of Global Environmental Crises', in Yong, *The Spirit Renews*, 117–34.

creation.⁷⁵ In the older perspective, the world is destined to be destroyed to make place for a radically discontinuous 'new' dispensation; in the more recent view, the kingdom of God is already being established on earth, and human beings are held responsible for their actions at the advent of a new creation.⁷⁶ The primary eschatological question from the perspective of the full gospel is how an apocalyptic imagination serves the understanding of the first creation and its continuity and discontinuity with the new creation. The most recent constructive proposals among Pentecostals suggest that answers are sought in the theological engagement with science.

Relating science to apocalypse is a necessary endeavour in Pentecostal theology where eschatological questions are asked typically within ordinary 'scientific' categories of the public mind 'as two distinct and intrinsically related forms of discovery'.⁷⁷ For most Pentecostals, the greater and ultimate eschatological realm certainly frames the lesser and present natural realm.⁷⁸ While the knowledge of the present natural and social world relies on the empirically precise and tangible, the knowledge of the coming kingdom depends on the revelation of the Spirit.⁷⁹ Yet, this contrast of discovery does not juxtapose the physical and the spiritual or the scientific and the religious dimensions but rather returns to the pneumatological perspective at the foundation of Pentecostal cosmology: God acts in the world teleologically or eschatologically through the Holy Spirit in ways that can be explained by both theological and scientific accounts.

A Pentecostal pneumatological theology of creation confronts and corrects any reductionist definition of creation as a purely physical reality reducible to material elements.⁸⁰ This kind of reductionism is a consequence both of a uncritical understanding of science and a spiritualized eschatology. The former exaggerates the empirical methods of science and their focus on the

---

[75] See Robby Waddell, 'Apocalyptic Sustainability: The Future of Pentecostal Ecology', in *Perspectives in Pentecostal Eschatology: World without End*, ed. Peter Althouse and Robby Waddell (Eugene, OR: Pickwick, 2010), 95–110.

[76] See Robby Waddell, 'A Green Apocalypse: Comparing Secular and Religious Eschatological Visions of Earth', in Swoboda, *Blood Cries Out*, 133–51.

[77] See Telford Work, 'What Have the Galapagos to Do with Jerusalem? Scientific Knowledge in Theological Context', in *Science and the Spirit: A Pentecostal Engagement with the Sciences*, ed. James K. A. Smith and Amos Yong (Bloomington: Indiana University Press, 2010), 15–33 (at 22).

[78] Ibid., 23.

[79] Telford Work, 'Pneumatological Relations and Christian Disunity in Theology-Science Dialogue', *Zygon* 43, no. 4 (2008): 897–908.

[80] See Amos Yong, 'The Spirit and Creation: Possibilities and Challenges for a Dialogue between Pentecostal Theology and the Sciences', *JEPTA* 25 (2005): 82–110.

causal mechanisms of nature.[81] The latter overemphasizes the spiritual nature of the kingdom of God and its displacement of the physical world.[82] A pneumatological eschatology, in contrast, imagines the realization of the coming kingdom precisely in terms of the incarnational nature of Christ and the outpouring of the Holy Spirit on the natural world. In other words, a Pentecostal account of eschatological divine action engages deeply in the teleological explanations of the scientific disciplines.[83] The belief that the Spirit brings about the coming reign of God in the present world can direct a Pentecostal theology of creation to the empirical world of the geosciences, including contemporary physics, chemistry, and biology, as well as to astronomy and physical cosmology, anthropology, psychology, and the social sciences.[84] Nonetheless, since such redirection is motivated by an eschatological vision, its ultimate concern is participation in the mission of God in creation. In this sense, Pentecostal theology can speak of creation endowed with the activity of the Spirit as a charismatic sacrament (see Chapter 4).

The eschatological agency of the Spirit in creation, while shaping the natural history of the world in accordance with the intentions of God, nonetheless remains hidden in the origin of the natural processes and laws of the world.[85] This hidden ubiquity of the Spirit, rather than a causal-evolutionary phenomenon, is a teleological principle inherent to the increasing emergence of complexity and its transition to life. Put theologically, however, not life itself but life's redemption forms the principle of the transformation of the world. For Pentecostals, the principle of ontological (and eschatological) transformation is tied not to an impersonal ground of being but to the personal nature of God realized by the Holy Spirit.[86] Spirit is in this sense the basic ontological category; yet, at the same time, Pentecostal pneumatology

---

[81] See Amos Yong, 'Reading Scripture and Nature: Pentecostal Hermeneutics and Their Implications for the Contemporary Evangelical Theology and Science Conversation', *Perspectives on Science and Christian Faith* 63, no. 1 (2011): 3–15.

[82] Thompson, *Kingdom Come*, 144–60.

[83] See Amos Yong, 'How Does God Do What God Does? Pentecostal-Charismatic Perspectives on Divine Action in Dialogue with Modern Science', in Smith and Yong, *Science and the Spirit*, 50–71.

[84] See Smith and Yong, *Science and the Spirit*, 75–91; Wolfgang Vondey, 'The Holy Spirit and the Physical Universe: The Impact of Scientific Paradigm Shifts on Contemporary Pneumatology', *TS* 70, no. 1 (2009): 3–36.

[85] Amos Yong, 'The Spirit at Work in the World: A Pentecostal-Charismatic Perspective on the Divine Action Project', *TAS* 7, no. 2 (2009): 123–40 (135).

[86] Rhys Kuzič, 'To the Ground of Being and Beyond: Toward a Pentecostal Engagement with Ontology', in Wariboko and Yong, *Paul Tillich and Pentecostal Theology*, 45–57.

is more restrictive when it demands a particular way that creation is being grasped by God's Spirit.[87] Redemptive pneumatology does not equate all spiritual dimensions with the Spirit of God. Nature and spirit remain in eschatological tension, and the laws of nature are merely teleological (real but not redeemed) 'tendencies' through which the Holy Spirit serves as agent of God's kingdom.[88] The activity of the Spirit at the Incarnation and at Pentecost manifests the beginning of new laws of the coming kingdom opening the world to charismatic participation, divine empowerment, and eschatological transformation.[89] Hence, physics as an engaging science is formed by a confluence of experiential, philosophical and spiritual dimensions, while theology as a spiritual discipline also includes the material, empirical, and causal dimensions of creation. This interactive engagement of the present world and the world to come in the Spirit forms the basis for the charismatic reality that permeates the transformation of creation. Pentecostal eschatology therefore demands both a missiological cosmology, in which all of the cosmos is invited to participate in the Spirit's work of redemption, and a cosmological missiology, in which the final goal of the Spirit's work is the redemption of the entire cosmos. In this sense of the interconnectedness of the Spirit's activity in the origin and history, sanctification and charismatic empowerment of the natural world and the human being, creation is the cosmic altar of redemption.

If this pneumatological redemptive trajectory of Pentecostal cosmology is accurate, then it is necessary to situate in this broad metaphysical framework also a functional theological anthropology, which can speak more closely to divine and human agency, a theology of society and culture, which can sustain a participatory soteriology, an ecclesiology that supports the particular Pentecostal trajectory of redemptive community and a theology that culminates in a corresponding cosmological doxology. Such is the task of the following chapters.

---

[87] Andreas Northlander, 'Pneumatological Participation: Embodiment, Sacramentality, and the Multidimensional Unity of Life', in Wariboko and Yong, *Paul Tillich and Pentecostal Theology*, 101–14.

[88] Amos Yong, 'Natural Laws and Divine Intervention: What Difference Does Being Pentecostal or Charismatic Make?' *Zygon* 43, no. 4 (2008): 961–89.

[89] Ibid., 979–80.

8

Humanity

Divine Image, Human Agency, and Theological Anthropology

Pentecostals have not produced a fully articulated anthropology, although the human being is unambiguously the object central to the narrative of the full gospel.[1] In principle, anthropology among Pentecostals can be identified by a traditional theological focus, that is, the human being is understood first of all (though not exclusively) in relation to God, created in God's image and utterly dependent upon God. The central focus on Jesus Christ as the subject of the full gospel places upon this theological anthropology a strong Christocentric focus: Jesus is both redeemer and prototypical image of redeemed humanity. Nonetheless, neither the classical theological approach to humanity from the image of God nor the well-worn Christological lens offers a particular ontological grounding to what might be termed a genuine Pentecostal anthropology. The full gospel proclaims that God chooses in Jesus Christ to save, sanctify, baptize with the Spirit, heal, and commission the human being for the kingdom of God (see part one). These particular Pentecostal affirmations raise important questions for theological anthropology about how divine action characterizes human nature and its embodiment of the divine image.

Pentecostals have challenged traditional theological and Christological approaches to human nature. Their particular concerns include a rational and intellectual bias towards the *imago Dei* as the exclusive ontological foundation for defining humanity, a theological lens that tends to suppress the reality of human embodiment, and a weak pneumatology that does not begin

---

[1] Delineating the parameters is Simon Coleman and Rosalind I. J. Hackett (eds), *The Anthropology of Global Pentecostalism and Evangelicalism* (New York: New York University Press, 2015).

the anthropological enquiry with the Spirit. In contrast, Pentecost as theological symbol enacted among Pentecostals today reaches deep into the environment of the altar and urges Pentecostal anthropology to remain indebted to the tangible concerns of human embodiment and practices. This chapter proposes that in the context of creation, identified previously as the cosmic altar of redemption, humankind is created to embody the image of God to the world through the reception of the Holy Spirit. The fullness of the gospel guides Pentecostals to articulate this embodiment of the image of God through a holistic anthropology that critically engages human agency in relation to God, self, and others. The following constructive account, indebted to the motifs of the full gospel, sketches the basic contours of a Pentecostal theological anthropology that begins with the Spirit and takes seriously the pneumatological imagination for understanding salvation, sanctification, Spirit baptism, divine healing, and eschatological mission.

Salvation and the image of God

On the basis of the Pentecostal theology of creation constructed along the core soteriological affirmations of the full gospel (see Chapter 7), theological anthropology shows a foundational indebtedness to the notion of redemption. Salvation is not only the eschatological goal but the metaphysical grounding for the creation, providence, redemption, and transformation of human nature.[2] Moreover, the affirmation that 'Jesus is Saviour' serves not merely as a recapitulating identification of the human condition *after* the Fall (sinful human beings necessitate the provision of salvation) but as existential identification and affirmation of human origin *before* creation (human beings are created into the providence of salvation). From the perspectives of the New Testament, human beings are predestined for salvation in Christ before the foundation of the world (see Eph. 1:4; 1 Pet. 1:20; Rev. 13:8).[3] Theologically

---

[2] See Frank D. Macchia, *Justified in the Spirit: Creation, Redemption, and the Triune God*, Pentecostal Manifestos 2 (Grand Rapids, MI: Eerdmans, 2010), 293–312; Amos Yong, *The Spirit Poured Out on All Flesh: Pentecostalism and the Possibility of Global Theology* (Grand Rapids, MI: Baker Academic, 2005), 91–98; Miroslav Volf, 'Materiality of Salvation: An Investigation in the Soteriologies of Liberation and Pentecostal Theologies', *JES* 26, no. 3 (1989): 447–67.

[3] For a Pentecostal reading of election, see James M. Henderson, 'Election as Renewal: The Work of the Holy Spirit in Divine Election' (PhD diss., Regent University, 2012).

speaking, salvation precedes creation in God's eternal intention for humankind. From the perspective of the full gospel, the primary soteriological question is certainly why human beings occupy this irrevocable position in God's redemptive providence. The traditional answers point to the creation of the human being in the *imago Dei* – without doubt 'the key concept of modern theological anthropology'.[4] Humankind exists for salvation because the human being is made in the image of God. Pentecostal theology affirms that the image of God in the human being 'is the most distinctive dimension of human existence'.[5] At the same time, the foundational Pentecostal emphasis on God as spirit suggests that the divine image occupies this central importance precisely because human beings possess a unique spiritual quality with which they are created and which affords them a unique place in the divine purpose of salvation.[6] Not only are the purposes of creation and salvation in this sense identical, but both find their grounding in the divine image actualized through the special spiritual quality of the human being.

The grounding of Pentecostal anthropology in the *imago Dei* defined by God as spirit raises both metaphysical and ontological questions with regard to the general constitution of human nature and its reflection of the divine image.[7] The first biblical creation account in Gen. 1:1–2:4, particularly Gen. 1:26–27, forms the classical theological backbone for a theology of the *imago Dei*. Created by God, the human being comes into existence in the likeness of God and with the ability to reflect the moral, intellectual, and spiritual character of the creator.[8] Yet, despite the immediate biblical reference to the manifestation of God as 'wind' or 'spirit' in the account of creation (Gen. 1:2), little attention has been paid traditionally to a pneumatological account of

---

[4] Bernd Oberdorfer, 'The Dignity of Human Personhood and the Concept of the "Image of God"', in *The Depth of the Human Person: A Multidisciplinary Approach*, ed. Michael Welker (Grand Rapids, MI: Eerdmans, 2014), 257–73 (at 258–59).
[5] French L. Arrington, *Christian Doctrine: A Pentecostal Perspective*, vol. 1 (Cleveland, TN: Pathway, 1992), 198. See also Guy P. Duffield and Nathaniel M. Van Cleave, *Foundations of Pentecostal Theology* (San Dimas, CA: L.I.F.E. Bible College, 1983), 123–25; Larry D. Hart, *Truth Aflame: Theology for the Church in Renewal*, rev. ed. (Grand Rapids, MI: Zondervan, 2005), 231–41.
[6] See Wolfgang Vondey, 'Pneumatology from the Perspective of the Spirit: A Historical and Theological Assessment', in *Third Article Theology*, ed. Myk Habets (Philadelphia: Fortress, 2016), 77–96.
[7] See Amos Yong, *Theology and Down Syndrome: Reimagining Disability in Late Modernity* (Waco, TX: Baylor University Press, 2007), 169–70.
[8] Arrington, *Christian Doctrine*, 1:198; Duffield and Van Cleave, *Foundations*, 250–53.

the divine image.[9] Rather, the theological interpretation of the divine image is widely cast in the interpretive context of the divine word (*logos*) noted in Gen. 1:3, even though the presence of God as spirit precedes the activity of God as word in the biblical text.[10] As a consequence of this overemphasis on the divine *logos*, Pentecostals lament that the manifestation of God as *pneuma* (both as divine person and divine attribute) has gradually disappeared.[11] In turn, the dominance of a rational or intellectual interpretation of the image of God in the history of theological anthropology has neglected the spiritual quality of human beings often at the exclusion of those who do not clearly reflect the attributes given to the rational image of the divine in human nature.[12]

Equally dominant in the history of theological anthropology is the functional view of God's image, which attributes to human beings the ability to serve as stewards of creation and agents of God's purpose: human beings are defined by what they do. The dominant biblical support for this perspective is lent by Gen. 1:26, a text that suggests God's intention for human beings is that they would exercise dominion and stewardship over the earth. Again, Pentecostals lament that this perspective eschews human beings who are not able to exercise such authority and responsibility,[13] and that the New Testament suggests no human being actually holds such position of authority.[14] While functional imagery may describe divine intention joined with human destiny, it does not embrace the factual reality of human practices.

Finally, the relational view of the *imago Dei*, increasingly popular in theological scholarship, attributes to human nature a unique ability for relationships and expressive communication reflecting the divine life, in general,

---

[9] See Lisa P. Stephenson, 'A Feminist Pentecostal Theological Anthropology: North America and Beyond', *Pneuma* 35, no. 1 (2013): 35–47; idem, *Dismantling the Dualisms for American Pentecostal Women in Ministry: A Feminist-Pneumatological Approach* (Leiden: Brill, 2012), 117–21.

[10] Stephenson, 'A Feminist Pentecostal Theological Anthropology', 40.

[11] See Steven M. Studebaker, *From Pentecost to the Triune God: A Pentecostal Trinitarian Theology*, PM 6 (Grand Rapids, MI: Eerdmans, 2012), 174–85; Andrew K. Gabriel, 'The Spirit Is God: A Pentecostal Perspective on the Doctrine of the Divine Attributes', in *Defining Issues in Pentecostalism: Classical and Emergent*, ed. Steven M. Studebaker (Eugene, OR: Pickwick, 2008), 69–98.

[12] Yong, *Theology and Down Syndrome*, 172–73. See also Jeff Hittenberger, 'Receiving God's Gift of a Person with Special Needs: Amos Yong's Theology of Disability', in *The Theology of Amos Yong and the New Face of Pentecostal Scholarship: Passion for the Spirit*, ed. Wolfgang Vondey and Martin William Mittelstadt, GPCS 14 (Leiden: Brill, 2013), 141–59.

[13] See Yong, *Theology and Down Syndrome*, 173.

[14] Arrington, *Christian Doctrine*, 1:200.

and echoing the life of Jesus Christ, as the prototypical image, in particular.[15] A foundational text for this view in Gal. 3:26-28 suggests that the *imago Dei* is defined not by the original event of creation but by the redemption of creation or new creation.[16] Yet, those unable to establish conscious mutual relationships remain excluded from this view of redeemed human nature.[17] Amidst the reality of often exclusivist, dysfunctional, and even hostile human communities, the factuality of uninhibited relationships is often reduced to an eschatological anticipation.

The underlying Pentecostal concerns with these dominant interpretations are that they departmentalize human nature and fellowship. Pentecost as a symbol of the uninhibited outpouring of the Spirit 'on all flesh' reflects with this emphasis not only the entirety of humankind but also the inclusiveness of human nature: the benefit of Pentecost is experienced not literally by 'flesh' and 'body' alone but by the whole person and fellowship of human beings. Although both, the dichotomist position that human beings consist of body and soul and the trichotomist position of body, soul and spirit, can be found among Pentecostals, the essential Pentecostal anthropological affirmation is that these dimensions represents what human beings *are* rather than what they *have*.[18] Human creation and destiny always involve human beings as a whole in their existence rather than exclusively in their possessive attributes. Proposals that emphasize polychotomous views of human nature frequently suppress a deeper understanding of the spiritual dimension of human existence, suffer from a dualistic anthropology with regard to gender, race, and disability or obscure the communal dimensions inherent in the redemption of all creation.[19]

The pietist notions of Pentecostal Christology emphasize that the acclamation of Jesus as Saviour derives from a theology of the atonement deeply rooted in the suffering and death of Christ.[20] On the cross, the image of God

---

[15] Yong, *Theology and Down Syndrome*, 173-74; Hart, *Truth Aflame*, 235-36; Arrington, *Christian Doctrine*, 1:205-6.
[16] Stephenson, 'A Feminist Pentecostal Theological Anthropology', 41-42.
[17] Yong, *Theology and Down Syndrome*, 173-74.
[18] See Edmund J. Rybarczyk, 'What Are Thou, O Man? Theo-Anthropological Similarities in Classical Pentecostalism and Eastern Orthodoxy', in *Ancient and Postmodern Christianity: Paleo-orthodoxy in the 21st Century: Essays in Honor of Thomas C. Oden*, ed. Kenneth Tanner and Christopher Hall (Downers Grove, IL: InterVarsity Press, 2002), 83-105.
[19] Stephenson, 'A Feminist Pentecostal Theological Anthropology', 35-37.
[20] See Shaibu Abraham, 'Ordinary Indian Pentecostal Christology' (PhD diss., University of Birmingham, 2011); J. M. Waliggo, 'African Christology in a Situation of Suffering', in *Jesus in*

is tied to both the 'ability' and the 'disability' of God manifested in Jesus.[21] The practice-oriented nature of Pentecostal soteriology in light of this dual christological emphasis embraces a 'conditional unity'[22] of body, soul, and spirit: Wrapped in the physicality of human nature, the volatile character of this unity becomes evident in human suffering and death as well as in resurrection and eternal life.[23] Human nature expresses the vulnerability of reflecting the *imago Dei* precisely through the possibilities of embodying this unity and an openness to human affections, emotions, intuition, and volition.[24] As a prototype of redeemed humanity, the incarnate Son of God (from Incarnation to ascension) exhibits the *imago Dei* most fully in his redemptive suffering and resurrection. The life of Christ manifests in the realms of this embodiment a consistent exhibition of the presence, power, and person of the Holy Spirit.[25]

In turn, from the perspective of a soteriological theological anthropology, human beings reflect the *imago Dei* through participation in the *imago Christi* including the possibility of temptation, suffering, and death.[26] Neither the rational, the functional, or the relational view of the *imago Dei* in human nature exhausts this potential for participation in the divine life while also allowing for the possibility that human life can contradict the divine purpose. In response, the remainder of this chapter shows that Pentecostal theology insists that the event of Pentecost sheds new light on human nature by virtue of the outpouring of the Spirit of Christ. The image of God in Christ is embodied by human nature through the reception of the Holy Spirit (*imago Spiritus*).[27] The direction of Pentecostal theology leads to a theological

---

African Christianity, ed. J. N. K. Mugambi and Laurenti Magesa (Nairobi: Acton, 1998), 92–111; Chris E. Green, 'The Crucified God and the Groaning Spirit: Toward a Pentecostal Theologia Crucis in Conversation with Jürgen Moltmann', *JPT* 19, no. 1 (2010): 127–42.

[21] See Nancy Eiesland, *The Disabled God: Toward a Liberatory Theology of Disability* (Nashville: Abingdon, 1994).

[22] Timothy Munyon, 'The Creation of the Universe and Humankind', in *Systematic Theology*, rev. ed., ed. Stanley M. Horton (Springfield, MO: Legion, 1995), 215–53 (at 245).

[23] See Edmund J. Rybarczyk, 'Pentecostalism, Human Nature, and Aesthetics: Twenty-First Century Engagement', *JPT* 21, no. 2 (2012): 240–59; James K. A. Smith, *Thinking in Tongues: Pentecostal Contributions to Christian Philosophy*, PM 1 (Grand Rapids, MI: Eerdmans, 2010), 54–61.

[24] Rybarczyk, 'Pentecostalism, Human Nature, and Aesthetics', 247.

[25] Stephenson, 'A Feminist Pentecostal Anthropology', 42.

[26] Stephenson, *Dismantling the Dualisms*, 128–33.

[27] Stephenson, 'A Feminist Pentecostal Anthropology', 43–44. See also Steven M. Studebaker, *A Pentecostal Political Theology for American Renewal: Spirit of the Kingdoms, Citizen of the Cities*, Christianity and Renewal-Interdisciplinary Studies (New York: Palgrave Macmillan, 2016), 141–73.

anthropology that is more fully trinitarian than attempted thus far.[28] The concrete embodiment of the full gospel further demands that the Pentecostal image of the human being speaks to the spiritual and physical, the personal and social, the individual and interdependent, the embodied and transcendent dimensions of human existence (see Chapter 9).

Sanctification and human transformation

The emphasis Pentecostal theology places on human practices, centred on the metaphor of the altar, raises the question how exactly a theological anthropology of the *imago Dei* manifests itself beyond a general ontology of human nature. Discussions of human nature and concomitant conversations about flesh, body, heart, soul, and spirit, are theologically fruitful insofar as they exist in practice together only in human persons.[29] A practice-oriented ontology of human persons constructed from a Pentecostal perspective may emphasize developmental and relational aspects of human beings in order to construct a general theological anthropology.[30] Such an approach points to human particularity and difference as essential components of reflecting the *imago Dei* in creation: not every human being embodies the divine image in the same way.[31] This assertion is not to suggest a difference in quantity of the *imago Dei* (as if some human beings possessed less of the image) but in the quality of its embodiment, that is, in the way the divine image is grasped, mirrored and communicated by a human person.[32] This qualitative difference not only distinguishes human beings from the rest of creation but also human persons from one another, albeit not in an anthropological but theological sense: a difference in quality of the divine image does not make a being less human but a person less like the divine. Strictly speaking, the image of God is not affected but the human mediation of that image. There is neither a radical dualism nor a complete identification of the human and the divine.

---

[28] Pentecostal theology is guilty of neglecting in particular a theology of God as Father.
[29] See Michael Welker, 'Flesh – Body – Heart – Soul – Spirit: Paul's Anthropology as an Interdisciplinary Bridge-Theory', in Welker, *The Depth of the Human Person*, 45–57.
[30] See Amos Yong with Jonathan A. Anderson, *Renewing Christian Theology: Systematics for a Global Christianity* (Waco, TX: Baylor University Press, 2014), 114.
[31] Yong, *Theology and Down Syndrome*, 181.
[32] Ibid., 182.

Rather, the theology of the Wesleyan-Holiness tradition and its influence on a Pentecostal theology suggests that the act of emulating the divine image is a process of the sanctification and perfection of human nature.[33]

The doctrine of creation highlights the uniqueness of the human being in its embeddedness in creation as a whole, and its distinction from other created beings, in a way that yields the foundation for both human dignity and human failure. The uniquely human position of reflecting the *imago Dei* is cast between the divine call for holiness and the reality of human sin.[34] Since the Fall, each person, although created in the image of God, exists in a state of sinfulness inherited from the sins committed by Adam and Eve (see Rom. 5:14–21).[35] This state of sinfulness is taken for granted by Pentecostals, not just by those in the Holiness tradition (see Chapter 3). The importance of this belief for Pentecostal anthropology lies in its radical presupposition of the unity of the human being: sin affects the entirety of human nature subsisting in each person. Put differently, with the effect of the Fall, the human being is sinful by nature, yet it is the human person who commits sin.[36] Theological anthropology can therefore not persist in generalizations of human nature: while locating sin in human nature can lead to a doctrine of impersonalized deprivation and determinism that leaves little room for the possibility of perfection, locating sin instead in the unity of the human person encourages a doctrine of embodied responsibility for sanctification.[37] Pentecostal theology resists a reduction of human sinfulness to either human nature alone or to human intellectual capacities, because sanctification is an existential struggle between human nature and each human person. Grounded in soteriology, Pentecostals therefore insist that human nature can be restored to the image of God in each human being through participation of each person in the image of Christ. Rooted in the pneumatological cosmology characteristic

---

[33] See Mark H. Mann, *Perfecting Grace: Holiness, Human Being, and the Sciences* (New York: T & T Clark, 2006), 21–52.

[34] See Edmund J. Rybarczyk, *Beyond Salvation: Eastern Orthodoxy and Classical Pentecostalism on Becoming Like Christ* (Milton Keyes: Paternoster, 2004), 213–39.

[35] See Keith Warrington, *Pentecostal Theology: A Theology of Encounter* (London: T & T Clark, 2008), 35–37; Bruce R. Marino, 'The Origin, Nature, and Consequence of Sin', in Horton, *Systematic Theology*, 255–90; Hart, *Truth Aflame*, 249–76.

[36] Hart, *Truth Aflame*, 264–67; Marino, 'The Origin, Nature, and Consequence of Sin', 278.

[37] See Terry L. Cross, 'The Yoke of Necessity: The Use of the Terms *necessitas* and *coactio* in the Thought of John Calvin', in *The Spirit and the Mind: Essays in Informed Pentecostalism*, ed. Terry L. Cross and Emerson B. Powery (Lanham, MD: University Press of America, 2000), 157–77.

for Pentecostals, such participation of the human being in the divine life is made possible by the Holy Spirit.

From a pneumatological perspective, the unity of the human being as person emerges from the divine Spirit, who 'as intermediary mediates the presence of the triune God such that God is recognized to be present with intermediate aspects of creaturely reality for the purpose of salvation'.[38] The spiritual presence of the Father and the Son is manifested in the human spirit through the Spirit of God who makes that unity possible.[39] God's Spirit is thus at work in all of creation in the widest possible manner (see Chapter 7) and in the human being in a particular manner that allows the human person to participate in the divine life.[40] Put differently, humanity is sanctified, in a universal sense, through the activity of God's Spirit at the creation of the world (see Gen. 1:2) and, in a particular sense, through the activity of the Spirit at the creation of the human being (Gen. 2:7). This sanctifying grace mediated by the Spirit places humanity in a unique relationship with God identified by human responsibility to both God and creation.[41] The sanctification of each person therefore begins with conception (not birth), although it is a dynamic reality that needs to be actualized in a subsequent development of the person, typically called the 'new birth' (see Chapter 2).[42] This development characterizes human spirituality as participation in the effort to overcome the polychotomy of body, soul, and spirit, as well as of divine Spirit and human spirit.[43] The integrative centre of human spirituality is the 'heart' composed of human affections, beliefs and practices.[44] Recognizably dominant in Pentecostal anthropology is human affectivity, the passions and desires, or 'abiding dispositions' of the heart, which play a central role in

---

[38] Mark J. Cartledge, *The Mediation of the Spirit: Interventions in Practical Theology*, PM 7 (Grand Rapids: Eerdmans, 2015), 65.
[39] Frank D. Macchia, 'Spiritual Presence: The Role of Pneumatology in Paul Tillich's Theology', in *Paul Tillich and Pentecostal Theology: Spiritual Presence and Spiritual Power*, ed. Nimi Wariboko and Amos Yong (Bloomington: Indiana University Press, 2015), 84–100.
[40] Andreas Nordlander, 'Pneumatological Participation: Embodiment, Sacramentality, and the Multidimensional Unity of Life', in Wariboko and Yong, *Paul Tillich and Pentecostal Theology*, 101–14.
[41] Arrington, *Christian Doctrine*, 1: 205–6.
[42] Steven J. Land, *Pentecostal Spirituality: A Passion for the Kingdom*, JPTS 1 (Sheffield: Sheffield Academic Press, 1993), 128.
[43] Tae Young So, 'Pentecostal Spirituality as Nurturing Vitality for Human Lives', *JPT* 18, no. 2 (2009): 246–62.
[44] Land, *Pentecostal Spirituality*, 132; Paul H. Pipkin, 'Know Your Heart', *PE* (June 17, 1962): 4–5.

Pentecostal accounts of human spirituality and the transformative encounter with God.[45] The affections display the logic or progression of Pentecostal soteriology and its pursuit of the sanctification and perfection of the human person.[46]

The affections are relational and objective dispositions of the heart, that is, they occur always in relation of the self to others and take an object towards which they are disposed (see Chapter 1). The affections in their unifying position can consequently grasp the human being as a whole and are powerful to direct a person towards any object. From a soteriological perspective, the affections should have 'their source and object in God' and thereby 'dispose the person toward God and the neighbor in ways appropriate to their source and goal in God'.[47] However, on its own, the heart is subject to all passions and desires of human nature and does not possess the power to pursue a consistent sanctified life apart from placing the affections in Jesus Christ.[48] The pursuit of the image of Christ in the human being is always an experience of the human spirit directed by and towards the Holy Spirit.[49] In this sense, the human person is transformed into the image of Christ only by embodying the image of the Spirit of Christ.[50] At the level of spirit, the perfection of the human spirit by the Spirit of God demands the submission of the human being (see Jn 3:6; 4:24; Rom.8:5, 9; 1 Cor. 2:11). This sanctification of the passions into right affections (*orthopathos*) requires the integration with right beliefs (*orthodoxy*) and right practices (*orthopraxy*) of the whole person.[51] From the formative metaphor of the altar, such integration, as an activity of the heart, requires holistic habits of the individual empowered by the divine Spirit and embodied in sanctifying practices of the human being in communion with others.[52] The centre of such active transformation, not only through imitation but also participation in the life of the triune God, is the baptism in the Holy Spirit.

---

[45] See Daniel Castelo, *Revisioning Pentecostal Ethics: The Epicletic Community* (Cleveland, TN: CPT Press, 2012), 35–38.
[46] Land, *Pentecostal Spirituality*, 147.
[47] Ibid., 134–36.
[48] Ibid., 128–29.
[49] Amos Yong, 'On Divine Presence and Divine Agency: Toward a Foundational Pneumatology', *AJPS* 3, no. 2 (2000), 167–88.
[50] See Samuel Solivan, *The Spirit, Pathos, and Liberation: Toward an Hispanic Pentecostal Theology*, JPTS 14 (Sheffield: Sheffield Academic Press, 1998), 27–28.
[51] Ibid., 60–69; Land, *Pentecostal Spirituality*, 41–46.
[52] Castelo, *Revisioning Pentecostal Ethics*, 59–82

Spirit baptism and human embodiment

Within the narrative of the full gospel, I have suggested that the baptism in the Spirit serves as a lens through which to order and interpret the other elements. Pentecostal theology can speak of the baptism in the Spirit as a sacramental encounter of the human person with the person of the Holy Spirit for the purposes of sanctification and charismatic empowerment (see Chapter 4). In the tangible environment of Pentecostal worship, Spirit baptism marks the transformative moment between coming to the altar and going into the world. In order to defend this central interpretive perspective in the context of a theological anthropology, the primary theological question is how the transformative emphasis of Spirit baptism speaks to an understanding of the human being. Important in this endeavour is not only the move from human nature to human person, demanded by the holistic emphasis on sanctification, but furthermore the relational identity of human persons in community, demanded by the exercise of the charismata. Spirit baptism for Pentecostals is 'both an intensely personal and a communal experience',[53] because the Holy Spirit, through the gifts of the Spirit, delivers the individual from isolation for the purpose of engaging in the transformation of the self and others in community. Put differently, the goal of human existence is the realization of the individual as part of the dedication of the self to God and to others, which is made possible by the outpouring of the Spirit on all flesh.[54] In anthropological terms, if relation is ontological to human existence, then reflection of the image of God in the world is always also a shared reality of human communion.[55] In turn, the image of God is then found not exclusively in human nature as manifested in each individual person but also in the embodied, interdependent, and relational existence of human beings with one another and with the world.[56] Pentecostals may then insist that only 'the Holy Spirit creatively enables and empowers our full humanity in relationship to ourselves, others and God'.[57] In order to be relevant to theological anthropology, the emphasis on Spirit baptism

---

[53] Frank D. Macchia, *Baptized in the Spirit: A Global Pentecostal Theology* (Grand Rapids, MI: Zondervan, 2006), 172.
[54] Ibid., 174.
[55] Ibid., 175.
[56] Yong, *Theology and Down Syndrome*, 180–81.
[57] Ibid., 181.

must therefore possess implications for the physical, biological, and social embodiment of human beings.

The motif of Spirit baptism rooted in the biblical language of Luke-Acts highlights the importance of embodiment in its root metaphor that the Holy Spirit is poured out 'on all *flesh*' (Acts 2:17).[58] Although the biblical passage places the outpouring of the Spirit at Pentecost in the broad context of creation, spanning from heaven to earth, the identification of the object of the Spirit's outpouring on 'flesh' is immediately qualified by anthropological references (see Acts 2:17–19).[59] Theologically significant in this context is not merely the anthropological focus as such but the 'sacramental' concentration on human embodiment as the object, element and sign of the baptism in the Spirit.

The sacramental language of 'baptism' holds significant implications for human embodiment particularly with regard to the *imago Dei*. Just as the apostle Paul illustrates water baptism with a 'putting on' or 'being clothed with' Christ (Gal. 3:26–28), as if to say that those who have been baptized now exist in the image of Christ, so, too, Luke-Acts describes Spirit baptism with the same words as a 'putting on' or 'being clothed with' the Spirit (Lk. 24:49; Acts 1:8).[60] Acts 2 depicts this metaphor with the experience of the outpouring of the Spirit on all flesh so that those who have been baptized in the Spirit now exist in the image of the Spirit.[61] Pentecostals may speak of this baptism as a point of encounter between the human spirit and the divine Spirit resulting in the sanctification of human nature and illumination of the image of God that together make possible an intensification of the *imago Dei*.[62] Spirit baptism therefore has an ontological effect on human beings as embodied, relational and developing creatures 'recreated' or 'born again' in the image of the triune God as revealed in Jesus Christ and sustained by the Holy Spirit.[63] This embodied transformation of humanity via the Spirit

---

[58] See Yong, *The Spirit Poured Out on All Flesh*, 27–30; Martin William Mittelstadt, *Reading Luke-Acts in the Pentecostal Tradition* (Cleveland, TN: CPT Press, 2010), 68–77.
[59] See Yong, *Spirit Poured Out on All Flesh*, 31–80.
[60] Stephenson, *Dismantling the Dualisms*, 129.
[61] Ibid., 129.
[62] See Amos Yong, *Spirit-Word-Community: Theological Hermeneutics in Trinitarian Perspective* (Eugene, OR: Wipf and Stock, 2002), 160–61; Frank D. Macchia, 'Baptized in the Spirit: Towards a Global Theology of Spirit Baptism', in *The Spirit in the World: Emerging Pentecostal Theologies in Global Contexts*, ed. Veli-Matti Kärkkäinen (Grand Rapids, MI: Eerdmans, 2009), 3–20.
[63] Yong, *Theology and Down Syndrome*, 181–91.

of Christ (see Jn 3:6) is the hallmark of relating the motif of Spirit baptism to theological anthropology.

Central to this transformation of human nature by the Spirit is the biblical affirmation of the outpouring of the Spirit on *all* flesh. This universal affirmation acknowledges and bridges existing distinctions of human existence between age, gender, social status, or ethnicity as the Spirit preserves and transforms the particular embodiment of human persons.[64] A restoration of the human embodiment of the *imago Dei* is nowhere more evident for Pentecostals than in the charismatic manifestations of Spirit baptism that are attributed without reservation to sons and daughters, young and old, slave and free, men and women, present and future generations (see Acts 2:17-19, 39). In these diverse contexts, the speaking with tongues is the most immediate unifying embodied manifestation of persons who, baptized in the Spirit, express their new identity through the gifts of the Spirit to the world.[65] Ontologically speaking, in Spirit baptism, charismatic being envelops human being in order to sanctify and empower the human person for the fullness of participation in the divine life.[66]

To speak of the outpouring of the Spirit as an ontological event remains defined within the horizon of the sacramentality of Spirit baptism (see Chapter 4). Embodiment here is existential (who a person is) and functional (what a person does) as well as transformational (who a person becomes) in light of putting on the Spirit. Sacramental embodiment in and through the gifts of the Spirit becomes the presupposition for the encounters of the heart with others and with God: the charismata invite participation of all dimensions of human being, doing and knowing in order to produce right affections, beliefs and practices for the sake of the transformation of the entire community.[67] In other words, charismatic practices (as expressions of the baptism in the Spirit) make God present to others through the whole person participating in the manifestation of the Spirit to the body of Christ.[68] Important

---

[64] See David Daniels, 'Pentecostals and Peoplehood in the 21st Century: Probing the Past Proleptically', *AJPS* 10, no. 1 (2007): 91–99; Stephenson, *Dismantling the Dualisms*, 134.
[65] See James K. A. Smith, 'Naturalizing Glossolalia? Prospects for a More Radically Pentecostal Ontology', *JPT* 20, no. 1 (2011): 149–54.
[66] See Mark J. Cartledge, *Charismatic Glossolalia: An Empirical-Theological Study* (Aldershot, UK: Ashgate, 2002).
[67] Land, *Pentecostal Spirituality*, 41–61.
[68] See Frank D. Macchia, 'Tongues as a Sign: Towards a Sacramental Understanding of Pentecostal Experience', *Pneuma* 15, no. 1 (1993): 61–76.

to Pentecostal anthropology is therefore that the charismatic dimension of human being cannot be reduced to the sanctification or empowerment of human nature alone (whether body, soul, mind, spirit, or flesh) but always represents gifts, enablements, and ministries celebrated by human persons as members in communion.[69] Embodiment of the *imago Dei*, because it is charismatic, is therefore never exclusively physical, spiritual, or intellectual but also social and relational.[70] This relational dimension of the transforming power of the Spirit runs against much of Western individualistic, spiritualized and internalized ideas of the charismatic life.[71] Pentecostal theology suggests that charismatic practices add an irreducible dimension to human existence precisely because a holistic anthropology places humankind irrevocably within creation, culture, history and world.[72] In these places, the image of God is reflected in humankind both as empowered and embattled persons-in-communion.[73] The charismatic dimension of human life speaks to the spirited existence of human persons, to which belong the physical reality and relationships with other human beings as well as their engagement with other spiritual realities that impact human life. The transformation of these realities is the subject of the Pentecostal theology of divine healing.

Divine healing and human nature

Healing manifests the most apparent engagement of human embodiment as a result of confrontation with other (e.g. physical, spiritual, emotional, intellectual, psychological) dimensions of creaturely existence. For Pentecostals, healings attributed to God form the most immediate signs and wonders of redemption (see Chapter 5). As part of a theological anthropology drawn on the canvas of soteriology as praxis, divine healing speaks to the need

---

[69] See Ben C. Aker, 'Charismata: Gifts, Enablements, or Ministries?' *JPT* 11, no. 1 (2002): 53–69 (esp. 58–65).
[70] Matthias Wenk, *Community-Forming Power*, 298–307; idem, 'Community Forming Power: Reconciliation and the Spirit in Acts', *JEPTA* 19 (1999): 17–33.
[71] Matthias Wenk, 'The Holy Spirit as Transforming Power within a Society: Pneumatological Spirituality and Its Political/Social Relevance for Western Europe', *JPT* 11, no. 1 (2002): 130–42.
[72] See Eldin Villafañe, *The Liberating Spirit: Toward an American Hispanic Pentecostal Social Ethic* (Grand Rapids, MI: Eerdmans, 1993), 163–92.
[73] See Wilma Wells Davies, *The Embattled but Empowered Community: Comparing Understandings of Spiritual Power in Argentine Popular and Pentecostal Cosmologies*, GPCS 5 (Leiden: Brill, 2010), 169–212.

to sketch not an idealistic and romanticized but critical and therapeutic image of human nature. The primary question raised in this context from the Pentecostal perspective is how divine healing qualifies the assertion that humankind is created in the image of God while also allowing for human frailty, suffering, and injustice.

From the outset, the affirmation of the full gospel that divine healing is a soteriological manifestation of Christ, who bridges the immanent physical and fallen world and the redemptive reality of the transcendent divine by the outpouring of the Spirit, rejects any artificial separation of the natural and supernatural, or the natural and spiritual, as opposite and unrelated dimensions of human existence (see Chapter 7). Instead, the outpouring of the Spirit on all flesh demands a holistic soteriology that resonates with the unity of the physical, material, spiritual, psychological, behavioural, and relational needs of human life.[74] Healing speaks not only to biomedical but also to social, economic, political, and moral justice as components of human conversion, reconciliation and transformation (see Chapter 9).[75] Despite the frequent ambivalence or even hostility Pentecostals show towards the sciences, a critical and therapeutic anthropology advanced by Pentecostals can connect a metaphysical pluralism of theological inquiry with a methodological naturalism.[76] The insistence on divine healing can here function to replace any static image of the human being as living between the promises of the atonement in the past and the awaiting of their eschatological fulfilment in a distant future with the emergence of a redeemed humanity in the present amidst (and in deliberate contrast to) the continued suffering, sickness, sin and evil in the world.

The human embodiment of the image of God, when placed in the context of sickness, suffering, disability and death, cannot be seen in a unilateral sense as either existing or not existing, destroyed or preserved, lost or restored. Created from the dust of the ground, filled with the breath of God (see Gen. 2:7), and created as male and female (Gen. 1:27), the divine image in humankind exists in the particularities of each person in relationship to God, creation and one

---

[74] Yong, *The Spirit Poured Out on All Flesh*, 117–20.
[75] See Amos Yong, *In the Days of Caesar: Pentecostalism and Political Theology* (Grand Rapids, MI: Eerdmans, 2010), 268–95; Nimi Wariboko, *The Pentecostal Principle: Ethical Methodology in New Spirit*, PM 5 (Grand Rapids, MI: Eerdmans, 2012), 134–41.
[76] See Amos Yong, *The Spirit of Creation: Modern Science and Divine Action in the Pentecostal-Charismatic Imagination*, PM 4 (Grand Rapids, MI: Eerdmans, 2011), 58–65.

another.⁷⁷ As creatures enlivened by God's Spirit (a metaphysical trait shared by all living creatures), human beings made in the image of God (an ontological trait unique to humankind) are given capacity to act as causal agents in the world in a way that differs from the rest of creation.⁷⁸ A holistic pneumatological perspective suggests that human beings are irreducible to the sum of their biological parts or a polychotomous view of human nature.⁷⁹ Rather, human embodiment is defined by emerging patterns of being-in-relationship that differ with each person in light of their biological, mental, social, and spiritual condition. Nonetheless, Pentecostals would argue that effective human agency on behalf of God requires the presence, power, and person of the Holy Spirit. A person baptized in the Spirit engages the world more consciously and critically on these different levels and in confrontation with the existential tension characterizing the human condition situated between the Fall and final redemption (see Chapter 6). Pentecostal anthropology is situated within a theology of spiritual warfare that takes seriously the spiritual dimensions of created existence and the resulting interdependent (and confrontational) relationships of spiritual powers affecting oneself and others (see Chapter 7). Human existence in these contexts is defined most clearly by the confrontational demands placed on human agency.

Divine healing sheds light on the confrontational demands of human agency by suggesting that the human reflection of the image of God is not conditioned by ontological status, physical embodiment, or personal performance of human beings. Human existence within the multifarious dimensions of a spiritual universe reflects the interdependent nature of life, in general, and the special character of human beings, in particular. Human agency in the world depends on God's particular bestowal of human dignity and affinity to God's own self granted to all human beings.⁸⁰ Nonetheless, this bestowal is cultivated in physical, spiritual, psychological, social, cultural, and other networks of embodiment that affect all of creation. Hence,

---

⁷⁷ See Amos Yong, 'Christian and Buddhist Perspectives on Neuropsychology and the Human Person: Pneuma and Pratityasamutpada', *Zygon* 40, no. 1 (2005): 143–65.
⁷⁸ Yong, *The Spirit of Creation*, 198–99. See also Celia Deane-Drummond, *The Wisdom of the Liminal: Evolution and Other Animals in Human Becoming* (Grand Rapids, MI: Eerdmans, 2014).
⁷⁹ Ibid., 64–65; idem, *Theology and Down Syndrome*, 188–91.
⁸⁰ See R. Jerome Boone, 'Created for Shalom: Human Agency and Responsibility in the World', in *The Spirit Renews the Face of the Earth: Pentecostal Forays in Science and Theology of Creation*, ed. Amos Yong (Eugene, OR: Pickwick, 2009), 17–29.

such confrontations with the realities of creation affect human agency but cannot be said to alter the image of God.[81] Sickness and suffering, disability and death can impact human embodiment but not, as a direct consequence, the human reflection of the *imago Dei*.[82] When Pentecostal theology insists that the integration of the different dimensions of human agency is a work of divine healing, Pentecostal anthropology draws significant distinctions between the healing and cure as well as between the self-giving (kenosis) and empowerment of the human being (see Chapter 9). Here, Pentecostal pneumatology and anthropology reflect their mutual interdependence.

Human nature has the ability to be cured, restored and healed. The difference between these states is significant for theological anthropology, since all three point to a positive development or action taken resulting in the improvement of a person's condition albeit with different results. While a similar affirmation can be made about all creatures, Pentecostals speak of the sickness of human nature, in general, and understand divine healing in the first place as an analogy for a spiritual remedy provided by Jesus Christ in the atonement and manifested by physical signs through the Holy Spirit. However, such generalizations have met with criticism by some Pentecostals who acknowledge the difficulty of maintaining a theology of divine healing when expectations of healing are not met (see Chapter 5). A distinction can be made here with regard to curing and healing of a particular condition: curing may be considered a restoration of health, the removal of symptoms and remedy of physical illnesses, while healing is not a localized restoration of the body to a former state but the holistic transformation of a person to a new state of being.[83] Theological anthropology cast in the image of Christ demands therefore also a theology of weakness reflecting the life of Jesus in human redemption marked by suffering and death.[84] Cast in the image of

---

[81] See Martin Lindhardt, '"If You Are Saved You Cannot Forget Your Parents": Agency, Power, and Social Respositioning in Tanzanian Born-Again Christianity', *JRA* 40, no. 3 (2010): 240–72; David A. Smilde, '"Letting God Govern": Supernatural Agency in the Venezuelan Pentecostal Approach to Social Change', *SR* 59, no. 3 (1998): 287–303.

[82] Boone, 'Created for Shalom', 20.

[83] Amos Yong, 'Disability, the Human Condition, and the Spirit of the Eschatological Long Run: Toward a Pneumatological Theology of Disability', *JRDH* 11, no. 1 (2007): 5–25; Donald F. Calbreath, 'Serotonin and Spirit: Can There Be a Holistic Pentecostal Approach to Mental Illness?' in Smith and Yong, *Science and the Spirit*, 133–52.

[84] See Keith Warrington, *Healing and Suffering: Biblical and Pastoral Reflections* (Milton Keynes, UK: Paternoster, 2005); Martin William Mittelstadt, *The Spirit and Suffering in Luke-Acts: Implications for a Pentecostal Pneumatology*, JPTS 26 (London: T&T Clark, 2004), 130–38;

the Spirit of Christ, the same theological anthropology suggests that human agency requires not cure but healing, a holistic integration of personal subjectivity and interpersonal agency that does not rely on restoring the body but on reconciling humanity in its multitudinous associations.[85]

In traditional Pentecostal lingo, divine healing is a form of empowerment by the Spirit of God who is poured out on all flesh for the transformation of all dimensions of life. Physical cure contributes to healing only if it includes also the transformation of other embodied, social, political, and economic conditions of human existence.[86] Human agency is consequently not bound to physical salvation alone but to the transformation of all dimensions of life opposed by suffering, discrimination, marginalization, oppression, and death.[87] Put differently, salvation aims at the healing (rather than curing or restoring) of humankind in relationship to God, creation and one another.[88] The human *imago Spiritus* functions therefore in the same manner as the human *imago Christi* as embodiment of the *imago Dei* through self-giving and surrender.[89] That human nature is empowered to surrender its dominance is a kenotic act of healing made possible by the charismatic presence of the Spirit who empowers human beings to empty themselves for the sake of others.[90] Divine healing is in this sense a charismatic experience of empowerment through kenosis in which the gifts of the Spirit act on behalf of creation despite the condition of the recipient. It is in this act of human agency that humankind differs from other created beings. When the human 'heart' bears witness to the experience of God, it is being healed in the interrelated complexities of its existence and transformed into a dwelling place for Christ to live by the Spirit.[91] When the result is that God lives in the human being in

---

Nancy A. Hardesty, *Faith Cure: Divine Healing in the Holiness and Pentecostal Movements* (Peabody, MA: Hendrickson, 2003), 129–47.
[85] Yong, *Theology and Down Syndrome*, 248–53.
[86] See Candy Gunther Brown (ed.), *Global Pentecostal and Charismatic Healing* (Oxford: Oxford University Press, 2011).
[87] Mittelstadt, *Spirit and Suffering*, 20–28.
[88] Yong, 'Disability, the Human Condition, and the Spirit', 15.
[89] See Veli-Matti Kärkkäinen, 'On a Theology and Spirituality of the Cross', in *Toward a Pneumatological Theology: Pentecostal and Ecumenical Perspectives on Ecclesiology, Soteriology, and Theology of Mission*, ed. Amos Yong (Lanham, MD: University Press of America, 2002), 167–78.
[90] See Peter Althouse, 'Implications of the Kenosis of the Spirit for a Creational Eschatology', in Yong, *The Spirit Renews the Face of the Earth*, 155–72; idem, 'Imago Dei and Kenosis: Contributions of Christology to the Study of Godly Love', in *The Science and Theology of Godly Love*, ed. Matthew T. Lee and Amos Yong (De Kalb: Northern Illinois University Press, 2012), 56–76.
[91] Terry L. Cross, 'The Divine-Human Encounter: Towards a Pentecostal Theology of Experience', *Pneuma* 31, no. 1 (2009): 3–34.

communion with others, then human nature has been more fully transformed into the image of God. To what extent such transformation can proceed in the human being and community can only be addressed by a teleological and eschatological anthropology.

The kingdom of God and human destiny

The preceding account of human nature suggests that the destiny of the human being is not a sudden eschatological transposition from one fixed state to another but a development through transformation via the Spirit into the image of Christ and thus towards the ultimate completion of humankind in the presence of God. Eschatology functions as an integrating theme that returns Pentecostal theology to its central concerns, albeit transformed by an apocalyptic urgency (see Chapter 6). For an understanding of human destiny, eschatology consequently speaks to the importance of cultivating transformative practices in the present, where human existence in charismatic fellowship – human agency empowered by the Spirit – converges in the experiences and encounter with the transcendent. The principal concern emerging from this perspective of the full gospel is how an eschatological anthropology speaks to the eternal development of human nature. Although not intended as teleological models, the scientific theories of evolution and emergence may offer a critical framework for constructing such an endeavour.

Pentecostals typically take a rather critical stance towards evolution or emergence. Most Pentecostals reject evolution and its proposal of a development of humankind from other species as well as a progression within the species recognized as human.[92] The central concerns raised by Pentecostals focus on the anthropic principle, the possibility of evolution and the mechanism(s) of evolutionary change that would allow for the existence of the human species.[93] An accidental arrival at humankind leaves little room

---

[92] See Steve Badger and Mike Tenneson, 'Does the Spirit Create through Evolutionary Processes? Pentecostals and Biological Evolution', in *Science and the Spirit: A Pentecostal Engagement with the Sciences*, ed. James K. A. Smith and Amos Yong (Bloomington: Indiana University Press, 2010), 92–116; Gerald W. King, 'Evolving Paradigms: Creationism as Pentecostal Variation on a Fundamentalist Theme', in Yong, *The Spirit Renews the Face of the Earth*, 93–114.

[93] See Ronald L. Numbers, 'Creation, Evolution, and Holy Ghost Religion: Holiness and Pentecostal Responses to Darwinism', *RAC* 2, no. 2 (1992): 127–58; Yong, *The Spirit of Creation*, 135–44.

for a theology of creation that relies on a strong intentional model of divine action and human particularity.[94] The theory of emergence, on the other hand, has been cautiously entertained by Pentecostals as suggesting a teleological reading of natural and human history that spans the primordial creation of the world, the emergence of life and the particularity of the human being, the history of humankind and election of Israel and the incarnational and Pentecostal events defined by Jesus Christ and the outpouring of the Holy Spirit.[95] In Pentecostal terms, salvation and the kingdom of God are the intended goal for humankind made possible through Christ and actualized by the Spirit.[96] This teleological emergence of human nature as a new creation realized in the Incarnation, baptism, death, resurrection, ascension, and glorification of the Son of God makes room for a pneumatological anthropology. In this theological model, regeneration, sanctification, Spirit baptism and divine healing, as elements of the full gospel, represent intensifying participations in the Spirit of Christ towards the same end.[97] Put in the terms of a theological anthropology, human nature is made for progress towards the kingdom of God.[98]

For Pentecostals, to speak of human nature as progressing towards eternity is more than to proleptically anticipate human destiny on the basis of divine action consistent with and deriving from past events. Regeneration, sanctification, Spirit baptism and divine healing are emergent realities of the eschatological 'already' actualized with the outpouring of the Spirit even if they constitute events of the 'not yet' fully consummated reality of eternal life in the Spirit.[99] Those who encounter the Spirit in the present exist 'between' (e)merging realities of this creation and that (new) creation by experiencing with intensifying measure both the fulfilment of God's promises of the past

---

[94] See Amos Yong, 'How Does God Do What God Does? Pentecostal-Charismatic Perspectives on Divine Action in Dialogue with Modern Science', in Smith and Yong, *Science and the Spirit*, 50–71.

[95] See David Bradnick, 'Spirits and the Stars: A Spirit-filled Cosmology', in *Interdisciplinary and Religio-Cultural Discourses on a Spirit Filled World: Loosing the Spirits*, ed. Veli-Matti Kärkkäinen et al. (New York: Palgrave, 2013), 213–26; Bradford McCall, 'Emergence Theory and Theology: A Wesleyan-relational Perspective', *WTJ* 44, no. 2 (2009): 189–207; Yong, *Spirit of Creation*, 63–65, 135–51, 162–72.

[96] Macchia, *Justified in the Spirit*, 221–312.

[97] Yong, *The Spirit Poured Out*, 81–120; idem, *The Spirit of Creation*, 167–68.

[98] See Frank D. Macchia, 'Jesus Is Victor: The Eschatology of the Blumhardts with Implications for Pentecostal Eschatologies', in *Perspectives in Pentecostal Eschatologies: World without End*, ed. Peter Althouse and Robby Waddell (Cambridge: James Clarke & Co., 2012), 375–400.

[99] Land, *Pentecostal Spirituality*, 98–110.

and a foretaste of the eschatological future of God's kingdom.[100] Yet, these ecstatic and charismatic experiences of the present still anticipate the resurrection and glorification of embodied creatures into the fullness of pneumatic existence.[101] The emphasis Pentecost places on the Spirit poured out on all flesh urges Pentecostal theology to articulate also a vision of the ultimate transformation of all flesh via God's Spirit.

Physical death and resurrection, typically found in traditional soteriology mainly in eschatological anticipation, form a significant part of a Pentecostal theology of spiritual warfare.[102] The juxtaposition of death and resurrection in the present is important to the Pentecostal view of emergence, since it suggests that death is not the end of human existence but is followed by a transition (sanctification[103] or healing[104]) towards a renewed existence.[105] This affirmation of a realized (because emergent) eschatology is first of all applied to the historical resurrection of Jesus and then, without distinction of dispensation, to the resurrection of his followers, even though they occur at different times: the resurrection of Jesus Christ and the resurrection of human beings are inextricably linked.[106] In theological terms, resurrection is no longer exclusively an eschatological event but a persistent emerging realization (or inbreaking) of a new creation.

This insistence on the eschatological resurrection of the body as an unexpected and spontaneous new possibility in the present logically and theologically requires the renewal of the physical cosmos.[107] Such renewal has been initiated with the resurrection of Jesus and the subsequent outpouring of the Holy Spirit at the hands of the ascended and glorified Christ.[108]

---

[100] Wolfgang Vondey and Chris Green, 'Between This and That: Reality and Sacramentality in the Pentecostal Worldview', *JPT* 19, no. 2 (2010): 243–64.

[101] Macchia, *Justified in the Spirit*, 251–54.

[102] See Päivi Hasu, 'Rescuing Zombies from the Hands of Witches: Pentecostal-charismatic Christianity and Spiritual Warfare in the Plural Religious Setting of Coastal Tanzania', *SM* 97, no. 3 (2009): 417–40.

[103] Yong, 'Disability, the Human Condition, and the Spirit', 17.

[104] See Miroslav Volf, 'Materiality of Salvation: An Investigation in the Soteriologies of Liberation and Pentecostal Theologies', *JES* 26, no. 3 (1989): 447–67; Althouse, 'Pentecostal Eschatology in Context', 205–31; Alexander, *Pentecostal Healing*, 241.

[105] See J. Ayodeji Adewuya, 'Constructing and African Pentecostal Eschatology: Which Way?' in Althouse and Waddell, *Perspectives in Pentecostal Eschatologies*, 361–74.

[106] See John A. Bertone, 'Seven Dispensations or Two-Age View of History', in Althouse and Waddell, *Perspectives on Pentecostal Eschatologies*, 61–94, esp. 71–72.

[107] Matthew K. Thompson, 'Eschatology as Soteriological: The Cosmic Full Gospel', in Althouse and Waddell, *Perspectives in Pentecostal Eschatologies*, 189–204 (202).

[108] Althouse, 'Pentecostal Eschatology in Context', 230.

Easter and Pentecost are therefore mutually indispensable events of Christ's human transformation.[109] Pentecost, and its continuation or repetition in the life of Pentecostals today, marks the nexus between the resurrection of Christ and the resurrection of the dead in the last days.[110] However, the resurrection in present history still includes marks of impairment, visible even at the hands and feet of the resurrected Jesus.[111] Hence, from the perspective of Easter, the bodily resurrection is also not the final event in the renewal of human nature but is succeeded by the transformation of Jesus as the second Adam into a spiritual being (see 1 Cor. 15:45). From the perspective of Pentecost, the baptism in the Spirit unites believers with the resurrection of Christ, even though a bodily resurrection still awaits all human beings.[112] In turn, the transformation of resurrected human beings via the Spirit remains incomplete until human nature also has been changed into spiritual nature.

The transformation (or reembodiment) of human nature into spiritual embodiment (see 1 Cor. 15:44) marks the climax of the work of God's Spirit in which the human being is glorified albeit without losing personal existence and identity.[113] The striving of human nature towards completion (or glorification) in the image of God finds its full realization in the arrival of the Spirit, first in Jesus, then through Pentecost in his followers, and finally in the unrestrained pneumatic existence of the kingdom of God.[114] Human nature participates in the power of the resurrection by virtue of the Spirit's life-giving act (see Rom. 8:11) rather than the quality of the resurrected body.[115] Nonetheless, the resurrection of the body must preserve and also transform personal identity.[116] Such transformation includes the eternal embeddedness and embodiedness of human persons in communion, both in continuity and discontinuity with present history, in which human reflection of the *imago*

---

[109] Ben Pugh, 'The Mind of the Spirit: Explorations in the Reciprocal Relationship between the Work of the Spirit and the Work of the Son', *JEPTA* 32, no. 1 (2012): 41–60.
[110] Yong, *The Spirit of Creation*, 90.
[111] Yong, *Theology and Down Syndrome*, 175.
[112] Yong, *The Spirit Poured Out on All Flesh*, 102; Frank D. Macchia, 'Sighs Too Deep for Words: Toward a Theology of Glossolalia', *JPT* 1, no. 1 (1992): 47–73 (57).
[113] Arrington, 3:239–40; Stanley M. Horton, 'The Last Things', in Horton, *Systematic Theology*, 597–638 (604); Duffield and Van Cleave, *Foundations of Pentecostal Theology*, 541.
[114] Yong, *In the Days of Caesar*, 327–47.
[115] Yong, *Theology and Down Syndrome*, 173.
[116] Gordon Fee, *The First Epistle to the Corinthians* (Grand Rapids, MI: Eerdmans, 1987), 776–77.

Dei is still realized.[117] Transformation into the image of Christ via the Spirit is therefore also transformation into the body of Christ via the fellowship of the Spirit. Since all perfection happens by virtue of participating in the life-giving Spirit, the glorification of humankind awaits the ongoing reconciliation of human beings with God, one another, and creation in the unity of the Spirit. Human bodies and human community are eternally awaiting transformation into the temple of the Holy Spirit (see 1 Cor. 3:16–17; 6:19–20). In other words, the glorification of human nature in person and communion likely remains the object of eternal transformation. Human nature cannot exist as pure spirit but only as embodied spirit – and that remains the eternal difference between human beings and God.

---

[117] Yong, *Theology and Down Syndrome*, 274–81; idem, 'Disability, the Human Condition, and the Spirit', 17–21.

9

Society

Civilization, the Common Good, and Cultural Theory

The previous chapters have illustrated that the full gospel provides an embodied, experiential, and relational narrative framework to articulate God's activity in the world: the encounter with God, narrated by the Pentecostal intuitions that Jesus is saviour, sanctifier, Spirit baptizer, divine healer, and coming king allows Pentecostals to envision creation as the cosmic altar of redemption (Chapter 7) where humankind embodies through the Spirit the image of God to the world (Chapter 8). The present chapter continues to explore the contributions of the full gospel to the wider theological conversation by probing the concrete, intertwined and complex realities of the public social, cultural, and political spheres underlying the theology of creation and theological anthropology provided thus far.

Pentecostals have been deeply entrenched in the messy realities of principalities and powers often manifested in poverty, persecution, marginalization, civil unrest, political, and cultural revolution. Nonetheless, the concurrent lack of theological articulation has fuelled contradicting stereotypes which argue that Pentecostals are either ambivalent towards issues of social justice, on the one hand, or that they are the new advocates of social engagement, on the other.[1] Extremes of triumphalism, individualism, and elitism are found alongside commitments to social, political, and economic welfare.[2]

---

[1] See Donald E. Miller and Tetsunao Yamamori, *Global Pentecostalism: The New Face of Christian Social Engagement* (Berkeley: University of California Press, 2007); Veli-Matti Kärkkäinen, 'Are Pentecostals Oblivious to Social Justice? Theological and Ecumenical Perspectives', *Missiology* 29, no. 4 (2001): 417–31.

[2] Wolfgang Vondey, 'The Impact of Culture and Social Justice on Christian Formation in Pentecostalism'. *JPT* 24, no. 2 (2015): 201–16.

Pentecostals are characterized at once as apolitical, political, and indirectly political,[3] ambiguous in different cultural sectors,[4] economically deprived and upward socially mobile,[5] sectarian and transformative,[6] individualist, separatist and migratory,[7] conservative and progressive.[8] These extremes represent internal and external sociocultural, cosmopolitical, and economic pressures of the movement that must be embraced as part of the current make-up of Pentecostal theology.[9] The full gospel navigates these territories through uniquely Pentecostal sensibilities, which, I suggest, encourage a soteriology of cosmopolitan redemption empowering cultural transformation and public welfare.[10] If Pentecost forms also the root image of the Pentecostal social imagination, then interpreting Pentecostal theology along this symbol demands that we identify how the actions of the full gospel are made socially meaningful. In the present chapter, I attempt to show how the Pentecostal story confronts, reinterprets and transforms society as a framework of meaning and agent of the common good by developing the notion of cosmopolitan redemption from the perspective of the full gospel. After applying Pentecostal soteriology to confrontation with the public life, the chapter traces the idea of sanctification as transformation of culture, applies Spirit baptism to the notion of the common good, interprets divine healing in terms of social welfare and relates the expectation of the coming kingdom as a question to the end of society.

[3] Amos Yong, *In the Days of Caesar: Pentecostalism and Political Theology* (Grand Rapids: Eerdmans, 2010, 4–14; Calvin L. Smith, 'The Politics and Economics of Pentecostalism: A Global Survey', in *The Cambridge Companion to Pentecostalism*, ed. Cecil M. Robeck Jr. and Amos Yong (New York: Cambridge University Press, 2014), 175–94.
[4] David Martin, *Pentecostalism: The World Their Parrish* (Oxford: Blackwell, 2002), 83–118.
[5] See Amos Yong and Katherine Attanasi (ed.), *Pentecostalism and Prosperity: The Socio-economics of the Global Charismatic Movement* (New York: Palgrave, 2012); Robert Mapes Anderson, *Vision of the Disinherited: The Making of American Pentecostalism* (Peabody, MA: Hendrickson, 1992).
[6] Miller and Yamamori, *Global Pentecostalism*, 99–128.
[7] Murray W. Dempster, Byron D. Klaus, Douglas Petersen (eds), *The Globalization of Pentecostalism: A Religion Made to Travel* (Paternoster: 1999).
[8] Bryant L. Myers, 'Progressive Pentecostalism, Development, and Christian Development NGOs: A Challenge and an Opportunity', *IBMR* 39, no. 3 (2015): 115–20; Michael Wilkinson and Steven M. Studebaker (eds), *A Liberating Spirit: Pentecostals and Social Action in North America* (Eugene, OR: Pickwick, 2010), 1–19.
[9] This is the premise of Wolfgang Vondey, *Pentecostalism: A Guide for the Perplexed* (London and New York: Bloomsbury T&T Clark, 2013).
[10] For similar connections of cosmopolitan and Pentecostal concerns, see Nimi Wariboko, *The Charismatic City and the Public Resurgence of Religion: A Pentecostal Social Ethics of Cosmopolitan Urban Life*, CHARIS 2 (New York: Palgrave Macmillan, 2014); Daniela C. Augustine, *Pentecost, Hospitality, and Transfiguration: Toward a Spirit-Inspired Vision of Social Transformation* (Cleveland, TN: CPT Press, 2012).

Salvation as cosmopolitan deliverance

Salvation, for Pentecostals, is fundamentally participation in the divine praxis of hospitality that involves the material and spiritual realities of being in the world (Chapter 2). Since all of creation is the economy of salvation, and creation is a spirit-filled cosmos, Pentecostal soteriology takes seriously the resulting interdependent and confrontational relationships of the spiritual and material dimensions of created existence (Chapter 7). A Pentecostal reading of the New Testament insists that salvation emerges from an expansive cosmological 'struggle … not against enemies of blood and flesh, but against the rulers, against the authorities, against the cosmic powers of this present darkness, against the spiritual forces of evil in the heavenly places" (Eph. 6:12). The primary theological question for a Pentecostal social vision is how this kind of confrontational soteriology translates into the concrete particularities of sociocultural existence. If salvation is deliverance from evil, sin, and death in its manifold global and particular forms, then soteriology must span the merging spheres of individuals enmeshed in social relations and networks comprising everyday activities across cultural, political, religious, economic, and institutional territories. The theological ideals of Pentecostal soteriology here are confronted with the tangible forms of the dominant cultural and social processes of modernization, globalization, transnationalization, and urbanization.[11] Amidst these contemporary forces, opportunities for deliverance are found (and created) amidst an emerging worldwide civilization, a cosmopolitan gathering of collective human activities and interactions. In what Pentecostals today might call a 'worldwide network of political, economic, cultural, religious, legal, corporate and technological forces and places without a controlling center',[12] the realist and pragmatic nature of Pentecostal spirituality and piety typically finds expression in a theology of spiritual socio-territorial warfare expanding throughout the regions, nations, ethnic groups, cities, neighbourhoods, institutions, and social networks of the world.[13] This confrontational soteriology has led Pentecostals to a frequent

---

[11] See André Droogers, 'The Cultural Dimension of Pentecostalism', in Robeck and Yong, *The Cambridge Companion to Pentecostalism*, 195–214.
[12] Wariboko, *The Charismatic City*, 11.
[13] See C. Peter Wagner (ed.), *Territorial Spirits: Practical Strategies for How to Crush the Enemy through Spiritual Warfare* (Shippensburg, PA: Destiny, 2012); Opoku Onyinah, *Spiritual Warfare: A Centre for Pentecostal Theology Short Introduction* (Cleveland, TN: CPT Press, 2012).

demonization of public life and culture.¹⁴ A more balanced, transformational account of Pentecostal theology acknowledges but redefines the importance of the notion of the demonic for the sociocultural, political, and economic spheres of a cosmopolitan soteriology.

The fundamental commitment of Pentecostal soteriology is that God in Jesus Christ confronts the substance of all existence. The outpouring of the Spirit at Pentecost expands the reach of Christ's presence to the ends of the earth in concrete spiritual and physical ways. At the same time, Pentecostal cosmology acknowledges also the universal extension of evil and the demonic in the world (see Chapter 7). A culturally adept demonology asserts that evil and the demonic are not merely symbols of social realities but 'conscious, metaphysical beings with ontological substance'.¹⁵ The way of salvation leads therefore inevitably through confrontation with the concrete embodiment of existence via the physical and social habitus that expresses the presence of diverse spirits.¹⁶ The reality of the demonic, although conceivable as immaterial fields of force with destructive powers, is recognized concretely in space and time in often personal incarnate forms. Accordingly, the chief insight of Pentecostal demonology is that principalities and powers are not encountered in the abstract but in the embodied realities of social, cultural, political and economic patterns of activity.¹⁷ Pentecostal demonology frequently connects with indigenous beliefs of witchcraft and sorcery and can find expression in militant ways of confronting, breaking, blocking, delivering, and destroying the demonic in its personal incarnations.¹⁸ But the embodiment of the demonic also transcends individual forms of physical materiality, and the concerns of salvation must therefore be expanded from concerns for individual conversion to the socioethical implications of the public, political, and economic life: to name the demonic is not only to

---

¹⁴ For a critical Pentecostal perspective see Charles Harris, 'Encountering Territorial Spirits', in *Power Encounter: A Pentecostal Perspective*, ed. Opal Reddin, rev. ed. (Springfield, MO: Central Bible College, 1999), 240–86.

¹⁵ See David Bradnick, 'The Demonic from the Protestant Era to the Pentecostal Era: An Intersection of Tillichian and Pentecostal Demonologies and Its Implications', in *Paul Tillich and Pentecostal Theology: Spiritual Presence and Spiritual Power*, ed. Nimi Wariboko and Amos Yong (Bloomington: Indiana University Press, 2015), 158–72.

¹⁶ See Jörg Haustein, 'Embodying the Spirit(s): Pentecostal Demonology and Deliverance Discourse in Ethiopia', *Ethnos* 76, no. 4 (2011): 534–52.

¹⁷ See Yong, *Beyond the Impasse*, 137–38.

¹⁸ See Sandra Fancello, 'Sorcellerie et délivrance dans les pentecôtismes africains', *CEA* 48, no. 189/190 (2008): 161–83.

recognize but to protest and resist the social and cultural manifestations of evil.[19] Salvation does not exist in confrontation alone but in the deliverance from confrontation.

Of course, Pentecostal demonology, and the prevalence of warfare imagery, lend themselves to an overtly dualistic worldview and omnipresent demonization of complex physical, psychological, and social structures.[20] Nevertheless, by casting sociocultural discourse in religious and spiritual terms, Pentecostal theology suggests that the discernment of evil is indispensable as a context for understanding the changing forces that challenge salvation amidst the concrete circumstances of social, economic, and political life.[21] Salvation as deliverance recognizes the demonic and destructive forces distributed across and integrating vastly different individual, familial, social and institutional entities. Salvation is therefore neither exclusively anthropocentric or individualistic but extends through the deliverance of human beings also to the spiritual strongholds manifested in societies, cultures, governments, corporations, economic, political, and technological systems.[22] Over-personalizing the demonic is just as problematic as demythologizing evil; both lend support for an abstract soteriology disconnected from human agency and its relational embeddedness in creation.

Pentecostal soteriology with its pervasive drive for practicability, and understood in the broad contexts of deliverance from principalities and powers, demands a phenomenology (not merely ontology) of divine, demonic and natural spheres of existence that accounts for the individual and social, the personal and public life in the cities, towns, villages, and neighbourhoods of an increasingly cosmopolitan world. Salvation as a confrontation of such realms involves exorcism and deliverance of the individual only insofar as the human person is always embedded in public life and its diverse

---

[19] See Amos Yong, *Discerning the Spirit(s): A Pentecostal-Charismatic Contribution to Christian Theology of Religions*, JPTS 20 (Sheffield: Sheffield Academic Press, 2000), 234–43.
[20] See E. Janet Warren, '"Spiritual Warfare": A Dead Metaphor?' *JPT* 21 (2012): 278–97.
[21] See Birgit Meyer, '"You Devil, Go Away from Me!" Pentecostalist African Christianity and the Powers of Good and Evil', in *Powers of Good and Evil: Moralities, Commodities and Popular Belief*, ed. Paul Clough and Jon P. Mitchell (New York: Berghahn, 2001), 104–34; idem, 'The Power of Money: Politics, Occult Forces, and Pentecostalism in Ghana', *ASR* 41, no. 3 (1998): 15–37; idem, '"Delivered from the Powers of Darkness": Confessions of Satanic Riches in Christian Ghana', *Africa* 65, no. 2 (1995): 236–55.
[22] Yong, *In the Days of Caesar*, 149; Walter J. Hollenweger, *Pentecostalism: Origins and Developments Worldwide* (Peabody, MA: Hendrickson, 1997), 204–17.

socioethical, political, and economic practices.[23] Soteriological practices are therefore ecclesial rites in a street-smart form that exist for the church as a 'portable' mode of public engagement in critical, if not alternative, forms of human agency resisting the destruction of God's created order.[24] The church, if it embraces and facilitates its worship, liturgies and rituals as soteriological practices, represents an alternative city amidst the powers and principalities of the world.[25] Yet, a confrontational soteriology cannot sustain a vision of the new Jerusalem without engaging in the transformation of the old.

The church does not exist as alternative city by virtue of the power of its own practices vis-à-vis the power of the demonic but because it resists entirely the demands of the competitive potentiality and performance governing the demonic in the world.[26] Church and world are not identical; the secular Babylon is not the heavenly Jerusalem.[27] The principle at work in this kind of soteriological resistance is the rejection of absolutizing any particular form of finite embodiment as a vehicle of the divine.[28] However, salvation as deliverance aims not at the destruction but the re-enchantment of the cosmopolitical domain, at the redemption of spiritual powers and principalities susceptible to demonic manifestations, and at the civilization of the affected social, political and economic spheres through rites of social exorcism formative of alternative human habits, character and agency.[29] Hence, Pentecostals deal with the demonic not exclusively through militant exorcism but also the liturgical practices of 'fasting, prayer retreats, researches on the dominant spirits possessing the gates of the communities, and ... prayer walking, traveling throughout the community, speaking and calling into being the good of the community'.[30] All rituals of the church are essentially capable of

---

[23] See Peter Versteeg, 'Deliverance and Exorcism in Anthropological Perspective', in *Exorcism and Deliverance: Multi-Disciplinary Studies*, ed. William K. Kay and Robin Parry, SPCI (Milton Keynes: Paternoster, 2011), 120–38.

[24] See Birgit Meyer, 'Aesthetics of Persuasion: Global Christianity and Pentecostalism's Sensational Forms', *SAQ* 109, no. 4 (2010): 741–63; Yong, *In the Days of Caesar*, 155–61.

[25] See ibid., 161–65; Wariboko, *The Charismatic City*, 169–93.

[26] See Nimi Wariboko, *The Pentecostal Principle: Ethical Methodology in New Spirit*, Pentecostal Manifestos 5 (Grand Rapids, MI: Eerdmans, 2012), 172–87; Wolfgang Vondey, *Beyond Pentecostalism: The Crisis of Global Christianity and the Renewal of the Theological Agenda*, PM 3 (Grand Rapids, MI: Eerdmans, 2010), 171–201.

[27] See Steven M. Studebaker, *A Pentecostal Political Theology for American Renewal: Spirit of the Kingdoms, Citizen of the Cities*, CHARIS 5 (New York: Palgrave Macmillan, 2016), 109–40.

[28] Wariboko, *The Pentecostal Principle*, 182.

[29] Yong, *In the Days of Caesar*, 155–65.

[30] Ogbu Kalu, *African Pentecostalism: An Introduction* (Oxford: Oxford University Press, 2008), 218.

carrying a soteriology of resistance. Pentecostal worship practices, as I have detailed them in the first part of this volume, extend from the church into the world and return from the world into the church. Under the symbol of the altar, these soteriological practices create not only ritual and liturgical space and time but also draw social and cultural realities into its ecclesial rhythm. The full gospel proclaims Jesus as saviour of the world precisely because his domain extends beyond a narrow idea of church and altar to the cities and public squares of the world.

With the church situated centrally amidst a soteriology of cosmopolitan redemption, Pentecostal theology is able to speak not only of the body of Christ as an alternative city but of the cities of the world as constituting the cosmopolitan body of Christ. The sociopolitical implications of Pentecostal soteriology demand that soteriological resistance cannot proceed exclusively in terms of displacement of the demonic or the secular. Instead, the body of Christ, from the perspective of Pentecost, both engages with and consists of the emerging cosmopolitan culture and character of the world and is able to transform and transcend its plurality as the temple of the Holy Spirit.[31] The politics of the Spirit, identified by Pentecostal rituals, are indeed intended to drive political and socioeconomic behaviour.[32] On the one hand, political and economic activism, even the controversial prosperity message, are unavoidable utilitarian tools in a soteriology of deliverance that seeks to transform social behaviour in order to bridge the chasm between the powerful and the marginalized, the rich and the poor, within the body of Christ.[33] On the other hand, a radicalized eschatological understanding of social and political activism as a form of building the kingdom of God on earth is equally inevitable in Pentecostal theology.[34] The principal power relations of a cosmopolitan life in the Spirit at work in Pentecostalism reach across the repertoires of the internal (believers and church), external (nonbelievers and society), and the transcendental (divine and demonic).[35] Ultimately, the

---

[31] Wariboko, *The Charismatic City*, 169–93.
[32] See Timothy J. Steigenga, *The Politics of the Spirit: The Political Implications of Pentecostalized Religion in Costa Rica and Guatemala* (Lanham, MD: Lexington Books, 2001).
[33] Smith, 'The Politics and Economics of Pentecostalism', 182–83; cf. Isabelle V. Barker, 'Charismatic Economies: Pentecostalism, Economic Restructuring, and Social Reproduction', *NPS* 29, no. 4 (2007): 407–27.
[34] See Bruce Barron, *Heaven on Earth? The Social and Political Agendas of Dominion Theology* (Grand Rapids, MI: Zondervan, 1992).
[35] Droogers, 'The Cultural Dimension of Pentecostalism', 208–11.

soteriological practices of the church are always directed at the fullness of the gospel: the way of salvation leads through the concrete struggles of sanctification, Spirit baptism, and divine healing towards the kingdom of God in the manifold pluralism of the here and now. As the centre and summit of a theology of the full gospel, the altar is the meeting place for the principal confrontation of good and evil, God and Satan, the divine and the demonic, the old and the new creation. The altar is therefore not the romanticized and exclusive possession of the church for its own liturgical celebrations but a place for the rituals of the world to be confronted with the presence of God. The remainder of this chapter sets out to describe the mechanisms of this confrontation. I suggest that when the church in the power of the Spirit reaches into the social, political, and economic spheres of the world, the altars of the church will reach beyond the church into the nations and governments, corporations, social networks, cultural, and economic ties. Put differently, cosmopolitan redemption is possible where the altars of the church have become the altars of the world.

Sanctification as transformation of culture

The Pentecostal notion of sanctification is closely intertwined with the emphasis on the original experience of conversion and deliverance and refers to an immediate or repeated sense of release from sin, addiction, sickness, demonic possession, or other oppressive experiences (see Chapter 3). This experience of deliverance is always embedded in the cultural life-world of a person's social networks and relations, economic status, cultural embodiment, and political ambitions. To be sanctified is God's act of purification and cleansing from sin, involving not only an intellectual, moral and physical conversion, but also a distancing of oneself from the world and its pollutants. Pentecostals have advocated an active stance towards separation from cultural ills, including gambling, television, alcohol, tobacco, mixed-bathing and many other socially accepted leisure activities.[36] More than personal pietism, sanctification is seen as purifying and consecrating by being relational

---

[36] See Robert Mapes Anderson, *Vision of the Disinherited: The Making of American Pentecostalism* (Oxford: Oxford University Press, 1979), 195–222.

and participatory, demanding a socio-cultural vision of salvation as deliverance. When the altars of the church are in the world and not apart from it, then sanctification as an image of redemption emphasizes the need for concrete individual and ecclesial practices that also initiate and sustain a socio-cultural ethical vision. The primary concern of the full gospel is whether a soteriology of deliverance supports not only counter-cultural resistance but also the redemption of culture. I suggest that sanctification acts as a catalyst that modifies a soteriological resistance through exposure to Pentecostal spirituality towards the goal of transforming culture by participation in the sanctified practices of the body of Christ.

The theological starting point for a Pentecostal social vision of sanctification can be traced back to the emphasis that sanctification originates with the work of the Holy Spirit (see Rom. 15:16; 1 Cor. 6:11; 2 Thess. 2:13; 1 Pet. 1:2) and that the biblical witness to the politics of the Spirit pursues 'simultaneously the rejection and redemption of culture'.[37] The solidarity of the Spirit with the oppressed and ostracized elements of society, echoing the ministry of Jesus (Acts 10:38), shows that deliverance is not exclusively the separation of individuals from the injustices of society but also the transformation of the institutions, structures, symbols, logics, systems and power dynamics in which they participate.[38] When conversion is merely separation, and sanctification merely consecration, the mission of the Spirit is stripped of its cultural garment made visible (and wearable) with the day of Pentecost. Instead, personal piety in the Spirit leads to public participation; individual and personal sanctification represent the cogs and wheels of civilization and social transformation. If culture is understood as a mechanism of continuity that preserves social identity (including the ailments of society), then participation in the mission of the Spirit produces both continuity and discontinuity.[39] On the one hand, salvation as deliverance takes seriously the ontology and cosmology of any given culture by situating sanctification within; on the other hand, the sanctification of culture struggles

---

[37] Yong, *In the Days of Caesar*, 195.
[38] See Matthias Wenk, 'Der Heilige Geist als Solidarität mit den Bedrängten und Ausgestoßenen', in *Das Evangelium den Armen: Die Pfingstbewegung im Spannungsfeld zwischen sozialer Verantwortung und klassischem Missionsverständnis*, ed. Marcel Redling (Darmstadt: FTHG, 2013) 95–124.
[39] See Joel Robbins, 'On the Paradoxes of Global Pentecostalism and the Perils of Continuity Thinking', *Religion* 33 (2003): 221–31; Droogers, 'The Cultural Dimension of Pentecostalism', 203–7.

against the principalities and powers thus made evident.[40] Sanctification is in this sense a necessary attribute of Pentecostal soteriology because it pushes the immediate concerns for conversion to their moral, social, and cultural consequences.

A helpful sociopolitical image to recast the tension between continuity and discontinuity is to speak of culture in terms of the centre and margins of society that have become particularly evident in today's cosmopolitan and urbanized world. The Pentecostal notion of sanctification takes seriously the mission of the Spirit to the marginalized, the disinherited, the poor and the outcasts of society in order to confound and deconstruct the powerful establishment of the centre.[41] Sanctification begins at these margins wherever human beings encounter the disturbing reality of what is considered acceptable, conventional, normal, or orthodox. The margins constitute a place of disturbance, a place of risk, tension and uncertainty open to resistance to the uncritical continuity of the status quo demanded by the cultural centre. People at the margins suffer and resist the complexity of cultural structures and symbols that continue to exist through the processes of cultural accommodation, systematization, and institutionalization.[42] Yet, because the mission of the Spirit is not exclusive to the margins but includes also the redemption of the powerful and dominant centre, sanctified practices must participate in transformation across the sociocultural spectrum.[43] The goal of sanctification is the dissolution of the centre/margin dichotomy by establishing a soteriological balance that opens up the space of deliverance to a social and cultural moral vision of human flourishing.

Sanctification identifies with civilization by posing a necessary principle for the transformation of culture that engages the world through a confronting social imaginary of redemption.[44] This sanctified aesthetic is concerned with the transitional phase of those who already have encountered the Spirit

---

[40] Robbins, 'On the Paradoxes of Global Pentecostalism', 223.
[41] See Cheryl Bridges Johns, 'Partners in Scandal: Wesleyan and Pentecostal Scholarship', *Pneuma* 21, no. 1 (1990): 183–97.
[42] Vondey, *Beyond Pentecostalism*, 196–201.
[43] See Heinrich W. Schäfer, 'Explaining Central American Pentecostalism within Social Inequality and Conflict: On *Habitus-Analysis* as a Clue to Describe Religious Praxis', in *Pentecostal Power: Expressions, Impact and Faith in Latin American Pentecostalism*, ed. Calvin Smith, Global Pentecostal and Charismatic Studies 6 (Leiden: Brill, 2011), 137–56.
[44] Yong, *In the Days of Caesar*, 205–10; James K. A. Smith, *Thinking in Tongues: Pentecostal Contributions to Christian Philosophy*, PM 1 (Grand Rapids, MI: Eerdmans, 2010), 80–85.

but are not yet perfected eternally and find themselves 'betwixt and between the positions assigned and arrayed by law, custom, convention and ceremonial'.[45] In this liminal state, individuals bond together in a volatile sanctified communion in which cultural assertions are transformed by the tarrying and waiting for the Spirit.[46] The embodiment of Pentecostal theology at the altar demands that this kind of cultural participation in the Spirit is clothed in concrete rituals and practices which serve both the reification and destructuralization of existing social configurations and values.[47] That means, not simply any cultural ritual is a sanctifying ritual, but the sanctification of culture requires 'a set of practices through which certain dispositions or practical skills for orientation towards the sacred are acquired and exercised'.[48] These practices must travel from the margins to the centre (and back again). Sanctification emerges through religious and cultural rituals in a structural ambiguity that is necessary for its purifying and consecrating functioning but which presents the soteriological vision of the church with two opposing theological demands: (1) sanctification as 'ritually cultivated embodied and linguistic dispositions for experiencing the sacred and reordering the behavioral environment'[49] must permeate the walls of the church if they want to remain a potential arena for transformation across social and cultural hierarchies; (2) consecration must remain a confrontation of these hierarchies with Christ in order to expose, identify and transform them by bringing them into the church and onwards to God.

Sanctification as ritual brings with it a double reification and objectification of religion and culture, that is, it places religious identity amidst cultural identification and vice versa.[50] Where the notion of conversion alone often presupposes and creates two opposite realms (e.g. world or God, society or church), sanctification demands a 'theologically responsible

---

[45] See Victor Turner, *The Ritual Process: Structure and Anti-Structure* (Chicago: Aldine, 1969), 94–97.
[46] See Daniel Castelo, *Revisioning Pentecostal Ethics: The Epicletic Community* (Cleveland, TN: CPT Press, 2012), 35–82.
[47] See Augustine, *Pentecost, Hospitality, and Transfiguration*, 126–38; Bobby C. Alexander, 'Pentecostal Ritual Reconsidered: Anti-Structural Dimensions of Possession', *JRS* 3, no. 1 (1989): 109–28.
[48] Martin Lindhardt, *Power in Powerlessness: A Study of Pentecostal Life Worlds in Urban Chile* (Leiden: Brill, 2012), 150.
[49] Ibid.
[50] See Ruth Marshall, *Political Spiritualities: The Pentecostal Revolution in Nigeria* (Chicago: University of Chicago Press, 2009), 54–68.

syncretism' that brings these realms together for the purpose of transformation and redemption.[51] Since a socioethical vision of holiness cannot be perceived apart from culture, sanctification and consecration must produce a culture acceptable and adoptable for the church. Rejecting, consuming and engaging culture are Pentecostal means to responsibly fit into different cultural contexts.[52] This diversity of interaction is possible because sanctification itself is impartial towards the object of transformation and aims as much at the purification of secular culture (to deliver it from the powers of evil, poverty, sickness, and hardship) as at the consecration and reformation of the existing ecclesial culture (its prejudices, isolation, stagnation). In other words, sanctification as a social ritual requires both ecclesial and cultural mediation; it is successful only if consecration does not preclude purification. Cultural resistance as a way of participation has the goal to harvest the culture for the church. Nonetheless, such harvesting must lead through both the threshing floor and the winnowing fan. A simplistic view on sanctification may suggest that the Pentecostal answer to social problems in the secular realm is their immediate confrontation with the Spirit of God. Yet, the goal of this Spirit-encounter is often the more difficult redirection of society towards the sacred as a way of preparing for the encounter with God: the ecclesial and secular are mutually enculturating realms of human and Christian existence. While the ultimate goal of sanctification is holiness, the way to purity cannot avoid the dirt, filth, and scum in the pit from which it needs to be redeemed. In other words, the altars of the sacred can stand within the secular only if the world is continually charged with the mystery and glory of God.

The sanctification of culture in its own right emphasizes that redemption includes 'many tongues and many cultures' of the world even if it does not provide a singular template for navigating the distance between separating from and participating in culture.[53] The difficulty of traversing the cultural terrain manifests itself particularly in the ambiguities towards certain areas of culture that systemically fit neither religious nor social concerns (e.g.

---

[51] Hollenweger, *Pentecostalism*, 132–43. Cf. Yong, *In the Days of Caesar*, 207.
[52] See Timothy H. Wadkins, 'Pentecostals and the New World Order in El Salvador: Separating, Consuming, and Engaging', in *Spirit and Power: The Growth and Global Impact of Pentecostalism*, ed. Donald E. Miller, Kimon H. Sargeant, Richard Flory (Oxford: Oxford University Press, 2013), 143–59.
[53] Yong, *In the Days of Caesar*, 194.

environmental care).⁵⁴ The continuing existence of these cultural ambiguities emphasizes the need to discern the Spirit's voice not only with regard to narrow social issues at stake but with respect to the broad beliefs and practices of the church that support or neglect all human flourishing.⁵⁵ Re-integrating sanctification in the narrative of the full gospel (for those who have neglected it) is important here, since sanctification in Pentecostal theology does not exist for its own purposes but points beyond itself to the wider purposes of salvation for the good of all creation.

Spirit baptism as a common good

Pentecostal theology takes seriously the biblical affirmation that with the day of Pentecost the Spirit of God has been poured out on all flesh. Pentecostals have interpreted this idea largely within an anthropological framework described as a baptism in the Spirit at the hands of Jesus (see Chapter 4). I have followed the idea that Spirit baptism serves as a lens through which Pentecostals view and interpret the other elements of the full gospel. However, the doctrines of Pentecostals may give the impression that this baptism is primarily a soteriological and missiological instrument tied to theological and religious concerns rather than to the social, political, or economic spheres of public life.⁵⁶ If a social vision of the full gospel goes beyond the notion of sanctification to the concerns of empowerment, Pentecostals face the question how the baptism in the Spirit can contribute from its central standpoint in the soteriological narrative to all concerns of human flourishing. I suggest that the charismatic manifestations of Spirit baptism can be interpreted as soteriological instruments that serve the public good. Salvation as deliverance in the image of Pentecost is interpreted charismatically as transpositional and self-transcending, liberating and transforming, confronting and building culture for the good of all.

---

[54] See Michael Wilkinson, 'Globalization and the Environment as Social Problem', in Wilkinson and Studebaker, *A Liberating Spirit*, 213–30.

[55] See Andrea Hollingsworth and Melissa D. Browning, 'Your Daughters Shall Prophecy (As Long as They Submit): Pentecostalism and Gender in Global Perspective', in Wilkinson and Studebaker, *A Liberating Spirit*, 161–84.

[56] See the overviews Chad Owen Brand, *Perspectives on Spirit Baptism: Five Views* (Nashville: Broadman and Holman, 2004) and Koo Dong Yun, *Baptism in the Holy Spirit: An Ecumenical Theology of Spirit Baptism* (Lanham, MD: University Press of America, 2003).

The biblical report of the outpouring of the Spirit on the disciples at Pentecost shows clear public manifestations. In its broadest sense, the outpouring of the Spirit 'on all flesh' is portrayed through an outpouring on a city (Jerusalem) gleaming with inhabitants 'from every nation under heaven' (Acts 2:5) gathering in a melting pot of cultures (vv. 9–11). The circle of impact is quickly widened beyond the Jewish audience gathered in Jerusalem to their sons and daughters and eventually to 'all who are far away' (v. 17, 39).[57] Following Peter's generous description of those who will receive the Spirit as 'everyone whom the Lord our God calls' (v. 39), the impact of the Spirit's outpouring is ultimately extended throughout the book of Acts beyond the Jewish culture to the Gentiles (see Acts 8:15–17; 10:44–47; 19:6), where the outpouring of the Spirit becomes a major point of confronting and reconciling the different cultures of the world.[58] A closer look at how the outpouring of the Spirit engages the public life leads immediately to the outward displays of Spirit baptism. More than merely physical (oral and audible) manifestations, the speaking with tongues, prophecies, dreams and visions experienced with the baptism are sociocultural phenomena that confound and rebuild culture.

The simultaneous confronting and building of cultures at Pentecost and beyond is often portrayed by Pentecostals (and others) in deliberate contrast to the confusion of languages that occurred at Babel.[59] The baptism in the Spirit reverses the attempt to build a singular public culture by going beyond Babel to embrace a diversity of voices and cultures that find 'expression in the move between individual and collective, sacred and profane, particular and general'.[60] However, a closer look at the altar of Pentecost shows that the sacramental qualities of the baptism in the Spirit *become* public qualities because the charismatic manifestations drive the Christians out of preoccupation with their own culture and put them in situations

---

[57] See Craig S. Keener, *Acts: An Exegetical Commentary*, Volume 1, *Introduction and 1:1–2:47* (Grand Rapids, MI: Baker, 2012), 780–836.

[58] Studebaker, *A Pentecostal Political Theology*, 109–40.

[59] See Daniela C. Augustine, 'Pentecost as the Church's Cosmopolitan Vision of Global Civil Society: A Post-Communist Eastern European Theological Perspective', in *A World for All? Global Civil Society in Political Theory and Trinitarian Theology*, ed. William F. Storrar et al. (Grand Rapids, MI: Eerdmans, 2011), 197–220; Frank D. Macchia, *Baptized in the Spirit: A Global Pentecostal Theology* (Grand Rapids, MI: Zondervan, 2006), 215–18; Yong, *The Spirit Poured Out*, 196.

[60] Andre Corten and Ruth Marshall-Fratani (eds), *Between Babel and Pentecost: Transnational Pentecostalism in Africa and Latin America* (Bloomington: Indiana University Press, 2001), 12.

(i.e. altars) where they meet the other as genuinely other by increasing their 'capacity for authentic encounter among humankind (including those who are not Christians)'.[61] The altar of Pentecost immediately exposes biases, misinformation and stereotypes about people from other cultures in those who observe them and leads them to ask questions about their own cultures, customs and views (see Acts 2:7-13). The speaking with tongues and prophecies of the body of Christ not only unmask differences in communication styles and values but respect the differences by communicating effectively across different ethnic status, races, cultures, classes, economic groups, and religions. The sights and sounds of those who are baptized in the Spirit ultimately fulfil the divine initiative at Babel by diversifying the tongues and publics that witness to God.[62] The charismatic manifestations of Spirit baptism confound the 'public square' and challenge its often limiting constitution by taking seriously its public essence and taking it to the extreme.

Christian theology typically underscores the biblical emphasis on the diversity of spiritual gifts, the distribution of charismata to various tasks and offices, and the unity of all gifts in the one Spirit (see Rom. 12:4-8; 1 Cor. 12:8-10, 28-30; 14:26; Eph. 4:11; 1 Pet. 4:10-11). However, less emphatic has been a connection of the public manifestation of the gifts of the Spirit with the emphasis that these manifestations are given 'for the common good' (1 Cor. 12:7).[63] The restriction of the charismatic life to the church alone is particularly problematic in the speaking with tongues and the prophetic gifts.[64] Tongue speech has disturbed, in a manner of speaking, the ability of Pentecostals to live quietly amongst their neighbours. Aside from the rich exegetical, historical, psychological, anthropological and devotional aspects of the practice, the sociocultural, ethical and political dimensions demand further attention.[65] Above all, the theophanic encounter of the human being with God expressed in the speaking with tongues has cemented their place as *between* demonstrative speech and ineffable 'sighs too deep for words' (Rom.

---

[61] Jean-Jacques Suurmond, *Word and Spirit at Play: Towards a Charismatic Theology* (Grand Rapids: Eerdmans, 1994), 201.
[62] See Macchia, *Baptized in the Spirit*, 216-19.
[63] See Mark J. Cartledge, 'Renewal Theology and the "Common Good"', *JPT* 25 (2016): 1-17.
[64] See Robert J. Gladstone, 'Sign Language in the Assembly: How Are Tongues a Sign to the Unbeliever in 1 Cor 14:20-25?' *AJPS* 2, no. 2 (1999): 177-93.
[65] See Watson E. Mills (ed.), *A Guide to Research on Glossolalia* (Grand Rapids: Eerdmans, 1986).

8:26).⁶⁶ Tongues are seen as attributes of empowerment by giving voice to a fuller image of God in the world, a restoration of the divine image through Spirit-empowered sights and sounds.⁶⁷ Although tongues may not be 'speech' in a linguistic sense,⁶⁸ they are nonetheless a demonstrative cultural speech-act that operates properly only through engagement with the public good.

The public good of speaking in tongues emerges from their divine origin and purpose as God's communication to humanity.⁶⁹ Tongues speech is a transpositional activity (from God to humanity)⁷⁰ that manifests in a more confrontational tone the divine-human encounter. Yet, as a divine instrument for the common good, the meaning of tongues is bound to semiotic and cultural identifiers without being restricted to discernible linguistic content. Speaking in tongues obtains its value when social and divine life meet to produce a cultural network of symbols that can transform lives.⁷¹ In this sense, speaking with tongues is not counter-cultural in the sense of entirely rejecting culture – tongues are inseparable from culture, even in their critical function. Yet, the uniqueness of speaking in an unlearned language (*xenolalia*) disarms cultural expectations of linguistic usage and development (especially among the poor and uneducated); the speaking in an unknown tongue (*glossolalia*) confounds the Babelian scepticism of a single universal language and that such (heavenly) language can be expressed with human tongues (and be understood). While the sight and sound of tongues alone confront the established culture, even when the tongues give forth no more than a groaning in the Spirit, the content of speech also contributes simultaneously to the building of an alternative public and symbolic narrative.⁷² The tongues,

---

[66] See Frank D. Macchia, 'Sighs Too Deep for Words: Toward a Theology of Glossolalia', *JPT* 1 (1992): 47–73; idem, 'Groans Too Deep for Words: Towards a Theology of Tongues as Initial Evidence', *AJPS* 1, no. 2 (1998): 149–73.

[67] See Blaine Charette, 'Reflective Speech: Glossolalia and the Image of God', *Pneuma* 28, no. 2 (2006): 189–201.

[68] See William Samarin, *Tongues of Men and Angels: The Religious Language of Pentecostalism* (New York: Macmillan, 1972).

[69] Harold Horton, *What Is the Good of Speaking with Tongues? An Enthusiastic Vindication of Supernatural Endowment* (London: Assemblies of God Publishers, 1960), 10–11.

[70] See Tony Richie, 'Transposition and Tongues: Pentecostalizing an Important Insight of C. S. Lewis', *JPT* 13, no. 1 (2004): 117–37.

[71] See Amos Yong, '"Tongues of Fire" in the Pentecostal Imagination: The Truth of Glossolalia in Light of R. C. Neville's Theory of Religious Symbolism', *JPT* 12 (1998): 39–65; Frank D. Macchia, 'Discerning the Truth of Tongues Speech: A Response to Amos Yong', ibid., 67–71; Amos Yong, 'The Truth of Tongues Speech: A Rejoinder to Frank Macchia', *JPT* 13 (1998): 107–15.

[72] See Wolfgang Vondey, 'The Symbolic Turn: A Symbolic Conception of the Liturgy of Pentecostalism', *WTJ* 36, no. 2 (Fall 2001): 223–47.

languages, dialects, and nations of Pentecost do not deprive people of their own culture but call them to integrate their cultural particularities in the plurality and freedom of the cosmopolitan world.[73]

When the content of speech meets with the expectation of divine intent (whether in the lingua franca of *xenolalia*, the interpretation of *glossolalia*, or as *akolalia* and its understanding in the mind of the audience regardless of the actual utterance), the culture-building function of the baptism in the Spirit has entered the realm of the prophetic. For many, prophetic discourse casts a more deliberate counter-cultural narrative often born from a conscientious experience of or identification with the injustices and ailments of society opposing the common good.[74] Both, tongues speech and prophecy, confront the public image of the good with the revelation of the goodness of God. However, whereas tongues may obtain an almost sacramental quality in their function as an 'audible medium for realizing the presence of God',[75] prophecy is a more literal (than semiotic) medium for realizing the opposition of God to the ideology of civil society and the state.[76] Prophetic discourse increases amidst a politics of oppression supported by an economy of affluence and a consenting religion.[77] The prophetic manifestation of Spirit baptism confronts the single-market culture of Babel in its totalizing reality and offers with Pentecost the vision of an alternative model that ultimately confronts human social, political and economic culture with God as the 'totally other'.[78] At the altar of Pentecost we find the prophethood of all believers – the charismatic functioning of all those baptized in the Spirit regardless of social, economic, religious or cultural standing, race, ethnicity and education, particularly the underprivileged, disestablished, and oppressed.[79] The aim of this public prophethood is not merely critical activity towards culture but the shaping of all cultures as testimony

---

[73] Augustine, *Pentecost, Hospitality, and Transfiguration*, 30–42; see also Samuel Solivan, *The Spirit, Pathos and Liberation: Toward an Hispanic Pentecostal Theology*, JPTS 14 (Sheffield: Sheffield Academic Press, 1998), 112–18.
[74] Augustine, *Pentecost, Hospitality, and Transfiguration*, 66–67.
[75] Frank D. Macchia, 'Tongues as a Sign: Towards a Sacramental Understanding of Pentecostal Experience', *Pneuma* 15, no. 1 (1993): 61–76.
[76] Yong, *In the Days of Caesar*, 249–52.
[77] Often cited by Pentecostals is Walter Brueggeman, *The Prophetic Imagination*, rev. ed. (Minneapolis: Augsburg Fortress, 2001), 21–37.
[78] Daniel A. Bruno, 'Pentecostés viene después de Babel: Integración económica, imperio y el "totalmente otro"', *CDT* 24 (2005), 163–75.
[79] See the literature in Vondey, *Pentecostalism*, 115–17.

to God, confronting and reinterpreting present conditions with an alternative imagination of hope.

The contribution of Spirit baptism to the common good should not be restricted to certain charismatic gifts; prophecy and speaking with tongues are merely its more immediate manifestation. Rather, Pentecostal theology is free to extend the Spirit-endowed nature of the body of Christ to all gifts of the Spirit shared with the world.[80] The vision of Pentecost confronts the public square not just with dramatic and inspired speech but also with visions and dreams, healing and exorcism, fellowship and prayer. At the heart of Pentecost stands a vision of the common good where all who believe are together and have all things in common (see Acts 2:44; 4:32). Yet, until that ideal is realized, the way to the common good resembles more of a 'hybrid' process of the intermixture of cultural values, identifications and confrontations.[81] Spirit baptism as an instrument for the emergence of the public good involves beyond tongues and prophecies the concrete hands and hearts of the people who live for the hope that the injustices which separate them (and the ambiguity of the process) will one day be removed. Such a soteriological vision requires that the common good emerges not merely from confrontation and resistance but also through peace, reconciliation and healing.

Divine healing as social welfare

The concern for healing is in the broadest sense a concern for welfare in any form. The emphasis of the full gospel on divine healing highlights the material and embodied dimensions of salvation (see Chapter 5). At the same time, the comprehensive soteriological orientation of the full gospel is at the core also a challenge to the perception that healing is concerned only with the physical realm or the human being. Instead, a theology that reaches deep into Pentecost demands also a social and cultural anthropology of human flourishing. Healing is concerned with any context that manifests the absence of health, and Pentecostals have applied the need for healing with particular

---

[80] Cartledge, 'Renewal Theology and the Common Good', 14.
[81] See Néstor Medina, *Mestizaje: Remapping Race, Culture, and Faith in Latina/o Catholicism* (Maryknoll, NY: Orbis, 2009); Eldin Villafañe, *The Liberating Spirit: Toward an Hispanic American Pentecostal Social Ethic*, 2nd ed. (Grand Rapids, MI: Eerdmans, 1993), 52–58.

enthusiasm to the restoration of social, cultural, ethnic, racial, political, religious and economic ailments.[82] Their approach to the broad scope of human illnesses in society and culture emerges naturally from the Pentecostal identification of salvation with cosmopolitan redemption and its confrontational soteriology.[83] Yet, the question whether the full gospel is an exclusively confrontational narrative remains a central concern for Pentecostal soteriology. I suggest that in the motif of divine healing, the full gospel reaches beyond resistance to engagement with society ultimately informed by a vision of cosmopolitan redemption, restoration and peace.

Throughout the book of Acts, healings take place overwhelmingly in the cosmopolitan settings of cities where they combine with the sociocultural and religious activities of public gatherings, marketplaces, meals and worship, not as unexpected and spontaneous but as planned and coordinated activities.[84] The social and cultural dimensions of healing in the wake of Pentecost are staggering. Seen as signs and wonders of God in the world, the altars of healing are established both by the inward move from the ailments of society towards the church and the outward move of the church into society. Signs and wonders attract the public, whether it is to receive a share in the healing or to dispute its powers (see Acts 6:8–15; 14:3–4). The inward movement is visible in the sometimes extreme measures taken by the sick to reach the apostles and call for the church in order to receive healing (9:36–43; 28:8–9), so that the people 'even carried out the sick into the streets' (5:15) and brought handkerchiefs and aprons to them (19:12). The outward consequences are visible in the movement of the disciples towards those who need healing (9:17–18, 32–35), resulting in the restoration of

---

[82] See, for example, Paul Alexander (ed.). *Pentecostal and Nonviolence: Reclaiming a Heritage* (Eugene, OR: Pickwick, 2012); Raymond Pfister, 'The Future(s) of Pentecostalism in Europe', in *European Pentecostalism*, ed. William K. Kay and Anne E. Dyer, GPCS 7 (Leiden: Brill, 2011), 357–81; Josephine Sundqvist, 'Reconciliation as a Societal Process: A Case Study on the Role of the Pentecostal Movement (ADEPR) as an Actor in the Reconciliation Process in Postgenocide Rwanda', *SM* 99, no. 2 (2011): 157–95; Martin W. Mittelstadt and Geoffrey W. Sutton (eds), *Forgiveness, Reconciliation, and Restoration: Multidisciplinary Studies from a Pentecostal Perspective* (Eugene, OR: Wipf and Stock, 2010); Jay Beaman, *Pentecostal Pacifism* (Eugene, OR: Wipf and Stock, 2009); Veli-Matti Kärkkäinen, 'Spirit, Reconciliation and Healing in the Community: Missiological Insights from Pentecostals', *IRM* 94, no. 372 (2005): 43–50.

[83] See Luke Bretherton, 'Pneumatology, Healing, and Political Power: Sketching a Pentecostal Political Theology', in *The Holy Spirit in the World Today*, ed. Jane Williams (London: Alpha International, 2011), 130–50.

[84] See Steven C. Muir, 'Healing, Initiation and Community in Luke-Acts: A Comparative Analysis' (PhD diss., University of Ottawa, 1998), 237–66.

power balance (8:9–13), the reintegration of the sick and impaired individuals in the community (9:18–28) and a disturbance to the established social environment, religious practices, and economic system (14:8–18; 16:16–19; 19:11–20).[85] Divine healing ascribes within the wider sociocultural setting new roles for those restored who now mediate the effects of physical healing to the public.

Pentecost as a theological symbol connects the outpouring of the Spirit inevitably with social healing and reconciliation. From Pentecost emerges a vision of society at peace with itself through the hands of a church at peace (Acts 9:31) carrying the gospel of peace (Acts 10:36) into the suffering, violence and hostility of the world.[86] Pentecostal theology, at the core identified by the full gospel, teaches that Jesus is the great physician who heals by the power of the Spirit. The significance of Pentecost is that with the outpouring of the Spirit there is now a continuation and expansion of Jesus's healing ministry at the hands of the disciples. A humanized view of public, social and cultural illnesses therefore demands that the outpouring of the Spirit as core of the symbol of Pentecost is carried by the healing community (those who heal and those who are healed) into the cracks and crevices (i.e. altars) of human networks and relations (and beyond into creation). The Pentecostal vision of healing includes social and economic justice and peace.[87] What is at stake at Pentecost is not only the healing and restoration of being as such (physical, individual, personal) but of being in common (social, political, historical, cultural, economic, religious) – now defined by the outpouring of the Spirit: the reconciliation of social roles and cultural expectations far exceeds the physical restoration of individuals because the touch of the Spirit transcends the limits of bodies and persons.[88] The construction and mediation of a new social identity retains the cultural values of language, race, nationality, education, status and wealth but confronts and transforms them with the symbols received from conversion, new kinship, and relations to the community.[89]

---

[85] For similar observation in Luke see Yong, *In the Days of Caesar*, 297.
[86] See Martin William Mittelstadt, 'Spirit and Reconciliation in Luke-Acts', in Mittelstadt and Sutton, *Forgiveness, Reconciliation, and Restoration*, 3–22.
[87] Milton, *Shalom, The Spirit of God and Pentecostal Conversion*, 204–23; Yong, *In the Days of Caesar*, 295–315.
[88] Wariboko, *The Pentecostal Principle*, 8–36.
[89] See Nicole Rodriguez Toulis, *Believing Identity: Pentecostalism and the Mediation of Jamaican Ethnicity and Gender in England* (Oxford: Berg, 1997), 165–211.

At the same time, the materiality of Pentecost resists a mere idealist vision of peace and human flourishing.[90] Although divine healing in the wake of Pentecost is irremovably located in a wider public environment, healing does not directly touch social networks and cultural institutions, in a mere symbolic sense of the altar, but impacts the public world always through the tangible restoration of individuals. The reciprocal relationship of personal healing and public life finds expression as society encounters the source of its own healing in the agency of the sick, and the sick find their healing not exclusively (or necessarily) in their physical restoration but through their (re)integration in the community.[91] Pentecostals, and others, have not always recognized the relationship of individual and communal health, physical and social well-being, material and public welfare. Nationalism and militarism can transform concerns for nonviolence and peace among people to casting stereotypes on the generalized and faceless anonymity of what is labelled gender, disability, race, nation or religion.[92] From the altar of Pentecost, however, the outpouring of the Spirit on all flesh extends the horizon of healing concretely to all human suffering, injustice and conflict.[93] The Pentecostal emphasis on the embodiment of the human person, often lamented as an expression of unfortunate individualism and isolationism, is helpful here to bring the need for social healing and reconciliation back to the level of persons, neighbours and the human touch. The more individuals suffer, the more does society, and the more society suffers, the more do individuals; the impact is reciprocal because of the presence of the Spirit at work in both. The Spirit's healing presence encountered in the tangible environments of the altar, now extended to the social sphere, 're-humanizes' wounded and separated institutions, nations and enemies and gives the 'other' a face that, like our own, endures human suffering and pain.[94] The Pentecostal response is found in forms of social activism, civil

---

[90] See Paul Alexander, 'Prophetic "Patriotic" Pentecostal Peacemaking: Early Assemblies of God Pacifism and the Twentieth Century', idem, *Pentecostals and Nonviolence*, 171–88.

[91] Yong, *In the Days of Caesar*, 310.

[92] See Paul Alexander, *Peace to War: Shifting Allegiances in the Assemblies of God* (Telford, PA: Cascadia, 2009).

[93] See Michael Beals, 'Toward a Pentecostal Contribution to the Just War Tradition', in Alexander, *Pentecostals and Nonviolence*, 229–49.

[94] Ibid., 248. See also Murray W. Dempster, '"Crossing Border": Arguments Used by Early American Pentecostals in Support of the Global Character of Pacifism', in Alexander, *Pentecostals and Nonviolence*, 121–42.

movements, economic progress, or political advocacy only if these can display the immediacy of manifesting the Spirit's presence and transforming power at the altar.

The move from the altars of the church into the world not only expands Christian rituals and weds them to the sanctified rituals of peoples and cultures, the practices of divine healing also manifest forms of socialization which establish and integrate individuals in a network of relations with the church, society and God.[95] In the environment of the altar, the practices of reconciliation are ordinary Christian practices that require no special abilities.[96] However, the outpouring of the Spirit expands and transforms what might be considered ordinary practices and rituals of Christian liturgy to the extraordinary environments of social illnesses, public diseases and civil cancers that form the cosmopolitan altars for the encounter with God. Pentecostal mechanisms for the healing of society include public confession and expressions of social, political, and collective forgiveness, communal prayer and worship, and cooperative service to one another; as both personal and social, individual and communal acts, the vocalization of faith encompasses in all its forms also a commitment to the healing of relationships; the laying on of hands to impart healing is extended to the joining of hands for humanitarian purposes; the washing of feet, with its religious implications for purification and holiness, extends to the washing of the sick, the homeless and the elderly; and the importance of the human touch, also intimately expressed in the anointing with oil, expands to the care for the dying and the dead. These expanded (altar) practices not only exist within society but penetrate the cultural, sociopolitical and economic environment to form within society an alternative model of the public good (see Acts 2:43–47).[97] The ultimate concern of this common good is the transformation and redemption of the present world in light of the coming of the kingdom of God.

---

[95] See Michael Wilkinson, 'What Happens When Canadian Churches and Governments Seek Forgiveness for Social Sins of the Past?' in Mittelstadt and Sutton, *Forgiveness, Reconciliation, and Restoration*, 177–96.

[96] See Paul N. Alexander, 'What Can Pentecostal and Charismatics *Do* for Peace with Justice in Israel and Palestine?' in *Christ at the Checkpoint: Theology in the Service of Justice and Peace*, ed. Paul N. Alexander (Eugene, OR: Pickwick, 2012), 61–74.

[97] See the various examples in Martin Lindhardt (ed.), *Practicing the Faith: The Ritual Life of Pentecostal-Charismatic Christians* (New York: Berghahn, 2011).

The coming Kingdom and the end of society

Eschatology is not the concluding theme of the full gospel, that is, the gospel narrative does not 'end' with the kingdom of God. Rather, a passion for the kingdom infuses Pentecostal spirituality throughout with both a consistent 'social identity and a sense of distinction between the church and the world'.[98] I have shown that eschatology functions as an integrating theme in the full gospel that returns Pentecostal theology to its central concerns, albeit transformed by an apocalyptic urgency (Chapter 6). This apocalyptic dimension of Pentecostal theology is necessary for the integrity of its confrontational soteriology: eschatology is a doctrine of conflict. The central concern for Pentecostal theology, in light of its vision of an apocalyptic struggle, is how Christians can avoid a violent political apocalypticism, on the one hand, and sectarian withdrawal from the world, on the other. I suggest that soteriological resistance is required only where civil rule and institution hinder the unfolding of the fullness of the gospel in light of the coming kingdom, so that political theology, public welfare, and social ethics are not opposites but corollaries of an apocalyptic eschatology. A confrontational soteriology does not demand a permanent state of conflict but seeks precisely the dissolution of destruction and death in order to realize the eternal state of salvation.

An apocalyptic social vision reaching deep into Pentecost arrives at the coming of the kingdom in light of the outpouring of the Holy Spirit. Pentecost initiates and preserves a 'pneumatological apocalypticism'[99] sustained by the continuation of the charismata throughout the world. The full gospel proclaims Christ as the coming king because it is with Christ that the coming of the kingdom has already begun. Yet, it is with Pentecost that the coming of Christ's reign is expanded eschatologically through the gifts of the Spirit 'in the last days' (Acts 2:17) towards 'the ends of the earth' (13:47). The charismata intensify the presence of the kingdom at the altars of the world through visible signs and audible sounds in individuals and communities in the space and time of the created order.[100] The apocalyptic dimension of Pentecost is

---

[98] Steven J. Land, *Pentecostal Spirituality: A Passion for the Kingdom*, JPTS 1 (Sheffield: Sheffield Academic Press, 1993), 102.
[99] Yong, *In the Days of Caesar*, 230–32; although Yong advocates redirecting Pentecostal political theology away from apocalyptic eschatology (p. 329).
[100] See Mark Cartledge, *The Mediation of the Spirit: Interventions in Practical Theology*, PM 7 (Grand Rapids, MI: Eerdmans, 2015), 90–98.

concentrated at the altars where the outpouring of God's Spirit finds tangible, embodied, physical, material, and spatial manifestations in the prophesies of sons and daughters, the visions of the younger and dreams of the older generations, signs and wonders in the heavens and on earth (Acts 2:17–21). Rather than withdrawal from the world, an apocalyptic social ethic emerges with Pentecost that initiates and enables charismatic participation in the world on behalf of the kingdom.

What comes into existence at the altars of the world with the outpouring of the Spirit is the ecclesial body of Christ manifesting in charismatic gifts the kingdom of God. The apocalyptic urgency of Pentecost prevents a radical ecclesiocentricity, since the church of Pentecost exists only as agent of the Spirit to the world (and thus neither apart from the Spirit nor apart from the world). While the kingdom is not fully manifest in the public square, the sociopolitical nature of Christ's reign becomes visible through the apocalyptic-charismatic acts of the church.[101] The eschatological Spirit determines the coming into existence of the church not only as the embodiment of the kingdom but also as the embodiment of the confrontation of the world with its own future.[102] Pentecostal eschatology has struggled with this determination caught between strong commitment to an apocalyptic vision and weak representation in wider public, political, and economic networks.[103] An important insight from this struggle is that the church does not abruptly come into existence with the outpouring of the Spirit at Pentecost but comes into being in the work of those who with Pentecost and beyond embody the presence of the Spirit in the world. In this sense, Pentecostals can speak of the eschaton as already present in the human being as such, in the social and cosmopolitan space out of which is formed the body of Christ.[104] Salvation, sanctification, Spirit baptism and divine healing are eschatological practices that transform the outside of the kingdom (society, culture, economics, politics, etc.) into the inside of the church.

---

[101] See Huibert Zegwaart, 'Apocalyptic Eschatology and Pentecostalism: The Relevance of John's Millennium for Today', *Pneuma* 10, no. 1 (1988): 3–25.

[102] See Macchia, *Baptized in the Spirit*, 209–11.

[103] See Peter Althouse, 'Apocalyptic Discourse and Pentecostal Vision of Canada', in *Canadian Pentecostalism: Transition and Transformation*, ed. Michael Wilkinson (Montreal and Kingston: McGill-Queen's University Press, 2009), 58–78.

[104] See Wariboko, *The Charismatic City*, 17 and 199.

An apocalyptic urgency prevents the active transformation of society from being exclusively a secular and humanitarian exercise. Pentecostal theology does not advocate the ideals of social justice, peace and reconciliation for their own purposes but always in light of the expectation that the confrontation of the public social world with the kingdom of God is about to be resolved when the present social world finds its culmination in the coming kingdom. At the crossroads of this struggle stands the church as a community 'saved, sanctified, filled with the Holy Spirit, delivered, and commissioned' for both the world and for the kingdom. This church of the full gospel is a socio-cultural entity because the Spirit is poured out on the world (see Chapter 10). The moral and ethical concerns of this community are grounded in the knowledge and experience of God amidst the eschatological horizon of the coming kingdom.[105] Ecclesial ethics is therefore social ethics because the church is compelled by the Spirit to take the realization of the common good into the world. In turn, social ethics is ecclesial ethics because the practices and rituals of the church are intended to compel society to be transformed in light of the coming of God.[106] In this sense, because this relationship between the church and the world sets the context for the altars of the church in the world, the church is the border between this world and that of the kingdom.[107] The church marks the 'end' of the public square not merely because as an eschatological community it announces the future to the present but because as an apocalyptic charismatic community the church *is* the future already present.

The coming into existence of the church by the Spirit of Pentecost compresses space and time so that the confrontation of society with the kingdom is an increasingly urgent event.[108] The practices of salvation, sanctification, Spirit baptism and healing do not have the 'time' and 'space' to unfold as social liturgies but remain always charismatic (urgent, ad hoc, spontaneous, enthusiastic) actions confronted with the return of Christ at any moment. This urgency is one of the central reasons why the Pentecostal vision of social justice cannot be separated from the movement's commitment to evangelization, and the

---

[105] See Castelo, *Revisioning Pentecostal Ethics*, 22–32.
[106] See Bernardo Campos, *De la reforma Protestante a la pentecostalidad de la iglesia: Debate sobre el Pentecostalismo en América Latina* (Quito, Ecuador: CLAI, 1997), 12–18.
[107] Yong, *In the Days of Caesar*, 352–54.
[108] See Wolfgang Vondey, 'The Holy Spirit and Time in Contemporary Catholic and Protestant Theology', *SJT* 58, no. 4 (2005): 393–409. See also Wariboko, *The Pentecostal Principle*, 200.

relationship between the church's mission and the destiny of society will have to be further developed.[109] My insistence on Pentecostal theology as a living rather than proclaiming of the full gospel highlights the primal and pragmatic nature of the Pentecostal apocalyptic imagination. The apocalyptic vision is a primal form of eschatology because it insists on the emergence of a radically new and better world that welcomes and participates in but does not presuppose the perfection of the public good.[110] It is a pragmatic vision because a Pentecostal vision of the 'end' of the world is 'willing to work within the social and cultural expectations of the age'[111] in order to find at these altars opportunities and venues for the Holy Spirit to save, sanctify, empower and heal human life. The logic of the primal and pragmatic impulses balance each other because they are held in tension by Pentecost as symbol, which upholds not only that redemption always originates sovereignly with God (and that the future is therefore radically new) but also that the new and better future breaks into the public life with unexpected possibilities for our participation.[112]

The resolution of difference between the present society and the kingdom of God marks for Pentecostals the climax of the work of Christ extended to the church through the outpouring of the Spirit. The altar as an eschatological metaphor for a cosmopolitan vision of salvation signals that the end of society is tied to the apocalyptic mission of the church, and vice versa. The body of Christ in the public square functions as the equivalent of the image of God in the human being so that, as public image of the coming kingdom of God, the church in the Spirit is a reflection of the completion of Pentecost. The redemption of society is cosmopolitan because it is defined by the confrontation, transformation and reconciliation of the cultures, ethnicities and nations of the world with the city of God. The festival of Pentecost is the image of the heavenly city, which reverberates with the sights and sounds of the presence of the Spirit among a people liberated for the cultures of the kingdom, which is the worship of the redeemed.

---

[109] See 'Selected Bibliography on Evangelization and Social Concern', *Transformation* 16, no. 2 (1999): 65–66.
[110] See Harvey Cox, *Fire from Heaven: The Rise of Pentecostal Spirituality and the Reshaping of Religion in the Twenty-First Century* (Cambridge, MA: DaCapo, 1995), 111–22.
[111] Grant Wacker, *Heaven Below: Early Pentecostals and American Culture* (Cambridge, MA: Harvard University Press, 2001), 13.
[112] See Peter Althouse, '"Left Behind" – Fact or Fiction: Ecumenical Dilemmas of the Fundamentalist Millenarian Tension within Pentecostalism', *JPT* 13, no. 2 (2005): 187–207.

10

Church

Mission, Movement, and Ecclesiology

The church originates with the day of Pentecost. Yet, these historical roots are shrouded in relatively few biblical records surrounded by what is often believed to be a short-lived apostolic period interpreted typically as the birth cry of an infant community succeeded by historical developments hardly recognizable as consequences of the original outpouring of the Holy Spirit. Although frequently the appeal of revival movements throughout Christian history, Pentecost had all but lost its significance for the Christian life until the arrival of the modern-day Pentecostal movement. From the beginning, the worldwide revivals were seen as manifestations of a movement of the Holy Spirit marking a historical turning point in the life of the church.[1] As I have outlined in part one of this volume, at the altars of these revivals, Pentecost was reborn, repeated, and rediscovered. Through the lens of this altar hermeneutics (see Chapter 1), Pentecostals have viewed themselves not so much as a new church tradition than a movement of the Spirit in and among the existing churches.[2] Because of Pentecost, the title 'church' is not seen as the property of a single institution but as the product of a movement of the churches together.[3] Pentecost is the symbol of the church because the movement of the Holy Spirit

---

[1] See Douglas Jacobsen, *Thinking in the Spirit: Theologies of the Early Pentecostal Movement* (Bloomington: Indiana University Press, 2003), 64; Harold D. Hunter, 'Global Pentecostalism and Ecumenism: Two Movements of the Holy Spirit?' in *Pentecostalism and Christian Unity: Ecumenical Documents and Critical Assessments*, ed. Wolfgang Vondey (Eugene, OR: Pickwick, 2010), 20–33.

[2] See Wolfgang Vondey, 'A Pentecostal Perspective on *The Nature and Mission of the Church*', ET 35, no. 8 (2006): 1–5.

[3] See Wolfgang Vondey, 'The Denomination in Classical and Global Pentecostal Ecclesiology: A Historical and Theological Contribution', in *Denomination: Assessing an Ecclesiological Category*, ed. Paul M. Collins and Barry Ensign-George (New York: Continuum, 2011), 100–116.

stands not only at its beginning but accompanies the Christian community throughout its history until its completion in the kingdom of God.

As a result, an institutional notion of the church has not developed among Pentecostals.[4] Instead, the formation of Pentecostal ecclesiology proceeds largely along experiential routes with their primary ground in the worship of the local assembly as the concrete fellowship of believers in which the movement of God's Spirit occurs.[5] The global diversity of the movement, especially the dominant contrast between different models of church government, as well as widespread denominational divisions, present significant obstacles to constructing a unified Pentecostal model of the church. Pentecostal ecclesiology sometimes borrows uncritically from congregational free-church traditions without easy reconciliation with the episcopal wing in the Pentecostal movement.[6] Much of Pentecostal thought remains reactionary and highly dependent on existing proposals from models of the church that take little account of Pentecost.[7] Consequently, some Pentecostals suggest that instead of a single ecclesiology there exists a plurality of ecclesial self-understandings and ecclesiological nuances in diverse expressions among the movement.[8] Disagreement exists between those who develop a view of the church solely out of a historical retrieval of early Pentecostal sources and those who construct their ecclesiology in conversation with contemporary ecumenical voices.[9] No single ecclesiological proposal has been generally accepted.

In this chapter, I argue that the full gospel offers a comprehensive proposal for a genuinely Pentecostal ecclesiology because it draws from

---

[4] Veli-Matti Kärkkäinen, *An Introduction to Ecclesiology: Ecumenical, Historical and Global Perspectives* (Downers Grove: InterVarsity, 2002), 73.

[5] Andy Lord, *Network Church: A Pentecostal Ecclesiology Shaped by Mission*, GPCS 11 (Leiden: Brill, 2012), 66; Shane Clifton, *Pentecostal Churches in Transition: Analyzing the Developing Ecclesiology of the Assemblies of God in Australia*, Global Pentecostal and Charismatic Studies 3 (Leiden: Brill, 2009), 7–26; Kärkkäinen, *An Introduction to Ecclesiology*, 75.

[6] See Dale M. Coulter, 'Christ, the Spirit, and Vocation: Initial Reflections on a Pentecostal Ecclesiology', *PEc* 19, no. 3 (2010): 318–39; idem, 'The Development of Ecclesiology in the Church of God (Cleveland, TN): A Forgotten Contribution?' *Pneuma* 29, no. 1 (2007): 59–85.

[7] See the absence of a Pentecostal model in Avery Dulles, *Models of the Church*, expanded ed. (New York: Image Books, 1987).

[8] See Wolfgang Vondey, 'Pentecostal Perspectives on *The Nature and Mission of the Church*: Challenges and Opportunities for Ecumenical Transformation', in *Receiving* the Nature and Mission of the Church: *Ecclesial Reality and Ecumenical Horizons for the Twenty-First Century*, ed. Michael A. Fahey and Paul M. Collins, EI 1 (London: T& T Clark, 2008), 55–68.

[9] See Mark J. Cartledge, 'Renewal Ecclesiology in Empirical Perspective', *Pneuma* 36, no. 1 (2014): 5–24.

Pentecost as the unifying theological symbol of the movement. Pentecostals have widely recognized that their proclamation of Jesus as saviour, sanctifier, Spirit baptizer, divine healer, and coming king holds diverse ecclesiological implications.[10] Underlying these concerns of the full gospel is the historical emphasis on Pentecostalism as a 'movement' and its distinctions from established ecclesial and institutional identities.[11] One could say that the full gospel identifies the central commitments of the church in the process of becoming: salvation, sanctification, Spirit baptism, divine healing, and the kingdom of God are never possessed entirely but always move the church forward towards its full realization in the kingdom of God. The full gospel contributes to the development of a consistent Pentecostal ecclesiology because it rejects any static and self-centred image that sees the church as a complete and self-sufficient entity deprived of its sociopolitical and economic implications and cultural garment (see Chapter 9). In contrast, a theology of the church emerging from the full gospel places the altars of the church squarely in the world.

In order to substantiate this claim, this chapter brings Pentecostal ecclesiology into conversation with the creedal traditions of the Christian community. Pentecostals have emphasized that the elements of the full gospel offer a critique and variation of the so-called creedal 'marks' or 'notes' of the church.[12] The day of Pentecost, identified throughout this book as the core symbol of Pentecostal theology, sheds a particular light on the unity, holiness, catholicity, and apostolicity of the church. A full-gospel ecclesiology can indeed be seen as an attempt both to enrich the historical self-understanding of the church and to contribute to contemporary ecclesiological and ecumenical

---

[10] See, for example, Veli-Matti Kärkkäinen, 'A Full Gospel Ecclesiology of *Koinonia*: Pentecostal Contributions to the Doctrine of the Church', in *Renewal History and Theology: Essays in Honor of H. Vinson Synan*, ed. Christopher Emerick and David Moore (Cleveland, TN: CPT Press, 2014), 175–93; John Christopher Thomas (ed.), *Toward a Pentecostal Ecclesiology: The Church and the Fivefold Gospel* (Cleveland, TN: CPT Press, 2010); Frank D. Macchia, *Baptized in the Spirit: A Global Pentecostal Theology* (Grand Rapids: Zondervan, 2006), 155–256; John Christopher Thomas, 'Pentecostal Theology in the Twenty-First Century', *Pneuma* 20, no. 1 (1998): 3–19.
[11] See Vondey, *Beyond Pentecostalism*, 151–55.
[12] Kenneth J. Archer, 'The Fivefold Gospel and the Mission of the Church: Ecclesiastical Implications and Opportunities', in Thomas, *Toward a Pentecostal Ecclesiology*, 7–43; Macchia, *Baptized in the Spirit*, 208, 241; Thomas, 'Pentecostal Theology in the Twenty-First Century', 18–19; Amos Yong, *The Spirit Poured Out on All Flesh: Pentecostal Theology and the Possibility of Global Theology* (Grand Rapids, MI: Baker Academic, 2005), 91, 120, 134–51; Amos Yong, 'The Marks of the Church: A Pentecostal Re-reading', *ERT* 26, no. 1 (2002): 45–67.

reflections.[13] The present task is to show how the full gospel offers a distinctive Pentecostal reading of authentic ecclesiality which can be brought into conversation with the creedal model of the church. By interpreting the church from each of the five facets of the full gospel, the chapter follows the procedure adopted throughout the second part of this book. Each section proposes a Pentecostal mark of the church and also issues a commentary on the creedal tradition. In this light, from the perspective of the full gospel, the church emerges as a charismatic, hospitable, empowered, egalitarian, and persistent movement of the Spirit of God.

Salvation and the charismatic church

Ecclesiology from the perspective of the full gospel begins with soteriology. The identity of the church, its core commitments and practices, are consequences of the Pentecostal emphasis on the redemptive practices of the community of faith (see Chapter 2). From this perspective, one is justified in saying that for Pentecostals 'soteriology takes precedence over ecclesiology'.[14] Nonetheless, the move from soteriology to ecclesiology is a logical one, in the sense that God's work takes primacy over the work of the church; it is not a strict theological division, since the practices of salvation *are* the practices of the church. In this sense, the full gospel is a testimony to the church's redemptive practices, and the possibility of the individual's participation arises out of the community's confession that Jesus is saviour.[15] The church as a movement towards salvation spans the full spectrum of soteriological experiences by being at once a community of the redeemed and a redeeming community that exists for those who are in need of redemption.[16] In other words, Pentecost symbolizes the full recognition of the historical character

---

[13] See Veli-Matti Kärkkäinen, 'A Full Gospel Ecclesiology of Koinonia: Pentecostal Contributions to the Doctrine of the Church', in *Renewal History and Theology: Essays in Honor of H. Vinson Synan*, ed. S. David Moore and James M. Henderson (Cleveland, TN: CPT Press, 2014), 175–93; idem, 'The Church as Charismatic Fellowship: Ecclesiological Reflections from the Pentecostal-Roman Catholic Dialogue', *JPT* 18 (2001): 100–21.

[14] Kenneth J. Archer and Andrew S. Hamilton, 'Anabaptist-Pietism and Pentecostalism: Scandalous Partners in Protest', *SJT* 63, no. 2 (2010): 185–202 (197).

[15] Kenneth J. Archer, 'A Pentecostal Way of Doing Theology: Manner and Method', *IJST* 9, no. 3 (2007): 301–14.

[16] Wynand J. De Kock, 'The Church as a Redeemed, Un-Redeemed, and Redeeming Community', in Thomas, *Toward a Pentecostal Ecclesiology*, 47–68.

of the economy of salvation and the importance of the church for the sake of embodying the continuity of redemption wrought by Jesus Christ. The central concern of Pentecostal ecclesiology is how the essence of the church, its authentic ecclesiality, is tied to the means by which creation, society, and the human being continue to participate in salvation. Answers, I suggest, arise from Pentecost taken as the core symbol of the church's origin and identity.

The continued participation of the world in the divine gift of salvation finds on the day of Pentecost an ecclesial centre, traditionally captured in Christian thought by the phrase 'outside the church there may be no salvation'.[17] The concentration of salvation in the church is tied directly to the lordship of Christ: as saviour, Jesus is the bridegroom of the church and head of the body. Pentecostal ecclesiology is without doubt Christologically centred because the church's practices of salvation are first and foremost experiences of Christ. In this sense, the church has traditionally been understood as originating with the Incarnation.[18] However, Pentecostal Christology is thoroughly pneumatological and interprets the historical presence of Christ in the church through the symbol of Pentecost primarily as the presence of the Holy Spirit. The continuation of Christ's ministry of salvation in the church is understood not with direct reference to the Incarnation but to the anointing of Jesus (see Chapter 2). Pentecost is the origin of the church because the church is now the continuation of the anointing of Christ with the Spirit. Christ, Spirit, and church are consequently intersecting entities that together identify Pentecostal ecclesiology.[19] Put differently, Christology, pneumatology, and ecclesiology are bound to each other in the symbol of Pentecost. From Pentecost, the church emerges as the difference between the indiscriminate outpouring of the Spirit 'on all flesh' (Acts 2:17) and the salvation received only by those who call on the name of the Lord (v. 21). Soteriology is constitutive of the church because it qualifies the very being of the church as a redemptive movement in the Spirit of Christ.

---

[17] *Extra ecclesiam non sit salus*; see Cyprian *Epistles*, 73.21, often rendered as *extra ecclesiam nulla salus*.

[18] See Michael J. Himes, *Ongoing Incarnation: Johann Adam Möhler and the Beginnings of Modern Ecclesiology* (New York: Crossroad, 1997).

[19] See Daniela C. Augustine, 'Pentecost as the Church's Cosmopolitan Vision of Global Civil Society: A Post-Communist Eastern European Theological Perspective', in *A World for All? Global Civil Society in Political Theory and Trinitarian Theology*, ed. William F. Storrar et al. (Grand Rapids, MI: Eerdmans, 2011), 197–220; Veli-Matti Kärkkäinen, 'Spirit, Church, and Christ: An Ecumenical Inquiry into a Pneumatological Ecclesiology', *OIC* 36, no. 4 (2000): 338–53.

Overcoming the difference between the anointing of Christ and the anointing of Christians is the constitutive element of the church manifested at Pentecost in the outpouring of the Spirit. It is therefore correct to speak of the church as the identity of the Spirit in Christ and in Christians.[20] Nevertheless, while this pneumatological *identity* preserves the historical continuity of the ministry of salvation in Christ and the church, and the church is in this sense the continuation of the anointing of Jesus, the historical distance between the church and the Incarnation (in which Christians do not participate) suggests that there is also a pneumatological *difference*: the church is body not head, bride not bridegroom, temple not Spirit.[21] Pentecostal ecclesiology is driven by pneumatology, because Pentecost reveals the property of the Holy Spirit specifically in constituting the church.[22] The Spirit of Christ now continues in the church as the mark of salvation (Eph. 1:13) and thus as the principle of identifying the church's redemptive activity as the work of Christ.[23] At the same time, the redemptive activity of the Spirit not only establishes but distinguishes the church from its origin in Christ, so that the church does not have a foundation in God without also possessing a mission in the world.[24] Spirit and church are inseparable domains of the mission of the triune God.[25] Because of this mission, Pentecost is necessary. Because of Pentecost, the difference between Christ and world is overcome in the church with the reception of the Spirit for the sake of the church's mission. Ecclesiology, from the perspective of Pentecost, therefore highlights that the birth of the church

---

[20] Heribert Mühlen, *Una Mystica Persona: Die Kirche als das Mysterium der heilsgeschichtlichen Identität des Heiligen Geistes in Christus und den Christen: Eine Person in vielen Personen*, 2nd rev. ed. (Paderborn: Schöningh, 1967). See Wolfgang Vondey, *Heribert Mühlen: His Theology and Praxis: A New Profile of the Church* (Lanham, MD: University Press of America, 2004), 99–160.

[21] See Miroslav Volf and Maurice Lee, 'The Spirit and the Church', in *Advents of the Spirit: An Introduction to the Current Study of Pneumatology*, ed. Bradford E. Hinze and D. Lyle Dabney (Milwaukee, WI: Marquette University Press, 2001), 383–409; see Mühlen, *Una Mystica Persona*, 207–13.

[22] See Simon Chan, 'Jesus as Spirit-Baptizer: Its Significance for Pentecostal Ecclesiology', in Thomas, *Towards Pentecostal Ecclesiology*, 139–56, esp. 142.

[23] See Amos Yong, 'The Marks of the Church: A Pentecostal Re-reading', *Evangelical Review of Theology* 26, no. (2002): 45–67; idem, *The Spirit Poured Out*, 134–51.

[24] See Andy Lord, 'Mission-driven Pentecostal Ecclesiology', *IJSCC* 11, no. 4 (2011): 279–87; Peter Althouse, 'Towards a Pentecostal Ecclesiology: Participation in the Missional Life of the Triune God', *JPT* 18 (2009): 230–45.

[25] See Chan, *Pentecostal Ecclesiology*, 74–92; Torbjörn Aronson, 'Spirit and Church in the Ecclesiology of Lewi Pethrus', *Pentecostudies* 11, no. 2 (2012): 192–211; Frank D. Macchia, 'The Spirit-Baptised Church', *IJSCC* 11, no. 4 (2011): 256–68; Lord, 'Mission-Driven Pentecostal Ecclesiology', 279–87; Clark H. Pinnock, 'Church in the Power of the Spirit: The Promise of Pentecostal Ecclesiology', *JPT* 14, no. 2 (2006): 147–65.

is not simply the result of the outpouring of the Spirit (who is poured out on *all* flesh) but more specifically of the anointing with the Spirit (which is manifested only in the church). Although in the world, the church differs from the world, which 'cannot receive' the Spirit (see Jn 14:17). The distinction between the outpouring and the anointing of the Spirit can be called the charismatic difference and the birth cry of the church.

The charismatic difference is the defining moment for the redemptive mission of the church to continue beyond the physical presence of Christ.[26] The upper room, Jerusalem, Samaria, and Judea cannot contain the church, but the anointing with the Spirit manifested in the charismata thrusts the church immediately into the world. The first mark of the church at Pentecost is therefore that the church is *charismatic*. Spirit and mission, although not a feature of all Christian ecclesiologies, are too general a category to identify and distinguish Pentecostal theology. The charismatic difference, however, is more than a commentary on the four creedal marks. The gifts of the Spirit initiate and sustain the mission of the church, even though they are not themselves the mission.[27] The full gospel does not proclaim the charismata. Ecclesiastical history may even suggest that the church can exist without the visible presence of charisms just as it can without visible unity, sanctity, catholicity, and apostolicity. Yet, the argument for the cessation of the charismata is at the core a threat to the essence of the church. From the perspective of Pentecost, the church is one, holy, catholic, and apostolic because it is charismatic.

The church as the fellowship of the Spirit (see 2 Cor. 13:14; Phil. 2:1) has been a dominant image for Pentecostal self-portrayal in ecumenical conversations.[28] This interdependence of church and Spirit suggests that the core of Pentecostal efforts is a pneumatological ecclesiology with focus on a charismatic fellowship.[29] From the perspective of the proclamation that Jesus is

---

[26] See Julie C. Ma and Wonsuk Ma, *Mission in the Spirit: Towards a Pentecostal/Charismatic Missiology* (Eugene, OR: Wipf and Stock, 2010), 43–49.

[27] See Mark J. Cartledge, 'Renewal Theology and the "Common Good",' *JPT* 25 (2016): 1–17; Macchia, *Baptized in the Spirit*, 241–44.

[28] See 'Perspectives on *Koinonia*. Final Report of the Dialogue between the Roman Catholic Church and Some Classical Pentecostal Churches and Leaders: 1985–89', in Vondey, *Pentecostalism and Christian Unity*, 133–58.

[29] See Veli-Matti Kärkkäinen, *Spiritus Ubi Vult Spirat: Pneumatology in Roman Catholic-Pentecostal Dialogue (1972–1989)* (Helsinki: Luther-Agricola Society, 1998); Paul D. Lee, 'Pneumatological Ecclesiology in the Roman Catholic-Pentecostal Dialogue: A Catholic Reading of the Third Quinquennium (1985–1989)' (SthD diss., Pontifical University of St. Thomas, Rome, 1994).

saviour, the charisms signal the continuation of the salvation made possible by Christ who is encountered in the church through the gift(s) of the Spirit. The traditional marks of the church are therefore subject to the interdependence of the soteriological dimension and the charismatic difference that identify the essence of the church.

The church is *one* because unity identifies the continuity of Christ manifested in the church by the gifts of the Spirit.[30] Through the ministry of the Spirit, both the community and the individual serve as signs and instruments of salvation amidst a potent cosmopolitan environment that both embraces and resists the gospel.[31] For the purposes of salvation, the church finds its unity in charismatic fellowship before it turns to other structural and institutional means.[32] Charismatic unity insists on diversity, the varieties of gifts, services, and activities 'for the common good' (1 Cor. 12:4-7).[33] Likewise, the *holiness* of the church emerges from this charismatic continuity in a compelling but volatile tension between the individuals and the communities confronted with outpouring of the Spirit.[34] The church is formed as a fellowship through Spirit-inspired speech and actions which both thrust the church into the world of sin and distinguish it from its environment as an instrument of redemption.[35] The church is *catholic* because it is oriented towards the whole purposes of salvation within the universal realm of God's creation.[36] Pentecostals can call the church 'catholic' because the gifts of the Spirit make possible the existence and expansion of the charismatic fellowship to the ends of the world so that fullness of catholicity is identical with fullness of the

---

[30] Kärkkäinen, 'A Full Gospel Ecclesiology', 181-83; Yong, *The Spirit Poured Out*, 90, 135-39; 'Perspectives on Koinonia. Final Report of the Dialogue between the Roman Catholic Church and Some Classical Pentecostal Churches and Leaders', in Vondey, *Pentecostalism and Christian Unity*, 133-58.

[31] 'Perspectives on Koinonia', (no. 94), 154.

[32] See Veli-Matti Kärkkäinen, 'The Church as the Fellowship of Persons: An Emerging Pentecostal Ecclesiology of Koinonia', *PentecoStudies* 6, no. 1 (2007): 1-15; idem, 'Church as Charismatic Fellowship: Ecclesiological Reflections from the Pentecostal-Roman Catholic Dialogue', *JPT* 9, no. 1 (2001): 100-121.

[33] See Stanko Jambrek, 'Unity and Fellowship of Christians from a Pentecostal Perspective', *KEJT* 2, no. 1 (2008): 61-77; 'Perspectives on Koinonia', (no. 36), 141.

[34] Yong, *The Spirit Poured Out*, 139.

[35] See Matthias Wenk, *Community-Forming Power: The Socio-ethical Role of the Spirit in Luke-Acts*, JPTS 19 (Sheffield: Sheffield Academic Press, 2000), 120-48.

[36] See Veli-Matti Kärkkäinen, 'Catholic, Full Gospel, and Fullness of the Spirit: A Pentecostal Perspective on the Third Mark of the Church', in *Pentecostal Issues, Ecclesiology and Ecumenism: Papers Presented in Theological Positions Colloquium, Continental Theological Seminary, 2011*, ed. Rikku Tuppurainen (Sint-Pieters-Leeuw: Continental Theological Seminary, 2011), 77-99.

Spirit.[37] The church catholic therefore requires the particularity, individuality, and diversity of the church charismatic.[38] Yet, the reason for this universality is soteriological: the church is catholic and charismatic because it is missionary. In turn, the church is *apostolic* because the pneumatological and charismatic life and worship of the church since the apostles continue dynamically through the missionary church of the ages.[39] Understood in terms of its apostolic mission, the church is a fellowship of salvation that stands in continuity with the mission of Christ because it stands in succession of the apostles' spiritual and charismatic example of the Christian life.[40] The Pentecostal dictum of apostolicity is not succession of office ('this succeeds that') but continuity ('this *is* that') of the fellowship of the Spirit.[41] Pentecostal ecclesiology is therefore less interested in the history than in the historicity of salvation, the imitation of Christ through participation in the Spirit, which is the sanctification of the church.

Sanctification and the hospitality of the church

From the perspective of Pentecost, the church is conceived by the Holy Spirit in the sanctity of a room filled with prayer, worship, and unity (Acts 2:1–4), yet the birth of the church takes place in the streets of the city. The previous chapter has traced the historicity of the church along the notion of cosmopolitan redemption where the church emerges in the world from soteriological practices amidst concrete and resisting social and cultural realities. The emphasis of the full gospel on sanctification (see Chapter 3) consequently raises immediate ecclesiological concerns: How can we speak of the church as holy when the church exists historically only amidst the sinful structures of the world? The answer to this question, I suggest, is rooted in the emphasis of

---

[37] Kärkkäinen, 'Catholicity, Full Gospel, and Fullness of the Spirit', 90–93.
[38] Yong, *The Spirit Poured Out*, 143.
[39] See Veli-Matti Kärkkäinen, 'Pentecostals and the Claim for Apostolocity', *ERT* 25, no. 4 (2001): 323–36.
[40] See Harold D. Hunter, 'Pentecostal Reflections on Apostolicity', *JEPTA* 33, no. 1 (2013): 1–13; Veli-Matti Kärkkäinen, 'The Apostolicity of Free Churches', *PEc* 10, no 4 (2001): 389–400; H. David Edwards, 'A Pentecostal Perspective of the Church', in *Roman Catholic-Pentecostal Dialogue (1977-1982): A Study in Developing Ecumenism*, vol. 2, ed. Jerry L. Sandidge (Frankfurt: Peter Lang, 1987), 404–21.
[41] See Glen W. Menzies, 'A Full Apostolic Gospel Standard of Experience and Doctrine', *AJPS* 15, no. 1 (2012): 19–32.

the full gospel on sanctification as a pursuit of holiness applied to the church in history. We can speak of the church as holy insofar as sanctification identifies the process of the community in becoming the church.

For Pentecostals, the holiness of the church stems from the sanctifying work of the Spirit of Christ who is received by both the community and the individual.[42] Pentecost as symbol for the church upholds the principle that the church exists as recipient of Christ's holiness not only because the church has received the Holy Spirit (once and in the past) but because the church exists as the continuing reception of the sanctifying Spirit throughout history (in a perpetual Pentecost). This continuing reception of the Spirit marks the church not only as charismatic but also as sanctified community, which is holy by being in a process of becoming holy amidst adverse contexts for living out and being held accountable to God's call to holiness.[43] The church can be identified with the biblical notions of both being 'called out' (*ecclesia*) and being 'sent' (*apostoloi*), a paradoxical mission originating with the calling of the disciples by Jesus and magnified with the day of Pentecost. Even though the church exists as a community of those who come out and are set apart from sin and evil (see Acts 5:11; 9:31; 14:27), and persecuted by the world (Acts 8:1–3; 11:19; 12:1), those who are called out cannot entirely distance themselves from the world because as the church they are also sent into the world (Acts 11:1; 13:1; 14:23; 15:3, 22). Sanctification cannot be separated from the charismatic mission of the church. In other words, holiness is a mark of the church insofar as the church comes into existence through sanctifying activities and practices that express and reaffirm the community's values in response to God's call.[44] Sanctification as part of the Spirit's mission in the world builds the church because the individual is unable to obtain and sustain a life of holiness apart from the sanctified community.[45] At the same time, the church endures in its this-worldly mission a constant struggle for the continuity of its identity as a community sanctified by the Spirit.[46] The sanctified community invites the world because sanctification

---

[42] See Simon Chan, *Pentecostal Ecclesiology*, 86–88; Kimberly E. Alexander, 'The Holiness of the Church: An Analysis of Wesleyan-Pentecostal Thought', *IJSCC* 11, no. 4 (2011): 269–78.

[43] See Frederick L. Ware, 'What Does It Mean to Be "Black" and "Holy"?' *BT* 6, no. 1 (2008): 119–31.

[44] Matthias Wenk, 'The Church as Sanctified Community', in Thomas, *Pentecostal Ecclesiology*, 105–35.

[45] Yong, *The Spirit Poured Out*, 141–42; Matthias Wenk, 'Community Forming Power: Reconciliation and the Spirit in Acts', *JEPTA* 19 (1999): 17–33.

[46] Wenk, *Community-Forming Power*, 278–306.

is a transformative process that cannot be reified and categorized apart from the world without compromising the Christian mission to the world.[47] The gifts of the Spirit are not simply expressions or manifestations but confrontations with and invitations to participate in the divine life. From the perspective of Jesus as sanctifier, the mission of the church is expressed in its radical hospitality to the world because of the hospitality of God manifested in the sending of Christ and the Holy Spirit. A second mark of the church from the perspective of sanctification is therefore that the church is *hospitable*.

Hospitality is not a romantic trademark of Pentecost.[48] In the diverse and often hidden contexts of sin, the unconditional hospitality of the church is risky and painful.[49] Nonetheless, just as Christ had fellowship 'with sinners and tax collectors' (Mt. 9:11; 11:19; Mk 2:16; Lk. 5:30; 7:34; 15:1), the church endures, resists, and confronts the sins of the world for the sake of redemption.[50] Displaying the hospitality of God, Pentecost becomes a symbol for the church to create the conditions for 'the cosmopolitanism of divine welcome'[51] to emerge across and despite the sinful structures of global social, cultural, political, economic, and religious divides. Hospitality as an expression of holiness constitutes the core value of redemptive practices after Pentecost: a form of Christ-like suffering the passions of the world for the sake of their transformation and salvation. The outpouring and anointing with the Spirit at Pentecost are followed by immediate opposition, rejection, and suffering that become a hallmark of the hospitality of the church.[52] A theology that reaches deep into the heart of Pentecost therefore cannot afford to romanticize and idealize the image of hospitality. Where the altars of the church extend into the world, sanctification becomes a continuous process of confrontation

---

[47] Daniel Castelo, 'The Improvisational Quality of Ecclesial Holiness', in Thomas, *Towards a Pentecostal Ecclesiology*, 87–104.

[48] See Daniela C. Augustine, *Pentecost, Hospitality, and Transfiguration: Toward a Spirit-Inspired Vision of Social Transformation* (Cleveland, TN: CPT Press, 2012); Amos Yong, *Hospitality and the Other: Pentecost, Christian Practices, and the Neighbor* (Maryknoll, NY: Orbis, 2008).

[49] On the 'weight' of holiness and hospitality see Chris E. W. Green, *Sanctifying Interpretation: Vocation, Holiness, and Scripture* (Cleveland, TN: CPT Press, 2015), 85–95.

[50] See my detailed treatment in Wolfgang Vondey, *People of Bread: Rediscovering Ecclesiology* (New York: Paulist, 2008), 105–242.

[51] Augustine, *Pentecost, Hospitality, and Transfiguration*, 43.

[52] See Chad M. Bauman, *Pentecostals, Proselytization and Anti-Christian Violence in Contemporary India* (Oxford: Oxford University Press, 2015); Harold D. Hunter and Cecil M. Robeck Jr. (eds), *The Suffering Body: Responding to the Persecution of Christians* (Milton Keynes: Paternoster, 2006); Martin William Mittelstadt, *The Spirit in Luke-Acts: Implications for a Pentecostal Pneumatology*, JPTS 26 (London: T & T Clark, 2004).

and transformation for the sake of the gospel. The charismatic church cannot withdraw from the world because it is driven into the world by the Holy Spirit. The church is called and empowered by the gifts of the Spirit for its mission to the ends of the world, and the missionary community follows the example of Jesus,[53] the holy one of God (Mk 1:24), who although he did not belong to the world was sent into the world, driven into the wilderness by the Spirit (see Lk. 4:1; Mt. 4:1; Mk 1:12), and sanctified himself through suffering, so that the church, now sent by Jesus, is sanctified (Jn 17:19) and suffers the truth that 'it is through many persecutions that we must enter the kingdom of God' (Acts 14:22). Out of Pentecost develops an ecclesiology that locates the church in the world because the church cannot avoid the world without deserting the divine hospitality at the root of its origin and anointing with the Spirit. The Spirit of Pentecost is also the Spirit of the cross and the resurrection and works through suffering to accompany, sanctify, and empower believers.[54] Anointing and charisma find in suffering and martyrdom the limits of hospitality.

The suffering of the church is the consequence of an inclusive approach to holiness demanded by the church's anointing with the Holy Spirit and movement into and out of the world.[55] Although the Spirit is poured out on *all* flesh, and thus initiates and sustains the cosmopolitan mission of the church, sanctification demands the environment *within* the church with its purifying and consecrating rituals. The church is holy because it shares in the suffering of Christ (see 1 Pet. 4:13) for the sake of redemption in every area where it faces the injustices, inequalities, and oppressions of the world in its own body. Hence, the church suffers the consequences of being in but not of the world when it realizes that its own temperament and negligence, rather than external discrimination and persecution, present the first obstacle to sanctification.[56] Racial discrimination, ethnic stereotyping, gender inequality, sexual harassment, and economic corruption are not simply external realities but sins that the communion of saints must face at the altars of the

---

[53] Wenk, 'The Church as Sanctified Community', 112–16.
[54] See Keith Warrington, 'A Spirit Theology of Suffering', in Hunter and Robeck, *The Suffering Body*, 24–36; Martin W. Mittelstadt, 'Spirit and Suffering in Contemporary Pentecostalism: The Lukan Epic Continues', in *Defining Issues in Pentecostalism: Classical and Emergent*, ed. Steven M. Studebaker (Eugene, OR: Pickwick, 2008), 144–73.
[55] Wenk, *Community-Forming Power*, 257–308.
[56] See Ioan F. Tipei, 'Persecution of the Romanian Church in the Twentieth Century: An Historical and Theological Perspective', in Hunter and Robeck, *The Suffering Body*, 127–52.

church.⁵⁷ The struggle for holiness is indicative of the difficulties to reconcile the pastoral, evangelistic, and prophetic dimensions of the church's mission.⁵⁸

The Pentecostal vision of a radical cosmopolitan hospitality therefore challenges and transforms the traditional marks of the church. The suffering of hospitality is the bridge between holiness and oneness, catholicity and apostolicity. From the proclamation of Jesus as sanctifier comes a theology of suffering as the affection of the entire body (see 1 Cor. 12:26), so that the entire body is transformed and sanctified (Heb. 2:10) through suffering for the kingdom of God (2 Thess. 1:2–5).⁵⁹ The church is *one* because the holy community acknowledges differences without demanding division, and it can do so because the Spirit of holiness (Rom. 1:4) is also the Spirit of unity (Eph. 4:3), communion (2 Cor. 13:14) and sanctification (2 Thess. 2:13; 1 Pet. 1:2).⁶⁰ In the hospitality of Pentecost, the church not only shares in the anointing of Christ through the gifts of the Spirit but also in the suffering of Christ through the quenching of the Spirit.⁶¹ The unity of the church is expressed in the hospitality of tongues, prophecies, exhortations, and practices that invite the world to the altar of God indiscriminate of language, culture, or confession.⁶² This hospitality is the ground for the ecumenical unity of the churches. The church is *catholic* because the hospitality of the Spirit invites the totality and fullness of local and diverse contexts throughout the entire world to participate in the divine welcome. The full gospel is a catholic gospel because it is hospitable to the fullness of the Spirit who is restricted neither to God nor to the church alone.⁶³ Catholicity requires holiness so that diversity and suffering lead neither to compromise nor division. However, if becoming catholic is a process of sanctification 'in the paradoxical sense of transcendence and existential involvement in the world',⁶⁴ then

---

[57] See Jim Pieterse, 'Managing Belief in a Hostile World: Experiencing Gifts of the Spirit at a Small Pentecostal Charismatic Church in Pretoria', *ASR* 39, no. 1 (2016): 1–13.

[58] See Japie La Poorta, 'Church and Society: A Pentecostal Perspective from the Southern Hemisphere', in *Pentecostal Mission and Global Christianity*, ed. Wonsuk Ma, Veli-Matti Kärkkäinen, J. Kwabena Asamoah-Gyady (Oxford: Regnum, 2014), 292–300.

[59] Tipei, 'Persecution', 143–46.

[60] 'Perspectives on Koinonia' (no. 70), 149.

[61] See Jon Ruthven, *On the Cessation of the Charismata: Protestant Polemic on Postbiblical Miracles*, JPTS 3 (Sheffield: Sheffield Academic Press, 1993).

[62] Macchia, *Baptized in the Spirit*, 218.

[63] Kärkkäinen, 'Catholic, Full Gospel, and Fullness of the Spirit', 86–97.

[64] 'Toward a Common Expression of Faith: A Black North American Perspective', in *Black Witness to the Apostolic Faith*, ed. David T. Shannon and Gayraud S. Wilmore (Grand Rapids: Eerdmans, 1985), 63–70 (66).

fellowship with other cultures, races, and ethnicities (within and without the church) is as much a necessary expression of the catholic mission as is hospitality to those of no faith or other faiths.[65] The church is *apostolic* because it shares in the experience of the anointing with the Spirit poured out on the apostles at Pentecost. Strictly speaking, the reception of the Spirit by the community and its members suggests that every individual in the church stands in succession from the apostles.[66] We can therefore speak of the whole church as apostolic only insofar as every member mediates this apostolic mission in a sanctified manner.[67] The church is apostolic not only by the traditioning of doctrine and faith but also by engagement with charismatic gifts and empowered practice.[68] These interpretations of ecclesial marks lead Pentecostals beyond holiness to concerns for the power of the church to accomplish its mission to the world.

Spirit baptism and the empowered church

The gifts of the Spirit are gifts of the hospitality of the church, and vice versa. Nonetheless, the church does not possess the marks in some absolute sense but is always challenged by them as gifts of grace.[69] Not every hospitable, charismatic act comprehends the fullness of the church. Since charisma and hospitality are always instruments but never the exclusive ends of the life of the church, these marks point beyond themselves to the further realization of the fullness of the presence of Christ. Amidst Pentecostal concerns for the fullness of the Christian witness, I have argued that the baptism in the Spirit functions as an interpretive lens at the centre of the full gospel narrative (see Chapter 4). In turn, in the context of the ecclesiological concerns discussed in this chapter, Pentecost as symbol points to Spirit baptism as a particular lens through which to view and order the marks of the church. Pentecostals

---

[65] See Tony Richie, *Speaking by the Spirit: A Pentecostal Model for Interreligious Dialogue* (Lexington, KY: Emeth Press, 2011); Amos Yong, *Discerning the Spirit(s): A Pentecostal-Charismatic Contribution to Christian Theology of Religions*, JPTS 20 (Sheffield: Sheffield Academic Press, 2000).
[66] Macchia, *Baptized in the Spirit*, 205-6.
[67] 'Toward a Common Expression of Faith', 69.
[68] For early Pentecostal reflections of apostolicity see Cecil M. Robeck Jr., 'Pentecostals and the Apostolic Faith: Implications for Ecumenism', *Pneuma* 9, no. 1 (1987): 61-84.
[69] Macchia, *Baptized in the Spirit*, 205.

most widely identify Spirit baptism with the reception of power.[70] On the way to the fullness of the church, the Pentecostal experience of Spirit baptism can be identified as both a heightened charismatic experience[71] and an amplified gift of divine hospitality.[72] Put differently, holiness and hospitality receive and reciprocate empowerment.[73] From the perspective of Jesus as the one who baptizes with the Spirit, the church is therefore not only charismatic and hospitable but also *empowered*. Receptive to the hospitality and gifting of Jesus, the church becomes a fellowship empowered by the Holy Spirit. The central ecclesiological concern arising from this proposal is how the church experiences a breakthrough in power that differs from the experience of grace in regeneration and the participation in the divine life through sanctification. The response, I suggest, must lead Pentecostal theology further to explore the sacramental nature of Spirit baptism and the church.

Empowerment as an ecclesial mark focuses on the measurable difference of the Christian community in its witness to the world. Spirit baptism identifies power as the interdependent element in the community manifesting the love of God and the presence of Christ by the gifts of the Holy Spirit for the sake of mission. Problematic for the ecclesiological use of power is the often overwhelmingly individual focus on Spirit baptism in the West.[74] Yet, if the role of Spirit baptism for a realization of the common good and the significance of the church for the transformation of society, identified in the previous chapter, are correct, then the primary significance of the outpouring of the Spirit is found in the missionary community, not the individual.[75] The church is a continuation of the anointing of Jesus only because it is a fellowship of the community in the Spirit embodied as the charismatic

---

[70] See Peter Althouse, *The Ideological Development of 'Power' in Early American Pentecostalism: An Historical, Theological, and Sociological Study* (Lewiston, NY: Edwin Mellen, 2010); William W. Menzies and Robert P. Menzies, *Spirit and Power: Foundations of Pentecostal Experience* (Grand Rapids, MI: Zondervan, 2000).

[71] See Donald L. Gelpi, *Pentecostalism: A Theological Viewpoint* (New York: Paulist Press, 1971), 219. See also Ralph Del Colle, 'The Pursuit of Holiness: A Roman Catholic-Pentecostal Dialogue', *Journal of Ecumenical Studies* 37, nos. 3–4 (2000): 301–20, esp. 314–15.

[72] See Daniela C. Augustine, 'The Empowered Church: Ecclesiological Dimensions of the Event of Pentecost', in Thomas, *Towards a Pentecostal Ecclesiology*, 157–80.

[73] See Ralph Del Colle, 'Theological Dialogue on the "Full Gospel": Trinitarian Contributions from Pope John Paul II and Thomas A. Smail', *Pneuma* 20, no. 1 (1998): 141–60.

[74] Kärkkäinen, 'A Full Gospel Ecclesiology', 186.

[75] Macchia, *Baptized in the Spirit*, 205; Simon Chan, 'Mother Church: Toward a Pentecostal Ecclesiology', *Pneuma* 22, no. 2 (2000): 177–208.

and hospitable reality of God's presence.⁷⁶ Christ does not restrain the divine power within himself but empties himself of the Spirit (see Mt. 27:50; Lk. 23:46; Jn 19:30). Likewise, the Spirit does not conserve the divine power but is poured out at Pentecost on all flesh.⁷⁷ The church embodies Christ in the Spirit in a similar manner because the communal embodiment of power differs from that of the individual, since the community exists also before, between and beyond individuals.⁷⁸ The convictions, habits, virtues, and practices of the church are the result of the life of the community existing not simply as the sum total of individuals but in the collective experiences of the community that exceed each person. In the same sense as the empowered community surpasses the gifting of each individual, the empowered church cannot contain the power of the Spirit within its fellowship. Pentecost as ecclesiological symbol identifies the church strictly speaking not as a community accumulating but disseminating divine power.⁷⁹ The power of the church exists in practice in the weakness and readiness of the church to share in the suffering of others. Yet, this kind of hospitality does not cast the charismatic life in the light of powerlessness. On the contrary, the paradox of charismatic power is that the divine presence increases with the decrease of the one manifesting the power.⁸⁰ Here we have arrived at the heart of charismatic sacramentality.

Spirit baptism signifies the empowerment of the Spirit in the Christian life as a charismatic sacrament (see Chapter 4). To say so is to emphasize that the existence of the empowered church, manifested by its charismatic hospitality, is a sacramental reality.⁸¹ While the baptism in the Spirit is already participation in the life of the Spirit, the signs of the baptism are broken symbols, transformative, but apophatic and provisional, and not absolute

---

[76] Daniela C. Augustine, 'Pentecost, Empowerment and Glossolalia', *IJSCC* 11, no. 4 (2011): 288–304.

[77] See D. Lyle Dabney, *Die Kenosis des Geistes: Kontinuität zwischen Schöpfung und Erlösung im Werk des Heiligen Geistes* (Neukirchen-Vluyn: Neukirchener Verlag, 1997).

[78] See William K. Kay, 'Gifts of the Spirit: Reflections on Pentecostalism and Its Growth in Asia', in *Spirit and Power: The Growth and Global Impact of Pentecostalism*, ed. Donald E. Miller et al. (Oxford: Oxford University Press, 2013), 259–76.

[79] See Frank D. Macchia, 'The Spirit-baptised Church', *IJSCC* 11, no. 4 (2011): 256–68.

[80] See Martin Lindhardt, *Power in Powerlessness: A Study of Pentecostal Life Worlds in Urban Chile* (Leiden: Brill, 2012); Wilma Wells Davies, *The Embattled but Empowered Community: Comparing Understandings of Spiritual Power in Argentine Popular and Pentecostal Cosmologies*, GPCS 5 (Leiden: Brill, 2010).

[81] See Wolfgang Vondey and Chris W. Green, 'Between This and That: Reality and Sacramentality in the Pentecostal Worldview', *JPT* 19, no. 2 (2010): 243–64.

but sacramental references to the divine presence.[82] Prophecy, speaking with tongues and other gifts of the Spirit are ascetic struggles within the liturgy of the church, a decreasing of the significance and meaning of the church for the sake of pointing (charismatically and sacramentally) to Christ.[83] The hospitable sacramental life does not serve self-proliferation but insists on the self-emptying of charismatic power on behalf of others and for the coming of the kingdom. That is why the church has arrived with the baptism in the Spirit at a threshold of its own identity: from filled and empowered by the gift of the Spirit to emptying and empowering with the gifts of the Spirit in service and mission to the world. This sacramental dynamic is cultivated through the charismatic practices, rituals, and sacraments of the hospitable community.

Pentecostal theology struggles with sacramentality understood as a special mode of God's presence that excludes the charismatic encounter of the church with Christ in the Spirit.[84] Any neglect of the charismatic dimension of the church from the sacramental reality is problematic because it omits the hospitable character of encountering the Spirit among those who also encounter one another in the sacramental act. The sacramental reality of the church is necessarily rooted in the church's worship and mission made possible by the outpouring of the Spirit.[85] Yet, the notion of a 'baptism' in the Spirit forsakes pure sacramental symbolism for the sake of the tangible embodied agency of the Spirit, so that the focus shifts 'to Christ's participation by the Spirit in the communal act and our communion with him and one another by the same Spirit'.[86] From the perspective of Pentecost, Spirit baptism functions as a mode of the divine presence in the community insofar as it expresses as sacrament the power of the charismatic hospitality of the church (see Acts 2:41–47).[87] Of course, the church is not a self-sufficient performance of liturgical

---

[82] See Amos Yong, '"Tongues of Fire" in the Pentecostal Imagination: The Truth of Glossolalia in Light of R. C. Neville's Theory of Religious Symbolism', *JPT* 12 (1998): 39–65.

[83] Augustine, *Pentecost, Hospitality, and Transformation*, 37–39; idem, 'The Empowered Church', 175–78.

[84] See Tom F. Driver, *The Magic of Ritual: Our Need for Liberating Rites That Transform Our Lives and Our Communities* (San Francisco: Harper, 1991), 208–9.

[85] Vondey and Chris W. Green, 'Between This and That', 252–54; Chris E. W. Green, *Toward a Pentecostal Theology of the Lord's Supper: Foretasting the Kingdom* (Cleveland, TN: CPT Press, 2012), 307–25; Simon Chan, 'The Use of Prosper's Rule in the Development of Pentecostal Ecclesiology', *IJSCC* 11, no. 4 (2011): 305–17.

[86] Macchia, *Baptized in the Spirit*, 255.

[87] See Wolfgang Vondey, 'Pentecostal Ecclesiology and Eucharistic Hospitality: Toward a Systematic and Ecumenical Account of the Church', *Pneuma* 32, no. 1 (2010): 41–55.

rites that produces the immediacy of the divine presence.[88] It is also not the charismatic or hospitable act as such that can be equated with the power of God. Rather, the divine presence is mediated immediately by the power of the anointing with the Spirit of Christ.[89] From the perspective of Pentecost, the immediate power of the Spirit cannot be manifested apart from the transformation of the participants who are shaped by the encounter into the likeness of Christ.[90] All sacraments of the church therefore function as rituals of discernment that the church is being transformed into the one, holy, catholic and apostolic community to which the presence and power of God bears witness through the Spirit.

Consequently, from the perspective of the community's empowerment by the Spirit, the marks of the church can be seen as sacramental. The church is *one* because it exists simultaneously as confronted with Jesus and united with Jesus in the Spirit (as saviour, sanctifier, Spirit baptizer, healer, and coming king). Pentecost as a theological symbol reminds the church that the power of the Spirit of Christ is both wedded to and resisting the church's institutional structures and rituals.[91] The unity of the church is found not in an unqualified possession of the charismata but in the weakness of mediating the divine power where the church itself is both consuming and consumed by the Spirit. Similarly, the church is *holy* because the community both receives and empties itself of the wholeness of divine power for the sake of its worship and mission.[92] The holiness of the church requires individual and corporate sanctity, which mutually condition one another.[93] At the same time, the sacramental holiness of the church also transcends and challenges individuals and the community because their source of power is found in the weakness of remaining dependent on God. The church is *catholic* because the Pentecostal community is filled beyond containment with the Spirit and overflows with flames of fire, tongues and prophetic speech,

---

[88] See Margaret M. Poloma, 'The Symbolic Dilemma and the Future of Pentecostalism: Mysticism, Ritual, and Revival', in *The Future of Pentecostalism in the United States*, ed. Eric Patterson and Edmund J. Rybarczyk (Lanham, MD: Lexington Books, 2007), 105–21.
[89] Green, *Towards a Pentecostal Theology of the Lord's Supper*, 286–93.
[90] Ibid., 74–181.
[91] See Frank D. Macchia, *Justified in the Spirit: Creation, Redemption, and the Triune God* (Grand Rapids, MI: Eerdmans, 2010), 54. See also Miroslav Volf, *After Our Likeness: Church as the Image of the Trinity* (Grand Rapids: Eerdmans, 1998), 221–57.
[92] Althouse, *The Ideological Development of Power*, 91–130.
[93] Macchia, *Baptized in the Spirit*, 222–23; Yong, *The Spirit Poured Out*, 142.

charismatic power, and hospitality into the world. This catholicity of the Spirit is born in the church at Pentecost, but as sacramental reality it must also subsist in the historical and institutional church.[94] As both divine gift and human task, the catholicity of the church must not only be believed by the local church and the communion of churches but also be practiced in universal dependence on one another and on God.[95] Hence, the church is *apostolic* because as the community filled and empowered with the Spirit, the historical church discerns and submits to the continuous reality of being called and sent by God.[96] Apostolicity is sacramental, since the church in the power of the Spirit is both sent away into the world and called back unto God. The gift of apostleship is manifested for Pentecostals undoubtedly in the authority and power accompanying the church's mission.[97] Nonetheless, apostolicity as empowered mission begins from below.[98] In the weakness of Pentecost the Spirit-baptized church continues to be a succession of apostolic faith, witness, worship, and service.

Divine healing and the egalitarian church

The emphasis the full gospel places on divine healing sheds further light on the character of the empowered church. Pentecostal healing practices, as I have shown, require, establish and transform the community of faith (see Chapter 5). Informed by a vision of cosmopolitan redemption, the previous chapter identified with the motif of divine healing also the transformation of society. Healing practices constitute a threshold of the community into the world and entrance of the world into the community of faith.[99] The willingness, ability, and empowerment of the healing community come from the confrontation with suffering and sickness at its own altars. At the healing altars of the church, we encounter the Christian at the frontline of the

---

[94] Macchia, *Baptized in the Spirit*, 224–29.
[95] Kärkkäinen, 'Catholicity, Full Gospel, and Fullness of the Spirit', 82–84.
[96] Macchia, *Baptized in the Spirit*, 235.
[97] See J. Kwabena Asamoah-Gyadu, '"You Shall Receive Power": Empowerment in Pentecostal/Charismatic Christianity', in Ma, Kärkkäinen, Asamoah-Gyadu, *Pentecostal Mission and Global Christianity*, 45–66; Ma and Ma, *Mission in the Spirit*, 59–71.
[98] See Veli-Matti Kärkkäinen, 'The Pentecostal Understanding of Mission', in Ma, Kärkkäinen, Asamoah-Gyadu, *Pentecostal Mission and Global Christianity*, 26–44.
[99] See Kimberly E. Alexander, 'The Pentecostal Healing Community', in Thomas, *Toward a Pentecostal Ecclesiology*, 183–206.

community's mission confronting the suffering and sicknesses of the world that have become the suffering and sicknesses of the church. A chief concern amidst these practices is that public ministry and service demand visible structures necessary for the mediation and reception of charismata, hospitality, and empowered mission. At the altars of the church, individuals and the community must embody the church's public ministry consistently as a recognizable fellowship of the Spirit in visible continuity with the ministry of Christ. The dominant expression of the visible structures of the church in Pentecostal ecclesiology is an individualist and pluralist understanding of community combined around Pentecost as symbol of the calling and mission of each and every Christian. This seemingly paradoxical combination is often difficult to reconcile with traditional notions of episcopal hierarchy and authority. In this section, I want to expand Pentecostal ecclesiology further under the notion of divine healing towards the reconciliation of ecclesiastical structures.

Pentecost as symbol of the universal outpouring of the Holy Spirit has immediate connotations for the visible structures of Christian ministry and service. Since the gifts of the Spirit are available to everyone, the church is at once the work of each person and of all people. However, this Pentecostal image of the church should not be confused with simply the mobilization of every person for the preaching of the gospel, evangelization or the healing of the sick. The outpouring of the Spirit leads to a deep saturation of the community with a calling into the fellowship of the Spirit that embodies the anointing of Christ as a unique vocation of each person.[100] Charisma, hospitality, and power function to embody this vocation across the divides of gender, age, race, ethnicity, class, or education, which are not indicative of the anointing of the Spirit and therefore do not imply a measure of authority or position.[101] The church after Pentecost emphasizes the variety of Christian vocations found in the New Testament: apostles, prophets, evangelists, pastors, teachers (Eph. 4:11), overseers, elders, and deacons (Phil 1:1), all distributed among believers in a manner evading a polarity between priest and people, ordained and laity, office and charisma, Jew or Gentile (see Acts 15:8–9), or any other similar distinction that locates the active exercise of the Christian mission in

---

[100] Coulter, 'Christ, the Spirit, and Vocation', 328–38.
[101] Vondey, *Pentecostalism*, 115–19.

the hands of a particular individual or group.[102] The principle of order is the hospitality of the Spirit distributed as the gift of hospitality to the people, who in turn function as different gifts of the Spirit throughout the church and for the benefit of all.[103] Put differently, an important mark of the church under the symbol of Pentecost is that the church is *egalitarian.*

The ideal of an egalitarian church is hardly realized among the Christian churches and serves as a reminder that the marks of the church are believed by faith even if they are not visibly present. Christian egalitarianism is therefore not a reference to the reality of equality already achieved but the social process of healing from exclusion, domination, and oppression. Nonetheless, an egalitarian ecclesiology that is closely associated with a theology of suffering remains the exception rather than the norm, even in Pentecostalism.[104] Episcopal and congregational forms of church structure continue to dominate church governance among Pentecostals without easy reconciliation.[105] The episcopal wing, on the one hand, favours hierarchical church governance without reconciling sacerdotal structures of ecclesiastical organization with a theology of the priesthood of all believers.[106] The free church tradition, on the other, and its emphasis on the ministry of all believers, often goes hand in hand with an uncritical rejection of traditional, hierarchical patterns in favour of congregational forms of government.[107] Instead, continuity with the anointing of Christ demands egalitarian structures of the church that are neither entirely voluntary nor exclusively institutional but follow the vocational patterns of Jesus as the bearer of the Spirit.

The vocation of the Christian can be seen as the consistent public expression of the anointing with the Spirit manifested in the life of the individual

---

[102] See Keith Warrington, *Pentecostal Theology: A Theology of Encounter* (London: T&T Clark, 2008), 138–43; Veli-Matti Kärkkäinen, 'The Calling of the Whole People of God into Ministry: The Spirit, Church, and Laity', *Studia Theologia* 54, no. 2 (2000): 144–62. Maintaining a Pentecostal notion of laity is Steven M. Fettke, *God's Empowered People: A Pentecostal Theology of the Laity* (Eugene, OR: Wipf and Stock, 2011).

[103] Gordon Fee, *God's Empowering Presence: The Holy Spirit in the Letters of Paul* (Peabody, MA: Hendrickson, 1994), 705–8.

[104] See Oliver McMahan, 'Grief Observed: Surprised by the Suffering of the Spirit', in Land et al., *Passover, Pentecost, and Parousia*, 296–314.

[105] See Volf, *After Our Likeness*, 29–125.

[106] See David G. Roebuck, 'The Development and Significance of Centralized Government in the Church of God', in *Passover, Pentecost and Parousia: Studies in Celebration of the Life and Ministry of R. Hollis Gause*, ed. Steven J. Land et al., JPTS 35 (Blandford Forum: Deo, 2010), 209–31.

[107] See Simon Chan, 'Mother Church: Toward a Pentecostal Ecclesiology', *Pneuma* 22, no. 2 (2000): 177–208.

and the community (e.g. in church, family, marriage, or work). Pentecostals do not understand vocation in terms of ordination or office but as a gift of the Spirit that precedes both public affirmations.[108] Instead, the public affirmation of the gifts of the Spirit must stand in continuity with the public anointing of Christ portrayed by the full gospel through the images of saviour, sanctifier, Spirit baptizer, healer, and coming king. The church as an egalitarian movement employs various vocations that realize the vocational identity of Jesus in the community over time.[109] These vocations of the body and its many members may not correspond directly to the identity of Jesus as head of the body, since the gift of the Spirit is manifested through the bestowal of different charisms (see 1 Cor. 12:4–11).[110] The move from the altars of the church into the world therefore requires the cultivation of diverse vocations distinguishing individuals and congregations on the basis of their particular response to the call of God.[111] Although all Christians can come to the altar, not all leave the altar transformed and commissioned in the same way.

There exist under the symbol of Pentecost different vocations of apostles, prophets, evangelists, pastors, and teachers, grounded in the charismatic life of the church and its gradual realization of continuity with the vocational identity of Jesus. Christian egalitarianism should therefore not imply that all people possess equal gifts and vocations. The much lamented privatization of faith and charism among Pentecostals helps create and shape new spaces for individual self-expression and authority in response to the voice of God.[112] At the same time, these expressions of the gifts of the Spirit in individuals are always integrated in and purposed for the life of the community and do not evade hierarchy.[113] Leadership by those elevated to a position of spiritual authority and the sharing of charisma among the people stand in close

---

[108] Volf, *After Our Likeness*, 245–57; 'Perspectives on *Koinonia*', 152.
[109] Coulter, 'Christ, the Spirit, and Vocation', 331–38.
[110] Ibid., 335. However, a direct correspondence is sought by Archer, 'The Fivefold Gospel', 40–43. Tying vocation more closely to Jesus' water baptism is Green, *Sanctifying Interpretation*, 7–25.
[111] See Opoku Onyinah, 'Pentecostal Healing Communities', in Thomas, *Toward a Pentecostal Ecclesiology*, 207–22.
[112] See Cerasela Voiculescu, 'To Whom God Speaks: Struggles for Authority through Religious Reflexivity and Performativity within a Gypsy Pentecostal Church', *SRO* 17, no. 2 (2012), available at http://www.socresonline.org.uk/17/2/10.html.
[113] See Naomi Haynes, 'Egalitarianism and Hierarchy in Copperbelt Religious Practice: On the Social Work of Pentecostal Ritual', *Religion* 45, no. 2 (2015): 273–92; Rachel Morgain, '"Break Down These Walls": Space, Relations, and Hierarchy in Fijian Evangelical Christianity', *Oceania* 85, no. 1 (2015): 105–18.

relationship for the realization of diverse vocations in the church.[114] Episcopal and congregational structures are not a hindrance to the egalitarian calling of God unless they cancel out the vocation of particular persons or groups (whether children, women, the disabled, or racial-ethnic minorities).[115] On the contrary, the distribution of vocations by the Spirit establishes a necessary interaction of egalitarianism and hierarchy intended to lead to new structures and positions of authority.[116] The principle of recognition that these structures of the church continue the vocational identity and anointing of Jesus is the community's spiritual discernment.

Spiritual discernment in the church is a way of distinguishing if and how the beliefs, actions, and affections of its members contribute to the fulfilment of the church's identity and mission. The full gospel casts the governance of the church unambiguously under the headship of Christ. The structures of the body of Christ emerge from the Spirit's continuous conferring of gifts to individuals and the community.[117] Pentecost as symbol portrays the government of the church therefore principally as theocratic under the headship of the risen and glorified Jesus who has poured out the Spirit. Discernment of this theocratic government is found in the church's consensus of what seems 'good to the Holy Spirit' and to the community (Acts 15:28) amidst hierarchical, congregational, and confessional structures. Hence, to say that spiritual discernment submits to the direction of the Holy Spirit is insufficient, since a pneumatological theocracy can function neither without divine revelation nor the discernment of the community.[118] The Spirit bestows the charisms necessary for the recognition of offices, but the exercise of charisms depends on the cooperation of the community of faith with the Spirit, not only charismatically but also priestly, politically, and prophetically.[119] That the egalitarian community is a discerning

---

[114] Poloma, *The Assemblies of God at the Crossroads*, 66–87.
[115] See Coulter, 'The Development of Ecclesiology', 74–82; Harold D. Hunter, 'A. J. Tomlinson's Emerging Ecclesiology', *Pneuma* 32, no. 3 (2010): 369–89.
[116] See Emilio Willems, 'Validation of Authority in Pentecostal Sects in Chile and Brazil', *JSSR* 6, no. 2 (1967): 253–58.
[117] Volf, *After Our Likeness*, 222–33.
[118] See Amos Yong, *Spirit-Word-Community: Theological Hermeneutics in Trinitarian Perspective* (Eugene, OR: Wipf and Stock, 2002), 275–310; Yong, *Discerning the Spirit(s)*, 243–55; Stephen E. Parker, *Led by the Spirit: Toward a Practical Theology of Pentecostal Discernment and Decision Making*, JPTS 7 (Sheffield: Sheffield Academic Press, 1996), 101–16.
[119] See Cheryl Bridges Johns, 'Spirited Vestments: Why the Anointing is not Enough', in Land et al., *Passover, Pentecost and Parousia*, 260–77; Margaret M. Poloma, *The Assemblies of God at the Crossroads: Charisma and Institutional Dilemmas* (Knoxville: University of Tennessee Press, 1989), 101–61.

community means that there is no aristocracy that can mediate discernment on behalf of the whole.[120] Instead, egalitarian discernment legitimizes never the leadership of the church alone but always points to the manifestation of the charismatic life throughout the whole church and the spiritual authority of all believers in interdependence with its leadership.[121] Since egalitarian instincts transcend also the governance of single congregations and denominations towards the holistic functioning of the entire body of Christ, the principle of Christian egalitarianism is the interdependence of leaders and people, congregations and denominations within the whole household (*oikoumene*) of God. This principle functions only if it is aimed at the continuous discernment of the structures in existence and their healing and restoration for the good of all.

Divine healing emphasizes that the church is characterized by the interdependence of its marks: egalitarianism directs and is directed by charisma, hospitality, and power towards the unity, holiness, catholicity, and apostolicity of the whole church. In this light, the church is *one* because the egalitarian principle is the mode of operation for the unity of charismatic diversity in any assembly hospitable to the empowerment of all. Unity is therefore a vocation of each individual embedded in relationships within the body of Christ discerning its service to God. The church is *holy* because the egalitarian Spirit sanctifies and transforms the structures of negligence, exclusion, and oppression. This sanctification is not a painless process but an active suffering in the Spirit by each member for the discernment of the vocations and structures possible in the whole church. The church is *catholic* because the Spirit directs the church in an outward movement from Pentecost towards a dynamic universality through the egalitarian distribution of vocations.[122] Catholicity is therefore both mark and mission of the church, since the vocations given by the Spirit are already contained within the church at Pentecost and yet expand the church through the plurality of persons towards the fullness of the new creation.[123] The church is *apostolic* because succession emerges from the discernment that the community's charismatic life stands in continuity with the anointing of Christ.[124] This

---

[120] Macchia, *Baptized in the Spirit*, 235; Volf, *After Our Likeness*, 152.
[121] See Chan, 'The Use of Prosper's Rule', 314.
[122] Lord, *Network Church*, 129–59.
[123] Volf, *After Our Likeness*, 264–69.
[124] Coulter, 'Christ, the Spirit, and Vocation', 338.

continuity is determined not simply by succession but by vocation, so that it is not only the community but each member of the church who is apostolic.[125] The marks of the church are bound to the government of the Spirit made evident in the historical, social, liturgical, and political structures affecting all individuals throughout the body of Christ. These egalitarian structures, if reflecting the divine hospitality, are not abolished with the coming of the kingdom. The final section of this chapter looks at the eschatological continuity of the church.

The kingdom of God and the persistent church

The eschatological emphasis of the full gospel (see Chapter 6) has not been widely applied to Pentecostal ecclesiology. In this final section, I suggest that ecclesiology under the symbol of Pentecost identifies the marks of the church as apocalyptic elements of the kingdom of God. The birth of the church with the outpouring of the Spirit at Pentecost is also the inauguration of the kingdom towards which the church moves.[126] The movement of the church as 'the way' (Acts 9:2; 19:9, 23; 22:4; 24:14, 22) towards the kingdom and the coming of the kingdom into the world are complementary expressions of an apocalyptic ecclesiology. In other words, Pentecost and kingdom are complementary ends of the church as a movement on this side of history 'on the way' to the fullness of redemption. The move of the church outward into history is therefore also a move forward eschatologically to the new creation. We can say that Pentecostal ecclesiology is formed by the mission of the kingdom. More precisely, however, this eschatological mission is shaped by the day of Pentecost as the bridge in history between the ascension and the return of Christ.[127] The chief concern of this apocalyptic ecclesiology is how Pentecostals retain the tension between the historical structures and the eschatological ideal of the Christian community. The answer to this question reveals that an important, and often neglected, facet of Pentecostal ecclesiology is its eschatological criticism of the church.

---

[125] See Macchia, *Baptized in the Spirit*, 235.
[126] Macchia, 'The Spirit-Baptised Church', 257.
[127] See Peter Althouse, 'Ascension – Pentecost – Eschaton: A Theological Framework for Pentecostal Ecclesiology', in Thomas, *Towards a Pentecostal Ecclesiology*, 225–47.

The critical element of Pentecostal ecclesiology is embedded in the day of Pentecost, which identifies the church not only historically but eschatologically.[128] Defined by the outpouring of the Holy Spirit, the church is a divine reality and gift as well as a human reality in the world. Pentecostals do not embrace a division between the visible and the invisible church because it implies a false distinction between spirituality and historicity or the church in its essence and the church in becoming.[129] Instead, Pentecost as symbol presents a theological critique of the church that involves a necessary realism of the tension between the divine calling and human response, gift and institution, the historical reality and eschatological purpose of the community. The heart of the Pentecostal critique is located precisely in the engagement of the church with the world, not the divine calling and mission as such, but the question of the continuity of historical structures to support the church's eschatological existence until the return of Christ. Whereas the day of Pentecost shows a church born free in the Spirit, Pentecostals paint the continuing historical picture as that of freedom captured by institutionalism, division, and creed.[130] This critical interpretation should not serve as justification of a Pentecostal isolationism and triumphalism (although it has). Pentecostal ecclesiology does not serve Pentecostals but the church as a whole. Nonetheless, taken seriously, this critical perspective has supported an eschatological mindset consisting primarily of a restoration of the ideal church seen at Pentecost, both as a form of primitivism by returning to the apostolic age and a form of dispensationalism interpreting modern-day Pentecostalism as the embodiment of the true church in the last days.[131] In other words, Pentecostal theology accepts Pentecost as symbol of both the historical beginning and the eschatological purpose of the church. The importance of this dual emphasis for ecclesiology lies not in the difference but in the continuity between the present and future creation. The church manifests in the historical expression of its charismatic, hospitable, empowered, and egalitarian marks also an eschatological *persistence*.

---

[128] See the literature in Vondey, *Beyond Pentecostalism*, 151–58.
[129] See Frank D. Macchia, 'The Nature and Purpose of the Church: A Pentecostal Reflection on Unity and *Koinonia*', in Vondey, *Pentecostalism and Christian Unity*, 243–55, esp. 251–54.
[130] See Dale M. Coulter, 'Pentecostal Visions of the End: Eschatology, Ecclesiology and the Fascination of the Left Behind Series', *JPT* 14, no. 1 (2005): 81–98.
[131] Ibid., 85–95; D. William Faupel, *The Everlasting Gospel: The Significance of Eschatology in the Development of Pentecostal Thought*, JPTS 10 (Sheffield: Sheffield Academic Press, 1996), 26–27.

The eschatological idea of the church at Pentecost should not be equated with a naïve hermeneutic removed from the historical tensions and limitations of the primitive community.[132] Pentecostals see themselves as thoroughly located in history, yet from an eschatological perspective which questions the extent of history's authority. The church at Pentecost emerges from the absence of the resurrected and ascended Christ.[133] The outpouring of the Spirit is no replacement of the presence of Jesus, but the church at Pentecost continues to long for Christ's return. The church suffers the departure of Christ as a historical reality in the brokenness of its symbols, institutions, and practices, not the least in the outpouring of the Spirit at Pentecost, which despite the thunderous praise of tongues bemoans the absence of the Lord.[134] The fact that the Pentecostal critique of the historical church does not reach back to the day of Pentecost underscores the primacy of the eschatological character of Pentecost as symbol and its function as an interpretive lens for the church in history. If it has any eschatological significance, Pentecost must also function as a symbol of the kingdom. Ecclesiological primitivism is therefore not historically but eschatologically motivated: the return to Pentecost is seen as a movement forward to the kingdom.[135] Both Pentecost events, the inauguration and the fulfilment of the kingdom, join earth and heaven, promise and fulfilment, already and not yet, old and new, in the fellowship of the eternal Spirit already poured out into history. Nonetheless, the church exists as a reminder that the two events still differ and that the difference is concentrated in the historical persistence of the Christian community. The church journeys through history as an apocalyptic movement in continuous dynamic expression of its mission from Pentecost to the world and to the kingdom of God.[136]

Apart from the church, any talk about the continuity of history and eternity, the present and the future creation, is meaningless. As an eschatological community, the church is incidental to its marks; it does not possess them with the day of Pentecost but is rather their eschatological product amidst transitory historical structures. For this reason, Pentecostals are hesitant to

---

[132] Macchia, 'The Nature and Purpose of the Church', 253.
[133] Althouse, 'Ascension – Pentecost – Eschaton', 234.
[134] See Frank D. Macchia, 'Sighs Too Deep for Words: Toward a Theology of Glossolalia', *JPT* 1, no. 1 (1992): 47–73.
[135] See Vondey, *Beyond Pentecostalism*, 151–55.
[136] See Vondey, 'Pentecostal Perspectives on *The Nature and Mission of the Church*', 65.

apply the term 'church' in an absolute sense to anything but the glorified community of saints eventually revealed in the kingdom.[137] Yet, because the continuity between Pentecost and kingdom already finds expression in the outpouring of the eschatological Spirit in history, the church as a product of the Spirit already manifests persistently the eschatological presence of Christ in history. This persistence of the church bridges both historical location and historical distance, because the distance between Pentecost and kingdom is not governed by history but transcends, transforms, and fulfils history.[138] On the one hand, the persistence of the church stands in radical contrast to the destruction of the world; it is the apocalyptic work of the Spirit, deliverance not participation, redemptive because it finds fulfilment only in the new creation. On the other hand, this persistence is apocalyptic because it is prophetic; it is historical, not otherworldly, and redemptive because it is critical and confrontational. Joining and reconciling these tensions, the church is constituted by its liturgy, the charismatic, hospitable, empowered, egalitarian, and persistent rituals and practices of the Spirit.[139] Only in worship the church exists fully as herself, the distance between Pentecost (on earth) and the kingdom (as the heavenly Pentecost) is overcome, and the marks of the church are complete.

The eschatological identity of the Christian community reminds the traditional marks of the church that the essence of being is in becoming. The church as movement towards the kingdom of God is *one* because unity is a mark of the kingdom to be manifested in the persistence of the church in history. Unity is the presupposition for persistence, so that continual repentance, reconciliation, and healing are liturgical acts of the church informed by and anticipating the eschatological union.[140] The church is *holy* because persistence acknowledges the existence of opposition and temptation in the world but denies them authority. The sanctity of the church is an eschatological mark of historical ecclesiality because the liturgy of the community embodies and enacts the holiness of God as both source and goal for transformation

---

[137] Vondey, 'The Denomination in Classical and Global Pentecostal Ecclesiology', 100–16.
[138] See Chan, *Pentecostal Ecclesiology*, 69; Murray W. Dempster, 'Christian Social Concern in Pentecostal Perspective: Reformulating Pentecostal Eschatology', *JPT* 1, no. 2 (1993): 51–64.
[139] Chan, *Pentecostal Ecclesiology*, 71–73. See also Simon Chan, *Liturgical Theology: The Church as Worshipping Community* (Downers Grove, IL: IVP Academic, 2006).
[140] Yong, *The Spirit Poured Out on All Flesh*, 138.

and redemption.[141] Since the church is the continuity between the present and the future creation, the universality of the kingdom demands the persistent realization of catholicity in the particularities of history. The church is *catholic* because as eschatological gift the universality of the church is already realized at Pentecost in the outpouring of the Spirit on all flesh yet takes shape historically through the expansion of the diversity of gifts. The church is *apostolic* because this eschatological expansion towards the coming kingdom cannot take shape apart from the unbroken persistence of vocations, beliefs, and practices embodied in the liturgy. Apostolicity is the faithfulness and continuity of the whole church with Christ anointed with and anointing with the Holy Spirit. Oneness, holiness, catholicity, and apostolicity are the marks of the church because they stand between the earthly Pentecost and the heavenly Pentecost as persistent eschatological signposts for the coming of God.

---

[141] Castelo, 'The Improvisational Quality of Ecclesial Holiness', 89–92; Alexander, 'The Holiness of the Church', 275–77.

11

God

Pentecost, Altar, and Doxology

The previous chapters have charted the course of Pentecostal theology in the light of the full gospel. The narrative of the full gospel presented in the first part of this volume has served as a lens for offering in the second part a constructive proposal for a Pentecostal theology of creation, theological anthropology, theology of society and culture, and ecclesiology. Implicit in the direction of these chapters is a certain doxology, the praise of God in Pentecostal worship, doctrine, and life. In this closing chapter, I therefore want to pick up my initial argument that the full gospel points to the worship of God as the beginning and end of Pentecostal theology. The metaphor of the altar adopted throughout this book specifies the significance of worship in Pentecostal life and doctrine in terms of a spiritual movement towards and mystical encounter with God in Christ through the Holy Spirit that empowers and transforms the world. Worship among Pentecostals is the anticipation and celebration (remembrance, repetition, and continuation) of Pentecost. However, despite the importance Pentecostals place on worship, a Pentecostal doxology has yet to be written.

Pentecostal theology is doxology insofar as it aims at interpreting all forms of lived experience as opportunities to glorify God. Surprisingly, Pentecostals have hardly pursued articulating their own understanding of God.[1] In order

---

[1] Biblical overviews and general introductions can be found in Keith Warrington, *Pentecostal Theology: A Theology of Encounter* (London: T & T Clark, 2008), 28–130; Larry D. Hart, *Truth Aflame: Theology for the Church in Renewal* (Grand Rapids, MI: Zondervan, 2005), 71–146; J. Rodman Williams, *Renewal Theology: Systematic Theology from a Charismatic Perspective* (Three Volumes in One), vol. 1 (Grand Rapids, MI: Zondervan, 1996), 47–81; Stanley M. Horton (ed.), *Systematic Theology*, rev. ed. (Springfield, MO: Gospel Publishing House, 1995), 117–77; French L. Arrington, *Christian Doctrine: A Pentecostal Perspective* (Cleveland, TN: Pathway

to address this lacuna, I want to bring the doxology implicit throughout this book into conversation with the doctrine of God. I suggest that the Pentecostal image of God is evident in the full gospel proclamation of Jesus as saviour, sanctifier, Spirit baptizer, healer, and coming king. Narrated under Pentecost as its core theological symbol, the witness of the full gospel to Christ is saturated with the outpouring of the Holy Spirit as the origin of the church's witness to God's redemptive activity. Since, for Pentecostals, the encounter with Christ through the Holy Spirit is always in some form an altar experience, Pentecostal doxology fundamentally engages the Pentecostal altar hermeneutics (see Chapter 1) in the concerns and practices of worship. If the altar serves as a metaphor for the human encounter with God, then it must also, to some extent, shed light on the divine initiative and activity towards creation. This approach serves as the interpretive lens for the Pentecostal story of God presented in this final chapter along the themes of salvation, sanctification, Spirit baptism, divine healing, and the coming kingdom. This chapter highlights that the goal of any doxology is not primarily epistemological but ontological and soteriological, reminding us that worship brings about transformation.[2] To speak of Pentecostal theology as doxology favours an interpretation open to the possibility that it is we who are the object of transformation by the mystery of God confronting us in the fullness of the gospel.

God who saves

The purpose of all worship is to glorify God. If we say that Pentecostal theology begins and ends with worship, we emphasize that Pentecostal theology is oriented towards an increasing experience of the glory of God.[3] The full gospel

---

Press, 1993), 85–184; Guy P. Duffield and N. N. Van Cleave, *Foundations in Pentecostal Theology* (San Dimas, CA: L.I.F.E. Bible College, 1987), 45–114.

[2] For recent theological approaches to Pentecostal doxology see Mark J. Cartledge and A. J. Swoboda (eds), *Scripting Pentecost: A Study of Pentecostals, Worship, and Liturgy* (London: Routledge, 2017); Monique M. Ingalls and Amos Yong (eds), *The Spirit of Praise: Music and Worship in Global Pentecostal-Charismatic Christianity* (University Park: Pennsylvania State University Press, 2015); Martin Lindhardt (ed.), *Practicing the Faith: The Ritual Life of Pentecostal-Charismatic Christians* (Oxford: Berghahn, 2011).

[3] For a typology of Pentecostal worship, see Peter Althouse, 'Betwixt and Between the Cross and the Eschaton: Pentecostal Worship in the Context of Ritual Play', in *Toward a Pentecostal Theology of Worship*, ed. Lee Roy Martin (Cleveland, TN: CPT Press, 2016), 265–79; Daniel Albrecht, *Rites in the Spirit: A Ritual Approach to Pentecostal/Charismatic Spirituality*, JPTS 17 (Sheffield: Sheffield Academic Press, 1999), 252–59.

identifies the distance between the beginning and the end of worship as the path of salvation: the direction of Pentecostal doxology is thoroughly soteriological (see Chapter 2). The central theological question emerging from this affirmation is what impact a soteriological doxology has on the Pentecostal doctrine of God. From the perspective of the full gospel, I suggest that the answer of Pentecostal theology points not in a general sense to 'God' but to the 'God who saves' as the starting point for articulating such a doctrine. Pentecostal worship embodies a fundamental witness to God's redemptive identity through the experience of God's redemptive activity. What is significant for Pentecostals is not immediately the experience that God saves but the revelation that God is saviour, because the latter enables the former.[4] A doxological starting point of the doctrine of God unfolds most immediately in the experience of the revelation of God as saviour.

The Pentecostal altar hermeneutic emerges from experience of the divine self-manifestation by way of a particular 'reading' of the biblical story of God.[5] Pentecostals undoubtedly seek a doctrine of God that is faithful to the biblical narrative from creation to the coming of the kingdom.[6] However, Pentecostal doxology is not in the strict sense a performance of the biblical story but aims at the experience of revelation and thus encounter with God beyond the literal text.[7] The experience of God can indeed precede the understanding that God saves. Hence, a soteriological doxology glorifies the God who saves through the experience of divine revelation in the church's worship (and its formational, devotional, communal, and spiritual functions).[8] The important hermeneutical step from the reading of the biblical texts to the encounter with God (and vice versa) is participation in the biblical story.[9] Entrance to this participation is made possible by the continuing revelation of

---

[4] See Peter Neumann, 'Whither Pentecostal Experience? Mediated Experience of God in Pentecostal Theology', *CJPCC* 3 (2012): 1–40.
[5] See Rickie D. Moore, 'Altar Hermeneutics: Reflections on Pentecostal Biblical Interpretation', *Pneuma* 38, no. 2 (2016): 148–59; R. Hollis Gause, 'The Nature and Pattern of Biblical Worship', in Martin, *Toward a Pentecostal Theology of Worship*, 139–51.
[6] See Amos Yong, *Renewing Christian Theology: Systematics for a Global Christianity* (Waco, TX: Baylor University Press, 2014), 297–326.
[7] Wolfgang Vondey, *Beyond Pentecostalism: The Crisis of Global Christianity and the Renewal of the Theological Agenda*, PM 3 (Grand Rapids, MI: Eerdmans, 2010), 71–77.
[8] Amos Yong, *Spirit-Word-Community: Theological Hermeneutics in Trinitarian Perspective* (Eugene, OR: Wipf and Stock, 2002), 260.
[9] Richard D. Israel, Daniel E. Albrecht and Randal G. McNally, 'Pentecostals and Hermeneutics: Texts, Rituals, and Community', *Pneuma* 15, no. 1 (1993): 137–61.

God in worship, doctrine, and life that captures the person and the community in the imagination of the heart and the fullness of its affective, spiritual, psychological, social, political, and public dimensions.[10] For Pentecostals, it is the particular experience of God identified with Pentecost that opens the ability to participate in the biblical story and thus to identify God as the God who saves.

The explorations of the full gospel in part one of this volume have shown how Pentecost serves as a hermeneutical entry point for interpreting the encounter with God. The experience of Pentecost holds hermeneutical primacy for Pentecostals in a way that deeply influences their theological perceptions.[11] At the altar, the story of redemption is read 'backwards' through Pentecost in order to arrive at a doxology that follows the path of experience as a faithful interpreter of the biblical revelation.[12] At the core of this altar hermeneutics, the experience that God is saviour identifies the centre of Pentecostal worship before arriving at a doctrine of God as Father, Son, and Holy Spirit, that is, the hermeneutical path beginning with experience has not led to a doctrine of the triune God for all Pentecostals.[13] Resolving this theological impasse between Oneness and trinitarian Pentecostals is possible only with a shared doxology.[14] I suggest that what unites Pentecostals is precisely the singular emphasis on the revelation of God as saviour: to understand God primarily as the God-who-saves speaks to the entire identity, character, and personality of God. Salvation is an ontological affair that involves God's eternal being. Because salvation is a relational act, God the saviour therefore must be described in relational terms. The result is a particular doxological emphasis that speaks to the traditional symbol of God through the symbol of Pentecost. The altar as a possibility of the continuing experience of Pentecost presents a lens with which to reconcile the traditional trinitarian language

---

[10] See Kenneth Archer, *A Pentecostal Hermeneutic: Spirit, Scripture and Community* (Cleveland, TN: CPT Press, 2009), 189–90; Yong, *Spirit-Word-Community*, 264.

[11] See Craig S. Keener, *Spirit Hermeneutics: Reading Scripture in Light of Pentecost* (Grand Rapids, MI: Eerdmans, 2016), 21–38.

[12] See Nigel Scotland, 'From the "Not Yet" to the "Now and the Not Yet": Charismatic Kingdom Theology 1960–2010', *JPT* 20 (2011): 272–90.

[13] For the Oneness position see David K. Bernard, *The Oneness of God*, rev. ed. (Hazelwood, MO: Word Aflame, 2001); Andrew D. Urshan, *The Almighty God in the Lord Jesus Christ* (Los Angeles: Andrew D. Urshan, 1919).

[14] See the 'Final Report of the Oneness-Trinitarian Pentecostal Dialogue', in *Pentecostalism and Christian Unity*, vol. 2, *Continuing and Building Relationships*, ed. Wolfgang Vondey (Eugene, OR: Pickwick, 2013), 268–90.

of doctrine with the soteriological language of Pentecostal worship.[15] To encounter God at the altar relates the worshipper to the manifold presence of God in the economy of salvation: if God is the God who saves, this designation must apply equally to the Father, the Son, and the Holy Spirit.

Despite this trinitarian affirmation, the full gospel identifies the God who saves clearly with Jesus, and most Pentecostals would not readily apply the same designation equally to the Spirit and the Father. This hesitancy stems from a lack of integration of the doctrine of the Trinity with a Pentecostal liturgy (a problem shared by other trinitarian traditions).[16] If my argument is correct that the full gospel serves to bridge this gap, then the foundational designation of Jesus as saviour speaks to all soteriological affirmations of the full gospel so that the experience of Jesus as saviour is also an experience of Jesus as sanctifier, Spirit baptizer, divine healer, and coming king. This full-gospel doxology outlined in part one of this book is a consequence of the fullness of the experience of Jesus anticipated in Pentecostal worship. Jesus clearly possesses doxological primacy in Pentecostal theology, yet the experience of salvation as participation in the divine life begins not with the Son but with the Spirit.[17] Interpreted through the doxology of Pentecost (Acts 2:14–40), the crucified and resurrected Jesus is 'exalted to the right hand of God' where he 'received from the Father the promised Holy Spirit and has poured out what you now see and hear' (v. 33). This doxology oriented at the biblical story is interpreted through the present experience of divine revelation at the altar as gaining access to the redemptive work of the Father through Jesus Christ in the Holy Spirit (see Eph. 2:18). In other words, the experiential affirmation of Jesus as the God who saves begins with the Spirit.

The experience of the Holy Spirit is also the experience of Christ and the Father because the Holy Spirit is the Spirit of Pentecost, the Spirit of Christ, and the Spirit of creation.[18] Nonetheless, from the perspective of Pentecost,

---

[15] See Jason Vickers, *The Making and Remaking of Trinitarian Theology* (Grand Rapids, MI: Eerdmans, 2008).

[16] See Stephen Dove, 'Hymnody and Liturgy in the Azusa Street Revival, 1906–1908', *Pneuma* 31, no. 2 (2009): 242–63. Attributing the problem to an overtly biblical theology is Gabriel, 'This Spirit is God', 75–76.

[17] See Peter Neumann, *Pentecostal Experience: An Ecumenical Encounter*, PTM 187 (Eugene, OR: Pickwick, 2012), 100–61.

[18] See William P. Atkinson, *Trinity after Pentecost* (Eugene, OR: Pickwick, 2013), 22; Steven M. Studebaker, *From Pentecost to the Triune God: A Pentecostal Trinitarian Theology*, PM 6 (Grand Rapids, MI: Eerdmans, 2012), 67.

God is 'experienced' and 'understood' most immediately in the reception of the Holy Spirit before Pentecostals interpret the experience and understanding of Christ and the Father. The Spirit enables our knowledge and participation in the saving work of Christ who is the fullest revelation of the Father.[19] Put differently, Pentecost gives access to the order of redemptive history in reverse – the order of interpretation follows the order of experience: the presence of the Spirit directs to the presence of Christ and so also to the presence of the Father.[20] The distinctiveness of these presences may only be evident in the reflection on the experience of divine love, personified by the Holy Spirit, incarnated by the Son, and shared by the Father.[21] Yet, this epistemology of the grace of God follows a distinctive ontological order: the Father sent the Spirit of his Son into our hearts (Gal. 4:6). While the love of the Father is manifested most fully in Christ in bodily form and poured out into our hearts by the Spirit (Rom. 5:5), the Father remains 'in unapproachable light' (1 Tim. 6:16) as the most fully transcendent. Similarly, the physical presence of Christ is not experienced immediately in worship, but the presence of the ascended and exalted Son is mediated by the Spirit.[22] Moreover, the Incarnation of the Son is a particular form of immanence in which God overcomes his radical otherness through human embodiment, whereas the immanence of the Spirit, as we have seen, possesses no particular form, so that the Spirit can be the presence of God in the cosmos (Chapter 7), the human being (Chapter 8), society (Chapter 9), and the church (Chapter 10). Salvation is expressed at the altar in a transformative encounter that moves from the immanent to the transcendent presence of God who saves. Put differently, worship engages three theological moments of the redemptive being of God as saviour: The Holy Spirit is the immanence of salvation, Jesus is the incarnation of salvation, and the Father is the transcendence of salvation. The distinctions of these theological experiences become evident only through the movement of

---

[19] See Yong, *Spirit-Word-Community*, 174–75.
[20] See Jim Purves, *Triune God and the Charismatic Movement: A Critical Appraisal of Trinitarian Theology and Charismatic Experience from a Scottish Perspective* (Carlisle, UK: Paternoster, 2005), 222–25.
[21] For a Pentecostal position see Amos Yong, *Spirit of Love: A Trinitarian Theology of Grace* (Waco, TX: Baylor University Press, 2012). Arguing for an indistinguishable presence is Chris E. Green, 'The Crucified God and the Groaning Spirit: Toward a Pentecostal Theologia Crucis in Conversation with Jürgen Moltmann', *JPT* 19 (2010): 127–42.
[22] Cf. Odette Mainville, *The Spirit in Luke-Acts* (Woodstock, GA: The Foundation for Pentecostal Scholarship, 2016), 66–96; Gabriel, 'This Spirit Is God', 85–93.

God 'from glory to glory' (corresponding to 2 Cor. 3:18) projecting the experiences narrated by the full gospel: salvation, sanctification, Spirit baptism, divine healing, and the reign of God are contemporary realizations of the fullness of God's eternal redemptive identity.

God who sanctifies

In the full gospel narrative, the way of salvation leads through the experience of sanctification. Typically considered from the perspective of the human being, sanctification is a transitional practice in which the person is transformed by the holiness of God and drawn closer into participation in the divine nature (see Chapter 3). Through the lens of an altar hermeneutics, I have argued that the experience of the divine presence in Pentecostal worship leads from the immanence to the transcendence of God. True transcendence, of course, is not simply the opposite of immanent presence; the transcendence of God stands above the distinction of presence and non-presence; more exactly, God's transcendence is prior to any possibility contained in the created order.[23] Moreover, if transcendence is a divine attribute, it cannot belong to the Father alone in an absolute sense but must apply to the Father, the Son, and the Spirit. Nonetheless, Pentecostal doxology manifests an acute sense for attempting to resolve the tension between divine immanence and transcendence concentrated in the experience of the revelation of God's presence.[24] God is saviour because the relational act of salvation can resolve the problem of the transcendence of God only in the experience of the presence of God's immanence. The holiness of God is for Pentecostals the synonym par excellence of divine transcendence: only God is holy (1 Sam. 2:2) and all other holiness is a derivative of the holiness of God (see Chapter 3). Considered a trait of God's transcendent being, the question emerges about what it means to speak of God ontologically as the God who sanctifies. I suggest that the

---

[23] See David Bentley Hart, 'Impassibility as Transcendence: On the Infinite Innocence of God', in *Divine Impassibility and the Mystery of Human Suffering*, ed. James F. Keating and Thomas Joseph White (Grand Rapids, MI: Eerdmans, 2009), 299–323.
[24] See Daniel Tomberlin, *Encountering God at the Altar: The Sacraments in Pentecostal Worship* (Cleveland, TN: Center for Pentecostal Leadership and Care, 2006), 1–38. For a similar argument, see Terry Cross, 'The Rich Feast of Theology: Can Pentecostals Bring the Main Course or Only the Relish?' *JPT* 8 (2000): 27–47.

answer of Pentecostal theology comes from the perspective of the divine initiative that stands at the start of Pentecostal soteriology: sanctification as the participation of creation in the divine life must be preceded and accompanied by a divine movement towards creation. Sanctification as an ontological trait of God resolves the tension between transcendence and immanence by a divine movement towards creation within the eternal being of God.

The eternal movement of God towards creation forms the presupposition for a soteriological doctrine of God. The theological principle for understanding the eternal movement of God has been articulated for much of contemporary theology in Karl Rahner's axiom that God's activity in the world reflects God's eternal being (and vice versa).[25] At the same time, Pentecost has not widely served as a point of entrance for trinitarian reflections in response to Rahner's paradigm. The traditional way to relate soteriology to the doctrine of God finds expression in the theological emphasis that the Father, the Son, and the Holy Spirit are but one principle of salvation, although each participates differently in the shared work according to a different property as person. If we want to open Rahner's paradigm for Pentecostal reflection, we must read it through the symbol of Pentecost, which allows us to say that the encounter with God the saviour is made possible by the experience of the Spirit who gives access to the redemptive activity of the incarnate Son because the Spirit poured out at Pentecost is also the Spirit in the life of Jesus.[26] The Spirit is thus essential to both Christ's redemptive work and the participation in that work by the worshipper.[27]

All acts of worship are Spirit-filled activities that function as a hermeneutical lens for approaching the revelation of God and its interpretation by the church. The theological focus of Pentecostal worship is clearly on Jesus Christ. Yet, part one of this book has shown that entrance to the work of God in Christ is given by Spirit-filled practices at the altar as the place where Pentecostals interpret and experience their own story in light of the redemptive story of God.[28] Worship is not only interpretation but participation by the Spirit in God's redemptive and sanctifying work because God is revealed

---

[25] Karl Rahner, *The Trinity*, trans. Jospeh Donceel (New York: Crossroad, 1988), 22.
[26] Studebaker, *From Pentecost to the Triune God*, 6–9.
[27] See Steven M. Studebaker, 'Pentecostal Soteriology and Pneumatology', *JPT* 11, no. 2 (2003): 248–70.
[28] Moore, 'Altar Hermeneutics', 155–57.

by the Spirit in the act of worship.[29] Furthermore, participation in worship is not a static reception of the Spirit but a dynamic development and intensifying presence of the Spirit in the human being and the community.[30] In this dynamic sense, sanctification is an experience of worship (and vice versa) as the worshipper is drawn into the holiness of God through the activity of the Spirit of Christ. The experience of the Spirit is therefore both a pneumatological and a Christological experience. In the work of the Spirit, the altar of the church is transformed into the altar of Christ and thus affords participation in Jesus's sacrifice, suffering, and death 'who through the eternal Spirit offered himself without blemish to God' (Heb. 9:14). At the same time, the altar of Christ points ahead to Pentecost and the outpouring of the Holy Spirit. This reciprocal emphasis embraces the significance of the Spirit's work in God's eternal being as the divine power enabling Jesus's sacrifice and Jesus's agency in the outpouring of the Spirit. The Spirit's agency is the sanctification of the believer which parallels the Spirit's work in the life of Jesus as the source for the Spirit's work after Pentecost.[31] Sanctification is the immanence of the Spirit at the altar of Christ which directs the worshipper in the work of the Spirit through the sacrifice of the Son to the Father. This trinitarian order becomes most explicit on the day of Pentecost.[32]

Pentecost is significant for a trinitarian doxology because with the reception of the Holy Spirit emerges most clearly the identity of the Spirit as person. The dominant evangelical Protestant position that Christ achieves salvation and the Spirit applies the benefits of salvation (i.e. sanctification) subordinates the Spirit's work to that of the Son.[33] Pentecostals are critical of this subordination because it distinguishes the Spirit as the primary agent of sanctification

---

[29] See Peter Althouse and Michael Wilkinson, 'Musical Bodies in the Charismatic Renewal: The Case of Catch the Fire and Soaking Prayer', in Yong and Ingalls, *The Spirit of Praise*, 29–44; Johnathan E. Alvarado, 'Worship in the Spirit: Pentecostal Perspectives on Liturgical Theology and Praxis', *JPT* 21, no. 1 (2012): 135–51.

[30] On the tension of ritual and worship in Pentecostalism see Andrew Mall, '"We Can Be Renewed": Resistance and Worship at the Anchor Fellowship', in Ingalls and Yong, *The Spirit of Praise*, 163–78, esp. 175.

[31] See Graham H. Twelftree, *People of the Spirit: Exploring Luke's View of the Church* (Grand Rapids, MI: Baker, 2009), 31–32; Steven M. Studebaker, 'Integrating Pneumatology and Christology: A Trinitarian Modification of Clark H. Pinnock's Spirit Christology', *Pneuma* 28, no. 1 (2006): 5–20.

[32] For a Oneness Pentecostal view on the divine economy see David A. Reed, *'In Jesus' Name': The History and Beliefs of Oneness Pentecostals*, JPTS 31 (Blandford Forum: Deo, 2008), 265–72.

[33] This was developed by Steven M. Studebaker, 'Beyond Tongues: A Pentecostal Theology of Grace', in *Defining Issues in Pentecostalism: Classical and Emergent*, ed. Steven M. Studebaker (Eugene, OR: Pickwick, 2008), 46–68; idem, 'Pentecostal Soteriology and Pneumatology', 248–70.

from the Son as the primary agent of redemption.[34] Nonetheless, the classical Pentecostal identification of sanctification and Spirit baptism as distinct works of grace subsequent to conversion has contributed to a fragmented image of the work of God at Pentecost.[35] Instead, an altar hermeneutics can be seen as joining these two elements amidst others as distinct yet complementary experiences of the full gospel. The distinctive contribution of sanctification to the Pentecostal doctrine of God is that the holiness of God demands divine transcendence. Only a transcendent God can create (*ex nihilo*) what is other than God and consecrate creation.[36] Yet, the holiness of God cannot sanctify creation in a state of absolute transcendence: the transformation of the human being by the holiness of the triune God is paralleled by a consecrating movement of the divine persons into the human person and the purification of the human being. Sanctification demands immanence through an encounter of the finite sanctity of the created being with the uncreated and infinite holiness of the divine life. From the perspective of God, overcoming the divide of holiness is possible only if God is both transcendent and immanent in relation to creation. More precisely, the divide of immanence and transcendence is bridged only in a becoming immanent (i.e. kenosis) of God. Pentecost contains this possibility of the divine self-emptying as the very presupposition for the reception of the Holy Spirit.

An appeal to the classical analogy of the Son and the Spirit as the two hands of the Father and to a trinitarian coinherence (*perichoresis*) of the divine persons serves as important reminder of the church's insistence that trinitarian theology requires a distinction but not separation of persons.[37] Pentecost identifies the experience of the triune God in the church through an immediate encounter with the Holy Spirit and a mediated encounter with the Son and the Father.[38] From the perspective of persons, Pentecost places the reception of the Spirit as an experience of immediate immanence 'before'

---

[34] Studebaker, 'Beyond Tongues', 49.
[35] See D. William Faupel, *The Everlasting Gospel: The Significance of Eschatology in the Development of Pentecostal Thought*, JPTS 10 (Sheffield: Sheffield Academic Press, 1996), 87–90.
[36] See Amos Yong, 'Oneness and the Trinity: The Theological and Ecumenical Implications of Creation Ex Nihilo for an Intra-Pentecostal Dispute', *Pneuma* 19, no. 1 (1997): 81–107.
[37] See Atkinson, *Trinity after Pentecost*, 152–57; Frank D. Macchia, *Baptized in the Spirit: A Global Pentecostal Theology* (Grand Rapids, MI: Zondervan, 2006), 120–21; Yong, *Spirit-Word-Community*, 50–59.
[38] Studebaker, 'Beyond Tongues', 62; David Coffey, *Did You Receive the Holy Spirit When You Believed? Some Basic Questions for Pneumatology* (Milwaukee, WI: Marquette University Press, 2005), 74–75, 87–88.

the experience of the mediated immanence of the Son and, ultimately, the Father. Nevertheless, the experience of the Spirit as person does not exist as an experience in its own right because the experience of the Spirit is always also the experience of the Son and the Father. More precisely, the immanence of the Spirit is realized in the world as the subsistent relation to the Son and to the Father, who by this relation participate in the presence of the Spirit. Pentecost is therefore the encounter with God as spirit (Jn 4:24) through the Holy Spirit, and the encounter with the Holy Spirit is the encounter with the spirit of the Son and the Father.[39]

Although also experienced immanently, the Father remains the most utterly 'other' person of the Trinity, whose kenotic activity occurs only through the Son and the Spirit.[40] The Father possesses no visible 'form' (Jn 5:37; also Jn 1:18; 6:46; 1 Tim. 6:16) and no proper mission but preserves his absolute holiness from the mission of the Son and the Spirit in which the Father is encountered as an immanent experience only through their kenotic movement. All sanctification stands in correlation to the absolute holiness of the person of the Father (see 1 Pet. 1:16). Experiencing the closeness of the Father in creation is therefore precisely an experience of the transcendent God made possible through the immanence of God (see John 17:20–26). A non-trinitarian Pentecostalism threatens to dissolve this distinction in a unilateral mode of being applied to God as only one divine person ('Jesus') who cannot extend from transcendence into immanence without surrendering one for the other.

In contrast, in a trinitarian Pentecostal view, the Son is revealed immanently in the 'form' of man (Phil. 2:8) through his own kenotic activity as a revelation of and yet distinct from the Father. Although the self-giving of the Son originates with the activity of the Father (Jn 3:16; Rom. 8:32), it is Christ who emptied himself (Phil. 2:7) and gave himself up (Eph. 5:2; 25; Gal. 2:20).[41] The Son is the only begotten of the Father, the Word of God made

---

[39] On the distinction see Wolfgang Vondey, 'Pneumatology from the Perspective of the Spirit: A Historical and Theological Assessment', in *Third Article Theology: A Pneumatological Dogmatics*, ed. Myk Habets (Minneapolis: Fortress, 2016), 77–96.

[40] For a proper kenosis of the Father argues Atkinson, *Trinity after Pentecost*, 130–36.

[41] This trinitarian scheme is indicated by Herbert Mühlen, 'The Person of the Holy Spirit', in *The Holy Spirit and Power: The Catholic Charismatic Renewal*, ed. Kilian McDonnell (New York: Doubleday, 1975), 11–33. For a Pentecostal adaptation see Gabriel, 'This Spirit Is God', 87–88.

flesh (Jn 1:14) so that seeing the Son is seeing the Father (Jn 14:9) and through the Son we have fellowship with the Father (1 Jn 1:1–3). Yet, the mission of the Son includes a further self-emptying to the point of death (Phil. 2:8) at which the 'holy one of God' (Mk 1:24) who was 'without sin' (Heb. 4:15) takes upon himself the sins of the world (Jn 1:29; 1 Jn 2:2) so that in the scheme of sanctification Jesus became sin for our redemption (2 Cor. 5:21). The immanence of the Son is not a static difference from the transcendent holiness of the Father but leads through a suffering of kenosis eventually to the absence of the Father on the cross (Mt. 27:46; Mk 15:34). Sanctification thus originates out of the distance of the immanent Son from the transcendent Father through which the Son of God can preserve his holiness despite taking on the sins of the world.

This relation of opposition marks the paradigm for the possibility of sanctifying creation. Participation in the proper mission of Christ is limited to the particular form of the Son's immanence as a human being and its apparent historical restriction to the time between the Incarnation and ascension. However, the immanence of the Son takes on a new form with his exaltation when Christ 'became a life-giving spirit' (1 Cor. 15:45), an event that stands between the ascension of Christ and the outpouring of the Holy Spirit (see Jn 16:7). Exalted to the right hand of God, the Father shares the outpouring of the Spirit with the Son.[42] Therefore, Pentecost can be the reception of God's Spirit, who is both the spirit of the Father (Joel 2:28; Acts 2:17) and the spirit of the Son (Gal. 4:6). In turn, sanctification as the proper mission of the Holy Spirit relates the human being to the Father through the Son (see Rom. 8:15–16). For this mission, the Holy Spirit takes on no particular form but enters as the spirit of adoption, and thus as the spirit of both the Father and the Son, into the hearts of human beings (2 Cor. 1:22). The sanctification of sinful human nature by the Holy Spirit marks a soteriological extension of the sanctifying sacrifice of the Son in which the Spirit is closer to the human spirit than the Son and the Father. This differentiation of the experience of the trinitarian persons forms the presupposition for the baptism with the Holy Spirit.

---

[42] Atkinson, *Trinity after Pentecost*, 133.

God who baptizes with the Spirit

Sanctification describes the eternal movement of God for the purpose of redemption in which the holiness of God extends from the Father through Christ and in the Spirit to creation. This principally pneumatological extension of the triune God demands the mutuality and reciprocity of the divine persons in order to preserve the eternal participation of each in the economy of salvation. The Pentecostal doctrine of Spirit baptism presupposes this movement.[43] At the same time, Spirit baptism insists on a distinct mode of receiving the divine presence: while both justification and sanctification have their origin in the indwelling Spirit, Spirit baptism marks the climax in the process of receiving the Spirit as gift.[44] This central emphasis at the heart of the full gospel raises the question what ontological significance the giving of the Spirit has for the doctrine of God. From the perspective of the human being, to be baptized *in* the Spirit connotes a 'coming' or 'falling' upon and a 'filling' with and 'receiving' of the Holy Spirit (see Chapter 4). In turn, from the perspective of God, to baptize *with* the Spirit must then denote in some form a 'going', 'outpouring', 'emptying', and 'giving away' of the Spirit. I suggest that Pentecostal theology captures the kenosis of God with the metaphor of the altar as a means to speak of the mission of God in Christ and the Spirit through which creation is transformed into a dwelling place for God's presence (see Eph. 2:22; 4:10; 1 Cor. 15:28). Pentecost is the altar of God's gift of the Spirit through which the gift of God's Son is made present to all flesh.

The altar has served throughout this book as a metaphor for the human encounter with God. Arguably, the primary direction of this metaphor is anabatic, from the human being towards God, although the direction of the second part of this volume has expanded this lens deliberately in reverse (katabatic) direction from its cosmological to anthropological, sociocultural, and ecclesiological implications. Seen from the perspective of God's redemptive activity, Spirit baptism marks a central point in the meeting of God and the human being identified by God's act of a 'baptism' with the Spirit. More

---

[43] Macchia, *Baptized in the Spirit*, 117.
[44] Ibid., 76–85.

precisely, the full gospel speaks unambiguously of Jesus as the Spirit baptizer. The Christological lens of the full gospel has served throughout this book as the core witness of Pentecostal theology. The preference for the Christological lens is primarily a result of the overwhelming soteriological focus of the Pentecostal theological narrative.[45] The historical testimony to Spirit baptism nonetheless possesses a strongly trinitarian structure: Pentecost reveals Jesus, the Spirit baptizer, as the Son of God, who anointed with the Spirit pours out this Spirit on all flesh (see Acts 2:17, 33). In turn, the Spirit poured out mediates the Son and the Father.[46] The baptism with the 'Holy Spirit' is a baptism with the 'Spirit of God' and the 'Spirit of Christ'.[47] It is the Father who has baptized the Son with the Spirit, that is, 'Spirit baptism basically describes the role of Jesus in pouring out the Spirit that comes from the Father'.[48] Hence, Spirit baptism becomes a metaphor for the life and mission of Jesus, sent by the Father, capturing his conception, baptism, transfiguration, death, resurrection, and exaltation (see Lk. 12:50).[49] In summary, the work of the Son happens principally because 'God anointed Jesus of Nazareth with the Holy Spirit' (Acts 10:38). Jesus's identity as the Spirit-bearing Spirit baptizer does not end with the ascension (his going-away) but continues beyond his return to the Father to Pentecost and his return as king.[50] However, the crucified, resurrected, and glorified Son can no longer carry out his work of redemption in the immanent mode of human flesh. The singular incarnate form of Christ changes after the resurrection by the Spirit (Rom. 8:11), so that Jesus, 'vindicated in spirit' (1 Tim. 3:16), is encountered now also in other 'forms' (Mk 16:12), more closely identified with spirit (Lk. 24:37), until Jesus, made alive in the spirit and by the Spirit (1 Pet. 3:18), is finally himself transformed into a life-giving spirit (1 Cor. 15:44–45).[51] It is this Jesus, conceived, baptized and transformed by the Spirit into spirit, who pours out the Holy Spirit at Pentecost. Having already given his human spirit for our redemption (see

---

[45] See Max Turner, 'The Spirit of Christ and 'Divine' Christology', in *Jesus of Nazareth: Lord and Christ*, ed. Joel B. Green and Max Turner (Eugene, OR: Wipf and Stock, 1999), 413–36.

[46] See Mark J. Cartledge, *The Mediation of the Spirit: Interventions in Practical Theology* PM 7 (Grand Rapids, MI: Eerdmans, 2015).

[47] Gordon Fee, *God's Empowering Presence* (Peabody, MA: Hendrickson, 1994), 835–42.

[48] Ibid., 118.

[49] See Kenneth J. Archer, *The Gospel Revisited: Towards a Pentecostal Theology of Worship and Witness* (Eugene, OR: Pickwick, 2011), 50–51; Macchia, *Baptized in the Spirit*, 118–19.

[50] Cf. Stanley M. Horton, *The Book of Acts: The Wind of the Spirit* (Springfield, MO: Gospel Publishing House, 1981), 16.

[51] Studebaker, *From Pentecost to the Triune God*, 84–87.

Mt. 27:50; Lk. 23:46; Jn 19:30),[52] Jesus at Pentecost shares with humankind his eternal spirit as an everlasting gift in the giving of the Holy Spirit (Jn 14:16, 23).

Although the Spirit of Pentecost is the spirit of the Son and of the Father, it is important to emphasize that the gift of Spirit baptism is the Holy Spirit (and not the Son or the Father). The distinction of the Holy Spirit from the Father and the Son is indispensable for the functioning of Pentecost as symbol of the outpouring of the Spirit of God, and the distinction between the Holy Spirit and the Son is indispensable for the declaration of the full gospel that Jesus is the one who baptizes with the Spirit.[53] I have argued so far that this distinction is made on grounds of the mode of divine presence. Moreover, Pentecost presupposes an exchange in the presence of the Son and the Spirit. The coming of the one is preceded by the going away of the other: Pentecost functions only because the Holy Spirit takes the place of Christ (Jn 16:7). Only with the Son exalted can the Son baptize with the Spirit (see Acts 2:33). In contrast to water baptism, the baptism in the Spirit is not an outward immersion into the reality of the Spirit but an immersion of the reality of the Spirit into the human being. The Spirit of Pentecost is present in the human being in a manner different from the presence of Christ or, more accurately, the baptism in the Spirit identifies a shift in the presence of the divine spirit in the human being.[54] The eternal mission of God begun with the Father's sending of the Son continues with Pentecost by way of the mission of the Holy Spirit towards the human spirit. In this kenotic movement of God, the presence of the Spirit intensifies in creation and in the human being (see Chapter 8). From the perspective of the human being, this intensification implies an increasing participation in the fullness of the divine presence.[55] The charismatic difference between the outpouring of and the anointing with the Spirit reflects this intensification of the divine presence (see Chapter 10). Pentecostal doxology emerges from this charismatic difference insofar as it is rooted in the kenosis of the divine persons. From the perspective of the divine persons, the

---

[52] On problematic interpretations of this notion, see William P. Atkinson, *The Spiritual Death of Jesus: A Pentecostal Investigation*, GPCS 1 (Leiden: Brill, 2009).
[53] For the difficulties of this view in Oneness Pentecostalism see Reed, '*In Jesus Name*', 279–303.
[54] See Andrew K. Gabriel, 'The Intensity of the Spirit in a Spirit-Filled World: Spirit Baptism, Subsequence, and the Spirit of Creation', *Pneuma* 34, no. 3 (2012): 365–82.
[55] See James K. A. Smith, 'The Spirit, Religions, and the World as Sacrament: A Response to Amos Yong's Pneumatological Assist', *JPT* 15, no. 2 (2007): 251–61.

intensification of the divine presence in creation speaks to the increasing of the giving away of the divine Spirit.

Although the dominant metaphor for the intensification of the Spirit's presence is the 'filling' with the Spirit, some Pentecostals tend to speak of a 'release' of the Spirit already given at regeneration.[56] From the perspective of God's activity, at least, the two ideas are complementary insofar as any filling of the human being presupposes a release of the Spirit by the Father through the Son. The traditional Pentecostal emphasis on being 'filled' with the Spirit holds perhaps greater figurative power in portraying an overwhelming presence of the divine life in the human being. In turn, the language of 'release' emphasizes that this overwhelming experience involves yet a further 'giving' and 'letting go' by God. The Father shares his right to give the Spirit with the Son,[57] and through the Son, in baptizing with the Spirit, shares this Spirit with the believer. Interpreted from the doctrine of God, this kenosis of the Spirit initiated by the Father through the Son continues with the extensive gift of the Spirit's self. The 'baptism' with the Spirit identifies the nature of this divine gift.

The baptism with the Spirit into the depth of the human being parallels the work of the Spirit in the life of Jesus. At the same time, with the gift of the Spirit at Pentecost, God is present in the church in the person of the Spirit in a way 'exceeding' the presence of God in the person of Christ. The overflow of the Spirit indicates a change not merely in the perception of divine presence but in the eternal mediation of the divine nature.[58] The Spirit's identity in sanctification resides in the Spirit's 'transitive presence'[59] as the continuing link between the divine immanence and transcendence so that the righteousness of God reaches us from the Father through Christ and in the Spirit and returns in the Spirit through Christ to the Father.[60] The Spirit's identity in Spirit baptism differs from sanctification in that the Spirit remains as gift with the human being and extends through indwelling the human person to

---

[56] Macchia, *Baptized in the Spirit*, 77. Cf. John R. Levison, 'Filled with the Spirit: A Conversation with Pentecostal and Charismatic Scholars', *JPT* 20, no. 2 (2011): 213–31 in response to the debate.
[57] Atkinson, *Trinity after Pentecost*, 132–33.
[58] See Cartledge, *The Mediation of the Spirit*, 90–98.
[59] Jim Purves, 'Water, Fire & Wind: Visiting the Roots of Pentecostal Pneumatology', *CV* 53, no. 3 (2011): 56–73.
[60] Studebaker, *From Pentecost to the Triune God*, 97–98.

the world, so that 'Spirit baptism empowers, renews, or releases the sanctified life towards outward expression and visible signs of renewal'.[61]

The Spirit continues in this personal mode of self-giving (i.e. baptism) by being both gift and giver.[62] More exactly, because the Holy Spirit is a gift given into the human being, the Spirit can continue the divine kenosis by giving to the human being the gifts of the Spirit's sanctification and power. The emphasis on Spirit baptism as power and charismatic endowment speaks primarily to the experience of the Spirit's work in the human person.[63] Viewed from the perspective of the divine kenosis, charismatic empowerment signifies a giving away and sharing of power with the human being, who receives the gifts of the Spirit for the ministry of salvation (see 2 Cor. 4:7).[64] In the exercise of spiritual gifts, the divine self-giving joins with the human self-giving and continues beyond the human being in witness and service to the world.[65] The climax of the self-giving of the Spirit is located in human empowerment as the result of the intensification of the divine presence manifested in the exercise of the gifts of the Spirit, which become a human potential despite the fact that they exceed the ability and authority of the human being.[66] The far-reaching outcome of God's baptism with the Spirit is the most immanent extension of God's eternal being through the gifts of the Spirit for the healing and reconciliation of the world.

God who heals

Spirit baptism marks a turning point in the practices of the full gospel as those who have come to the altar are transformed and empowered to leave the altar filled with the Holy Spirit. Yet, despite a dominant emphasis on the

---

[61] Frank D. Macchia, 'The Kingdom and the Power: Spirit Baptism in Pentecostal and Ecumenical Perspective', in *The Work of the Spirit: Pneumatology and Pentecostalism*, ed. Michael Welker (Grand Rapids: Eerdmans, 2006), 109–24 (119).

[62] See Craig S. Keener, *Gift & Giver: The Holy Spirit for Today* (Grand Rapids, MI: Baker, 2001).

[63] See William P. Menzies and Robert P. Menzies, *Spirit and Power: Foundations of Pentecostal Experience* (Grand Rapids, MI: Zondervan, 2000).

[64] On the sharing of divine power by the Spirit see Gabriel, *The Lord Is the Spirit*, 183–204.

[65] See Joshua D. Reichard, 'Toward a Pentecostal Theology of Concursus', *JPT* 22, no. 1 (2013): 95–114; Terry Cross, The Divine-Human Encounter Towards a Pentecostal Theology of Experience', *Pneuma* 31, no. 1 (2009): 3–34.

[66] See Nimi Wariboko, *The Pentecostal Principle: Ethical Methodology in New Spirit*, PM 4 (Grand Rapids, MI: Eerdmans, 2012), 1–41.

transformative encounter with God, Pentecostals have said virtually nothing about what it means to speak of this experience in terms of the divine Spirit indwelling the human spirit. From the perspective of human experience, those who have received the Holy Spirit are empowered to take the altars of the church into the world in order to bring the world to God. In this Spirit empowered mission, the church is a witness to the confrontation of the healing power of God with the sicknesses, sufferings, and sins of the world (see Chapter 5). The altar narrative of the full gospel suggests, that we can speak in some form of a directional intensity of God's presence in the church and the human being.[67] The Spirit-filled believer is directed and empowered by the Spirit to participate in the church's mission to the world. From the perspective of the eternal mission of God, this assertion raises the question on whether and how the immanent involvement of God in confrontation with the world affects the divine being. Contemporary theology has challenged the classical assertion of divine impassibility primarily through a focus on the suffering and death of Jesus.[68] I suggest that Pentecostal theology can speak further of the kenosis of God through the notion of divine healing. If my argument is correct that the outpouring of the Spirit extends the horizon of healing to all forms of suffering (see Chapter 9), then the divine kenosis traced thus far can be extended further to include the Spirit's participation in the suffering of creation.

Impassibility refers to the classical notion that God is not subject to involuntary passion. Pentecostal thought is divided over the possibility of divine participation in suffering. Those who uphold the notion of impassibility seek to safeguard the divine transcendence and epistemological distance between God and creation so that suffering does not modify the being of God ontologically.[69] Those who reject a strict adherence to the notion of divine impassibility wish to emphasize the immanence of God particularly evident in the outpouring of the Holy Spirit.[70] Both sides share the concern that when

---

[67] See Smith, 'The Spirit, Religions, and the World as Sacrament', 256.
[68] See Jürgen Moltmann, *The Crucified God: The Cross of Christ as the Foundation and Criticism of Christian Theology*, 40th anniversary ed., trans. Margaret Kohl (London: SCM Press, 1974, 2015).
[69] See Daniel Castelo, 'An Apologia for Divine Impassibility: Toward Pentecostal Prolegomena', *JPT* 19 (2010): 118–26; idem, *The Apathetic God: Exploring the Contemporary Relevance of Divine Impassibility* (Colorado Springs, CO: Paternoster, 2009).
[70] See Andrew K. Gabriel, 'Pentecostals and Divine Impassibility: A Response to Daniel Castelo', *JPT* 20 (2011): 184–90; Green, 'The Crucified God', 127–42; Samuel Solivan, *The Spirit, Pathos, and Liberation: Toward an Hispanic Pentecostal Theology* (JPTS 14; Sheffield: Sheffield Academic Press, 1998).

suffering is seen as an entirely static, passive, and involuntary attribute, any participation of God in suffering threatens the assurance of divine simplicity, immutability, and sovereignty. Yet, in light of the account given thus far, we can also interpret the two sides as being interested in the concurrent depiction of divine transcendence *and* immanence as joint attributes of the trinitarian pathos.

The Pentecostal approach to a theology of divine pathos emerges from the experiences and practices of suffering at the altar. However, the hermeneutical starting point for Pentecostal theological reflections is typically not suffering but healing. Many Pentecostals recognize this as a dilemma for theological reflection.[71] The expressions of suffering have their place in Pentecostal worship insofar as they are always embedded in and aimed at the practices of divine healing.[72] These practices presuppose suffering as unresolved healing for which God has provided a remedy in the atoning suffering of Christ (see Chapter 5). The full gospel speaks therefore unambiguously of Jesus as healer, yet it does so by way of a theology of atonement which operates fundamentally through the mode of divine suffering. In other words, the believer's experience of Jesus as healer passes through Jesus's experience of and victory over suffering.[73]

Pentecostal theologians have processed the notion of divine suffering in Christ almost exclusively through a theology of the cross.[74] The work of

---

[71] See Chris E. Green, 'The Crucified God and the Groaning Spirit: Toward a Pentecostal *Theologia Crucis* in Conversation with Jürgen Moltmann', *JPT* 19 (2010): 127–42; Martin William Mittelstadt, 'Spirit and Suffering in Contemporary Pentecostalism: The Lukan Epic Continues', in Studebaker, *Defining Issues in Pentecostalism*, 144–73; Veli-Matti Kärkkäinen, 'Theology of the Cross: Stumbling Block to Pentecostal/Charismatic Spirituality?', in *The Spirit and Spirituality: Essays in Honour of Russel P. Spittler*, ed. Wonsuk Ma and Robert P. Menzies (London: T&T Clark, 2004), 150–63; William W. Menzies, 'Reflections on Suffering: A Pentecostal Perspective', in Ma and Menzies, *The Spirit and Spirituality*, 141–49.

[72] See Jospeh Quayesi-Amakye, 'Christ, Evil, and Suffering in Ghanaian Christian Liturgy', *PentecoStudies* 14, no. 1 (2015): 9–41; Andrew M. McCoy, 'Salvation (Not Yet?) Materialized: Healing as Possibility and Possible Complication for Expressing Suffering in Pentecostal Music and Worship', in Ingalls and Yong, *The Spirit of Praise*, 45–59; Melvin L. Butler, 'The Weapons of Our Warfare: Music, Positionality, and Transcendence among Haitian Pentecostals', *Caribbean Studies* 36, no. 2 (2008): 23–64. See also Candy Gunther Brown (ed.), *Global Pentecostal and Charismatic Healing* (New York: Oxford University Press, 2011).

[73] Green, 'The Crucified God', 129.

[74] See Christopher A. Stephenson, 'Should Pentecostal Theology Be Analytic Theology?' *Pneuma* 36, no. 3 (2014): 246–64; Green, 'The Crucified God and the Groaning Spirit'; Kärkkäinen, 'Theology of the Cross;' Daniel Castelo, 'Moltmann's Dismissal of Divine Impassibility: Warranted?' *Scottish Journal of Theology* 61, no. 4 (2008): 396–407; Peter Althouse, *Spirit of the Last Days: Pentecostal Eschatology in Conversation with Jürgen Moltmann*, JPTS 25 (London: T&T Clark, 2003).

Jürgen Moltmann, in particular, has helped Pentecostals to see the cross as a trinitarian event of suffering: The Son suffers the loss of his life in the absence of the Father; the Father suffers the loss of his Son and thus the death of his own fatherhood; and the Spirit suffers alongside the Son and in the separation of the Son and the Father.[75] The consequence is not an unqualified rejection of divine impassibility, since the divine persons do not participate in suffering in the same manner. Rather, cast in the language of divine transcendence and immanence, the Father suffers in his transcendence as a means of assuring the most radical form of separation from his crucified Son, while the Son suffers immediately in his own suffering and in his separation from the transcendent Father. The Holy Spirit participates in the suffering of this separation because the divine Spirit is the Spirit of both the Father and the Son and thus stands between them despite their distance. Put differently, the Father and the Son suffer individually, in their respective different modes of divine presence, and jointly in the Spirit. The Spirit mediates both the immanent and transcendent suffering of God.

If Pentecostal theology indeed arrives at this conclusion, it does so through the pneumatological lens of Pentecost.[76] However, this hermeneutical choice views a theology of the cross from the perspective of the outpouring of the Holy Spirit and therefore as a consequence of the resurrection, ascension, and exaltation of the crucified Christ (see Acts 2:32–33). Hence, strictly speaking, it is not a theology of the cross reaching for a theology of glory but the reverse that characterizes the Pentecostal insistence on divine healing.[77] The divine transcendence cannot redeem the reality of sin and death in apathetic distance and total separation; healing comes out of suffering. Yet, the divine choice to redeem suffering by entering into a human form serves only to underscore that suffering is ultimately alien to God and to creation.[78] While a theology of the cross must come to terms with the notion of divine impassibility in order to explain the suffering of God in Christ, a theology of glory comes to terms with this suffering precisely by insisting on the eschatological significance of divine

---

[75] See Green, 'The Crucified God', 130–38; Stephenson, 'Should Pentecostal Theology Be Analytic Theology?' 253–54.
[76] See the discussion of immanence and transcendence in Maltese, *Geisterfahrer*, 179–225.
[77] See David J. Courey, *What Has Wittenberg to Do with Azusa? Luther's Theology of the Cross and Pentecostal Triumphalism* (London: Bloomsbury, 2015), 185–255.
[78] Cf. Castelo, 'Moltmann's Dismissal', 406.

impassibility.⁷⁹ In the voluntary separation from his Son, the Father protects the divine transcendence from the inclusion of evil, death, and sin in the divine life, while in the voluntary separation from the Father, Christ suffers the consequences of taking on the sins of the world, so that healing is mediated by the immediate suffering of the Son (1 Pet. 2:24; Isa. 53:5) in his distance from the transcendent Father. The death of the Son is the death of his impassibility; separated from the Father, the Son heals the world by dying to God and to his own transcendence. However, a theology of glory embracing the reality of the cross insists that this absolute solidarity of Christ with a suffering creation cannot find its meaning in the affirmation of suffering but must lead to its resolve.⁸⁰ If the goal of redemption is the end of all suffering (see Rev. 21:4), and in this sense impassibility, then the Son must participate in achieving this end even in his death and despite the distance from the Father.⁸¹ Moreover, the characterization of the cross in terms of the distance between the Father and the Son risks a binitarian reductionism that excludes the participation of the Holy Spirit. From the perspective of Pentecost, the distance between the impassible transcendent Father and the passion of the incarnate Son is bridged by the eternal Spirit.

In the life of Christ, both suffering and healing are signs of the Spirit's presence. The Incarnation is in some sense a form of mediated transcendence of the Son by the Spirit, so that by becoming human the Son forever surrenders his absolute transcendence. In turn, the kenosis of the Spirit is a voluntary giving of the Spirit into the immanent suffering of the Son (and of creation) as the very possibility of divine healing, so that the Spirit of the cross is the Spirit of the resurrection and the Spirit of Pentecost.⁸² Poured out on all flesh, therefore, the kenosis of the Spirit at Pentecost is oriented towards suffering because it comes out of the historical suffering of Christ and the Father for the eschatological purpose of the healing and redemption of creation.⁸³ Pentecost

---

79 See Castelo, 'Toward Pentecostal Prolegomena II: A Rejoinder to Andrew Gabriel', *JPT* 21 (2012): 168–80.
80 See May Ling Tan-Chow, *Pentecostal Theology for the Twenty-First Century* (Aldershot, UK: Ashgate, 2007), 102–4.
81 See D. Lyle Dabney, '*Pneumatologia Crucis*: Reclaiming *Theologia Crucis* for a Theology of the Spirit Today', *SJT* 53, no. 4 (2000): 511–24.
82 On the continuity of the Spirit and suffering see Martin William Mittelstadt, *The Spirit and Suffering in Luke-Acts: Implications for a Pentecostal Pneumatology*, JPTS 26 (London: T&T Clark, 2004).
83 See Peter Althouse, 'Implications of the Kenosis of the Spirit for a Creational Eschatology', in *The Spirit Renews the Face of the Earth: Pentecostal Forays in Science and Theology of Creation* (Eugene, OR: Pickwick, 2009), 155–72.

is the result of God's own overcoming the distance between the Father and the Son in the kenosis of the Spirit. Whereas the Son suffers by assuming the sins of the world, the Spirit suffers as the one who transforms the suffering on behalf of the Father and the Son. In the human experience of suffering, the Holy Spirit continues as the least objective and the most immediate presence of God in the mediated distance of suffering creation from the Son and the Father.[84] Pentecost does not abolish this distance but opens the history of the world to the activity of the eternal Spirit. Transformation and healing of the suffering creation involves the Spirit's own grieving and groaning.[85] In solidarity with the suffering world, the groaning of the Spirit is the cry of the Son to the Father for eternal redemption.

God who reigns

The outpouring of the Spirit at Pentecost marks a crucial threshold in the history of salvation as the Son baptizes the church with the Spirit of the Father. Pentecostals have taken account of this dimension of Pentecost primarily in the context of eschatological expectations that interpret the outpouring of the Spirit as a harbinger of the return of Christ.[86] Only recently, in the wake of shifting eschatological expectations, Pentecostals have begun to speak of Pentecost also as the possibility of participating in the eternal life of God.[87] The theological significance of Pentecost as symbol is therefore neither primarily Christological or pneumatological but the completion of the revelation of the triune God in history. The decisive question Pentecostal theology poses to the doctrine of God is in what sense we can speak of Pentecost as an eternal event in the divine life. The answer given by Pentecostals, I suggest, directs the attention from Pentecost to the kingdom of God. When seen not only as

---

[84] Speaking of 'mediated immediacy' is Yong, *Spirit-Word-Community*, 229; see also Maltese, *Geisterfahrer*, 198–201.

[85] Gabriel, *The Lord is the Spirit*, 125–48; Green, 'The Crucified God', 135–38.

[86] For the history of interpretation, see David William Faupel, *The Everlasting Gospel: The Significance of Eschatology in the Development of Pentecostal Thought*, JPTS 10 (Sheffield: Sheffield Academic Press, 1996).

[87] See Studebaker, *From Pentecost to the Triune God*, 87–94; Amos Yong, *In the Days of Caesar: Pentecostalism and Political Theology* (Grand Rapids, MI: Eerdmans, 2009), 331–32; Macchia, *Baptized in the Spirit*, 97; Steven J. Land, *Pentecostal Spirituality: A Passion for the Kingdom*, JPTS 1 (Sheffield: Sheffield Academic Press, 1993), 191–207.

a historical but as an eschatological category as well, Pentecost emerges as the final revelation of God's kingdom before the return of the Messiah.

The preceding reflections could be interpreted mistakenly as advocating that Pentecostal theology leans towards a form of tritheism. Indeed, the emphasis Pentecostal theology places on the economic Trinity often gives predominance to the divine persons at the neglect of reflections on the divine nature. Nonetheless, Pentecost as symbol of the outpouring of the Spirit crosses this artificial divide with a 'foundational pneumatology' that traverses conversations on the divine persons and the divine nature.[88] While the key to this conversation offered by Pentecostal theology is undoubtedly pneumatological, a reconciliation of the biblical affirmation that God by nature is spirit (Jn 4:24) with reflections on the Holy Spirit as person has been neglected in the history of pneumatology and trinitarian theology.[89] A revision of the doctrine of God from the perspective of Pentecost witnesses to a different participation of the Father, the Son, and the Spirit in the ontic structures of the world that is grounded in the divine nature as spirit. The eschatological motif of the kingdom of God clarifies the importance of this pneumatological unity envisaged in the Pentecostal image of the triune God.

Pentecostal eschatology flows from the day of Pentecost and Jesus's teachings on the kingdom of God announcing the coming of the Holy Spirit (see Acts 1:3–6). The full gospel narrates the eschatological consequences of Pentecost in the terms of an apocalyptic vision of the kingdom of God (see Chapter 6). Salvation, sanctification, Spirit baptism, and divine healing are eschatological practices because they are apocalyptic reconstructions of time and space by the Spirit of Christ in the image of the kingdom of God.[90] My description thus far of the self-giving of God and intensification of the divine presence in the world obtains coherence with the eschatological image of the kingdom as the experience of the eternal reign of God. From the perspective of the transcendent Father, the kingdom of God 'coming' means a 'sending' and 'giving' of the Son and 'outpouring' of the Spirit. The kingdom is not the static presence of God but an eternal increasing of God's immanence in the

---

[88] See Yong, *Spirit-Word-Community*, 83–118.
[89] See Vondey, 'Pneumatology from the Perspective of the Spirit', 77–96.
[90] See Wolfgang Vondey, 'The Holy Spirit and the Physical Universe: The Impact of Scientific Paradigm Shifts on Contemporary Pneumatology', *TS*70, no. 1 (2009): 3–36; idem, 'The Holy Spirit and Time in Contemporary Catholic and Protestant Theology', *SJT* 58, no. 4 (2005): 393–409.

world and in that sense always a newness of the experience of the divine transcendence in which all three divine persons participate by virtue of the one divine nature.[91] In the coming of the kingdom, God is 'already' present to the world in Christ, and even 'more already' in the Spirit at Pentecost, but does 'not yet' fill all of creation. At the same time, the kenosis of God does not lead to an empty God, and we cannot say that God becomes more immanent at the cost of forsaking the divine transcendence. We must rather say that, through the kenosis of the divine persons, humankind is taken into the divine nature as we are transformed into the image of the Son by the Spirit.[92] The path to the kingdom leads through repentance, baptism, and the gift of the Holy Spirit (Acts 2:38) because the path itself is an attribute of the divine nature.

The atonement tradition has argued that the way of salvation cannot be external to God's nature but must belong to God's self. Hence, the coming of God's kingdom is identical with the coming of God. This 'coming' is eschatological insofar as the movement of the kingdom emanates from the divine nature and does not come from within creation. Yet, since the fullness of the divine nature is present in each of the divine persons, how can theology speak of a 'coming' of God? The insistence of Pentecostal theology on the apocalyptic dimension of the kingdom can serve as an important reminder that, despite the kenosis of the Son and the Spirit, the eschatological 'arrival' of God happens unexpectedly. Conversion and transformation are appropriate categories to capture this confrontational nature of the reign of God.[93] The return of Christ is undoubtedly the central image of this apocalyptic eschatology. With the Incarnation of the Son the kingdom is already 'near' (see Mk 1:15; Mt. 4:17) albeit not as near as at his second coming (Rev. 19:11–16). In the same sense, with the coming of the Spirit the kingdom of God is 'nearer' than with the incarnation insofar as the Spirit reveals and intensifies the presence of the glorified Jesus and anticipates his return. The proleptic encounter with the kingdom in the experience of the outpouring of the Spirit is therefore also the consummation of God's work of redemption before the final arrival of the king.[94] Put differently, because the Holy Spirit poured out is the spirit of the Father and the Son, we can also speak of God's spirit as the presence of

---

[91] Macchia, *Baptized in the Spirit*, 96–97.
[92] Land, *Pentecostal Spirituality*, 199–200.
[93] Ibid., 95.
[94] Studebaker, *From Pentecost to the Triune God*, 89.

the kingdom. Jesus's exclamations that the kingdom of God is near are clearly speaking to the presence of the Spirit (Mt. 12:28) and are therefore ultimately references to Pentecost.

Pentecost as the nearness of the kingdom identifies the eschatological presence of God in a way that cannot be extended beyond the kenosis of the divine persons although it can intensify with the fullness of the kingdom.[95] In other words, the fullness of the kingdom is identical with the fullness of the divine persons. However, if the kingdom of God is the fullness of the presence of God in creation through Christ and the Spirit, then the fullness of the kingdom presupposes the eschatological continuity of the work of the cross through and beyond Pentecost.[96] For the doctrine of God, this eschatological continuity means that the giving of Christ and the Spirit are both 'once and for all' (see Heb. 10:1–18), historically completed but continuing evermore, so that Pentecost is an eternal symbol of how God relates to creation through Christ and the Spirit.[97] The central Pentecostal metaphor of the 'filling' with the Holy Spirit presupposes an eternal divine 'releasing' of salvation, sanctification, the baptism with the Spirit and healing as the realizations of the kingdom. Filled with the Spirit released by the Father and the Son, the groaning of God's Spirit in solidarity with creation stands at the core of both God's eternal kenosis *and* creation's reaching out to eternal redemption (Rom. 8:22).[98] Salvation, sanctification, empowerment, and healing are thus attributes of the filling and transformation of creation by the coming kingdom, which is the reign of the triune God.

However, from the perspective of the divine persons, the day of Pentecost still stands in discontinuity with the ultimate fullness of God's presence. The outpouring of the Spirit as the final harbinger of the kingdom in the last days still looks forward to 'the coming of the Lord's great and glorious day' (Acts 2:20). The present age represents the continuation of Pentecost and the anticipation of God's kingdom already present.[99] Yet, the continuing Pentecost still

---

[95] Viewing Pentecost as the completion of the divine kenosis is Matthew K. Thompson, 'Eschatology as Soteriology: The Cosmic Full Gospel', in *Perspectives in Pentecostal Eschatologies: World without End*, ed. Peter Althouse and Robby Waddell (Cambridge, UK: James Clark and Co., 2010), 189–204 (198).
[96] Ibid., 89–90.
[97] See Yong, *Renewing Christian Theology*, 242–47.
[98] Macchia, *Baptized in the Spirit*, 96.
[99] For different Pentecostal views on the kingdom, see Peter Althouse, *Spirit of the Last Days: Pentecostal Eschatology in Conversation with Jürgen Moltmann*, JPTS 25 (London: T&T Clark International, 2003), 61–107.

anticipates the final coming of the Lord in judgement (see Acts 2:19–20).[100] Only when the kingdom is fully present will the Son be fully revealed as king, and the glorious manifestation of the king will also be the manifestation of the full glory of the Spirit.[101] The coming of the king includes the wrath of God on those who have known but neglected the gift of Christ and the Spirit (see Heb. 2:1–4; 6:4–8; 10:26–39; 12:25–29).[102] The continuity and discontinuity of Pentecost and the kingdom meet in the return of the Spirit baptizer as the king so that Christ will then be present in unmediated immediacy as the glorified Son and in mediated immediacy through the glory of the Spirit. With the full consummation of the kingdom, there is no further intensification of the divine presence (see 1 John 3:2), and this fullness of the divine glory is eternally mediated by the divine persons in the pattern of Pentecost. Put differently, the fullness of God's glory remains mediated eternally through the Son as king and the Spirit poured out as the kingdom.[103] This is the eternal Pentecost.

In the fulfilment of the kingdom, the Spirit prepares creation for the eternal reign of the Son, and the Son hands over the kingdom to the Father (see 1 Cor. 15:22–26) so that we can speak of the new creation as the dwelling place of God (Rev. 21:3). That the Revelation of John shares a vision of this fullness of the kingdom in the terms of a 'new Jerusalem' and 'tabernacle' of God suggests continuity with the history of God's people leading to the day of Pentecost.[104] The arrival of the kingdom completes the building of God's people into the temple of the Spirit with Christ as the chief cornerstone (Eph. 2:19–22). At the same time, the presence of God in the temple will then be no longer mediated through the tabernacle and altar of the old Jerusalem. Instead, in the eternal Pentecost, the divine persons will have themselves taken the place of the altar. Worship will then mean the experience of the glory of God through participation in the eternal reign of the divine persons in the manner of Pentecost – the way to which is the fullness of the gospel.

---

[100] See Matthew K. Thompson, *Kingdom Come: Revisioning Pentecostal Eschatology*, JPTS 37 (Blandford Forum, UK: Deo, 2010), 123–26.
[101] Thompson, 'Eschatology as Soteriology', 201.
[102] Yong, *Renewing Christian Theology*, 246.
[103] Macchia, *Baptized in the Spirit*, 95–107.
[104] See John Christopher Thomas and Frank D. Macchia, *Revelation*, The Two Horizons New Testament Commentary (Grand Rapids, MI: Eerdmans, 2016), 365–66; R. Hollis Gause, *Revelation: God's Stamp of Sovereignty on History* (Cleveland, TN: Pathway, 1983), 265.

Conclusion

Living the Full Gospel

The present volume on Pentecostal theology has identified Pentecost as the core theological symbol of the movement. The logic of Pentecost as symbol has unfolded along the lines of a narrative called the full gospel. In the presentation of this narrative in the first part of this book, I have focused on the particular practices of Pentecostals concentrated at the altar and how these practices relate to Pentecostal doctrine. The second part applied this method to a constructive exploration of Pentecostal perspectives on creation, humanity, society, the church, and the doctrine of God. The intention of this process was to show that the full gospel represents both a comprehensive narrative descriptive of Pentecostal rituals and practices and a framework for the constructive and systematic articulation of Pentecostal theology. The surprising conclusion we can draw from this exercise is that Pentecostal theology is at heart a liturgical theology.

From a liturgical perspective, the first part of this volume has presented the full gospel as the shared 'text' of Pentecostal theology: salvation, sanctification, Spirit baptism, divine healing, and the coming kingdom form the narrative structure of Pentecostal liturgy. At the same time, the chapters have also paid attention to semiotic concerns, variants, and developments in the narrative, with particular interest in the transformations generated by the practices. The second part of the book continued to follow the fivefold structure of the full gospel adopted in this volume as the narrative of Pentecostal liturgy but leaving behind purely synchronic and structural concerns by turning instead to the reality beyond the literal narrative. Shifting to what might be seen as a poststructuralist discourse of Pentecostal liturgy, I have raised speculative questions about the implications, continuities, and discontinuities of the full gospel, which go beyond the immediate concerns of the narrative. This method was adopted in order to avoid misrepresenting the full gospel as a fixed text, hard theological boundary or dogmatic system for a movement widely seen as the very disallowance of creeds, strict rituals, and rigid liturgies. More importantly, this direction beyond the form and content of the liturgy highlights that Pentecostal theology is doxology only insofar as it is able to interpret all forms of lived experience as opportunities to glorify God. Consequently, Pentecostal theology as liturgical theology is a hermeneutical exercise that aims to make explicit theologically the image of God in the worship of the people: the full gospel is essentially a Pentecostal doxology oriented around the altar. The strict motivation for Pentecostal worship exists in neither the call to nor the release from the altar (although both constitute the boundaries of the Pentecostal liturgy), but in what is articulated in this volume as taking place (mystically) between both practices: at the heart of Pentecostal theology stands the glory of God. The full gospel as the narrative of this encounter at the altar is not an abstraction of particular ideas but a testimony to transformative events on the way of salvation. In the language of Pentecostalism, the rationale for worship, the key event, and thus the motivation for Pentecostal theology, can be articulated with a single word: Pentecost.

That Pentecost forms the core symbol of Pentecostalism has not been taken seriously for an articulation of Pentecostal theology. Certainly, the importance of Pentecost for the self-identification of Pentecostalism is undisputed (even if only as a namesake for labelling the movement). Yet, for the most part, Pentecost as a hermeneutical lens has been reduced to a reference point defined either by Scripture (thus identifying Pentecostal theology as apostolic biblicism), history (identifying Pentecostal theology as primitivist restorationism) or experience (identifying Pentecostal theology as charismatic reductionism). While these references may explain how Pentecostals look at Pentecost (through the apostolic, primitivist, charismatic lens), they do not identify how Pentecost functions for the development of Pentecostal doctrine and thus yield a distorted image of Pentecostal theology. Instead, the chapters of this book have shown the interdependence of (1) Pentecost as the theological symbol of Pentecostal theology, (2) the full gospel as the theological narrative of this symbol, and (3) the altar as the liturgical heart of this narrative to support the central proposal that Pentecostal theology reaches deep into the heart of Pentecost. Into this focus we can integrate the biblical, historical, experiential, and doctrinal concerns of Pentecostals and articulate the three core dimensions of Pentecostal theology: the symbol of Pentecost, the narrative of Pentecostal theology, and the Pentecostal liturgy.

The symbol of Pentecost

Every symbol points beyond itself to another reality in which it participates. Every symbol invites participation. At first hand, Pentecost points to a particular experience of God. However, to label 'God' a core symbol of Pentecostal theology is not sufficient in itself to distinguish the Pentecostal tradition from other theological confessions. Moreover, Pentecostals have not widely engaged the notion of symbol. If the account of Pentecostal theology given in this volume can be trusted, what is significant for Pentecostals is that principally Pentecost can be seen as a symbol for God's outpouring of the Holy Spirit and for the experience, interpretation, and response of the human being to God's redemptive activity. The definition of a religious symbol must therefore engage the dimension of worship in a significant manner: Pentecost as symbol (1) cannot be replaced (2) because it participates in the worship of God and thus (3) points to a new level of reality beyond ourselves (4) that reveals hidden dimensions within our own being corresponding to that new reality, (5) which cannot be produced intentionally (6) and which express the pilgrimage of the community.[1] These dimensions identify the crucial conditions for designating Pentecost as the theological symbol of Pentecostalism made evident throughout this volume.

(1) Pentecost as symbol identifies the encounter with God made possible by the outpouring of the Holy Spirit. The full gospel describes this symbol as an encounter with Jesus Christ as saviour, sanctifier, Spirit baptizer, divine healer, and coming king. To replace Pentecost with another symbol (e.g. the Holy Spirit, Spirit baptism, glossolalia, etc.) would fundamentally alter

---

[1] This is an adaptation of the definition of symbol in Paul Tillich, *Dynamics of Faith* (New York: Harper & Row, 1957), 42–43. For my own engagement with religious symbols see Wolfgang Vondey, *People of Bread: Rediscovering Ecclesiology* (New York: Paulist Press, 2008), 13–35.

the narrative and change the identity of the reality in which Pentecostal theology aims to participate. Jesus is undeniably the subject of the full gospel but not its symbol. Despite its strong focus on the redemptive work of Christ, Pentecostal theology is not simply identical with Christology. Yet, to replace Pentecost would alter the manner in which the Pentecostal witness to Christ is experienced and interpreted through the symbol of Pentecost, namely, existentially with reference to the outpouring of the Holy Spirit. Here, also, Pentecost maintains its significance, since the Holy Spirit can function as symbol of Christ only in the terms of a particular experience of the Spirit in the life of Jesus and its interpretation (i.e. Spirit-Christology), which does not function apart from the event of Pentecost and its experience and interpretation by the church. Pentecostal theology is not synonymous with pneumatology, since Pentecostal theology is determined by Pentecost as symbol of Christ before its focus on the Holy Spirit. As symbol, Pentecost is determinative for the entire hermeneutical focus of Pentecostal thought and praxis on the revelation of God through Jesus Christ and the Holy Spirit.

As a symbol of revelation, the fullness of that reality we name 'Pentecost' always transcends the religious, confessional, and embodied character of Pentecostalism. The first part of this book has illustrated how the symbol of Pentecost informs and transcends the concrete biblical interpretations, doctrines, and practices of Pentecostals. Nonetheless, without Pentecost, the narrative that informs Pentecostal theology collapses and is dispersed among individual elements unable to carry Pentecostal doctrines beyond isolated concerns. Spirit baptism, speaking with tongues, divine healing, and other dominant concerns are consequences of Pentecost and apart from that symbol represent only an addendum to other theological narratives. The second part of this book has suggested how Pentecost can function as a comprehensive symbol for a diversity of broad theological concerns that participate in the reality of that symbol. Pentecost as symbol identifies the outpouring of the Holy Spirit in terms of radical experiences of the self and the community that together shape Pentecostal perceptions of reality. In each of the chapters of the second part, and in each of the sections of these chapters, I have identified the central questions and concerns emerging from Pentecost as symbol. The resulting answers should demonstrate that a theological narrative constructed around Pentecost can indeed be articulated.

(2) Pentecost as symbol is not primarily a conceptual tool or hermeneutical lens or representative event. Pentecost is not the signpost of Pentecostal theology pointing to Pentecost as the reality beyond Pentecostalism. In other words, Pentecostal theology is not disconnected from Pentecost so that Pentecost as symbol functions to establish an empirical link between the event and the movement. Rather, Pentecostal theology emerges from Pentecost as the historical event and tangible experience of which the symbol is not an added dimension but an existential expression. The chief implication of this emphasis is that Pentecostal theology in the present can never be an abstraction of, but must always remain, a participation in the event it identifies as 'Pentecost'. With part one of this book I have accentuated the participatory nature of Pentecostal theology through the language of verbs. Pentecost is not only the name for the event identified with God's outpouring of the Spirit but an active participation in that event. Consequently, the doing of Pentecostal theology cannot be accomplished without the possibility of participating in the reception of the Spirit. This participation in a Pentecost for our times relies on the participation of the historical Pentecost in God's outpouring of the Spirit, so that Pentecost as symbol today must be a perpetual principle of the gospel rather than a singular or multiplied event. The conditions for participation in this principle are narrated theologically in terms of the possibilities of being saved, sanctified, baptized in the Spirit, healed, and commissioned for the coming of God's kingdom. These possibilities exist not because the necessary conditions for participation are found among Pentecostals (in an exclusive sense) but because Pentecostals are those who participate (in an inclusive sense) in shaping the conditions for the possibility of the event. The practices of this participation are concentrated in worship at the altar. Participation in Pentecost means worship. Worship is the overarching referent of all Pentecostal symbols and therefore the underlying motivation for Pentecostal theology.

(3) Pentecost is the indispensable and irreplaceable symbol of Pentecostal theology because it points to a new level of reality: salvation, sanctification, Spirit baptism, healing, and the coming kingdom are experiences beyond ourselves otherwise unreachable. As event, Pentecost marks a new revelation of God's Spirit in the world: the tongues and prophecies, sounds and sights of Pentecost cannot be anticipated. As symbol, this new revelation

confronts theology with what stands beyond it and has to be expressed in ways that exceed existing terms of theological articulation. The theological struggle of Pentecost, visible in the biblical records, is echoed in the symbol of Pentecost: because what happens at Pentecost is a new revelation, taking Pentecost as theological symbol accepts the confrontation with this newness in terms of an encounter with the Spirit. To engage in Pentecostal theology therefore requires that other theological symbols (e.g. cross, resurrection, redemption) are submitted to the revelation of Pentecost and transformed by the possibility of a new encounter with God. Catholic, Eastern Orthodox, and Protestant theologies cannot engage Pentecostal theology without being fundamentally transformed by the challenge of Pentecost and its call to the altar of worship. Because this new reality always escapes us as continuing possibility, Pentecostal theology has no recourse in triumphalism. The worship of God is forever a calling of Pentecost as symbol that can only be lived in the perpetual experience of Pentecost as event. Both as symbol and event, Pentecost calls for further theological exploration.

(4) Worship as the principal outcome of Pentecostal theology points to the existential, affective, and spiritual dimensions of Pentecost. As an entirely new reality beyond ourselves, Pentecost confronts us because it reveals new dimensions corresponding to that reality hidden within our own being. For those engaging in Pentecostal theology, this means that to take Pentecost seriously as theological symbol involves taking seriously theology as doxology. The interiority of Pentecost cannot be reduced to psychological or physiological functions; the outpouring of the Spirit produces affective and spiritual transformations which yield participation in the liturgy of worship. This subjective character of Pentecost represents one of the principal challenges to engaging with Pentecostal theology: while Pentecostal theology can be done by everyone who accepts Pentecost as symbol of a new revelation, it remains incomplete without the experience of Pentecost within ourselves. Although the symbol of Pentecost is the outpouring of the Spirit on all flesh, only those who receive the Spirit can participate in that reality. However, it is precisely Pentecost as a symbol within ourselves that keeps Pentecostal theology from becoming an exclusivist and triumphalist exercise. As long as Pentecost remains an external event confronting us from beyond ourselves, Pentecostal theology remains elusive. The altar of Pentecost is not accessible

unless we find it within ourselves to enter the way of salvation by way of the Spirit of Christ. Only when the possibility of Pentecost confronts us from within our own being can Pentecost as symbol be the existential possibility of theology. For these reasons, Pentecost can neither be produced intentionally nor invented by any theological agenda. Through Pentecost we become aware of our participation in the divine life in a way not possible through other symbols.

(5) Pentecost as symbol is not a conscious construct of the Pentecostal community or of individuals. Although the practices of Pentecost are shaped intentionally and function as the church's liturgy, the community is reduced to waiting and tarrying for the outpouring of the Spirit. The event can be anticipated and reasonably constructed from the revelation received before Pentecost, yet these data provide only the means for receiving and not for creating the event. Pentecost comes into existence with the reception of the Spirit by the church, which originates in worship with the outpouring of the Spirit. That Pentecost as symbol cannot be produced intentionally but comes from the unexpected collective pathos of the community in which it is manifested ('Pentecostals') speaks to the importance of worship as the primary expression of the communal experience ('Pentecost'). Many of the problems in the development of doctrine among Pentecostals, highlighted throughout this book, suggest that they spring from intentional attempts to (re)create theological symbols apart from the collective liturgy. The nuances and variances in Pentecostal rituals and practices form an important step towards identifying the scope and terrain of Pentecostal theology. While knowing (and practicing) this liturgy cannot produce the theological symbol, the path towards a unified Pentecostal hermeneutic and constructive future leads inevitably through a participatory study of the Pentecostal liturgy.

(6) An important commentary on the previous aspect is the emphasis that symbols change and can also cease to function. Pentecost as symbol creates Pentecostal theology and is nourished by the liturgy of the Pentecostal community. Yet, symbols also express the pilgrimage of the community from where they arose and, transferred to other cultures and communities, can fail to speak with their original clarity or cease to function when they no longer yield an appropriate response. Since Pentecost as symbol is neither the invention nor exclusive possession of the Pentecostal community but belongs

to the whole church, the historical neglect and inaccessibility of Pentecost in some Christian traditions speaks to the dying of the symbol. Where salvation, sanctification, baptism in the Spirit, divine healing, and the coming kingdom do not (any longer) produce response, Pentecost cannot function as theological symbol. Even within Pentecostalism, the weaknesses, divisions, and debates of Pentecostal theology are witness to the ongoing transformation of the traditional rituals and practices of the group where they originally found expression and to their substitution with other practices not directly related to or influenced by the symbol. The unprecedented worldwide growth of Pentecostalism should not give the impression that the movement can afford a triumphalist attitude towards its own symbols. For these reasons, the present volume alerts the theological community as much to the symbol of Pentecost as to the importance of the community receiving this symbol. As symbol, Pentecost cannot function apart from a receptive community. The life of Pentecost as symbol of the Pentecostal movement depends heavily on the traditioning of the symbol. Symbols, however, cannot be handed on as pure symbols to subsequent generations; the tradition of Pentecost as symbol demands the continuity of the event and the continuing recognition of its experiences by the community. Since Pentecostalism is a global community, the full gospel elaborated as the core narrative of Pentecostal theology must also be able to speak to Pentecostals (and others) around the world. This book has provided a general narrative for the traditioning of Pentecost in the form of the full gospel. The survival of Pentecost as symbol of Pentecostal theology depends on the survival of the collective narrative of the group in which Pentecost has emerged as symbol.

The narrative of Pentecostal theology

One of the challenges of proposing with Pentecost an innate symbol of Pentecostal theology is whether all Pentecostal theological currents and concepts can be translated into (or out of) this symbol. Continuing theological discussions may not always directly anticipate, use or embed this symbol explicitly in the conversation. Intimately related to this challenge is the question to what extent a symbol also reflects ordinary Pentecostal theology in the streets. For this reason, I have argued that a theological symbol cannot function without a corresponding theological narrative. Pentecost as the story of God who pours out the Holy Spirit is told in Scripture through narrative, including prophecy, preaching, tongues, and metaphors. Narrative expands and articulates symbol. Yet, although Pentecostals embrace Pentecost as their core theological symbol, Pentecostal theology has been slow to develop a corresponding theological narrative. I have argued that the full gospel is the narrative of Pentecost. More precisely, the full gospel is a particular narrative concerned with the recovery of the biblical revelation as the universal story of God revealed in Jesus Christ: its particularity lies in the insistence that the fullness of the gospel demands the inclusion of Pentecost as an event identifying the eternal outpouring of the Holy Spirit. The theological articulation of the full gospel marks an attempt to overcome the reduction of the gospel to a purely biblical narrative (however understood and interpreted) that might obscure considerations of how this narrative can function historically, theologically, liturgically, culturally, and ethically. The coherence of Pentecost as symbol of Pentecostal theology is rooted in the articulation of the Pentecostal narrative.

Pentecost functions as symbol only as long as the full gospel as narrative retains its power to direct Pentecostals towards the story of God in the light of Pentecost. Although the symbol does not derive from the story, Pentecostal theology has suffered the poverty of its symbol(s) primarily because of a lack of development of its core theological narrative. This book has proposed not only that Pentecostal theology possesses a coherent and comprehensive theological narrative but that this narrative encompasses Pentecostal doctrine, liturgy, and worship. The grammar and logic of the full gospel has been presented in the first part of this volume along the theological metaphor of the altar: the full gospel is essentially an altar narrative. This insight has led to the portrayal of the Pentecostal narrative as drawing worshippers into the story of God through a call to, tarrying at, transformation, release from, and return to the altar. In the language of verbs, the full gospel can be stated succinctly: saved, sanctified, baptized with the Holy Spirit, healed, and commissioned for the kingdom! Taking these popular expressions of Pentecostal piety seriously, the full gospel speaks to the subjective, affective, embodied, cultural, spiritual, and ecclesial configurations of the Pentecostal imagination. Further work in these areas will not only have to clarify the details of the Pentecostal story neglected in this volume, it will also have to provide direction for the global expansion of the Pentecostal narrative, which always remains open to the fullness of the revelation of God.

The full gospel is in the first place a theological narrative oriented towards doxology; its purpose is to direct to the worship of God. Hence, Pentecostal theology embraces the conviction that without a full narrative of the gospel, Christian worship of God is incomplete. The soteriological direction of the full gospel emphasizes that for Pentecostals participation in worship is not a consequence of but presupposition for participation in the fullness of salvation. The central concern of the full gospel is to direct our soteriological vision and activities to all possibilities of participating in the redemption of the world created with the outpouring of the Spirit at Pentecost. The language and character of the full gospel are therefore never exclusive: salvation, sanctification, Spirit baptism, divine healing, and the coming kingdom are invitations to a shared soteriological narrative. The full gospel invites personal story and testimony, yet it also serves as a corrective communal story for Pentecostals, since the plot of the full gospel is global, diverse, and inclusive. The second part of this volume has expanded this story towards cosmological, anthropological, sociocultural, ecclesial, and doxological extensions of the original narrative. The contours of this broadened narrative will need to be filled in with the colours of robust theological inquiry without losing sight of the core motifs of the Pentecostal story and yet with a vision for overcoming any sectarian narrowness that would turn Pentecost in on itself as the exclusive centre of the gospel. If the themes identified in this volume give rise to a distinctive and relevant gospel, then Pentecost as symbol allows and invites openness to different contexts, local and global dialects. Nonetheless, these variations of the Pentecostal story should not subtract from but only add to its hospitality as a 'full' gospel.

Designating the Pentecostal story as 'gospel' points to a particular function and authority of the narrative. As gospel, the story of Pentecost speaks to the historical narrative of the Christian church. As historical narrative, the full gospel is a telling of the Christian gospel through the perspective of Pentecost. Simply put, the chief contribution of the full gospel is its insistence on Pentecost as a lens for telling the gospel of Jesus Christ. That the full gospel gives prominence to experiences of the Holy Spirit must consequently become subject of further theological pursuit for understanding the fullness of the Pentecostal witness. At the very least, the designation as gospel indicates that Pentecostal theology seeks more than narrative and story-telling. While Pentecost as symbol already participates in the reality which it identifies as the lens for reading the gospel of Christ, the concern of the full gospel is to tell the story of that participation in order to enable our own participation in the event. Pentecost, with its diversity of tongues, bewilderment of the community and unrestrained manifestations of the Spirit, resists the distortion of revelation through overt focus on a single perspective or agenda. As gospel, the Pentecostal story remains unambiguously a testimony to the redemptive activity of God in Jesus Christ. Yet, the importance of Pentecost is precisely that it makes available the universal possibility of participating in the gospel of Christ through many entrances into a life in the Spirit. Pentecostals narrate the world through participation, celebration, and practices that tell of the possibilities of redemption opened with Pentecost. The full gospel is in this sense a form of living the Christian life that demands our confrontation with the fullness of the revelation of God. Symbol and narrative are not themselves the means to participation in this fullness. Rather, Pentecostal theology insists that the only way to participate in the fullness of the gospel is by living it. In practice, the full gospel is not merely story but liturgy.

The Pentecostal liturgy

The chief conclusion of this book is that Pentecostal theology represents a liturgical tradition oriented around the altar. The full gospel forms the narrative of a Pentecostal liturgy that makes possible the participation in Pentecost as symbol of the outpouring of the Holy Spirit. That Pentecostal theology is therefore liturgical theology is central to its recognition and integration in other theological traditions. The long-lasting and persistent denial that Pentecostalism is a liturgical tradition, and the consequent lack of attention paid to developing and interpreting these liturgical qualities, is largely responsible for the slow development of and late ecumenical engagement with Pentecostal theology. The further development of Pentecostal theology, systematically and contextually, practically, and methodologically, depends on a deeper understanding of the liturgical qualities of Pentecostalism as a religio-cultural tradition. The 'ordinary' of the Pentecostal liturgy, so to speak, is formed by the altar call and response rite: the call to the altar, the tarrying at the altar, the transformation at the altar, the release from the altar, and the return to the altar.

The first part of this volume integrated these elements of the altar liturgy into a programmatic altar hermeneutics of Pentecostal theology embodied through the central motifs of the full gospel: salvation as praxis, sanctification as ritual, Spirit baptism as sacrament, divine healing as sign and wonder, and the coming kingdom as mission of the church. The surprising insight gleaned from these characterizations of the core elements of Pentecostal theology is that support could be offered from within a wide range of Pentecostal rituals, practices, and beliefs. This broad support suggests that the altar at the centre of the Pentecostal liturgy provides an underlying thematic unity for studying, interpreting, and ordering Pentecostal practices, rituals, sacraments, and other forms of embodied experiences narrated by the full gospel and directed towards participation in Pentecost. At the same time, although it can be seen as a hermeneutical metaphor, the altar remains at the core a doxological praxis. The study of Pentecostal theology as a liturgical task must therefore be submitted to an understanding of the complexities of Pentecostal worship. A phenomenology of the Pentecostal altar, as I have attempted it throughout this volume, demands further research and attention to nuances and discrepancies with the homogeneous account given here for the sake of offering a programmatic proposal. Pentecostal theology must ultimately be able to give a comprehensive account of Pentecostal doxology.

The second part of this book expanded the proposal of a liturgy of the altar towards a theological metaphor shaping Pentecostal cosmology, theological and sociocultural anthropology, ecclesiology, and doxology. In the terms of this metaphor, creation appears as the cosmic altar of redemption, sanctification, empowerment, transformation, and eschatological mission. Humankind is created to embody the image of God to creation through the reception of the Holy Spirit. And with this reception, the domain of Christ extends into the cities and public squares to enable a cosmopolitan redemption as the altars of the church become the altars of the world. The marks of the church portray the altar as the principal meeting place for the confrontation with good and evil, God and Satan, the divine and the demonic, the old and the new creation. At the heart of the church's liturgy, the altar calls the world to God. Only in worship does the church exist fully as herself, and God is manifested as saviour, sanctifier, baptizer, healer, and king.

The book ends with a return of the liturgy to the symbol of Pentecost. Not all worship is embodied liturgy; the full gospel always transcends the materiality of Pentecostal theology towards the prospect of an immediate encounter with God. Pentecost as symbol of this encounter always remains a possibility that cannot be prescribed fully in liturgical activities. The playfulness of Pentecostal theology indicated at the start of this book has been given new contours throughout: what Pentecostals play is Pentecost, its logic is that of the full gospel and its playing field is the Pentecostal liturgy. The ludic character of Pentecostal theology remains yet to become the subject of sustained theological analysis. At a minimum, my articulation of the character of Pentecostal theology as play should aid in rejecting this volume as a strict programmatic proposal for doing Pentecostal theology. No unyielding fivefold structure and ordering of doctrine is the intention of this book but rather the longing to escape this order through worship as the constant opportunity to break out of the limitations of pathos, beliefs, and practices. Put in this perspective, the full gospel identifies the longing of God that salvation, sanctification, Spirit baptism, divine healing, and the coming kingdom become the longing of creation for the sake of its eternal redemption. The way to the fulfilment of this longing is marked by Pentecost as the symbol of eternal pilgrimage in the Spirit of Christ to the fullness of fellowship with God.

****

Pentecost symbolizes the pathos of the Pentecostal movement, the full gospel narrates Pentecostal beliefs, and the Pentecostal liturgy holds together the array of traditions, rituals, and practices of the Pentecostal community. Each element of this triad of pathos, belief, and praxis mutually intersects and conditions the other to create through symbol, narrative, and liturgy what is labelled with this book as 'Pentecostal theology'. This kind of Pentecostal theology is not a system closed in on itself, no circular movement satisfied with its intersecting sources. Rather, each element contributing to the whole is a pathway to the worship of God. Orthopathy, orthodoxy, and orthopraxy, when in tune with the Spirit, are elements of doxology and thus the ultimate purpose of theology. Pentecostal theology calls us to the altar where salvation, sanctification, Spirit baptism, divine healing, and the coming kingdom are never ends in themselves but pathways to the full experience of God's presence. Worship is the beginning and end of Pentecost, the full gospel and the Pentecostal liturgy. And yet, we must be careful not to interpret worship as the 'end' of Pentecostal theology. Principally speaking, the aim of Pentecostal theology is an eternal Pentecost. Doxology does not have an end but is an eternal return to the pathos, beliefs, and practices that nourish our worship of God. The end of Pentecostal theology is therefore the same as its beginning: Pentecost as living the fullness of the gospel.

Index

affections 5, 7, 9, 14, 17–18, 24–7, 28, 30, 33, 54, 86, 88, 90, 93, 95, 103, 110, 134, 144, 149, 166, 180, 183–4, 187, 221, 237, 247, 258, 272, 275, 286, 289 *see also* spirituality

agency
  divine 10, 59, 73, 85, 122, 124–5, 156, 166, 173, 175, 194, 241
  human 10, 54, 124, 166, 170, 173–4, 176, 190–3, 203, 204, 219, 241, 263 *see also* anthropology

altar 5–10, 31–2, 37, 40–5, 47, 49, 51, 55–57, 59–66, 69–72, 79, 83–5, 87, 89–90, 101–3, 105, 107–15, 120, 126, 132–3, 136, 138, 151, 155–6, 174, 176, 181, 184–5, 199, 205–7, 209–10, 212–13, 215, 217–24, 225, 227, 235–7, 243–4, 246, 255–64, 267, 271–3, 280–2, 285–6, 289, 291–4 *see also* metaphor

altar call and response 9, 10, 31, 34, 37, 40, 42–4, 47, 49, 55, 56, 59–62, 69, 84, 95, 104, 132, 151, 182, 201, 215, 217, 229, 232, 234, 246, 282, 286, 289, 292 *see also* ritual

altar hermeneutics 9, 16, 23, 31, 101, 104, 125, 126, 132, 135, 141, 142, 147, 149, 155, 156, 225, 233, 251, 256–8, 261, 264, 287, 292

anointing 48, 52, 54, 55–7, 65, 87, 88, 90, 98, 113–14, 117, 126, 136, 171, 220–4, 225–31, 235–9, 242, 244–8, 253, 268, 269

anthropology 5, 9, 10, 41, 45, 47, 52, 54, 72, 119–21, 155–6, 162, 164, 166, 167, 169, 173–4, 175–94, 196–7, 199, 203, 213–14, 216, 255, 266, 269, 278, 281, 292 *see also* agency, human

apocalypticism 131–3, 136–51, 156, 167, 171–2, 193, 221–4, 249, 251–2, 277–8 *see also* eschatology

apostolicity 95, 114, 124, 133–4, 137, 143–4, 225, 227, 231, 233, 237–8, 242–3, 248–50, 253, 282 *see also* church, marks of the

ascension 38, 60, 100, 180, 194–5, 249, 251, 260, 266, 268, 274

atonement 48–9, 52, 116–7, 119, 121, 130, 179, 189, 191, 273, 278 *see also* Christology; cross; soteriology

Babel 139, 212–13, 215

baptism *see* Spirit baptism; water baptism
  in the Spirit *see* Spirit baptism
  of Jesus 54, 98–101

born again *see* new birth

catholicity 227, 231–3, 237–8, 242, 243, 248, 253 *see also* church, marks of the

cessationism 122, 124–6, 231 *see also* spiritual gifts

charismata *see* spiritual gifts; *see also* church, marks of the

Christology 15, 19, 21, 22, 25–7, 33, 37–40, 43–9, 51–8, 59–60, 62, 64–80, 84, 85, 87, 90, 92, 99, 100–2, 104, 105, 109–12, 114–19, 121, 126, 130, 131, 133–7, 139–45, 147, 149, 150, 157, 159, 160, 163, 165–7, 169–70, 173, 175, 176, 179, 180, 182, 184, 186, 187, 189, 191–7, 199, 202, 205, 207, 209, 211, 213, 216, 218, 220–4, 255–6, 258–60, 262–3, 265–70, 272–80, 283, 284, 289–92 *see also* God, doctrine of; Jesus Christ

church 5, 9, 10, 20, 26, 27, 40–3, 52–7, 61, 62, 67, 72–80, 92, 94, 95, 99–105, 109–10, 112–14, 116, 120, 121, 125, 129–51, 155, 161–3, 166–8, 170, 204–7, 209, 210, 211, 213, 217, 218, 220–4, 225–54, 256–7, 260, 262–4, 270, 272, 276, 281, 284, 287, 288, 290, 292, 293 *see also* ecclesiology
  marks of the 10, 14, 44, 45, 79, 84, 85, 90, 99, 122, 147, 164, 165, 185, 196, 223, 224, 227, 231–2, 234, 237–8,

242, 245, 248–53, 266, 267, 271, 276, 285, 289, 292 *see also* apostolocity; catholicity; holiness; oneness
civilisation 201, 204, 207, 208 *see also* common good; culture; society
Commission, Great 60, 135, 150, 175, 223, 246, 285, 289
common good 10, 200, 211–16, 220, 223, 224, 232, 239 *see also* society; welfare
community 14, 19, 20, 22, 23, 25, 42, 43, 47, 50, 53, 61, 62, 65, 72, 78, 80, 91, 96, 99, 102–5, 119–21, 129, 130, 134–5, 143, 146–8, 162, 167, 170, 174, 179, 185, 187, 193, 197, 204, 218–20, 223, 225–8, 232, 234, 236–44, 246–52, 257–8, 263, 283, 284, 287, 288, 290, 291, 293 *see also* ecclesiology; society
consecration 72, 78, 207, 209, 210 *see also* sanctification
conversion 44–50, 54–6, 59, 63, 68–72, 74–6, 80, 84, 87, 92–4, 97–8, 103, 108, 111, 125, 132, 143, 189, 202, 206–9, 218, 264 *see also* soteriology
cosmology 9, 126, 128, 155, 156, 158–67, 169–74, 182, 190, 195, 201, 202, 207, 260, 292 *see also* creation; pneumatology; spirits; worldview
cosmopolitan deliverance 201–6 *see also* deliverance
creation 2, 5, 7, 9, 29, 41, 48, 49, 52, 55, 56, 58, 60, 72, 103–5, 116, 117, 119, 121, 123–8, 130, 132, 135, 139, 140, 143, 150, 155–74, 176–9, 181–3, 186, 188–92, 194, 195, 197, 199, 201, 203, 206, 211, 218, 229, 232, 248–53, 255–9, 262, 264–70, 272, 274–6, 278–81, 292, 293 *see also* cosmology
creed 227, 228, 231, 250 *see also* tradition
crisis 13, 43, 69, 70, 72, 92
cross 15, 39, 43, 46, 52, 75, 87, 118, 179, 236, 259, 266, 268, 273–5, 279, 286 *see also* atonement; Christology; soteriology; suffering
culture 2, 3, 9, 23, 30, 47, 49, 77, 79, 95, 107, 109, 119, 161, 170, 174, 188, 190, 199–203, 205–12, 214–20, 222–4, 227, 233, 235, 237, 255, 289, 292 *see also* society

death 43, 44, 46, 51, 70, 75, 108, 110, 112, 115–18, 121, 126, 128, 129, 139, 146, 179, 180, 189, 191, 192, 194, 195, 201, 220, 221, 263, 266, 268, 272, 274, 275, 288 *see also* suffering
deliverance 50, 56, 64, 65, 80, 108, 118, 128, 137, 143, 160, 167, 201–6, 207–8, 211, 252
demons 64, 116, 118, 121, 125, 128, 160, 165, 168, 169, 202–6, 293 *see also* pneumatology; spirits
disability 128–9, 179–80, 189, 191, 219, 247 *see also* divine healing
dispensationalism 92, 139–43, 147–50, 171–2, 195, 250 *see also* eschatology
divine healing 6, 21, 24, 27, 33, 34, 37, 42, 45–9, 59, 65, 67, 80, 107–30, 131–3, 135–6, 143, 145, 149, 151, 155–6, 160, 167–71, 172–6, 188–93, 194–5, 199–200, 206, 216–20, 222–4, 227, 243–9, 252, 256, 259, 261, 271–6, 277, 279, 281, 283–5, 288–90, 292–4
doctrine 7–15, 17–33, 46, 49, 59, 60, 67–8, 70–71, 73, 79, 83–4, 91, 93, 95, 97, 100, 108, 115–16, 121–3, 127–8, 132–3, 138–9, 141, 145–9, 155–7, 168, 182, 211, 221, 238, 255–9, 262, 264, 267, 270, 276–7, 279, 281–4, 287, 289, 293 *see also* prolegomena
doxology 3, 10, 26, 30, 31, 162, 174, 255–9, 261, 263, 269, 282, 286, 290, 292, 294 *see also* worship

ecclesiology 5, 9, 10, 20, 26–7, 40–3, 52–7, 61–2, 67, 72–8, 80, 92, 94–5, 99–105, 109, 110, 112–14, 116, 120–1, 125, 129–32, 134–41, 143–51, 155, 161–3, 166–8, 170, 174, 204–7, 209–11, 213, 217, 218, 220–53, 255–7, 260, 262–4, 270, 272, 276, 281, 284, 287, 288, 290, 292, 293 *see also* church
ecology *see* environment
ecumenism 3, 5–7, 9, 83–4, 93, 96–7, 108, 132, 141, 226–7, 231, 237, 291 *see also* ecclesiology; unity
egalitarianism 228, 243–9, 250–2 *see also* church, marks of the; disability; ecclesiology; gender; race
embodiment 8, 14, 27, 29, 30–3, 40, 44, 47, 52, 56, 62, 65–6, 71, 74, 78, 80, 86, 88, 112, 115–16, 119, 130, 161, 163–4, 175–6, 179–84, 185–8, 189–92, 195–7,

199, 202, 204–7, 209, 213, 216, 219, 222, 224, 229–30, 236–7, 239–41, 246–50, 253, 260, 284, 289, 292, 293 *see also* liturgy; materiality; ritual
emergence, theory of 3, 47, 122, 170, 173, 189, 193–5, 216 *see also* cosmology; evolution, theory of; science
empowerment 4, 17, 38, 39, 47, 48, 50, 53, 56, 60, 65, 69–72, 84, 87, 91–9, 102–4, 107, 110, 112–14, 116–18, 120–1, 123, 125, 129, 134–7, 143–4, 148, 150, 156, 163–8, 170, 174, 180, 184–5, 188, 190–2, 196, 204–7, 211, 214, 218, 220, 238–43, 244, 248, 263, 270–2, 279, 289, 292 *see also* agency; power; Spirit baptism
encounter 1, 4, 7, 8, 13, 15, 18–20, 23–30, 33–4, 41, 43–7, 49, 51, 55–7, 60, 62, 65, 73, 83–5, 87, 89, 101–3, 111, 115, 117, 132, 136–7, 140, 143, 150, 158–59, 161, 184, 186–7, 193–4, 199, 202, 208, 210, 213–14, 219–20, 232, 241–3, 255–60, 262, 264, 265, 267–8, 272, 278, 282–3, 286, 293 *see also* experience; liturgy; ritual
sacramental 84, 101–2, 104, 164, 166, 185
environment 5, 10, 32, 43, 50, 61, 63, 77, 114–15, 120–1, 136, 138, 162–3, 168–71, 176, 185, 209, 211, 218–20, 232, 236 *see also* nature
epistemology 24, 25, 55, 137, 172, 223, 260 *see also* reason; worldview
eschatology 4, 6, 21, 24, 27, 29, 34, 41, 45, 48, 51–2, 55–6, 59, 72, 73, 80, 87, 103–4, 115–17, 119, 121, 125–8, 130–51, 155–6, 162, 164, 167, 169, 171–6, 179, 189, 193–7, 200, 205–6, 220, 221–4, 226–7, 236–7, 241, 249–53, 256–7, 274–80, 285, 288, 289–90, 292–4 *see also* apocalypticism; kingdom of God; teleology
ethics 56, 63, 71, 78, 80, 120, 141, 148–50, 162, 177, 180, 189, 196–7, 204, 206–8, 213, 221, 223, 232, 278 *see also* holiness; sanctification
evangelisation 57, 72, 138, 143, 146–8, 156, 223, 244 *see also* mission
evil 111, 126, 129, 149, 158, 160, 165–6, 169, 189, 201–3, 206, 210, 234, 275, 293

evolution, theory of 156, 193 *see also* cosmology; science
exorcism 64, 108, 118, 135, 137, 143, 171, 203, 204, 216 *see also* deliverance; demons; spirits
experience 2, 4–10, 12–17, 18–20, 21–34, 38–9, 43–5, 47–51, 54–6, 59–61, 63–72, 76–7, 80, 83–5, 87–102, 104, 107–9, 112–13, 115–20, 126–9, 131–7, 140, 142–3, 149–51, 156, 158, 160–1, 169–70, 184–6, 192–3, 195, 206, 215, 223, 228–9, 238–40, 255–66, 270–3, 276–8, 280, 282–8, 291, 292, 294 *see also* altar; epistemology; materiality

faith 2, 40, 42, 46–7, 52, 57, 68, 74–6, 87, 96, 109–14, 116, 119–20, 123, 126, 129, 133, 143–4, 220, 228, 238, 243, 245–7
vocalization of 109–11, 220
Fall 51–2, 116, 125, 139, 160, 165, 176, 182, 190, 214 *see also* sin
finished work 46, 70–1 *see also* Christology
foot washing 63, 65–7, 74, 77–78, 113, 196, 220 *see also* ritual; sacrament
full gospel 1, 5–10, 15, 20, 21–4, 25–7, 29–30, 32–4, 37–9, 43–52, 57, 59, 68, 72, 81, 83–5, 87–8, 92–5, 99–100, 102–3, 107–8, 115–16, 118, 122, 128, 131–3, 135–7, 142, 145, 148–51, 155–7, 161, 163, 169, 171–2, 175–7, 181, 185, 189, 193–4, 199–200, 205–7, 211, 216–18, 221, 223–4, 226–8, 231–4, 236–8, 243–4, 246–7, 249, 255–9, 261, 264, 267–9, 271–3, 277, 280–5, 288–94 *see also* narrative; story

gender 71, 109, 179, 187, 219, 236, 244 *see also* egalitarianism
glorification 26, 37, 52, 71, 72, 76, 79, 125, 194–7, 247, 252, 268, 278, 280 *see also* eschatology; kingdom of God
glory 53, 118, 131, 161, 210, 256, 261, 274–5, 280, 282 *see also* doxology; encounter; eschatology; kingdom of God
glossolalia 12, 19, 39, 42, 64, 65, 87–90, 95–7, 101–2, 104, 110, 135–7, 143, 187, 210, 212–16, 237, 241–2, 251, 283–5, 289, 291 *see also* xenolalia

God, doctrine of 4, 5, 7–10, 12–15, 18–31, 33, 34, 39–59, 61–70, 72, 74–80, 83, 84, 86–8, 90, 93, 95–6, 99–101, 103–4, 108–10, 112–13, 116–38, 141–51, 155–67, 170–97, 199, 202, 204–6, 209–24, 226–8, 230, 232, 234–7, 239–49, 251–3, 255–81 *see also* Christology; Jesus Christ; Oneness Pentecostalism; pneumatology; Spirit-Christology; Trinity

grace 29, 45–7, 49, 50, 53, 59, 67–71, 73–5, 77–8, 80, 93, 96, 98–100, 104, 116, 128, 139, 145, 165, 183, 238, 239, 260, 264

healing *see* divine healing

hermeneutics 16, 22, 23, 24, 32, 38, 39, 48, 68, 69, 71, 80, 93, 95–8, 104, 109, 114, 125–6, 132–3, 135, 137, 139–40, 142, 147–50, 156, 164, 178, 215, 250–1, 256–7, 260, 262, 276, 283–4, 287 *see also* altar hermeneutics; epistemology; Scripture

holiness 42, 57, 59, 62, 67–73, 75–6, 80, 92, 95, 103, 182, 210, 220, 227, 231–9, 242, 248, 252–3, 261, 263–7 *see also* church, marks of the; sanctification

Holy Spirit 4, 12, 14–15, 17–20, 22, 25–8, 32, 38–41, 43–4, 48–50, 52–7, 60–2, 64–5, 67–9, 71–6, 79–81, 83–98, 100–3, 107, 117–19, 121, 125–7, 131, 133–6, 140–1, 143–4, 149, 151, 156, 159–66, 172–4, 176, 180, 183–6, 188, 190–1, 194–5, 197, 205, 207, 211, 217, 221, 223–4, 225–6, 229–30, 233–6, 239, 244, 245, 247, 250, 253, 255–6, 258–60, 262–9, 271–2, 274–9, 283–4, 289, 291–2 *see also* pneumatology

hospitality 6, 8, 9, 10, 34, 45, 55–7, 60, 86, 103, 157, 201, 228, 233–8, 236–45, 248–50, 252, 290 *see also* church, marks of the

humanity *see* anthropology

imago Dei 52, 175–82, 185–93, 196, 199, 214, 224, 256, 282, 292 *see also* anthropology

immanence 20, 127, 189, 260–6, 268, 270–8 *see also* kenosis; transcendence

impassibility 272, 274–5 *see also* God, doctrine of

Incarnation 52, 54, 159, 165, 174, 180, 194, 229, 230, 260, 266, 275, 278 *see also* Christology; Spirit-Christology

initial evidence 91, 94–7, 104 *see also* Spirit baptism; glossolalia

intensification, of the Spirit 86, 113, 137, 149, 164, 186, 269–71, 277–8, 280 *see also* cosmology; God, doctrine of

intercession 110, 137 *see also* prayer; praying through

Jesus Christ 15, 19, 21, 22, 25–7, 33, 37–40, 43–9, 51–60, 62, 64–80, 84–5, 87, 90, 92, 99–102, 104–5, 109–12, 114, 116–19, 121, 126, 130–1, 133–7, 139–47, 149–50, 157, 159–60, 163, 165–7, 169–70, 173, 175–6, 179–80, 182–4, 186–7, 189, 191–7, 199, 202, 205, 207, 209, 211, 213, 216, 218, 220–4, 226–42, 244–53, 255–6, 258–60, 262–3, 265–70, 272–80, 283–4, 289–92 *see also* Christology; God, doctrine of; Spirit-Christology

justice 10, 138, 168, 170, 189, 199, 218, 223 *see also* church; egalitarianism; public square; society; welfare

justification 10, 47, 49, 60, 67–8, 70, 73–8, 80, 102, 228, 250, 267 *see also* ordo salutis; soteriology

kenosis 56, 159, 170, 191–2, 264–72, 275–9 *see also* Christology; cosmology; pneumatology

kingdom of God 4, 6, 21, 24, 27, 29, 34, 41, 45, 55, 59, 80, 87, 103–4, 116, 119, 125, 130–4, 136–7, 140–51, 155–6, 164, 167, 171–5, 193–7, 200, 205–6, 220–4, 226–7, 236–7, 241, 249–53, 256–7, 276–80, 285, 288–90, 292–4 *see also* eschatology

language 2, 3, 12, 25, 33, 48, 52–3, 64–5, 69, 95–6, 100, 102, 127, 137, 163, 186, 214, 218, 237, 258–9, 270, 274, 282, 285, 289, 290 *see also* doctrine; xenolalia

Latter Rain 133, 134, 143 *see also* apocalypticism

laying on of hands 89, 90, 97, 102, 103, 112–14, 126, 220 *see also* ritual liturgy 31, 32, 40, 41, 53, 55, 64, 66, 70, 77–8, 89, 96, 98–100, 146, 150, 204–6, 220, 241, 249, 252–3, 259, 281–3, 286–7, 289, 291–3 *see also* ritual; sacrament

marks of the church *see* church, marks of
materiality 8, 30, 48, 50, 89, 114, 118–19, 127–8, 160–1, 172, 174, 189, 201, 202, 216, 219, 222, 293 *see also* embodiment; ritual; soteriology
metaphor 5, 7, 8, 13, 37, 40, 41, 45, 57, 59, 83, 84, 93, 103, 107, 109, 118, 132, 134, 135, 164, 166, 181, 184, 186, 224, 255, 256, 267, 268, 270, 279, 289, 292 *see also* altar
metaphysics 20, 122, 123, 125, 126, 159, 161, 174, 176–7, 189, 190, 202 *see also* ontology
millennialism 140–2, 144 *see also* apocalypticism; dispensationalism; eschatology
miracles 4, 40, 107, 108, 122–5, 127, 129, 133, 136, 142–3, 151, 166, 167, 188, 217, 222 *see also* cessationism; signs and wonders; spiritual gifts
mission 52, 72, 92, 94–5, 121–2, 132, 134–8, 142–4, 145–51, 156, 159, 168–70, 173–4, 176, 207–8, 211, 224, 230–1, 233–9, 241–4, 247–51, 265–9, 272, 292 *see also* ecclesiology; evangelization; Great Commission
movement 225–9, 236, 246, 248, 249, 251, 252, 255, 260, 262, 264, 265, 267, 269, 278, 281, 282, 285, 288, 293 *see also* ecclesiology

narrative 1, 4–10, 14–15, 17–27, 30–4, 37–40, 43–4, 46, 51–2, 54, 59–61, 69, 73–4, 83–5, 88, 107, 109, 112, 132–3, 135, 144, 155, 157, 158, 160, 163, 171, 175, 185, 199, 200, 211, 214–15, 217, 221, 238, 255–9, 261–2, 268, 272, 281–4, 288–91, 293 *see also* full gospel; story
nature 12, 15, 18, 28, 47, 57, 64, 67, 68, 70–1, 74, 77, 79, 81, 93, 95, 97, 114, 119–20, 123–8, 130, 148–9, 164–7, 169–70, 173–4, 175–82, 185, 188, 190–4, 196–7, 201, 216, 222, 224, 239, 261, 270, 277, 278, 285 *see also* cosmology; creation; environment; supernaturalism
new birth 15, 44–7, 49, 50, 74, 156, 183, 186, 215, 225, 230, 231, 233, 243, 249, 250 *see also* ordo salutis; regeneration; soteriology

Oneness Pentecostalism 46, 56, 70, 159, 253, 258, 263, 264, 269
oneness, of the church 225, 228, 231, 232, 236, 237, 239–43, 245, 248, 252 *see also* church, marks of the; ecclesiology; ecumenism
ontology 73, 77, 79, 148, 159, 161, 164–6, 173, 175, 177, 181, 185–7, 190, 202, 203, 207, 256, 258, 260, 262, 267 *see also* metaphysics
ordo salutis 45, 70, 72, 74, 77, 79, 93 *see also* soteriology
outpouring (*of the Holy Spirit*) 12, 13, 27, 39, 40–1, 43–4, 49, 52–3, 61, 68–9, 80, 85, 88–9, 98, 100–1, 105, 109, 121, 126–7, 131, 133, 135–7, 141, 143–4, 149–51, 161–5, 170, 173, 179–80, 185–7, 189, 192, 194–5, 202, 211–12, 218–24, 225, 229–32, 235–6, 238–41, 244, 247, 249–53, 256, 259–60, 262–3, 266–9, 272, 274, 276–80, 283–91 *see also* Pentecost, as symbol; Pentecost, day of; Pentecost, plot of; pneumatology

participation 3, 9, 14, 17, 19, 25, 29, 30, 33, 34, 37, 40–4, 47, 49, 52–7, 61–2, 64, 67, 74–7, 79–80, 85, 90, 101, 104, 110–11, 120–1, 126–7, 130, 144, 147–9, 159–61, 163–6, 173–4, 180–4, 187, 201, 207–10, 222, 224, 228–30, 233, 235, 237, 239–41, 252, 257–63, 265, 267, 269, 272–5, 277–8, 280, 283–7, 290–2 *see also* ecclesiology
Pentecost
as symbol 1–6, 8–22, 24–8, 31, 33–4, 37–46, 48–50, 54, 56–7, 59–61, 65, 83, 88, 89, 92, 95, 98–101, 107–8, 111, 121, 125, 127, 129, 131, 133–5, 141, 143–4, 148, 150–1, 155–7, 159, 161–5, 174, 176, 178–80, 186, 195–6, 200, 202, 205, 209, 211–13, 215–19, 221–31, 233–53, 255–6, 258–60, 262–70, 274–80, 283–8, 289–94 *see also* symbol

day of 2–7, 12–14, 17, 19, 22, 24, 28, 30, 34, 38–43, 47, 60–2, 68, 83–5, 89, 92, 100–1, 105, 108–9, 133–6, 143, 161–2, 164, 207, 211, 225, 227, 229, 234, 249, 250–1, 263, 277, 279, 280
  plot of 5, 21, 37–40, 55, 290 *see also* narrative; story
persistence 34, 78, 115, 128, 129, 195, 228, 249–53, 291 *see also* church, marks of the; eschatology
play 12–14, 29, 32, 80, 132, 133, 183, 293 *see also* liturgy; prolegomena
pneumatology 5, 18, 25, 43, 45, 48, 49, 53–5, 58, 61, 72–3, 76, 85, 115, 117–18, 121, 125–7, 134, 142–4, 149–50, 156–63, 165–6, 169–77, 182–3, 190–1, 194, 221, 229, 230–1, 233, 247, 263, 267, 274, 276–7, 284 *see also* Holy Spirit; Spirit-Christology
political theology 2, 10, 50, 93, 95, 118, 129, 138, 141, 150, 171, 189, 192, 199–207, 211, 213, 215, 217–18, 220–2, 235, 249, 258 *see also* civilisation; common good; public square
postmillennialism *see* millennialism
power 4, 17, 38–9, 47–8, 53, 56, 60, 65, 69–71, 87, 92–3, 98–9, 104, 107, 110, 112–14, 116–18, 120–1, 123, 125, 129, 134–7, 143–4, 148, 163–7, 170, 180, 184, 188, 190, 196, 204–7, 218, 220, 238–44, 248, 263, 270–2, 289 *see also* empowerment
practices 16, 18, 23, 26, 28, 31, 34, 37, 40, 42–4, 51, 55, 59–67, 69–70, 73–80, 84–90, 97, 102, 107, 110–14, 132, 134, 148, 180–1, 213, 238, 240, 243, 261, 291 *see also* embodiment; liturgy; praxis; ritual; sacrament
praxis, Pentecostal 6, 23, 28–30, 51–3, 55–6, 58–9, 61, 67, 71, 74, 78, 84, 99, 108, 119, 120, 134, 144, 156, 169, 188, 201, 284, 292, 293 *see also* practices
prayer 19, 38, 41, 42, 53, 61–6, 78, 85–90, 97, 102, 103, 108, 110, 112–14, 136–7, 146, 204, 216, 220, 233 *see also* praying through
praying through 86–7, 97, 102, 110 *see also* prayer; ritual
preaching 75, 87–9, 90, 97, 112, 244, 289

premillennialism *see* millennialism
prolegomena 6, 11, 12
prophecy 16, 19, 26, 39, 42, 65, 88, 90, 92, 95, 99, 104, 133, 137, 141, 144, 170, 213, 215–16, 237, 242, 252, 289 *see also* spiritual gifts
public square 2, 9, 10, 16, 51, 54–5, 57, 75, 99, 111, 113, 163, 172, 199–200, 202–5, 207, 211–24, 244–6, 258, 292 *see also* culture; political theology; society

race 109, 138, 179, 215, 217–19, 244, 247 *see also* egalitarianism
reason 24, 25, 28, 33, 77, 122, 123, 175, 178, 180, 233, 251, 289 *see also* epistemology
redemption 30, 47–9, 53, 59, 102–4, 108, 112, 116, 118–19, 121, 125–7, 129, 140, 150, 156–7, 160, 164–7, 169, 173–6, 179–80, 188–91, 199–200, 204–8, 210, 217, 220, 224, 228–9, 232–3, 235–6, 243, 249, 253, 258, 264, 266–8, 275–6, 278–9, 286, 290–3 *see also* soteriology
regeneration 44–5, 48–50, 53, 68–9, 71, 84, 92, 94, 194, 239, 270 *see also* new birth; *ordo salutis*; soteriology
relationality 26, 51, 81, 89, 116, 118, 121, 158–60, 169–71, 178, 180, 181, 184–6, 188–9, 194, 199, 203, 206, 258, 261
religion 49, 50–1, 63, 93, 95, 109, 114, 123–4, 134, 172, 201, 203, 209–11, 215, 217–20, 235, 283–4
renewal 7, 9, 15, 42, 44, 47, 65, 74, 95, 97–9, 169, 171–4, 195, 196, 271
responsibility 75, 95, 162, 171, 178, 182, 183 *see also* justice; welfare
resurrection 15, 26, 38, 43, 46, 51, 52, 75, 116–17, 180, 194–6, 236, 251, 259, 268, 274, 275, 286 *see also* Christology; pneumatology; Spirit-Christology
revelation 15, 19, 23, 42, 125, 140, 172, 215, 247, 257–62, 265, 276–7, 284–7, 289–91
revival 4, 14, 42, 47, 57, 78, 133, 137, 140, 225
ritual 5, 7, 9, 20, 31, 32, 38, 39, 41–3, 55, 57, 60–5, 67, 69, 73–81, 83–91, 97, 102–4, 108, 110, 112–14, 118–19, 122, 147, 150, 168, 204–6, 209–10, 220, 223,

236, 241–2, 252, 263, 281–2, 287–8, 292–3 *see also* liturgy; practices, Pentecostal; sacrament

sacramentality 32, 40, 41, 53, 55–7, 66, 74, 84, 96, 97–105, 114, 120, 126–7, 129–30, 147, 164, 166–7, 185–7, 212, 215, 239–43 *see also* encounter, sacramental; sacrament

sacrament 9, 32, 42, 53, 74, 76, 77–9, 97–105, 146, 241–2, 292 *see also* liturgy; ritual; sacramentality; Spirit baptism

sacrifice 40, 57, 263, 266

salvation *see* soteriology

sanctification 6, 21, 24, 26–7, 34, 37, 49, 59–81, 82–5, 87, 91–5, 98, 102–4, 107–9, 112, 116–17, 125, 127, 131–3, 135–6, 143, 145, 149, 151, 155–6, 160–4, 166, 169–70, 174, 176, 181–4, 185–6, 188, 194–5, 200, 206–11, 220, 222–3, 227, 232, 233–8, 242, 248, 252–3, 256, 261–6, 267, 270–1, 277, 279, 281, 285, 288–90, 292–4 *see also* consecration; holiness

science 119, 123, 124, 172–4, 193 *see also* cosmology

Scripture 15–17, 21, 25, 33, 37–40, 43–4, 48, 60–1, 63, 65, 68, 79, 83–93, 95, 108–16, 118–19, 124–5, 133–6, 139–40, 145, 148, 155, 157, 161, 164, 168, 177–8, 186–7, 202, 207, 211–13, 225, 234, 255, 257–9, 277, 283–4, 286, 289 *see also* hermeneutics; revelation

sickness *see* divine healing; suffering

signs and wonders 2, 4, 40, 62, 96, 99, 108, 122–30, 133, 136–7, 142–3, 151, 166–7, 188, 191, 217, 221–2, 232, 240, 271, 275 *see also* miracles

sin 44, 49, 51, 59, 64, 66, 68–72, 74, 78–80, 93, 112, 115, 116, 125, 129, 145, 160, 165, 169, 176, 182, 189, 201, 206, 232–5, 266, 274–5

soaking prayer 63–5, 78 *see also* ritual

society 2, 5, 9, 10, 47–8, 50, 56, 58, 78, 95, 99, 118, 120, 122, 129, 138, 140–2, 144, 147–8, 150, 155–6, 161, 163, 168, 170–4, 181, 186–90, 192, 199–211, 214–24, 229, 233, 235, 239, 243, 245, 249, 255, 258, 260, 281 *see also* culture; public square

soteriology 6, 15, 20, 21, 24, 27, 30, 34, 37–58, 59–61, 67–8, 70–2, 74, 76–9, 84–5, 92–4, 98, 100, 104, 107–9, 111, 115–16, 118–22, 125–36, 139–41, 143, 145, 148–9, 151, 155, 157–63, 164, 166, 169–70, 174, 176–82, 183–4, 188–9, 192, 194–5, 200–9, 211, 216–17, 221, 223–4, 227, 228–33, 235, 256–61, 262–3, 266–8, 271, 276, 278–9, 281–2, 285, 287–90, 292–4 *see also* conversion; justification; *ordo salutis*; redemption; regeneration

soul 50, 86, 116, 119, 130, 179, 180–1, 183, 188 *see also* anthropology

Spirit baptism 6, 21, 24, 26–7, 34, 37, 59, 63, 68, 70–2, 83–105, 107–9, 111, 112, 114, 117, 125–7, 129, 131–3, 135–6, 143, 145, 149, 151, 155, 156, 160, 163–7, 169, 176, 185–8, 190, 194, 196, 200, 206, 211–16, 222–3, 227, 238–43, 256, 261, 264, 267–71, 277, 281, 283–5, 288, 290, 292–4 *see also* empowerment; spiritual gifts

Spirit-Christology 4, 15, 25, 45, 48, 64, 162–3, 180, 184, 192, 194, 229–30, 234, 242, 259, 263, 268, 277, 284, 287, 293

spirits 158–61, 166, 168–9, 202, 204 *see also* cosmology; pneumatology

spiritual gifts 4, 9, 21, 41, 42, 49, 63, 64, 65, 78, 87, 88, 90–100, 102–4, 125, 127–9, 135, 137, 140, 143–4, 149–51, 163–6, 168, 170, 173–4, 185, 187–8, 192–3, 195, 211–13, 215–16, 221–3, 228, 231–4, 236, 238–42, 244, 246, 248, 250, 252, 269, 271, 282

spiritual warfare 43, 95, 117–18, 121, 125, 128–9, 137, 151, 165–70, 188, 190, 191, 195, 200–3, 206, 209–10, 216, 222–4, 235, 243, 272, 286, 291, 293 *see also* deliverance, exorcism

spirituality 2, 3, 5, 7, 9, 12, 14–18, 19, 21–2, 23, 24, 26, 28, 31, 33, 62, 118, 129, 183–4, 201, 207, 221, 250 *see also* affections; experience

story 1, 5, 7, 14, 15, 17–18, 21–4, 25, 27, 33, 52, 69, 109, 112, 160, 200, 256–9, 262, 289–91 *see also* full gospel; narrative; Pentecost, plot of

subjectivity 124, 159, 160, 192

subsequence 7, 37, 38, 67–9, 76, 80, 85, 91–4, 97, 164, 183, 195, 264, 288 *see also* Spirit baptism
suffering 3, 104, 110, 111, 113, 115–18, 120, 127, 129, 169, 179, 180, 189, 191, 192, 208, 218–19, 235–7, 240, 243–5, 248, 251, 263, 266, 272–6, 289 *see also* divine healing; sacrifice
supernaturalism 42, 50, 95, 123–8, 161, 165, 189 *see also* agency, divine; cosmology; creation; nature; science
symbol 1, 3–6, 9–12, 16–20, 26–8, 31, 34, 38, 41, 45, 51, 57, 59, 61, 75, 83, 84, 102, 107, 108, 131, 155, 159, 176, 179, 200, 205, 214, 218–19, 224–5, 227, 229, 234–5, 238, 240, 242, 244–7, 249–51, 256, 258, 262, 269, 276–7, 279, 281–91, 293 *see also* Pentecost, as symbol

tarrying, at the altar 38, 47, 60–5, 84–7, 107, 110, 132, 209, 287, 289, 292 *see also* altar; ritual
teleology 161, 173, 174, 193–4 *see also* eschatology
testimony 14, 18–20, 26, 28, 33, 46, 54, 99, 110, 128, 131, 134, 136–7, 215, 228, 268, 282, 290, 291 *see also* ritual
this-is-that *see* altar hermeneutics
tongues, speaking in *see* glossolalia; xenolalia
tradition 1, 2, 5, 9, 10, 12, 15, 21, 23, 28, 31–4, 39, 40, 43, 50, 53, 61, 68, 69–70, 77–8, 91–2, 107, 128, 146–7, 159, 175, 177, 182, 192, 195, 225, 228, 232, 237, 244–5, 252, 258, 262, 270, 278, 283, 288, 291, 292 *see also* community; epistemology; hermeneutics
transcendence 123–5, 127, 150, 159, 167, 181, 189, 193, 237, 260–2, 264–6, 270, 272–5, 277–8 *see also* cosmology; immanence; kenosis
transformation 8, 20, 27, 30, 34, 42, 44, 51–3, 56, 63–5, 71–3, 77–9, 84–5, 87–8, 90, 95, 103–4, 107–8, 113, 117, 119, 127, 129, 131–2, 135–6, 141, 144, 146–9, 156, 162–4, 166–7, 169, 171, 173–4, 176, 181–4, 184–9, 191–3, 195–7, 200, 204–5, 207–210, 214, 219–24, 235–7, 239, 242–3, 246, 252, 256, 261, 263–4, 267–8, 271, 278–9, 286, 288–9, 292 *see also* affections; encounter; experience, Spirit baptism
Trinity 46, 56, 140, 159, 164, 167, 181, 183, 184, 186, 230, 242, 258–9, 262–8, 270, 273–4, 276–7, 279 *see also* God, doctrine of

unity 4, 119, 161, 167, 180, 182–3, 189, 197, 213, 227, 231, 232–3, 237, 242, 248, 252, 277, 292 *see also* church, marks of the; ecclesiology; ecumenism; oneness, of the church

vocalization (of faith) 109, 110, 111, 220 *see also* faith; ritual
vocation 162, 244–9, 253 *see also* church, marks of the; ecclesiology; egalitarianism

water baptism 40, 50, 56, 65–7, 69, 74, 89, 94, 98–100, 135–6, 186, 246, 269 *see also* sacrament
welfare 2, 122, 139, 146, 199, 200, 208, 211, 216–20, 221 *see also* common good; egalitarianism; justice; society
worldview 26, 74, 80, 91, 118, 123–5, 127–8, 130, 167–9, 203 *see also* cosmology; epistemology
worship 5, 9–10, 14, 19, 26, 29–33, 40–2, 57, 62–4, 75, 88, 95, 98, 103, 120, 136, 146–7, 185, 204–5, 217, 220, 224, 226, 233, 241–3, 252, 255–63, 273, 282–3, 285, 286–7, 289–90, 292–4 *see also* doxology

xenolalia 137, 214, 215 *see also* glossolalia; language; spiritual gifts

Made in the USA
Columbia, SC
16 June 2021